CW01337862

Derek Collett was born on t
in 1965. He was brought up in
the county today. Educated at h
Southampton University, he ob
and has worked in scientific, tec
for almost 30 years, latterly in a freelance capacity.

Derek read his first Nigel Balchin novel, *The Small Back Room*, in 1991 and has been obsessively reading and re-reading the author's works ever since. In recent years he has used his love of Balchin's fiction as the springboard to launch a new career for himself as a literary writer and *His Own Executioner: The Life of Nigel Balchin* represents the first significant fruit of those labours.

HIS OWN EXECUTIONER

THE LIFE OF NIGEL BALCHIN

DEREK COLLETT

SilverWood

Published in 2015 by SilverWood Books

SilverWood Books Ltd
14 Small Street, Bristol, BS1 1DE, United Kingdom
www.silverwoodbooks.co.uk

ISBN 978-1-78132-391-5 (paperback)
ISBN 978-1-78132-392-2 (ebook)

British Library Cataloguing in Publication Data
A CIP catalogue record for this book is available from
the British Library

Set in Adobe Garamond Pro by SilverWood Books
Printed by Imprint Digital on responsibly sourced paper

For my mother

Contents

Foreword   11
1   *Simple Life*   17
2   *Psychology Welcomes a New Recruit*   33
3   *How to Run a Chocolate Factory*   53
4   *Making a Good Beginning: The Hamish Hamilton Years*   69
5   *One Night in the West End*   91
6   *Darkness Falls from the Air*   110
7   *Marital Discord 1: As Easy as EBCD*   125
8   *No More Square Pegs in Round Holes: Transforming*
    Morale in the British Army During World War Two   133
9   *The Small Back Room*   144
10   *Mine Own Executioner*   157
11   *A Very Thorough Demobilization*   172
12   *Socially Minded Donkeys and a Chinese Examination*   180
13   *Finding the Key to the Film World*   196
14   *Mr. Balchin's Formula: Too Much the Mixture as Before?*   211
15   *Marital Discord 2: 'People Do What They Want To'*   225
16   *Finding a Way Through the Wood*   240
17   *A Return to Elbow Grease*   248
18   *Before Hollywood*   269
19   *The Man Who Never Was*   291
20   *'A Very Destructive Period': Florence 1957–1962*   304
21   *All These Bloody Things*   321
22   *Return Journeys*   336
23   *Failing to Achieve Lift-Off*   351
24   *Balchin and Drink*   366
25   *Death of a Famous Writer*   372

Afterword   386
Acknowledgements   390
Photo Credits   394
Appendix: Selected Works of Nigel Balchin   395
Notes   400
Index   434

Author's Note

This book includes, as a series of stand-alone features, plot summaries for all fourteen of Balchin's novels. My intention is to allow the reader to quickly and easily assimilate what a particular novel is like without having to tease this information out of the main text of this book. So if you read a Balchin novel at some point in the past but have forgotten what it was called then these plot summaries might help you to remember! Alternatively, if you are seeking reading recommendations then I hope that my précis will provide you with a concise and accurate impression of the contents of each book. Although I have tried hard to remove all 'plot spoilers', it was not possible in one or two cases where I wished to discuss certain plot points in the main text. Therefore, if you are the sort of person who dislikes being told what a book is about before you've read it then I would respectfully suggest that you should skip the plot summaries until such time as you've read the books in question. If, on the other hand, you want to learn more about an individual novel then longer plot summaries—together with details of how to obtain each book—are available from my website: www.nigelmarlinbalchin.com.

Foreword

C. S. Lewis once described Kipling as 'first and foremost the poet of work'.[1] Nigel Balchin (pronounced 'Bol-chin') has a very strong claim to be considered the novelist of work. Or to be more specific, because his central characters were almost exclusively male, Balchin should rightly be considered the novelist of *men at work*.

Balchin's finest novels exemplify this 'men at work' theme. Thus *Darkness Falls from the Air* was about a temporary civil servant waging a lonely battle against governmental bureaucracy during World War Two; *The Small Back Room* described a weapons researcher trying to devise new ways of winning the same war; *Mine Own Executioner* brought to life the daily round of a psycho-analyst; biochemical research workers were the focus of *A Sort of Traitors*; and *Sundry Creditors* anatomized the internal workings of an engineering works.

But there is much more to Balchin's novels than just fascinating accounts of the working lives of his male protagonists. He also wrote compellingly about the troubled and chaotic private lives of his heroes, depicted the everlasting battle of the sexes with honesty and perception and put disabled characters into his books when it was very unusual to do so. Other standout features of Balchin's fiction include sparkling dialogue, bone-dry humour, convincing characterization, psychological insight, a wealth of period detail and a beautifully economical prose style. Balchin's best novels are characterized by their rapid-paced, streamlined plots and all of them are enriched by the 'devilish readability'[2] (as the *Guardian* once put it) that is one of the principal hallmarks of his work.

In my opinion though, the finest quality possessed by Balchin's writing is its intense realism. More perhaps than the works of any other writer, the two novels that Balchin published during the Second World War capture what it must really have been *like* to have lived and worked in London during the conflict. Simultaneously, Balchin's grumbling, embittered and disenchanted protagonists, always on the verge of exploding with anger when confronted with evidence of incompetence or corruption in high places, give the lie to the modern-day 'Keep Calm and Carry On' stereotype that has a tendency to be applied in blanket fashion to those civilians who lived through the Blitz.

After graduating from Cambridge with a degree in Natural Sciences, Balchin began his working life in the early 1930s as an industrial psychologist. Whilst on secondment to the confectioners Rowntree's he coordinated pioneering market research that led directly to the launch of the popular chocolate assortment Black Magic. Balchin also devised the distinctive black box in which the chocolates were packaged, a design classic that has endured for over eighty years. During the Second World War, Balchin performed work of national importance for the army in the areas of personnel selection and scientific research. So useful did he make himself to the military that in 1945 he was appointed Deputy Scientific Adviser to the Army Council and promoted to brigadier at the astonishingly young age of thirty-six. The work that Balchin carried out during the war years provided him with material for the three great novels on which his reputation largely rests: *Darkness Falls from the Air*, *The Small Back Room* and *Mine Own Executioner*.

When the war was over, it soon became apparent to Balchin that his plot-driven, dialogue-rich novels would lend themselves easily to cinema adaptation. Scripted by the book's author, *Mine Own Executioner* was filmed in 1947 and was greeted ecstatically by the nation's movie critics, one of their number remarking that it represented only 'the fourth notable British post-war film'.[3] *The Small Back Room* followed *Mine Own Executioner* onto the big screen two years later. Again very well received by cinema reviewers, Powell and Pressburger's atmospheric adaptation of

Balchin's book—a film that was shown regularly on terrestrial television in Britain until quite recently—ranks as one of the finest movies of the period.

The pinnacle of Balchin's career as a screenwriter came in 1957 when he was awarded the accolade of 'Best British Screenplay' by the British Film Academy for his accomplished script for the absorbing espionage thriller *The Man Who Never Was*, a film depicting an elaborate piece of deception successfully perpetrated by the Allies during World War Two. The military operation on which Balchin's script was based, Operation Mincemeat, was restored to public attention in 2010 by Ben MacIntyre's best-selling book of the same name.[4]

On the back of successes such as *The Man Who Never Was*, Balchin spent three lucrative years in Hollywood writing film scripts for Twentieth Century Fox. Separated from his wife and young son, he was lonely and fretful and drank too much. His film work was consequently uneven and he whimsically described the most memorable artefact that he crafted whilst in Hollywood as 'the first folio edition of *Cleopatra*',[5] this being his draft screenplay for the Elizabeth Taylor/Richard Burton extravaganza that very nearly bankrupted Fox.

In keeping with the situation he described for many of his fictional characters, Balchin's private life suffered badly in comparison with his extremely successful professional one. His first marriage, to fellow Cambridge graduate Elisabeth Walshe, ended in divorce after more than fifteen years when she left him to begin cohabiting with the (much younger) painter and sculptor Michael Ayrton. It is an indictment of Balchin's qualities as both a husband and father that his daughter, renowned child psychologist Penelope Leach, has stated publicly that she is glad that the divorce happened, as she and her mother were much happier living with Ayrton than they had ever been with Balchin. Balchin's second marriage, to Yovanka Tomich, a Yugoslavian émigré twenty-two years his junior, was a turbulent affair haunted by the ever-present spectre of divorce.

As the writer and critic Clive James has observed, 'Balchin is remembered by his contemporaries as the kindest of men.'[6]

He was a compassionate individual whose concern for his fellow human beings is apparent from reading his novels, especially those written during the 1940s and 1950s. For an example of Balchin's generosity of spirit, one need only look as far as an incident that took place after Ayrton had effectively stolen Balchin's wife. Both men were members of the Savile Club in London and a group of Savilians who were outraged by Ayrton's behaviour proposed that he should be thrown out of the Club as a punishment. But instead of relishing the chance to exact revenge on the man who had cuckolded him, Balchin let it be known that he would resign himself if Ayrton's membership was rescinded and so the proposal was quietly dropped.

Yovanka has described her late husband as 'a fascinating person to be with—deeply serious, but with a sense of humour.'[7] A large part of his fascination must have stemmed from the breadth of his interests; as he said himself, 'there is practically nothing in which I am not or can not be intensely interested.'[8] A cultured man, Balchin had read extremely widely before embarking on a career as a writer. He had acquired a thorough knowledge of poetry and the Bible, and his favourite authors included L. P. Hartley, Aldous Huxley, H. G. Wells and E. M. Forster. Balchin collected oil paintings and other artworks, and was a passionate devotee of the craft of woodcarving. His other enthusiasms included playing and watching sport, playing and listening to classical music and gardening, in particular the growing of fruit. He was also an authority on oriental rugs and carpets.

Balchin's damaging dependence on alcohol, which had been apparent to those closest to him since the late 1940s (and was undoubtedly exacerbated during his unhappy stay in Hollywood), escalated during the 1960s. The descent into alcoholism greatly impaired his ability to write to his previously exalted standard and it was principally this, together with a paucity of interesting subjects to write about in the absence of a full-time job, that brought his career as a novelist to a premature end.

Since Balchin's death in 1970, the best critical analysis of him has been provided by James.[9] Published in 1974, James's article consisted mainly of detailed synopses of most of Balchin's novels, augmented by a small amount of biographical information. The originality of the piece stemmed from James subjecting Balchin to the sort of searching psychological examination that some commentators in the 1940s and 1950s felt that Balchin should have applied to his own characters, but consistently sidestepped.

Only a small number of newspaper and magazine articles have been devoted to Balchin in the forty-one years since James's essay appeared and this biography represents the first attempt to tell the story of Balchin's eventful life in depth. In 2004, Oscar-winning scriptwriter Julian Fellowes observed that 'Balchin has been absurdly overlooked for too long'[10] and that he fully deserves to be restored to 'his proper place among the great masters of English fiction'. I hope that my book will go some way towards accomplishing that laudable and necessary objective.

1

Simple Life

In the early autumn of 1945, the Glaswegian publishers William Collins brought out *Mine Own Executioner*, the sixth novel by a recently demobilized thirty-six-year-old Wiltshireman, Brigadier Nigel Balchin. The author's early novels had been greeted with only cautious approval by the book reviewers and it was not until the publication of *Mine Own Executioner*'s predecessor, *The Small Back Room*, at the end of 1943 that Balchin had finally achieved his long-coveted goal of critical respect combined with large sales.

The reviews of *Mine Own Executioner* were everything that Balchin could have hoped for. Among more than a dozen notices for the book that I have accumulated from newspapers and literary magazines, only one can be described as negative; the remainder are predominantly adulatory and peppered with phrases such as 'an exceptionally good novel', 'this most accomplished book', 'a triumphant success', 'feverish reading' and 'an exciting, intelligently written novel'.[1] Among the celebrated writers lining up to extol the virtues of *Mine Own Executioner* were the likes of Elizabeth Bowen, Monica Dickens, John Betjeman and L. P. Hartley. In the course of his review in the *New Statesman and Nation*, poet Henry Reed described Balchin as 'a brilliant novelist'[2] and Pamela Hansford Johnson in *John o'London's Weekly* pronounced that 'Mr. Balchin's books are the most poised and complete of their class'.[3]

Launched down the slipway to success by the publication of numerous complimentary reviews, *Mine Own Executioner* flew off the shelves of bookshops. The novel sold well in excess of a quarter of a million copies worldwide, putting it second only to *The Small Back Room*, Balchin's signature work, as his most commercially successful title.

To judge by the ecstatic critical reception it was accorded on first publication, *Mine Own Executioner* marks the highpoint of Balchin's career as a novelist; thereafter, his star swiftly began to wane and just about the kindest adjective one can use to describe his subsequent output is 'uneven'. But with *Mine Own Executioner*, Balchin firmly established himself as one of the foremost popular novelists of his era, as witnessed by the many garlands bestowed on him by his peers in 1945.

Balchin is fortunate that he lived long enough to have any garlands bestowed on him at all as he very nearly failed to survive his own childhood:

> ...when I was about eighteen months old I knocked over a large kettle of boiling water and scalded myself so badly that I was not expected to live.[4]

A couple of decades before this painful incident, which thankfully had no lasting deleterious effects, another domestic event had taken place in the Balchin household that *did* have serious ramifications for the family. Its genesis was related by Balchin in an Author's Note[5] that preceded his compendium of short stories *Last Recollections of My Uncle Charles*:

> One day in the year 1887 my grandfather, who up till that time had been a hardworking farmer of 800 acres in Surrey, remarked at luncheon that he was tired of the farm and could not be bothered with it any more. After the meal, instead of going out to his work in the normal way, he settled down at the fireside with his pug dog, and hardly left it again, except to eat and to go to bed, until he died three years later.

The grandfather that Balchin wrote about, George Martin[6] Balchin (1830–1898), was descended from a line of wealthy and successful Surrey farmers who cultivated the land around Godalming, Dorking and Guildford. George married Sarah Ann Puttock (1833–1917) and the couple had seven children, the youngest of whom, William Edwin (1872–1958), was Nigel Balchin's father. George's impromptu decision to take early retirement from agricultural life drastically affected the future prosperity of his family. By the time that Nigel was born, the wealth of his forebears was little more than a distant memory. Out of necessity, a work ethic was instilled in Balchin from an early age and persisted until the very end of a writing career characterized above all else by industriousness:

> My father worked his head off to raise me and my brother and sister. I have worked mine off in order to bring up my children.[7]

In 1899, William Edwin Balchin married Ada Elizabeth Curtis in Potterne, Wiltshire. William had been born in Godalming. Ada, the daughter of a railway guard, was born in Wolverhampton in 1870. The newly-weds moved into a house in an area of Potterne known as The Butts. Here William worked as a baker, later extending his repertoire to include the running of a grocer's shop. The couple's first child was a boy born in 1900 and given the same two forenames as his father. A girl followed four years later: born in 1904, she was baptized Monica Coralie.

Nigel Marlin Balchin was born on 3 December 1908 and baptized at the church of St Mary the Virgin in Potterne on 10 January 1909. The earliest surviving photograph of William and Ada's third and final offspring was taken when he was just a few months old. Dressed in a voluminous white smock and seated in the corner of a couch, a chubby, healthy-looking boy who seems entirely at ease with himself smiles broadly back at the photographer. The glossy, luxuriant locks of dark hair and the distinctive oval face are familiar from studio portraits of the best-selling author of the 1940s and 1950s. Describing this image many years later, Balchin suggested that his youthful good looks may have deteriorated rather sooner than he would have liked:

> Rather a splendid chap I must say – what a pity it couldn't last.[8]

When Balchin was a small child the population of Potterne only just exceeded three figures, the 1911 census reporting the village's numerical strength as 1,145. It was a rural community situated about three miles south of Devizes on the main road to Salisbury and many of its residents earned a living from some form of agricultural activity. Balchin's birthplace had suffered a troubled past. During the nineteenth century it was said to be 'notorious for hooliganism'[9] and favourite activities of the villagers included rumbustious sporting contests, heavy drinking, gambling, quarrelling and fighting. An 1834 report noted that 'This parish of Potterne is filled with a very discontented and turbulent race'. So flagitious were the villagers, and so often did they find themselves in trouble with the law, that they were given the ironic appellation 'The Potterne Lambs' and when the law court was in session the magistrate would often exclaim exasperatedly 'Another case from Potterne!'.[10] The poor of the parish even went so far as to pool their meagre resources so that they could buy a legal textbook and use it to bamboozle the magistrate whenever a Potterne resident was summonsed.

By the time that Balchin was born, Potterne, partly as the result of a strong church influence, had succeeded in mending its ways and had become a much more law-abiding place. In an autobiographical sketch published in 1964, Balchin recalled his childhood in some detail, describing an essentially primitive existence:

> There was, of course, neither running water nor electricity. Water was from a pump, or drawn up in buckets from a well. Lighting was by paraffin oil lamps, both in the house and in the street—if the street was lit at all.[11]

The oil lamps that lined the main street running through Potterne were illuminated only for a two-hour period in the evening, just long enough to allow village residents to make their way safely to the pub and back. As Balchin indicated, the lamp-lighting operation was endearingly eccentric:

> ...the man in charge of lighting the lamps was an old gentleman with the rather appropriate name of Noah Dark. Well Noah was old, the street was long and he was not a fast mover. So what he used to do was to start at one end of the village and light the lamps, go up through the street lighting them and by the time he got to the last lamp it was just about time to put them out again. So he used to light the last lamp, immediately put it out and then go down the street turning out all the other lamps too.[12]

The house in which Balchin grew up—which has long since been demolished—was small, with what he described as 'exceptionally low ceilings',[13] and perhaps he was recalling certain features of his childhood home when he wrote about the humble abode of Elsie Pearce, widow of hit-and-run victim Joe, in his novel *A Way Through the Wood*:

> The Pearces lived in one of those cottages that are all right as long as you only have to see them from the road— thatched and built of lovely old brick, and with creeper over the front, like a sentimental chocolate box. Inside there are about four tiny rooms, very dark, with brick floors that are always damp, and ceilings so low that a tall man can't stand upright.

A strong value system was instilled in Balchin as a child: 'The ideas in which I was brought up are based on the assumption that there is such a thing as right & wrong'.[14] Although he claimed in 1952 that one of the great formative influences to which he had been subjected when young was 'a somewhat Puritan upbringing, which emphasized the importance of loyalty, duty, & self-abnegation', there is no evidence that Balchin's childhood was not a happy one. The environment in which he was raised was warm and loving, even if that love was only implicit:

> I was brought up in a singularly undemonstrative family, whose affections for each other were singularly deep & enduring. We took our basic love for one another entirely for granted, & to us love was something you *did*, not something that you said, or even something that you merely felt.

Another factor that had a profound effect on Balchin's future development was the breathtaking scenery surrounding his house:

> For me, perhaps the strongest formative influence in my early years was Salisbury Plain itself. I thought, and still think, that those bare windswept chalk downs were one of the most beautiful places in the world...[15]

It is apparent from reading his first two novels that Balchin was exceptionally fond of the great outdoors as a young man. Growing up in sight of Salisbury Plain had given him 'a love of space and tumbling wind, a liking for big sweeping views, and a preference for scenery which depends for its beauty on line rather than on decoration.' Long walks in the country are a prominent feature of several examples of Balchin's fiction and it seems likely that, in his youth, he took advantage of the magnificent countryside on his doorstep by walking extensively on the Wiltshire downs.

In Balchin's second novel *Simple Life*, the vast majority of the narrative is set in and around the writer's old stamping ground. Rufus Wade, the advertising copywriter who escapes the noise and dirt of London in search of a simpler existence, first encounters 'the great bare sweeps of Salisbury Plain' as the furniture van in which he hitches a lift to St Ives passes through rural Wiltshire. Soon afterwards, when the van suffers a breakdown, Rufus gets out, looks around and is struck by the open space surrounding him:

> To the left the brow of a hill mounted sharply only a hundred yards away. But to the right there was nothing. Nothing but bare green downland and far-away sky.

Later, after a lengthy stroll, it is the paucity of habitation that makes the greatest impression on Rufus:

> Untired by his walk, he was still intoxicated by the sheer grandeur of space and silence through which he had passed. He had walked for nearly three hours and had seen no human thing. There had been two or three distant outlying farms, and twice there had been men [sic] and horses moving, pygmy-like and slow, over vast expanses of brown earth. He had heard a dull far-away booming and had seen the weather-worn notices warning the passer-by from artillery ranges.

The proximity of Salisbury Plain to Balchin's house in Potterne brought him into contact with military manoeuvres—such as those referred to by Rufus in *Simple Life*—when still only a small child. The Plain was occupied by army encampments and aerodromes by the time of the First World War and, speaking in 1964, Balchin recalled his first sighting of an aeroplane there at the age of six:

> I remember it very well because it was just after the outbreak of World War One and I'd been taken to see a battalion of the Wiltshire Regiment going off to France. An aeroplane arrived and my father put me on his shoulders to look at this extraordinary affair which as I remember it seems to have consisted mainly of piano wire and canvas flaps.[16]

During the Second World War, Balchin may well have cast his mind back to his childhood locale when he came to devise locations and plot lines for his most famous novel, *The Small*

Back Room. Salisbury Plain probably supplied the inspiration for Graveley Bank ('a bare, bleak place with a tearing east wind that never stopped blowing'), the setting for the weapons trials witnessed by Sammy Rice in the novel. The legendary film director Michael Powell obviously sensed a Wiltshire connection when he filmed Balchin's novel in 1948, selecting Stonehenge as the location for this scene. An ancient stone circle would not seem to be a very practical place for testing experimental weaponry, but it was of course situated in close proximity to a heavily militarized area and the guns were pointing away from the monoliths, which provided an attractive backdrop and presumably had some resonance for the film's overseas audience.[17]

The most important plot thread of *The Small Back Room* may also have been inspired by Balchin's early experiences of living in Wiltshire. On 7 February 1918, the *Wiltshire Gazette* carried an article written by a Marlborough doctor warning of the perils of interfering with live munitions. Small boys playing on the downs had been hitting unexploded bombs with hammers and had suffered severe hand injuries as a result, with one child losing parts of both his thumb and forefinger. It was the doctor's belief that the devices had been dropped from aeroplanes as part of military exercises. With due allowance for the non-fatal outcome, the account given by the newspaper is startlingly similar to the situation that occurs in *The Small Back Room* when a young girl plays with a booby-trapped bomb dropped by the Luftwaffe and is blown to pieces. There is no way of knowing whether Balchin read this particular issue of the *Wiltshire Gazette* as a boy, but the parallel is certainly uncanny and it seems likely that he either knew of this particular incident or else had heard of similar ones.

Before the First World War was over, the Balchin family had moved away from Potterne. They established themselves three miles closer to Salisbury in West Lavington, a small village at the foot of Salisbury Plain. The house in which they resided, Holly Cottage in the High Street, also served as headquarters for the newly established firm of William E. Balchin & Son, bakers, with its lower floor functioning as a combined bakery and teashop in which Nigel's father and brother could ply their trade.

The Balchins presumably relocated to West Lavington so that Nigel could begin his secondary schooling because within a year or two of moving house he had begun to attend The Dauntsey Agricultural School, just a few hundred yards' walk from Holly Cottage.

*

Dauntsey's School—by which abbreviated name it has been known since 1923—was founded in 1542 and has occupied the same picturesque location just off the High Street in the centre of West Lavington since 1895. It was probably in 1918 that Nigel Balchin made his way up the attractive tree-lined drive towards the imposing red-brick facade to begin his schooling there.[18] The mission of the establishment was to provide an agricultural training for its pupils to enable them to pursue a career on the land once they had completed their education. Many of Dauntsey's pupils were thus farmers' sons who left the school at the earliest possible opportunity so that they could become farmers themselves. The most celebrated example was Arthur George (A. G.) Street (1892–1966), who wrote a string of novels based on his farming experiences and became a fixture on the radio from the 1930s onwards as a contributor to programmes that made use of his agricultural knowledge and commonsensical approach to life, most notably *Any Questions?*. Other boys who attended Dauntsey's in the 1920s came from a similar social stratum as Balchin, being the sons of tradesmen such as brewers, dairymen and builders.

In 1992, a renowned writer of children's fiction penned an account of his schooldays at Dauntsey's.[19] Wilbert Vere Awdry, better known to his readers as 'The Rev. W. Awdry', began writing 'The Railway Series' of books in 1945, his best-known fictional creation being Thomas the Tank Engine. Awdry entered Dauntsey's at the end of 1924. His first experience of the school had come a little earlier when he had sat the entrance examination, the chief invigilator on that occasion having been Balchin.[20] Bullying had apparently been rampant in Balchin's early days at Dauntsey's; six years on, a somewhat unhealthy atmosphere continued to pervade its corridors according to the future churchman:

> ...the School was still a rather rough place, populated for the most part by farmers' sons, with bad language often to be heard. Some of the pupils had ended up there as a result of being asked to leave their former seats of learning.[21]

Less than a year after Balchin began his secondary education a new headmaster arrived at Dauntsey's. George Olive had previously been a housemaster at Oundle, a public school in Northamptonshire that was then in the throes of transforming itself into a renowned centre for science and engineering; under his leadership, the direction of the Wiltshire establishment was decisively altered for the better. As well as stamping out the bullying (which must surely have worked to the advantage of the quiet, studious Balchin), Olive quickly steered Dauntsey's curriculum away from its previous dependence on agriculture and, in Oundle fashion, towards more conventional academic subjects such as languages, engineering and the hard sciences. The reforms instituted by the new headmaster were to have a significant influence on Balchin's scholastic development and ultimately helped him to win a place at Cambridge.

Outside the classroom, a full and varied sporting programme also existed during Balchin's time at Dauntsey's. Two open-air fives courts were built in 1924, when he was fifteen, allowing him to play a game generally associated with more illustrious schools. Rugby was introduced at the school in the same year. As a tall, well-built young man, Balchin made a natural back-row forward, and he packed down in the Dauntsey's First XV scrummage on many occasions. In addition to captaining his school at cricket, Balchin opened the batting. Unsurprisingly, given the overlapping skill sets required, he also kept wicket for the cricket team and played in goal for the hockey side. The love affair with sport that blossomed for Balchin whilst a pupil at Dauntsey's would prove to be a permanent one, although after the Second World War he generally preferred spectating to participation, deriving particular pleasure from watching tennis at Wimbledon and cricket at Lord's.

In his senior years at Dauntsey's, Balchin's achievements are documented with increasing frequency in the school magazine, the *Dauntseian*. His annus mirabilis was 1926, when he captained the school at cricket and soccer, won colours for hockey and rugby, played fives, hockey and rugby for the school, helped to produce the school magazine and was presented with two prizes at the annual Speech Day presentations on 30 June by the Duchess of Atholl: the Headmaster's prize and the Elocution prize. The award of the latter trophy bears testament to the patient efforts of Dauntsey's teaching staff to eradicate his broad Wiltshire accent:

> I had a rather splendid one as a child, but when I went to school they painstakingly educated it out of me, so that I, to whom Saint Peter had been 'Zent Pedur', now learnt to call him 'Sent Petah' like a proper gentleman. They meant well, but whenever I have heard Mr A. G. Street talking on radio or television, and contrasted my niminy-piminy, plum-in-the-mouth accent with his, I have felt that they were mistaken.[22]

Balchin might also have received prizes at the 1925 Speech Day had the event not been cancelled because of a bizarre fatality that plunged the whole school into mourning. The Duchess of Atholl, a Unionist politician nicknamed 'The Red Duchess' as a result of her support for the Republican side in the Spanish Civil War, had been the intended guest of honour on that occasion too. (The Duchess subsequently served as a guardian to the young Yovanka Tomich, who became Balchin's second wife in 1953.) On the morning of the Speech Day, two boys were deputed to go and shoot a bird with an air rifle in order to obtain a specimen for a demonstration of anatomical dissection that could then form the centrepiece of a display of work mounted to impress both the Duchess and visiting parents. Evidently the rudiments of accurate rifle shooting did not form part of the Dauntsey's curriculum because one of the two boys, instead of shooting a sparrow or blackbird, accidentally shot and killed his fellow pupil.[23] This strange tragedy was echoed many years later in Italy, when Nigel and Yovanka Balchin were able to rent a Florentine villa principally because the lady of the house refused to live there any longer after one of her sons was killed by his brother in a comparable shooting accident.

In 1927, Balchin's final year at Dauntsey's, he came close to rivalling his achievements of the year before when he was made captain of the school, represented it at hockey and rugby, was again awarded colours for rugby and retained the Headmaster's prize. Although a case can be made that Balchin was merely a big fish in a small pond—Dauntsey's had sixty-nine pupils when he arrived at the school and 113 when he left—his scholastic career was indubitably one of unalloyed success, both in the classroom and on the sports field.

Some idea of what Balchin was like as a schoolboy is provided by reminiscences from two of his contemporaries. John Cox attended the school between 1921 and 1926. In Cox's final year at the school, Balchin 'was having extra tuition, possibly in preparation for his Cambridge entrance'.[24] Cox recalled that Balchin was 'a quiet and studious boy who did not stand out in a crowd'. This view was echoed by Eddie Look, who spent five years at Dauntsey's from 1922 onwards before leaving at the age of fifteen to work on his family's farm. In Look's opinion, Balchin was 'very quiet and modest'[25] and impressed him as someone who had an unassuming nature despite his intelligence and obvious academic ability.

He may not have stood out in a crowd, but the unassuming Balchin is easy to spot in the 1925 school photograph. Taller than most of his fellow pupils and also than some of the teachers, he can be quickly recognized by virtue of his oval-shaped face and prominent ears. If he weren't attired in the school uniform of black jacket and grey trousers, the sixteen-year-old could almost be taken for a young master in his first teaching post after leaving university, such is his height and air of erudition and self-possession. When Balchin was interviewed for admission to Peterhouse a year or so later, the Senior Tutor of the Cambridge college, Paul Cairn Vellacott, scribbled the words 'rather self-confident, intelligent'[26] in pencil at the bottom of the schoolboy's application form.

When he was not occupied with his school work, Balchin played an active part in the social life of his village. Together with his father and brother, he belonged to the West Lavington Sports Club, which gave him the opportunity to participate in sports such as cricket, billiards and tennis. Balchin's mother was a stalwart of both the Women's Institute and the Mother's Union and his sister Monica was a long-time member of the church choir. In Yovanka's opinion, all of Balchin's family were churchgoers when he was a child and her husband was 'Very influenced by religion'.[27] Whether it was acquired in church, in the classroom or elsewhere, Balchin accumulated a vast repository of biblical knowledge in his youth—'he could quote the Bible by heart' according to Yovanka—and some of that knowledge was later integrated into his fiction, most notably in *Lord, I Was Afraid*.

The Balchins were evidently a very public-spirited family as there are numerous reports in the *Wiltshire Gazette* in the 1920s and 1930s of fetes in aid of the church, the Sunday School outing fund or the Sports Club in which they played a role, helping to run stalls such as darts for a pig, clock golf or the coconut shy, and Balchin brought this experience to life in the opening scenes of *A Way Through the Wood*.

Making music was another important aspect of Balchin's adolescence. In 1954 he revealed his *Desert Island Discs* to a radio audience.[28] He told the programme's host, Roy Plomley, that he had been:

> ...brought up in a Wiltshire village in the days when transport was a great deal more difficult than it is now and, where, if you wanted to be amused, you rather had to amuse yourself. My brother and sister were both very fond of music and we used to make a good deal of music together.

This musical ability is corroborated by several reports in the *Wiltshire Gazette*, such as one from 16 April 1925, in which the orchestra performing at the West Lavington Sports Club Dance on Easter Monday included 'the Balchin family with their jazz instruments'. Balchin informed Plomley that he had been the leader of a dance band for a while shortly before he was due to leave Dauntsey's and he added self-deprecatingly that he had also endured a reputation when a schoolboy as 'the worst cellist in three counties'.

Another of Balchin's interests as a teenager was church organs and, in particular, trying to play the works of Johan Sebastian Bach on them. At about the age of eighteen, Balchin would seek out churches in the vicinity of West Lavington and beg the vicar to allow him to use the organ. Many years later, Balchin recalled:

> ...sitting there in the organ loft, alone in an empty church that was usually perishingly cold, wrestling with the little E Minor. The bits of it that I could play sounded magnificent. The rest was a terrible row.[29]

Balchin and his two siblings ran the West Lavington Choral Society and once took part in a performance of Bach's 'St Matthew's Passion'. The youngest of the three Balchin children would retain a lifelong interest in classical music, and an especial love of Bach.

In the 1960s, Balchin disclosed that he had undertaken occasional trips to Devizes in his teens to perform 'tentative efforts at girl-hunting'.[30] His first known crush was a local beauty by the name of Mary Thomas:

> I never knew her, or even spoke to her, for I was sixteen and very shy, and Miss Mary Thomas must have been 21, and by my standards very sophisticated. But I loved her passionately from afar.

In the light of his subsequent facility at writing film scripts, it is a little surprising that Balchin's forays to Devizes rarely took him inside the doors of the town's cinema, as he admitted that he had seen only a very small number of films when he was living in West Lavington.

After passing examinations in English, Chemistry and Biology, Balchin was awarded his Higher School Certificate for Natural Sciences on 29 July 1926. He then gained a scholarship from the Ministry of Agriculture under the Sons and Daughters of Agriculture Workers Scheme; the fact that his father was a baker would appear to have made him eligible. These scholarships, which were intended to train agricultural scientists, were in great demand. Having been fortunate enough to secure one, Balchin decided that he would like to try for admission to Peterhouse. His cause was aided by his headmaster, who wrote a letter to the Senior Tutor commending his star pupil:

> Comparing him with many other boys at Ouncle and Dauntsey, I am of opinion that he ranks as one of the best boy biologists I have known.[31]

Balchin was interviewed by Vellacott, succeeded in the obligatory Latin examination and was formally admitted to the University on 5 January 1927. Vellacott originally refused to consider the Dauntsey's pupil as part of the 1927–1928 undergraduate intake, but later relented and squeezed him in at the eleventh hour after special pleading on the part of the Ministry of Agriculture.

One feature of school life would remain difficult to shift from Balchin's mind for many years afterwards. The awfulness of the food that emerged from the Dauntsey's kitchens is evident from this anecdote related by Awdry:

> Arriving back after holidays in about 1925 all boys found inside the lids of their desks a list of injunctions, of which the most memorable read: "Tuck is a luxury and not a necessity, for the food supplied is good in quality and ample in quantity. These regulations are to prevent greediness and the bad habit of eating between meals." There was perhaps a certain inevitability about the ignoble fate suffered by this

high sentiment—to be chanted irreverently in the dining hall, particularly on those occasions when less than generous portions were doled out.[32]

Compare this with the following extract from *How to Run a Bassoon Factory*, Balchin's first non-fiction book, written less than seven years after he had left Dauntsey's:

It is not difficult to draught [sic] a prospectus. Remember the prospectus of your old school and stick to about the same standard of accuracy and veracity. I don't want to put ideas into your head, but you may remember that your old school described its food as 'scientifically balanced, plentiful, appetising and nutritious'. Now think of what its food was really like, and you will see my meaning.

2

Psychology Welcomes a New Recruit

The University Lecturer in Abnormal Psychology lived in Old Court. The porter directed Milne to the staircase in the far corner and he read the list of names at the bottom of B. Staircase.

W. M. Tew.
A. J. P. Richmond.
Lord Islip.
J. W. Graham.
Dr. W. R. Field.

    Milne paused for a moment just to make absolutely sure that his decision was made, and that it was the right decision. He had no real doubt about it. But he was just twenty-one, and it was an autumn evening, and Old Court was very impressive. He thought again of the words in which he had decided to put it to Dr. Field. "It seems to me, sir, that this stuff is so important that if one really believes in it, there isn't much choice but to devote one's life to it—" Simple, noble words, as became the response to a Call—the realisation of a vocation. And Dr. Field would stretch out a hand, in slightly emotional silence, to welcome this new recruit to the cause...
        – Nigel Balchin, *Mine Own Executioner*

The extract above is part of the prologue to Balchin's 'psychological' novel *Mine Own Executioner*, in which the third-year medical student Felix Milne seeks advice from one of his lecturers on the best way to direct his studies so that he can fulfil his ambition of becoming a psychoanalyst. There are clear differences between Milne and Balchin. Milne studied Physiology, Anatomy and Chemistry for Part I of his Tripos, for which he achieved a First; Balchin took Botany in place of Anatomy and could manage only a Second. Milne studied Medicine in his third year whereas Balchin concentrated largely on Agriculture. And so on. But there are sufficient similarities between the two men—such as their evident shared interest in psychoanalysis and abnormal psychology and the fact that, during their first two years at university, they had both read Natural Sciences and passed their first and second Bachelor of Medicine degrees, so that they would only have needed to do hospital work in order to have qualified as doctors—to make it excusable to believe that at least some of this piece of fiction may have been inspired by a real event. For W. R. Field read F. C. Bartlett.

Frederic Bartlett was Director of the Cambridge Psychological Laboratory and Reader in Experimental Psychology when Balchin was at Peterhouse. Had Balchin knocked on Bartlett's door one evening, in comparable fashion to Milne, he would probably have received both an enthusiastic welcome and a sympathetic hearing ('Bartlett was kindly, encouraging, and informal. He inspired enthusiasm'[1]). The aura of the eminent psychologist, allied to the appeal of his subject, exerted a powerful attractive force on Cambridge students:

> His weekly lecture-discussions were a festive performance which nobody would have dreamed of missing, so that every corner of the small room was crammed.[2]

Balchin seems to have approached Bartlett at some point during his third year and begged the psychologist to allow him to study his subject. Accosting Bartlett would have been a straightforward process:

> It was incredibly easy to approach him, both because the modern hurdles of secretaries and ante-rooms were missing, and also because of the beaming and attentive welcome with

which he would greet brash and ignorant potential students or importunate and worried postgraduates.

In marked contrast, Milne in *Mine Own Executioner* receives a discouraging response from Dr Field, a deaf and obstructive old man who is convinced that the would-be psychoanalyst would be better off completing his medical studies first:

"I should go on and qualify and then think it over," he said rather wearily. "You've got plenty of time."

Balchin did not have plenty of time. His student days were drawing rapidly to a close and he was determined to get the most out of his final term having abandoned his Agriculture course. Studying Psychology under Bartlett (who became the first Cambridge Professor of Experimental Psychology a year after Balchin went down, a post he held for over twenty years) gave Balchin the chance to begin laying the foundations for a career as a psychologist. Many of the successes of the first half of his adult life can be traced back to his brave and momentous decision in February 1930 to turn his back on the prospect of a life on the land and instead embrace the newer, more exciting discipline of Psychology.

At the beginning of his third year, Balchin had intended to read for Part II of the Natural Sciences Tripos, in the subject of Botany. He did not have a free hand in the matter: the Ministry of Agriculture was paying for his university education by way of a large scholarship and, not unnaturally, they wished him to study for a Diploma in Agriculture Science either as well as, or instead of, the Tripos, a programme that would have taken two more years to complete. Midway through the Lent term Balchin rebelled against the Ministry's demands, advising them that it was pointless for him to continue to study Agriculture as he had no intention of pursuing an agrarian vocation when he left Cambridge. After a lengthy wrangle between Balchin and the Ministry, the student got his own way: he was released from the agricultural obligations of his scholarship and given the opportunity to determine the nature of the remainder of his studies. This is when he would have approached Bartlett and asked if he could study Psychology during his final term. Balchin came to the new subject with great excitement and enthusiasm, as he made clear in 1964 when he recalled the feelings that had been engendered by the discipline during his time as a student:

> When I was an undergraduate at Cambridge, I was convinced and a lot of other people were convinced, that there was a new heaven and a new earth just round the corner. We felt that in the discoveries of Freud and Ardler [sic] and Yung [sic] a door had been opened to the understanding of the minds and emotions of men.[3]

Balchin's desire to study Psychology was perhaps triggered by his burgeoning curiosity where human sexuality was concerned (the root of which remains obscure). Eric St Johnston, who subsequently became Chief Inspector of Constabulary for England and Wales, was a Mathematics freshman at Corpus Christi whom Balchin befriended during his final year at Cambridge. The innocent mien, clean-cut good looks and fresh-faced charm of the young Balchin must have been at odds with the intrusive lines of questioning he sometimes adopted when pursuing his new interest amongst his contemporaries, as St Johnston remembered:

> Nigel was an odd character with an intelligent, inquiring mind and a disconcerting habit of turning his upper lip inside out when he smiled, which was often. He kept copious notes of conversations that he had and would question all his friends and acquaintances about their dreams and, if they would discuss it, about their sexual thoughts and experiences. This was not for prurient reasons, but because of his scientific interest. In later life he told me that, with much regret, he was forced, owing to other commitments, to refuse a contract to re-edit and modernise Havelock Ellis's *Psychology of Sex*.[4]

This revealing anecdote is the earliest evidence we have of Balchin's lifelong interest in the scientific and psychological facets of the sexual experience. His second wife Yovanka stresses that her husband was 'very sexually aware [...] he loved talking to prostitutes [...] And he read all the sort of junk paper, all the books that arrive in brown envelopes and things like that.'[5] Prominent among the sexual literature that would clatter through the Balchin letterbox during his second marriage was 'anything to do with spanking'. Once one is made aware of this predilection then it is almost impossible to read any Balchin novel without uncovering at least one mention of the practice. Spanking is usually introduced into a narrative with a knowing wink towards its pleasurable connotations and Jim Manning in *A Way Through the Wood*, a character who is similar in some ways to Balchin, declares that 'I only put people across my knee for amusement'. Balchin's novels (mainly the later ones, but also earlier works such as 1942's *Darkness Falls from the Air* and 1948's *The Borgia Testament*) also attempt to periodically titillate the reader by mentioning witches' Sabbaths, striptease, voyeurism and orgies.

Balchin's daughter Penelope Leach has indicated that her father always had a 'passionate desire'[6] to be a psychoanalyst. Although diverted into other career avenues in early adulthood, he maintained an amateur's interest in the subject and even claimed in 1939 that he had practised as an abnormal psychologist ever since leaving Cambridge. In addition to turning down the opportunity to revise Ellis's work, Balchin planned to write a book of his own on a related subject in the 1960s. Provisionally entitled *The Language of Sex*, the proposed volume would have discussed why many people find it difficult to write and talk about sex, but would also have contained chapters on topics such as pornography, swearing and representations of sexual activity in film, theatre and literature. It remained unfinished when Balchin died.

*

When Balchin went up to Cambridge in 1927 he found himself surrounded by a talented collection of students who were already making their mark on University life in an assortment of ways.

Anthony Blunt (later to become Surveyor of the Royal Pictures before being outed as a Russian spy in the 1970s) was engaged in vitriolic arguments about art in one of the student newspapers. Michael Redgrave—who in 1947 starred in a film for which Balchin had written the script—affected an aesthetic pose (he was never seen in public without a book under his arm) in preparation for becoming one of the most revered stage and screen actors of his generation. The University's chess team numbered among its members both Jacob (*The Ascent of Man*) Bronowski and Maurice Kendall (later to become a friend of Balchin's and to be knighted for services to the theory of statistics).

A contemporary of Balchin's, the future surrealist painter Julian Trevelyan, who wore a large black felt hat as a student and bicycled through the streets of the town clad in carpet slippers, observed in his memoirs that 'Cambridge about 1929 was remarkable for its poets'.[7] The most brilliant of these was William Empson, already a published poet by the time he arrived at Magdalene. Empson and Bronowski edited the magazine *Experiment*, the content of which was influenced by some of the ideas of Magdalene English don Ivor Armstrong (I. A.) Richards, who tutored Empson. Other aspiring student poets of the late 1920s included the likes of John Lehmann, Julian Bell and Redgrave himself, who, with assistance from Blunt, launched *The Venture*, a rival publication to *Experiment* and one that adhered to a Bloomsbury ideology.

Other Cambridge undergraduates of Balchin's era who would achieve fame after going down included the documentary film makers Humphrey Jennings (director of *Fires Were Started* and co-founder of Mass-Observation) and Basil Wright (co-director of *Night Mail*), the writer and fiction reviewer John Davenport (described by Trevelyan as 'Fat, witty, bibulous, charming, bawdy' whilst at Cambridge and who, in 1955, contributed a rapturous review of Balchin's novel *The Fall of the Sparrow* to the *Observer*), the novelist Malcolm Lowry (author of *Under the Volcano*), the inventor of the hovercraft Christopher Cockerell and three future stars of television and radio: the vituperative Gilbert Harding (*What's My Line?*), who first established a reputation as a vigorous debater at the Cambridge Union, Arthur Marshall of *Call My Bluff* fame, drag star of numerous student drama productions, and Alistair Cooke (*Letter from America*).

Balchin may never have spoken to any of these fellow students. Perhaps he knew one or two of them by reputation or passed them occasionally in the street, but he did not enjoy the same exalted status as some of these characters whilst an undergraduate. What is beyond doubt is that the experience of meeting a very different type of person at Cambridge than he had previously been exposed to later rubbed off on Balchin's writing. This can be seen especially in the plays he wrote in the mid-1930s, a recurrent theme of which is a sort of horrified fascination with degenerate Oxbridge students, and also in *The Fall of the Sparrow*, in which the Cambridge aesthete Simon Grieves is referred to as 'an open sewer'.

Balchin took up residence in Cambridge on 5 October 1927. His home during his first year as an undergraduate was 7 Tennis Court Road, a two-storey terraced house that functioned as a College lodging and was situated just a few hundred yards away from Peterhouse. A student whose time in Cambridge overlapped with that of Balchin, and who lived at 7 Tennis Court Road himself in the 1931–1932 academic year, wrote a reminiscence of his Peterhouse days shortly before he died. As a non-public schoolboy—he attended Bradford Grammar School—from a poor background, Frank Walbank's experience of being a student in the 1920s was probably reasonably similar, at least from the domestic angle, to that of Balchin.

Life in Tennis Court Road would have been quite spartan for the former Dauntsey's pupil. College lodgings were not noted for their comfort and the provision of even routine modern conveniences could not be taken for granted. So when Balchin wanted a bath he may have been required to set foot outside his front door as Walbank recalled that 'Since lodgings often did not provide bathing facilities, you might not infrequently see men in pyjamas and a dressing-gown hurrying down Fitzwilliam Street in the early morning to take their place in the queue for the two College baths'.[8]

Although Balchin's accommodation was run by a landlady, one of her principal functions, prioritized perhaps above the welfare of her guest, was to act as a gatekeeper: the doors of College lodgings were routinely locked at 10 pm and any student seeking ingress after that time was reported to his tutor and fined accordingly. The duties of Balchin's landlady might not even have extended as far as cooking her lodger a meal in the morning because Walbank recalled that 'Breakfasts were delivered to College lodgings [...] on a bicycle'. Certainly Balchin would have eaten his evening meal at the College as 'Peterhouse dinner in Hall was reckoned to be the best in Cambridge [...] Attendance was compulsory, but you were allowed to sign off once a week (which I usually did as an economy measure).' Balchin probably did likewise, as he would not have had very deep pockets whilst living in Tennis Court Road. Walbank stated that 'To get by at Cambridge in those days (without any extravagance) cost around £220 p.a.'. Balchin's scholarship only amounted to about £200 a year (about £11,000 a year today[9]) and it is unlikely that his father would have had sufficient funds at his disposal to have topped up that sum in any meaningful way.

Founded in 1284, Peterhouse is the oldest of the thirty or so constituent colleges that make up Cambridge University. In Balchin's time, it was also the smallest of the Cambridge colleges: Balchin was one of only fifty-two students admitted in 1927–1928, joining 105 other undergraduates already in residence. The centrepiece of Peterhouse, and the most attractive building ranged around its central courtyard, is the seventeenth century chapel, a building that Balchin became very well acquainted with when he joined the College choir. Today, a statement on the College's website declares that Peterhouse 'has been and is somewhere that values the bold, the characterful and the committed above the commonplace, the familiar and the mundane'.[10] This is a creed that Balchin seems to have wholeheartedly embraced during his three years as a member of the College.

As a freshman, Balchin continued to pursue the interest in sport that had been so well nourished at Dauntsey's. His prowess at rugby remained untarnished, a report in the March 1928 edition of the *Dauntseian* stating that Balchin 'was the only fresher to get a place in the Peterhouse 1st XV' and that 'he has been given colours this term.' Over the same period he had also 'played for the college hockey XI occasionally'. Back at Dauntsey's on 21 January 1928, having become a member of the Old Dauntseians Association that winter, Balchin turned out for the Old Boys against the School, this time as an outfield player, not a goalkeeper, and was on the wrong end of a 3-2 scoreline. A team photograph has survived to memorialize this encounter: the burly Balchin, seated in the middle of the front row, gripping his hockey stick tightly in both hands, looks a good deal bigger and stronger than some of his team-mates, suggesting that the best dinner in Cambridge had succeeded in bulking him up and that the fresh air and exercise that were part and parcel of playing sport for his college were having a positive effect on his health.

It is curious, given Balchin's schoolboy prowess at cricket, that he does not appear to have played the sport—at least not to a level where he would have attracted notice—whilst at Peterhouse. Possibly, as a diligent scholarship student, Balchin felt that the protracted extent of many cricket matches would have kept him away from his books for too long. Alternatively, it may just have been that he had found the company too daunting, bearing in mind that, had he attempted to obtain a Blue in his first year, one of his competitors for a place in the Cambridge First XI would have been K. S. Duleepsinhji, a batsman good enough to have gone on to average well over fifty in a brief England Test career truncated by persistent illness. Similarly, had Balchin wished to try out for the University golf team then he would have struggled to displace incumbents such as Henry Longhurst (later to become a respected golf journalist and television commentator), who was sufficiently adept at the sport to win both a Blue as a freshman and the German amateur title in 1936.

When Balchin was not being distracted by the lure of sport, his development as a scientist was undoubtedly aided by the fact that the University of Cambridge boasted a glittering teaching faculty in the 1920s and 1930s. As well as Richards, Bartlett and the Austrian philosopher Ludwig Wittgenstein, who began lecturing to undergraduates on the subject of Philosophical Logic in Balchin's final year, the University's staff also numbered two very distinguished biochemists. As Balchin said himself, 'It was difficult not to be a fair bio-chemist under Gowland Hopkins and Haldane'.[11,12]

In the last week of May 1928, Balchin sat the written papers for his Intercollegiate Examination in Natural Sciences, with practical examinations continuing into early June. He was placed in Class I when the exam results were published and rewarded with a prize in books. In an article written for *Punch* some years later, Balchin joked about the circumstances of this recognition of his academic ability:

> ...through a clerical error on the part of my examiners (who, presumably, added the date in with my marks), I won a prize at Cambridge. It wasn't two hundred pounds. I think, in point of fact, it was three guineas.[13]

Balchin's exam result also led to him being awarded an Exhibition (a minor scholarship) for Natural Sciences, to the value of £40. When added to his £200 Ministry of Agriculture scholarship, this would have taken him above the £220 threshold that one was required to attain in order to 'get by at Cambridge'.

Balchin left his lodgings in Tennis Court Road in the summer of 1928. When he returned to Cambridge in October that year he moved into a College room in New Court. James Gerstley was a Petrean who came up to Cambridge the year before Balchin and 'kept' in Old Court. It may have been situated on the other side of Trumpington Street but Balchin's accommodation is likely to have resembled, in most of the important particulars, that of Gerstley:

> Our rooms in those days consisted of a small bedroom, a small pantry and a nice sitting room which had a fireplace.

[…] There was no bathroom as such – a bedside chamber pot and a hip bath were the accessories supplied. A college servant […] emptied the chamber pot each day and left a can of hot water for the hip bath.[14]

In terms of his academic studies, Balchin may have taken his foot off the pedal in his second year at Cambridge. He certainly seems to have broadened his range of extra-curricular activities: perhaps with the security of his First in the Intercollegiate Examination behind him, he felt justified in slackening off to an extent and attempting to get more out of the Cambridge experience in his middle year. This impression is reinforced by Paul Vellacott, Senior Tutor of Peterhouse, in a letter written at the beginning of Balchin's final year detailing how the student had occupied his leisure hours during the 1928–1929 academic year:

…all these interests, in the direction of literature, music, and various societies, have shown that he has a genuine keenness and capacity to get the best out of his time here.[15]

Living in College accommodation would have meant that Balchin was closer to the heartbeat of student social life than he had been as a freshman. His schoolboy passion for music was reawakened during his second year. In the Michaelmas term he was awarded a Choral Exhibition, which may have permitted him to have his voice professionally tested and to pay for singing lessons. Balchin sang in the Peterhouse choir and it was with one of his fellow choristers that he forged one of the most enduring friendships of his life.

James Neville Mason, the son of a textile merchant from Huddersfield, came up to Peterhouse in autumn 1928 to study Classics. After two terms he transferred to an Architecture course, eventually achieving a First. He took up acting whilst at Cambridge and later became one of the most highly acclaimed screen actors of the twentieth century. According to Balchin, his friend was 'a rather shy, very handsome and completely charming undergraduate'[16] and could hold a note almost as proficiently as he was later able to deliver a line of dialogue:

> I suppose the only *really* distinguished thing about me is that I sang in the college choir with Mr. James Mason. And very good he was too.[17]

Michael Powell (director of the film adaptation of Balchin's novel *The Small Back Room*) described Mason, a few years after he had left Cambridge, as having 'a voice and bearing second to none'[18] and suggested that Balchin's first encounter with the Yorkshireman had taken place 'down at the boats'. As Mason rowed as part of the second-string Peterhouse 2 crew in his first year he may have met Balchin during the May Races held on the Cam in June 1929 or while he was in training for them. Powell recounted how the strapping young Mason had first come to the attention of Balchin:

> Nigel described a tall, black-haired, magnificently built man in white rowing shorts and singlet which modelled the graceful shape of his muscular limbs. Nigel was a master of words and phrases, and in that moment I saw that wonderful young man exactly as Nigel had seen him on that sunshiny morning. I also realised that Nigel had been in love with James all their lives, and I thought with tenderness and understanding, how beautiful the love of one man for another can be.

Any homo-erotic undertone discernible in Powell's reminiscence should probably be discounted and treated merely as a piece of mischief-making on the part of the auteur, given his impish sense of humour and flair for over-dramatization. As late as 1969 though, Balchin declared that he was 'very fond of James'[19] and he remained friends with him for many years after going down from Cambridge. The relationship would have been partly sustained by the two men's mutual interests in theatre and film. Mason starred in a Balchin-scripted play in the West End in 1937, and although he never collaborated with his friend on a movie, he was spoken of as an ideal choice for the role of the Caliph in a film adaptation of James Elroy Flecker's *Hassan* that Balchin was working on towards the end of his life.

Balchin's involvement with the College magazine devoured a significant amount of his time during his second year at Peterhouse. *The Magazine of the Peterhouse Sexcentenary Club*[20] (always known by the faintly titillating diminutive *The Sex*) was a long-running periodical that was published termly whilst Balchin was associated with it. His first engagement with *The Sex* came in Michaelmas term 1928, when he was made its Sub-Editor. By the following term he had risen to become the Editor. In May term 1929, with his Tripos examinations imminent, he ceded the editorship to another student.

The Sex comprised a jocular blend of College gossip, sports reports and interviews with prominent students. Balchin's efforts in commissioning articles for the magazine and coordinating its production seem to have largely prevented him from putting pen to paper himself. In fact his sole contribution to the issue of *The Sex* that he compiled[21] was a brief editorial. In this, he lamented that his desire to improve the magazine by means of the introduction of serious articles and illustrations had foundered owing to a lack of time as his Tripos examinations loomed. Amongst the excuses, some intriguing hints were dropped as to the matter-of-fact nature of the literary career that the outgoing Editor of *The Sex* would soon begin to follow:

> But though we could not have the magazine of our dreams, we have striven to produce the next best thing, and with that end in view we have practically abandoned the well-meant but boring straight-stuff which few read. We deplore semi-serious literature.

Undoubtedly the twenty-year-old undergraduate's tongue would have been wedged firmly in his cheek when he formulated that last sentence. But despite this proviso, Balchin would receive more attention for his humorous writings than for his attempts at serious literature for more than a decade after leaving Cambridge; it was not until the middle of the Second World War that he finally abandoned the dependence on flippancy and absurdity that had characterized his earlier books and magazine articles and concentrated all of his efforts on producing serious literature. The self-deprecating sense of humour that would soon resurface in Balchin's non-fiction books of the mid-1930s was already in place in his editorial:

> ...deep down in our mind is the hope that Someday Somebody of literary tastes, with wide acquaintance and PLENTY OF TIME, will come forward and produce a magazine worthy of the college—a feat of which we know ourselves to be quite incapable.

The intense study required to be successful in Part I of his Tripos, plus his involvement with the College magazine and participation in other extra-curricular activities, must have meant that there was little space remaining in Balchin's timetable for sport. *The Sex*[22] does report that he played golf once for Peterhouse in 1929, being part of a weakened team that endured a crushing 5-0 defeat at the hands of Magdalene. The golf correspondent's sense of levity cannot quite disguise Balchin's facility at a game he would continue to play at a social level deep into middle age:

> Mr. Balchin played a very pretty shot from the first tee, straight as a dye [sic] and at least 20 yards. Maintaining this excellent standard of play he soon secured a commanding lead of three holes. Unfortunately the pace was too hot to last. Reserving some of his really worst shots for the last few holes, Mr. Balchin nevertheless emerged from a furious contest with a great moral victory. Under the circumstances the fact that his opponent won by 2 and 1 is of no great importance.

Between 20 May and 7 June 1929, Balchin spent a total of forty-six hours at the Cambridge Examination School and in various laboratories dotted around the city, sitting four (day-long) written papers and three practical and oral examinations. The reward for this heroic feat of endurance was a Second in Part I of the Natural Sciences Tripos (Chemistry, Botany and Physiology). In a letter written a few months later, Vellacott expressed some disappointment at this result, although a ready explanation was to hand:

> We were somewhat surprised that he did not get a First Class in Part I of the Natural Sciences Tripos [...] I think perhaps he has had rather too many interests up here to allow full justice to himself in his Tripos...[23]

Balchin may have failed to live up to Vellacott's expectations but his Exhibition—still to the value of £40—was nevertheless renewed.

The Exhibitioner returned to Cambridge in October 1929 to begin his final year's studies. His home for the next eight months was to be 12 Fitzwilliam Street, a three-storey end-terrace house only a short walk from Peterhouse and with a view of the front elevation of the Fitzwilliam Museum on offer had he cared to stick his head out of one of its upstairs windows. With a heavy heart, Balchin abandoned his plan to take Part II of the Natural Sciences Tripos and fell in line with the Ministry of Agriculture's stipulation that he should study instead for a Diploma in Agriculture Science.

As he ploughed his way through tedious lectures and seminars about the science of farming, Balchin's mood would have been lightened by thoughts of two young women he had recently become acquainted with. Elisabeth Evelyn Walshe, born in Worplesdon, near Guildford in Surrey in 1910, was an attractive, statuesque redhead who had studied firstly at Sutton High School on the southern edge of London and later at Sherborne School for Girls in Dorset. Her journalist mother had died in 1929 when only in her late forties and a desire to avoid being detained at home in Surrey to care for her father and two younger siblings is very likely to have played a part in Elisabeth's decision to go up to

Newnham College to read English. Douglas Walshe, Elisabeth's father, was also a journalist as well as being a popular novelist with many successful books to his name who later collaborated with Balchin on the latter's 1936 play *Peace in Our Time*.

Elisabeth's best friend at the all-female Newnham College was Dorothy ('Dorrie') Gertrude Jackson, another woman who escaped a difficult home life—relations were strained between her mother and father and Dorrie did not get on well with either parent—in order to read English. Born in 1909, Dorrie was a slim, petite brunette who lived at Herne Hill in South London and attended nearby Sydenham High School before going up to Cambridge in October 1929, where she first met Elisabeth. The closeness between the two undergraduates is underlined by the fact that they both achieved Lower Seconds—with almost identical marks—in their first-year examinations and in Part I of the English Tripos, before transferring together onto an Archaeology and Anthropology course and both being awarded Lower Seconds in Section B of that Tripos. Dorrie's son John Stein, now a distinguished physiologist at Oxford University, believes that his mother may have fallen in love with Balchin during her first year at Newnham, but it is unclear to what extent (if any) her interest in him was reciprocated. Yovanka Balchin is also of the opinion that Dorrie was 'at some point in love with Nigel'[24] but remembers that, before he met Elisabeth, Balchin had eyes only for a girl called Olive, who strenuously rebuffed all of his advances.

It is not known how Balchin first encountered Elisabeth. Dorrie Jackson met her first husband, Alan Fitzgibbon Stewart, then a Pembroke undergraduate, for the first time at a college tea party when she was still a fresher. Balchin later worked with Stewart at the National Institute of Industrial Psychology (NIIP) and was best man when Stewart married Dorrie in 1932, just a few weeks after she had graduated. Assuming that Balchin and Stewart were already friends by this stage, it is possible that Balchin accompanied him to the same tea party and made Elisabeth's acquaintance on that occasion. Stewart's son Jeremy believes that it can only have been an attraction of opposites that drew his parents together. The precise nature of the attraction between Balchin and Elisabeth is equally nebulous but it may have had something of the same quality, with the shy, diffident Newnham undergraduate being lured towards the older Peterhouse man with his charm and outward air of confidence. Elisabeth would also have been aware that, upon graduation, the unappealing prospect lying in wait for her was to return home to look after what remained of her family. If she could attract a potential suitor whilst at university then she would have a legitimate excuse to pass up the opportunity to reprise her role as her father's housekeeper.

In the 1920s, male and female students tended to inhabit separate universes at Cambridge, Walbank recalling how 'women students usually sat in groups together in lectures and there were few opportunities to get to know them'.[25] As relations with female undergraduates were thus 'somewhat restricted', college tea parties represented a rare chance for men to consort with members of the opposite sex. In Walbank's opinion, the life of an undergraduate 'suffered in many ways from restrictions which today would appear almost mediaeval'. So, in order to comply with the rule-based Cambridge University doctrine extant when Balchin began pursuing Elisabeth, if he had wished to spend time with the redhead in her room then technically he would first have had to have been vetted by the Newnham authorities and then another student (Dorrie perhaps) would have been required to have been present throughout his visit. Balchin would have needed to make himself scarce even before dinner was served as the College rulebook decreed that all male visitors had to vacate the premises by 6.45 pm. It is tempting therefore to speculate that Dorrie and Elisabeth may have taken turns to act as a chaperone as each of the two male students visited his respective Newnham girlfriend. However, Walbank observed that the chaperone stipulation was 'frequently ignored' and it is difficult to overlook the fact that Balchin, as a talented young athlete, would probably have possessed the necessary physical dexterity and fleetness of foot to have shinned down drainpipes, scaled college walls and outpaced the marauding proctors had he desired to prolong his stay beyond the prescribed time.

*

At the behest of Bartlett, Balchin completed his psychological studies by carrying out an experiment on the Cambridge University Farm during the last fortnight of May 1930. This allowed him to combine his earlier interest in agriculture with his new-found love of psychology. Balchin observed four farm labourers hoeing a field of kale. He found that they worked at a level well below their maximum capacity and that this slacking was attributable more to boredom than fatigue. When the men were offered a financial incentive to work harder they did so, almost doubling their output. Balchin concluded that his experiment afforded 'yet further evidence of how much might be hoped from the large-scale application of Industrial Psychology to English agriculture'.[26]

In order for Balchin to receive a degree, Vellacott had to convince the University authorities that his student had been in residence for three further terms after passing Part I of his Tripos, that he had been 'engaged upon academic studies suited to his attainments'[27] and also that he had been 'regular and diligent therein'. A Certificate of Diligent Study was issued to Balchin to cover his third year and this, together with his result in Part I of the Tripos, was sufficient to entitle him to receive a Bachelor of Arts (Honours) degree in Natural Sciences, which he was duly awarded in person at Senate House on 24 June 1930. This unusual route to a degree still exists today (although is very seldom used); the student receives a B.A. but no class is specified, and this was thus the case with Balchin.

In his appeal to the Ministry of Agriculture in February 1930 asking them to release him from the terms of his scholarship, Balchin had seemed rather confused as to exactly what sort of career he intended to follow when he left Cambridge. Thus, in one paragraph of his letter he wrote 'I do not wish to pursue a scientific career if it can be avoided'[28] but two paragraphs further on stated that he proposed to 'go down at the end of this year and enter on a career that may or may not be scientific in nature'. Quite possibly, what Balchin was really seeking was a career that combined elements of both science and business. If so, then the prospect of working for the NIIP must have seemed a heaven-sent opportunity.

Founded in 1921, the NIIP was a pioneering organization that had been established with the aim of applying psychological techniques in an attempt to solve some of the practical problems encountered in industry. Bartlett was associated with the NIIP in 1930 as a member of its Scientific Committee. It seems plausible that, as Balchin was one of his students during the May term of that year, Bartlett would have suggested to him that he should apply for a job with the NIIP. Had it been sold to him in the right terms, this may well have seemed like the perfect fit for Balchin. A job as an industrial psychologist would have been a 'scientific' post, but one with very different terms of reference from those of an agricultural scientist. Balchin would also have been involved in the business world, which is something that is known to have appealed to him. With or without help from his mentor, Balchin was taken on by the NIIP and asked to begin work before the end of the summer.

In the eight weeks that he spent at his parents' home in West Lavington between graduating and starting work at the NIIP there seems to have been only one thing on Balchin's mind: playing cricket. As a member of the Wiltshire Club and Ground squad,[29] he built on the promising start he had made the previous summer, when he had accumulated 64 runs in his sole appearance for them. Sometimes combining the roles of opening batsman and wicketkeeper (a physically demanding thing to do), Balchin played six times for the team in 1930, scoring 126 runs at a creditable average of 31.5. He also turned out for West Lavington Sports Club and Dauntsey's Wanderers (the Old Boys' side).

The high point of Balchin's cricketing career occurred during the course of two days in early August. On Friday the 8th and Saturday the 9th, the young batsman/wicketkeeper made his debut for Wiltshire, then, as now, a Minor County, in an away match against Berkshire held in Reading. The *Wiltshire Gazette* does not record whether Balchin kept wicket in this match, but he batted in the lowly number nine position, recording scores of 1 in his first innings and an unbeaten 12 in his second. As Balchin had not originally been selected as part of the Wiltshire side announced in the newspaper the previous week, he was probably a 'late call-up' designed to plug a hole in the team caused by the withdrawal of a more accomplished player.

Balchin may only have turned out once for Wiltshire but it was still a notable achievement for a cricketer who had played little—if at all—at Cambridge to have suddenly been catapulted to a level immediately below that of first-class cricket. Although the sport has inspired a rich literature and many eminent writers have been devoted to the game, most of them, such as J. M. Barrie, P. G. Wodehouse, Kingsley Amis and Harold Pinter, have been much more skilled with a pen in their hands than either a bat or ball. Among significant literary figures, only Samuel Beckett and Arthur Conan Doyle, both of whom participated in a very limited number of first-class cricket matches, have played the sport at a more exalted level than Balchin.[30]

After reaching its peak in August 1930, Balchin's sporting career soon traced a downward trajectory as he adopted an increasingly sedentary lifestyle. From this point onwards he was never much more than a casual sportsman, taking part in social games of golf, cricket, tennis, snooker or squash and specializing, as he put it himself, in 'looking like a good player out of practice'.[31]

3

How to Run a Chocolate Factory

> The constitution of the N.I.I.P. is to a great extent unique. It was called into being to fill a national need. It is not a private enterprise. It does not seek to make profits. It victimizes nobody. On the industrial side it seeks to make life easier and more happy for the employee, and in doing so, to benefit at once employee, employer and society in general.
>
> – Nigel Balchin[1]

On 30 December 1931, one of the directors of Brown & Polson Ltd. (Corn Flour Manufacturers, Paisley) wrote a letter to the National Institute of Industrial Psychology (NIIP) complimenting one of the Institute's staff and making admiring remarks about his competence.[2] The worker in question was Nigel Balchin, a young industrial psychologist who had recently completed the second of two investigations for the company. It was by no means the only such letter that the NIIP received about Balchin during the four and a half years he spent working for them.

Balchin reported for work at Aldwych House, the NIIP's London headquarters in Aldwych, for the first time on 18 August 1930. He would have been pleased to find a very familiar face on the premises: Alan Stewart, his Cambridge friend, had also secured a post with the Institute and took up his duties on the same day.

Balchin's job title was 'Investigator' and his remit included going into factories and other places of work, assessing the procedures that were in operation and utilizing scientific methods to improve their efficiency. He was taken on initially for a six-month training period, during which he received no salary but was paid 7s 6d per day (about £20 per day in present-day terms) as a living allowance. He was fortunate in this regard because some of his predecessors had been forced to pay £20 (roughly £900 today) out of their own pockets in order to cover the cost of their training.[3]

Although clients paid for work carried out by the Institute, fees were set at a level designed to merely cover the costs of an investigation. Membership subscriptions were also received both from industrial concerns and from private individuals with an interest in psychology. This latter grouping included prominent figures from public life as well as philanthropic members of the aristocracy, a glance down the list of subscribers for the 1933–1934 financial year throwing up names such as H. G. Wells, The Viscountess Bearsted, The Lady Bingham and The Dowager Countess of Listowel.[4] Generous donations were initially provided by confectionery companies such as Cadbury's and Rowntree's, who continued to support the work of the Institute for many years to come. But because it had no reliable, long-term source of significant income, the NIIP operated on a hand-to-mouth basis for the majority of its fifty-year lifespan: belt-tightening, appeals for funds and threats to close itself down were commonplace.

Balchin's work at the NIIP largely revolved around treating workers as human beings instead of mere production units and trying to improve their comfort and well-being. 'The human factor' was a catchphrase in common currency in industrial psychology circles in the 1920s and 1930s, and one commandeered by the Institute to provide the name for its in-house journal. Balchin paid attention to such human factor aspects as the elimination of unnecessary movements, making the working day less boring for employees, removing handicaps and revising factory layouts, all with a view to simultaneously helping both the employer (by increasing production) and the worker (by ensuring that increased productivity was not achieved at the expense of the welfare of the human cogs at the heart of the industrial machine).

Within two weeks of arriving at Aldwych House, Balchin had already embarked on his first industrial investigation. The NIIP believed very strongly in the merits of on-the-job training and so Balchin was probably just made familiar with the rudiments of his chosen profession and then trusted to use his intelligence and judgement as he saw fit in order to solve problems as they arose. In 1970, shortly before the Institute's activities were suspended, its long-time Director, Clifford Frisby, gave this assessment of the methods adopted by the NIIP at around the time when Balchin first joined them:

> The Institute's investigators had no ready-prepared remedies to apply; they had in effect to make a diagnosis of the situation they found and to seek for improvements from the human point of view wherever they thought it possible to make them.[5]

On 1 September, Balchin, Stewart and a more experienced investigator, Leonard Hunt, turned up at Rowntree's Cocoa Works in the Haxby Road in York, a complex of tall, angular red-brick buildings that occupied a sizeable tract of land on the northern edge of the city. The three men had been dispatched from London to begin work on an investigation for the chocolate manufacturers blandly entitled 'Individual Packing'. For Balchin, this unpromising beginning nevertheless laid the platform for an extremely profitable association with Rowntree's that lasted some twenty-five years and helped him to make his name not just as an industrial psychologist and businessman but also, and more importantly perhaps for him, as a writer and novelist.

Despite being sent to York as part of a three-man team, Balchin soon seems to have realized that he would make more of an impact if he struck out on his own. Writing to Paul Vellacott exactly two and a half months after beginning at Rowntree's, he informed the Senior Tutor at Peterhouse that 'I came here originally to watch another man[6] getting results but I became interested in the packing, and as I had the luck to bring a new method off, my companion very sportingly offered to turn the work over to me'.[7] Balchin also described a working environment that offered him ample opportunity to impress his bosses if he were able to introduce economy measures in the chocolate packing section:

> There are 7,000 employees, so that it is not difficult to find plenty of scope, and to get results that appear quite impressive on paper. There are 900 packers in the room in which I am working, and we pack over 1,000,000 boxes of chocolates per month. Thus, if I can save them 1/8 th of an ounce of chocolate per box, I am saving them over £63,000 [about £3.3 million today] per year!

In his letter to Vellacott, Balchin expressed his desire to 'get away from York for a week end [sic] in Cambridge soon'. He must have done so during the months that followed because Vellacott later claimed to have seen his former student whilst he was still on probation at the NIIP. Balchin's weekend in Cambridge would have allowed him to continue his courtship of Elisabeth Walshe, now in her second year at Newnham.

As part of his first (solo) Rowntree's investigation, Balchin helped to design a new bench at which the chocolate packers sat whilst they worked. This was preferred by the workers and increased output by 10% (a fine demonstration of the NIIP's creed of helping employer and employee simultaneously). Balchin may have been overoptimistic when predicting how much money he would be able to save Rowntree's, but his implementation of a better packing method did result in an eventual cost saving of at least £4,000 a year (equivalent to more than £200,000 today).[8]

While he watched his chocolate packers at work, Balchin made an observation that led to his first recorded appearance in print since leaving Cambridge.[9] He noted that there were two distinct methods adopted by the women who packed the chocolates into boxes. Balchin felt that one of these two methods should theoretically have been better than the other because it involved less total movement. Interestingly, however, he found that the packing of the boxes proceeded more efficiently when the individual was allowed to adopt the method for which she was psychologically and physiologically best suited, rather than having the theoretically superior method imposed on her.

It is reasonable to assume that Balchin's early successes at Rowntree's—and particularly his ability to save the company money—quickly made him a favourite with his superiors. The Chairman of Rowntree's in the 1930s was Benjamin (Seebohm) Rowntree, son of the company's founder Joseph and also a prominent member of the NIIP's Executive Committee. He would have noted with interest the sure-footed progress of the young industrial investigator and may perhaps have invited him to a Rowntree's social evening that he hosted with his wife at the beginning of 1931. The *Cocoa Works Magazine* (the company's in-house journal) carried a report on the event in its Easter 1931 edition:

> ...even had there been a lot of ice in the atmosphere, it would have been most effectively broken by Stainless Stephen, who came to entertain us. Greatly to our surprise, he was found to be an intimate friend of many of the staff, and gave his audience highly diverting side-lights on their characters. The political and civic interests of directors and recreative or other hobbies of managers etc. alike provided material for his facile wit—and later, conversation for the supper tables.[10]

There is little doubt that Balchin wisely used his time with the NIIP (and particularly that portion of it spent at Rowntree's) to gather material for his subsequent writing career. If he was not present at this particular staff party then he must either have been informed about it subsequently or else attended similar socials during his association with the chocolate-makers. This much is clear from a scene in his novel *Sundry Creditors*, in which a comedian hired to entertain the guests at Lang's annual

Works Party gives the impression that he is closely acquainted with the company chairman, Gustavus Lang:

> "*Oh* yes," said the entertainer. "*Oh* yes. I can always depend on Gus. Of course me and Gus is like *that*. Went down there the other day. Maid said: 'He's out looking at the pigs.'[11] I said: 'I'll go out and find him.' 'All right,' she said. 'You'll know him. He's the one with the hat on.'"

Having successfully completed his six-month training period during his time in York, Balchin was confirmed as a permanent member of the NIIP's staff on 18 February 1931. He was put on six months' probation—which passed without mishap—and awarded an annual salary of £396, roughly twice the national average.[12] Less than eighteen months after the Wall Street crash, with 2.5 million people unemployed in the UK and the bitingly cold wind of what Prime Minister Ramsay MacDonald referred to as the 'economic blizzard' sweeping through British industry, this was therefore a substantial starting salary.[13] The pay awarded by the NIIP was deliberately intended to be attractive to young graduates:

> It has been essential in the growth of the Institute that it should be able to attract investigators of first-class ability. For this reason salaries have been initially higher than an honours graduate would obtain in other professions, and they have tended throughout to be appreciably higher than those paid in academic walks of life, although, of course, somewhat lower than those of successful business careers.[14]

Balchin was soon displaying evidence that he possessed all the qualities required to become an investigator of first-class ability. His initial tenure at Rowntree's (which spanned ten months in total) concluded with an investigation that took four months to complete and which he appears to have carried out on his own. Balchin's report of his work carried the uninformative title 'Third Report of Investigation at Messrs. Rowntree & Co. Ltd.,

York'[15] but the style in which it was written was characteristic of the novelist he was later to become, with periodic hints of books such as *No Sky* and *Sundry Creditors*. Balchin's study aimed to improve both the efficiency of chocolate production and the quality of the chocolate leaving the factory. However, as a central tenet of NIIP philosophy in its early years was 'the removal of handicaps, mainly material, which wasted the worker's energy, so that he could perform more effectively and with less fatigue',[16] Balchin also recommended improvements such as the centralization of instrumentation panels and enhanced lighting. Balchin's report landed on the desk of Seebohm Rowntree himself, no doubt elevating his standing in the eyes of the Rowntree's Chairman.

With his duties at Rowntree's at an end for the time being, Balchin embarked on a demanding schedule between September 1931 and June 1932, performing a total of six studies for companies such as Creamola Ltd. of Glasgow and the aforementioned Brown & Polson in locations a long way away from London, and mostly in Scotland. The investigations carried out during this period mostly concerned factory organization, such as the redesign or optimization of layouts, improvements in transport procedures and the introduction of mechanized packing routines. However, Balchin also focused his attention on confronting problems like time-wasting, poor morale, organizational slackness and friction between employees.

When Balchin was between investigations and thus working at Aldwych House rather than outside London there is a strong likelihood that he lodged with Winifred Raphael at her house in the Brompton Road on the edge of South Kensington. Raphael, once aptly described as 'the Institute's loyal matriarch',[17] began work for the NIIP as an investigator in 1922, rising to become Assistant Director by the time she retired in 1961. In the words of a long-time colleague, Raphael was 'warm, friendly and encouraging, but with a very sharp intellect'.[18] The possibility that she may have been Balchin's landlady can be divined from an inscription contributed by the author to a copy of his pseudonymous second book, 1934's *How to Run a Bassoon Factory*, which satirized his work for the NIIP:

> To Winifred—at whose hearth so much of it was written—before 10 a.m. in the main—or after 5 p.m. at night. Nigel Balchin (Mark Spade).

Balchin had a pleasant duty to perform soon after his return to London following his nine-month working tour of northern Britain. Stewart married Dorrie Jackson on 16 July 1932 in the bride's home town of Herne Hill in South London and Balchin acted as best man. Both Dorrie and Elisabeth had graduated from Newnham just a few weeks previously.

Shortly before Stewart's wedding, the NIIP had embarked upon one of the largest and most important industrial investigations in its history. This study would last thirty-three months, involve a total of thirteen investigators (including Balchin, Raphael and Stewart) and send shockwaves through the Institute at a critical period in its history. Its greatest achievement was the creation of Black Magic, the perennially popular assortment of plain chocolates housed in the distinctive black box which is still to be found on the shelves of supermarkets up and down the land today.

The success of Black Magic derived from a fortuitous combination of circumstances. The NIIP had been in financial difficulty throughout the early years of the 1930s. There was little demand for its expertise in training and personnel selection and when it asked industry if it would like help in suggesting ways in which to increase production, the reply it received was 'We can't sell what we've made'.[19] Selling was the sticking point and so the NIIP's Director, George Miles, decided to dip a toe into the murky waters of market research. He picked an opportune time to do so. In 1932 it had become clear to Rowntree's that its most urgent problem was how to stop losing its market share of the chocolate assortment trade to its bitter rival Cadbury's.[20] Sales of Rowntree's high-class chocolate assortments were only a third of what they had been in 1925 and, as Cadbury's were cutting their prices, the York-based firm was in danger of haemorrhaging yet more of its market share if it didn't do something quickly to hit back at its main competitor. A low-cost, high-quality alternative to Cadbury's market-leading King George assortment was a clear priority and, perhaps with a hint of desperation, Rowntree's allocated the sum of £3,000 (about £165,000 today) to the NIIP for an investigation of the chocolate assortment market. The advertising agency J. Walter Thompson (JWT) had won the Rowntree's account in 1931 and they were also to function as another important piece in the Black Magic jigsaw.

Balchin was put in charge of coordinating the market research behind Black Magic, as made clear by Miles ('Nigel Balchin [...] very ably organized the experimental work and the complicated analysis of field surveys'[21]) and JWT's Head of Art George Butler ('Nigel Balchin [was] the active person there doing the work'[22]). Balchin's team of investigators interviewed 7,000 people in seven British cities and the surrounding areas: London, Birmingham, Cardiff, Glasgow, Leeds, Manchester and Newcastle upon Tyne.[23] Investigators were dispatched to factories, offices, schools, colleges, universities, institutions and 'one very superior garden party!'. Each interviewee completed a questionnaire designed to establish their idea of what constituted the perfect chocolate assortment. Analysis of the vast amount of data that accrued was simplified by the use of punched-hole 'Hollerith' cards,[24] an early and rudimentary form of computerization that Balchin later poked fun at in *How to Run a Bassoon Factory*:

> The basic idea of the punched card system is that you punch cards. That is to say, you take a card, and punch holes in it on a sort of Braille system. Then you put all your cards into a large machine (something between a pianola and a penny-in-the-slot machine), which understands Braille, and press a button and it makes a noise like a sewing machine and hands you a piece of paper with the answer.

To help Balchin construct a profile of the potential Black Magic consumer, 2,500 shopkeepers also filled in questionnaires. The headline findings of the two surveys were that 65% of chocolate assortment buyers were men, and that 60% of those men were buying the chocolates as presents for women (and would thus be prepared to pay more than women for the privilege, so as not to appear parsimonious in the eyes of the recipient).

Once he had processed all the data using a Hollerith machine, Balchin could begin to conduct tasting tests, something he would do a lot more of in the course of the following six years. The most popular assortments from the UK and Europe were scoured for inspiration and the chocolatiers at Rowntree's then created twelve enticing new centres that Balchin's team of tasters preferred to the established favourites and that were therefore used to fill the first boxes of Black Magic.

Rowntree's were very keen to economize on the packaging of Black Magic and to use the money saved to optimize the quality of the chocolates: the dual aims were to produce a high-quality assortment that retailed at the relatively low price of 2s 10d (about £8 today) per pound. Here Balchin stepped in again with a brilliant and far-sighted piece of lateral thinking. After undertaking his own impromptu piece of market research, he disclosed the result to Butler: 'Looking into any confectioner's window, there's every colour but black'.[25] Before Black Magic came into being, what we now understand by the pejorative term 'chocolate box art' was exemplified by cartons adorned with soft-focus paintings of adorable kittens and puppies, idyllic creeper-clad country cottages or angelic rosy-cheeked children and fussily decorated with frills and foils. Balchin's idea of a stark black box was therefore a radical departure from received wisdom. Further consumer tests were conducted, with Balchin's packaging concept being pitted against a variety of other colour schemes and designs. The monochrome box triumphed, being deemed more attention-grabbing, more memorable and easier on the eye. Importantly, a black-and-white box was also considered to be less feminine than traditional designs and thus there was a lower risk of it alienating the important constituency of male buyers.

Almost fifty different variants on the black-and-white theme were mocked up. The winning design, created by the Head of the Packaging Department at JWT, was a plain black box decorated with white lines that were visible from any angle, ensuring that the new product stood out from the competition. But Balchin's box was more than just an eye-catching break from tradition: the no-nonsense design and restricted colour palette meant that it was also cheaper to produce than existing packaging. The enduring popularity of Balchin's design for Black Magic is attested to by the fact that Rowntree's resisted the temptation to tamper with it for several decades after its introduction and the box remains predominantly monochrome more than eighty years later.

In commercial terms, Black Magic was a slow-burner: launched onto the market in January 1933, sales during the first twelve months were unspectacular, despite an enthusiastic response from the trade. However, when Seebohm Rowntree presented his 1935 Chairman's Report on 28 February 1936 he was proudly able to announce that:

> The steady increase in the sale of Black Magic is also extraordinarily satisfactory, because this is not a stunt sale: it should prove a staple.[26]

Rowntree was right. The brand performed steadily for the remainder of the 1930s and then flourished when post-war production was resumed in 1947. Balchin was handsomely rewarded for his work on Black Magic: by the end of 1933, his salary had risen to £550 (about £32,000 today), an increase of almost 40% in less than three years.

In the same month that Black Magic was launched, Balchin married Elisabeth Walshe in London, the wedding taking place on 21 January at Chelsea Old Church in the parish of St Luke. The newly-weds moved into 172 Portsdown Road, W9, a red-brick end-terrace house situated just a couple of hundred yards away from Maida Vale Underground station, and thus convenient for Balchin's daily commute to Aldwych.

More than eighty years after their wedding, it is impossible to say whether Balchin and Elisabeth married for love or if other factors had come into play. But, as detailed in Chapter 2, Elisabeth might have wanted to marry Balchin partly to avoid an obligation to keep house for her father. For his part, one cannot totally rule out the possibility that when Balchin tied the knot he may have had one eye on the future success of his career as an industrial psychologist. Balchin's bosses at the NIIP were very keen for him to promote the Institute by infiltrating organizations such as the Rotary Club and the London Chamber of Commerce. It is not difficult to appreciate that he would have been more likely to have ingratiated himself into the sober London business circles of the mid-1930s as a respectably married man than as an unattached one.

By the time of his wedding day, Balchin's publication history appears to have comprised a grand total of two articles in the NIIP's journal. About nine months later, on 4 October, he made his debut in *Punch*, the leading satirical magazine of the day. His first contribution was a ten-part series of articles which he summarized as:

> An alphabet containing much good advice and also numerous useful hints concerning things one should not believe in,[27]

'The Compleat Modern' was an A to Z detailing views that Balchin believed 'modern' people—and he evidently included himself under this heading—were obliged to hold on subjects such as art, music, poetry and the occult in order not to be out of step with enlightened contemporary thinking. The series was quirky and gently comic but the prose that Balchin deployed to write it (chatty and wordy, in common with most of his 1930s writing) bore no resemblance at all to the dry, terse reportage with which he would make his name during the 1940s.

Whilst at Cambridge, Balchin had apparently written 'short

stories on scientific themes'.[28] During the autumn of 1933 he began to find outlets for his fiction and it was the short-story format that he opted to exploit. Balchin's earliest known piece of published fiction is 'Publicity Pays', which appeared in the story magazine *The Passing Show* in September. 'Publicity Pays' was a light, humorous tale about a wallflower who marries an actress. She encourages him to enter society and he proceeds to behave so outrageously in public that he gets his name into the gossip columns of the newspapers at the expense of hers, putting her nose badly out of joint. To her relief, the husband then resumes a quiet life, which is what he had been scheming to bring about all along.

A much more characteristic Balchin story, 'That Feller Oates', was printed in the *20 Story Magazine* two months later. In Balchin's first novel *No Sky*, the protagonist, George Ordyne, signs up for a correspondence course in fiction-writing. One of the exercises that George undertakes is to write a short story based on the following scenario: 'Martin Peele, an elderly doctor, has married a young and charming wife some thirty years his junior. All goes well until Freddie Forbes comes into her life.' This plot outline is the starting point for 'That Feller Oates', but here the doctor is called Henry Herbert and his much younger wife is Sheila. Herbert overhears his wife talking to a junior medical colleague of his, Tommy Richards. He realizes that the two of them are very much in love and are planning how to break the news to him. Before they can do so, Richards is admitted to hospital with an infected hand and demands that Herbert operates. He does, and the operation is a success. But then a short while later Herbert himself is hospitalized with a similar infection and this time it has spread too widely for surgery to be practicable. Shelia visits her husband in hospital, where one of the doctors tells her that it is very unlike Herbert to have been so careless as to have pricked himself during his operation on Richards. With the life draining out of him, Herbert tells Shelia that Captain Oates—who gives the story its title—was a remarkable man because he courageously sacrificed himself for others. In Herbert's opinion, it would not be right for him to prevent Shelia from experiencing happiness with a younger man. He then dies. 'That Feller Oates' is thus the first recorded example of Balchin utilizing what Herbert refers to as 'The Eternal Triangle' as the backbone for a piece of fiction.

The 'deathbed scene', such as that enacted between Herbert and Shelia, would also become a feature of Balchin's fiction, occurring in one form or other in more than half of his novels. There is one in *No Sky*; all of his famous wartime trio of novels contain one; and his award-winning screenplay for *The Man Who Never Was* includes one with a novel twist: the body in the bed, 'William Martin', already being dead when the scene begins.

*

At the NIIP, Balchin was becoming increasingly groomed for a role in business administration. During his student's final year at Peterhouse, Vellacott had stated that:

> My own view is that Mr Balchin is likely to do much better on the administrative, rather than on the technical, side of business.[29]

On 1 December 1932, shortly before the launch of Black Magic, Balchin had been sent as the investigators' representative to the inaugural meeting of the Investigations Subcommittee, which had been formed 'to discuss new methods of interesting firms in the services provided by the Institute'.[30] Balchin continued to report to the Subcommittee until he left the NIIP in 1935 and was appointed its Secretary in September 1933. He also functioned as the first point of contact for industrialists wishing to avail themselves of the NIIP's services. In this capacity, he carried out initial surveys of a large number of British factories, offices and organizations. Balchin's familiarity with these working environments would later inform both his debut novel and his first non-fiction book.

Raphael once claimed that one of the factors that contributed to the NIIP's near-permanent penury was a failure to promote itself effectively ('Few of its staff were good at speaking or writing about its work'[31]). Balchin can certainly be exempted from this criticism as he did a great deal to publicize the work of the NIIP during his time with the Institute. He wrote a total of eight papers for its journal that touched on most of the areas in which he had been active and also delivered a number of public lectures.

Some of Balchin's journal articles were transcripts of the lectures he had given and were therefore written in a very accessible, light-hearted style. The most interesting of these articles is 'The Psychological Difficulties of the Institute's Work',[32] in which the young psychologist recounted various examples of misunderstandings of the Institute's aims he had encountered during his tenure as an industrial investigator. Confronting outdated and boneheaded prejudices was a particular challenge faced by Balchin:

> A remark once made to us by a director of the old school is typical. 'Want to make work easier do you?' he said. 'You people will be wanting me to give 'em cushions to sit on next'. We pointed out that there was nothing intrinsically absurd in that. A man might work better sitting on a cushion. His reply was worth recording—'I don't care if he would. I pay a man to come here to work, not to have a good time. In my day we *worked*—twelve hours a day, standing up.'
>
> In his day they worked—twelve hours a day standing up. No matter how much they produced—no matter how tired they were—no matter how bad and foolish and unnecessary it was—that was how they did it. And quite probably he felt that, in some queer way, the fact that it was unpleasant and uncomfortable was somehow connected with his own success. Firmly fixed in his mind was the idea of work as something unpleasant and exhausting. And anything which made it less so must lower efficiency. This attitude is rare nowadays. We wish it were non-existent.

*

The Balchins' first child was born while they were living in Portsdown Road: Elisabeth gave birth to a girl on 16 September 1934 at a private maternity clinic in Sutherland Avenue, Maida

Vale and she was christened Prudence Ann.

During Elisabeth's pregnancy, Balchin had conceived the idea for a project that he hoped would enable him to make his debut as a radio broadcaster. On 11 May, Leonard Moore of the literary agency Christy & Moore, George Orwell's long-time agent, submitted 'the roughest of rough ideas'[33] to Charles Siepmann, Director of Talks at the BBC. Moore wished Siepmann to consider 'the possibility of Mr. Balchin giving a series of talks under some such title as IN DEFENCE OF OUR YOUNGER GENERATION' but, five days later, the proposal was flatly dismissed by the Corporation.

This sort of setback would soon become a thing of the past for Balchin. In Moore's letter to Siepmann, Balchin's agent had informed the BBC man that 'I have just arranged for the publication of his first novel'. Balchin's luck was about to turn: he was now on the verge of becoming both a regular broadcaster and a published novelist.

4

Making a Good Beginning: The Hamish Hamilton Years

Mr. Balchin has made a good beginning; you can believe
every word in his book.

– Ralph Straus[1]

Nigel Balchin's first book, an 'industrial' novel entitled *No
Sky*, was accepted by the first publisher it was sent to, Hamish
Hamilton, and appeared in bookshops in September 1934.[2]
Founded in 1931 by the energetic half-Scottish, half-American
Jamie Hamilton, who had won a rowing silver medal for
Great Britain at the 1928 Olympics, the publishing company
was on the lookout for exciting young writing talent when the
manuscript of *No Sky* arrived at its London office. It had been
sent by Balchin's agent Leonard Moore, who succeeded in
negotiating an advance of £30 for the novel, not an atypical sum
at the time for an author's first work.[3]

Why did Balchin start writing novels? He tackled this question head-on in 1955, during the course of a radio interview with
the writer and critic Walter Allen, and in so doing suggested that,
in addition to penning short stories, he had also experimented
with another fictional format before turning to the novel:

Why did I start? I suppose because I had a story which
I wanted to tell which for some reason I felt went into the
novel medium more easily than into the play medium or
the short story medium.[4]

'I'm nearly always trying to express some general idea' was
Balchin's reply when Allen asked him what he was attempting to

do as a novelist. The interviewee then revealed that the concept underpinning each of his novels could be reduced to a simple written summary:

> I usually start with a novel by writing down one line which is always a generalisation to define what I'm really trying to say to people...

If it were possible to go back in time to the mid-1930s in order to rifle through the paraphernalia on Balchin's desk in search of the general idea behind *No Sky* then one might perhaps come across a scrap of paper on which he had scribbled something like 'Don't become enslaved by your job' because that is the book's most prominent message.

No Sky is an accomplished debut. The authorial voice is confident, the plotting assured. Balchin had chosen an unusual theme—the work of the time-and-motion men in a large factory—and the novelty of this subject matter was applauded in the *Daily Telegraph* by crime writer Anthony Berkeley Cox, writing under the pseudonym Francis Iles,[5] who said that the book contained 'glimpses of the work and methods in the huge engineering shops; and I found this side of the book of the highest interest.' The working routines described in *No Sky*—although not as well integrated into the narrative as those in some of his later fiction—are convincingly portrayed and Balchin obviously leant heavily on his experiences of working in factories in order to write them.

The domestic side of *No Sky* was also influenced by Balchin's own recent memories. There are brilliant descriptions of the lonely existence of the hero, George Ordyne, in lodgings and of his struggle to find something to do with the leisure time on his hands, especially at weekends ('the mere necessity of keeping sane had made one go to the pictures regularly three times a week'). Balchin was writing from direct experience here, and probably referring back to the period he had spent in York whilst working for Rowntree's, as a parallel quote can

No Sky (1934)

Whilst studying at Cambridge, George Ordyne is informed of the death of his father. He is therefore forced to abandon his Medicine course and try to obtain work in order to support his mother and sister. He succeeds in being taken on as an unpaid trainee by a Lancashire engineering firm called Hanly's and begins work in their rate-setting department. On his first day, George is warned by one of his colleagues, Masters, that the job he is performing is tantamount to a slow death.

George harbours ambitions as a writer and so begins a correspondence course in short-story construction. But when he is offered a permanent job by Hanly's he accepts it and ditches his literary aspirations.

The tight rates imposed by George's department stir up trouble on the shop floor. The shop steward protests and orders his men to work more slowly than usual when George is timing them, forcing the piece-rate to be set artificially high. When George points out this sharp practice he is accused of being a lackey of the bosses. Angered, George decides that he will stop being essentially fair-minded in future and will instead side with his rate-setting colleagues. He proposes a way of setting tight rates that does not require any worker involvement and is congratulated on it by his boss.

George meets a working-class girl at a dance and soon becomes very fond of her. Despite the social and intellectual chasms between them, George proposes to Lily and she accepts. The story ends with the young rate-setter ensnared by his profession, just as Masters had predicted he would be, and the couple trapped in a loveless marriage.

be found in his 1936 non-fiction work *Income and Outcome: A Study of Personal Finance*:

> ...I have been marooned for months in a northern manufacturing town so desperately dull and depressing that about three visits to the cinema a week were essential, merely to pass the time and to keep myself sane.

The opening plot line that acts as the mainspring for the chain of events that unfolds in *No Sky*—the death of George's father and its effect on the young man's education—may have been suggested to Balchin by Dorrie Jackson, either directly or via her best friend Elisabeth Balchin. Dorrie's second husband Eric Stein, whom she married in 1937, had been obliged to give up his desire to be a doctor (he had won a place at Oxford to read Medicine) when his father died, leaving insufficient resources to fund Eric's university education. Aged eighteen in 1926, Eric had entered the family business instead, reluctantly beginning work in the drinks industry. Dorrie met Eric for the first time on holiday in Cornwall in the summer of 1933, at about the time when Balchin would have been plotting *No Sky*.

As might be expected of a first novel, *No Sky* has some obvious weaknesses. The pace of the story is leaden throughout and the book is overlong, tailing off towards the end as its conclusion becomes inevitable. All the events depicted in its pages are reported on from George's point of view and he is insufficiently engaging as a central character to be able to bear this burden. Most of the other characters are *types* rather than individuals, and although Balchin would later become extremely adept at creating quirky and amusing minor figures with which to enliven his narratives, those in *No Sky* make little impression on the reader. Balchin's prose tends to be stiff and forced and the author himself appreciated this deficiency, remarking in 1962 that 'I tried to write in sentences and phrases instead of *using words*. [...] I was self-conscious about the style.'[6] But despite these misgivings, Balchin had undoubtedly 'made a good beginning' to his novel-writing career and it is noteworthy that the key theme of his mature period—the difficulties faced by men in both their professional and private lives—was in place as early as 1934.

Only a small handful of national newspapers devoted space to reviews of Balchin's debut novel, but such notices that did appear were broadly enthusiastic. In the *Sunday Times*, Ralph Straus,[7] one of the most influential literary critics of the 1930s (and a man who played cricket against Balchin on occasions), described *No Sky* as 'a first novel of some little distinction'. This tenor of praise was echoed by Iles,[8] who said that 'No Sky is a first novel not only of promise but of achievement'. A few nice notices were also published in the regions, the *Liverpool Post*[9] for example characterizing *No Sky* as 'An excellent first novel... Mr. Balchin has a nicely satirical touch and real readability.'

Even with the assistance of these encouraging reviews, sales of the book were disappointing. Balchin later claimed that *No Sky* had sold 'about 600 copies'[10] but that may have been an overestimate as Jamie Hamilton complained that the volume of sales had not been sufficient to enable the company to claw back the £30 they had advanced the author for the book.

Balchin was quickly given another opportunity to earn some money for the firm as *How to Run a Bassoon Factory; or Business Explained* was published within a few weeks of *No Sky*. Only his close friends and family would have been aware that the two books had been written by the same person as the new publication appeared under the pseudonym Mark Spade. Still employed by the National Institute of Industrial Psychology (NIIP) when the book was being printed, Balchin was careful not to rub his employers up the wrong way by disclosing the identity of its author:

> I had to use a pen name because it wouldn't have done for me to reveal that I found anything funny about business life.[11]

How to Run a Bassoon Factory is an extension of a series of ten articles that had originally appeared in *Punch*.[12] Balchin's book purports to be an instructional manual for budding businessmen about to embark on a career in industry, with the principles required for success being illustrated with examples pertaining to the running of the imaginary musical instrument factory that gives the book its title. In fact it is nothing of the sort: it is instead a chance for Balchin to satirize and, at times, belittle his occupation. (Although Balchin always spoke with respect and enthusiasm for industrial psychology when addressing an invited audience, privately, when talking to Eric St Johnston for example, he described it in altogether more cynical terms, and he once told his Cambridge friend that his work for the NIIP had mainly involved 'seeing a good idea in Factory A and selling it to the manager of Factory B'.[13])

As *How to Run a Bassoon Factory* contained chapters devoted to Motion Study, Time-Study and Costing, Market Research, Advertising and The Psychology of the Worker, Balchin clearly drew on material gleaned from his day job to write the book and some of the anecdotes included in it had already been utilized in the ostensibly more serious articles he had written for the NIIP's in-house journal. However, the joshing and score-settling are often underpinned by sound common sense and a lot of the advice dispensed is based on established business principles. If one strips away the levity it is possible to obtain some idea of what it was really like to have been an industrial psychologist in the 1930s, and Balchin himself claimed in 1969 that his book was 'required reading in certain business training'.[14]

The humour deployed by Balchin in *How to Run a Bassoon Factory* belongs to a bygone era and has dated rather badly (introducing a reissue of the book in 1950, the author admitted that it exuded 'an odour of old-world lavender'). It can mostly be characterized as a relentless brand of chirpy flippancy that the modern ear may soon find tiresome and grating. Some of it is more successful, for example Balchin's pithy definitions of a Managing Director as 'a man who really knows where the factory is, and even goes there sometimes' and a foreman as 'a man who does not think it can be done'. This extract, detailing how a Managing Director should delegate his work, gives a representative flavour of the book's funnier moments:

> Supposing one winter's day it becomes so dark in your office that you can't see the print of your paper. Now your first instinct is probably to get up and switch on the light. But pause a moment. Is that quite fair to the firm? A good organiser would reason like this: 'In the next office is my secretary. The cost of her time to the firm is only one seventh of the cost of mine. Clearly we shall save money if I ring for her and let *her* switch the light on.' You see? The good organiser sees at once how to get the job done as economically as possible.

How to Run a Bassoon Factory is a landmark of Balchin's early writing career. As with his debut novel, the author had abstracted information gathered whilst working in the factories he had frequented as an industrial psychologist and woven it into a book that is by turns entertaining, thought-provoking and educational. This alchemical ability to transform the dull metals of working life into written gold was a skill that would remain part of Balchin's armamentarium for several more decades.

Balchin's second book generated negligible press interest, with only *The Times Literary Supplement* according it even a cursory review. When Hamish Hamilton reissued *How to Run a Bassoon Factory* at the end of 1950 in the same binding as its successor, *Business for Pleasure*, the reception it received was very different, with three anonymous reviewers united in their praise for the book. The *Financial Times*[15] described the combined volume as an 'hilarious treatise on factory management', the *TLS*[16] referred to the two books as 'Those pre-war amusing skits on business methods' and the *Economist*[17] considered that for those people who took business too seriously a remedy was at hand: 'an almost infallible specific; seven and sixpence worth of Mr. Mark Spade'.

The paucity of reviews for the 1934 release of *How to Run a Bassoon Factory* led to disappointing sales initially. On

5 February 1935, a couple of months after it had been published, Jamie Hamilton wrote to Balchin to tell him that his book was 'still selling about 100 a week and is obviously being talked about'.[18] The author had set his sights rather higher, as elucidated in a letter to Hamilton sent the week before:

> I wish to God I knew what to do about the Bassoon Factory. I have an awful suspicion that we are missing the boat, and yet I don't know what to suggest. Your sales wallah was quite right. The thing has a potential five figure sale. But how can we *get* it to people? Smiths [i.e. W H Smith] may have got it, but they seem to be concealing the fact with real skill. I suppose there's no point in trying to start a riot in the press about who wrote it? I have heard it variously attributed to a director of I.C.I., a director of Lyons, Professor John Hilton,[19] and three other people.[20]

The outlook for Balchin's first non-fiction book may have appeared bleak in 1935 but, helped by positive notices for the 1950 combined volume, both *How to Run a Bassoon Factory* and *Business for Pleasure* continued to sell steadily over a very long period. So much so that, in 1962, Balchin was able to announce that:

> The remarkable thing is that those two little books, published in the mid-1930's, are still in print and still selling in quite substantial quantities. Only recently I heard that they have sold 30,000 copies in Holland…[21]

Whilst Balchin mulled over the problem of trying to increase sales of *How to Run a Bassoon Factory* he had a more important dilemma to resolve in his working life. Although the market research at which he had excelled had been incredibly successful, and had brought in much-needed revenue for the NIIP at a perilous stage in its existence, it had not been greeted with universal approval within the portals of Aldwych House. The NIIP's Director, George Miles, summed up one school of thought concerning the Institute's adventures in consumer psychology:

> Some people had a rather snobbish attitude towards these investigations and looked on them as lowering to the dignity of the Institute. They were also 'commercial' and 'opportunist'.[22]

The issue of whether or not the Institute's impartiality had been fatally compromised as a result of its market research activities needed to be addressed. Rowntree's had paid the NIIP considerable sums of money for its work on a range of products (most notably Black Magic) and was receiving the Institute's undivided attention in this area. The company's Chairman, Seebohm Rowntree, was eager that this state of affairs should continue. Other large chocolate companies were also making substantial donations to the NIIP's coffers (£700 a year throughout the 1930s in the case of Cadbury's,[23] which is roughly equivalent to £35,000–40,000 a year today) and yet their sweetmeats were not receiving the benefit of the Institute's burgeoning expertise in the field of consumer psychology. Understandably, they kicked up a fuss about being excluded from these market research activities.

The matriarchal Winifred Raphael described the schism that developed at the NIIP as the 1930s proceeded:

> As always when a number of intelligent young psychologists are working together, there were strong divisions of opinion [...] Did market research come properly within its scope? It was later decided that market research did not...[24]

Balchin, Miles, Raphael and others were in favour of doing more consumer research; Charles Myers, the Institute's principal, may well have been against it. The 'noes' won this ideological battle and the NIIP abandoned its market research activities. As Balchin had been working in this area with considerable success for the best part of three years he would probably have been upset at the loss of the Institute's consumer psychology programme. This is likely to have been a major reason why, in the first few weeks of 1935, he decided to leave the NIIP.

Balchin's resignation was accepted by the Institute's Executive Committee on 7 February, to be effective the following day. A position had been offered him by Rowntree's and he had decided to accept it. Despite the Executive Committee's assurance that it was 'convinced of the good faith in which Rowntree and Company Limited had acted',[25] it is hard for a modern observer not to feel that, in contemporary parlance, Balchin had been 'tapped up'. This is borne out by a minuted account of Seebohm Rowntree's statement to the Executive Committee describing the circumstances behind the approach made to Balchin:

> Mr. B. S. Rowntree explained that his company would not have considered making such an offer to Mr. Balchin had they not learnt that he had decided to resign from the Institute's staff. They had intimated to Mr. Balchin that they would be prepared to offer him a position, but had urged that this offer should not prevent him from remaining with the Institute if, after receiving his resignation, the Executive Committee made him an offer to remain with the Institute.

It is not known what financial carrots, if any, were dangled in front of Balchin's nose to persuade him to stay with the NIIP but as he had received a £50 salary increase just three months earlier, on 1 November 1934, bringing his annual salary to £600 (about £35,000 today), his employers were probably not prepared to go much higher. As the Institute's financial situation continued to be a parlous one, salaries for the investigations staff were cut by 5% just over eighteen months after Balchin resigned. He may therefore have left the NIIP at a mutually opportune time: he didn't want to stay with them and they couldn't afford to keep him. According to Raphael, the NIIP's management were 'furious'[26] when Balchin left as he was seen as one of their

Simple Life (1935)

On his twenty-ninth birthday, London-based advertising copywriter Rufus Wade, after a short period of soul-searching, concludes that he hates his sedentary, urban existence and needs to swap it for a more active, rural one. So he chucks in his job and walks out on his fiancée. He then meets a couple of men who are about to drive a furniture van to St Ives overnight and hitches a lift with them. When the van breaks down next morning near Salisbury, Rufus decides that Wiltshire is as good a place as any in which to begin living his 'simple life'.

The Londoner goes for a long walk on the downs, loses his bearings in a heavy snowstorm and collapses with exhaustion. He wakes up to find himself in a farmhouse with a man called Pip Mendel, who had rescued him from a snowdrift the night before. Mendel and his girlfriend Ruth are living the sort of life that Rufus is seeking, doing just as they please without paying attention to the clock or eating meals at regular intervals and indulging in a range of physical pursuits, such as walking, tobogganing, furniture-making and woodcarving.

Rufus chooses to stay with the couple and, with some encouragement from Mendel, soon falls in love with Ruth, sleeps with her and starts trying to prise her away from the other man. After a gradual build-up of friction between them, Rufus and Mendel fight for Ruth's affections. Rufus emerges victorious and Ruth agrees to run away with him. But she then reverses her decision, choosing instead to stay with Mendel and leaving the abandoned Rufus to catch the first train back to London so that he can resume his old life.

brightest stars and as someone who might well have gone on to become the Director of the Institute.

By leaving the NIIP and joining Rowntree's, Balchin was able to continue performing tasting tests on chocolate and thus remain working in the field of consumer psychology, something that obviously appealed to him. There was also no longer any need for him to spend months away from home engaged on industrial investigations; he had to take occasional trips to York for meetings but generally he could work much closer to his wife and young child than when he had been an NIIP employee.

Balchin had already delivered the manuscript of his second novel to his publisher by the time he left the Institute. *Simple Life* (for which he was advanced £40, about £2,300 today) was a different sort of novel from *No Sky* and constituted a marked improvement on the earlier book. The writer and critic Clive James first encountered *Simple Life* almost forty years after its publication, and was impressed by its content:

> Most of Balchin's future themes are already present in this novel, and so is a good deal of his peculiar skill.[27]

Simple Life provided Balchin with a narrative setting in which he could expound a philosophy, the nature of which he elucidated in a letter to Hamilton:

> …a life where time means nothing, there is no work, no conventions, and superficially no difficulties, is, in actual fact, completely bogus and impossible.[28]

In Balchin's view, the two 'simple lifers' he describes in his novel, Mendel and Ruth, and others like them, have buried their heads in the sand and refused to engage with the world around them:

> …you can't just detach from life the things you [don't] like and keep the rest. If you want to be alive you've got

to stay in the scrap and win. Otherwise the thing you get isn't life at all.

With *Simple Life*, Balchin introduced the love triangle plot into a novel for the first time; this was one of the 'future themes' that James identified when he read the book and it was a device that Balchin would continue to hone throughout the entirety of his writing career. This triangle is always in danger of collapsing into a straight line for precisely the same reason: a male outsider tries to extricate a woman from a long-established relationship with a male partner. In *Simple Life*, Rufus, the interloper, attempts to lure Ruth away from Mendel. To give but three further examples, this prefigures Stephen's efforts to win Marcia from Bill in *Darkness Falls from the Air*, Bule conducting an affair with Jill in *A Way Through the Wood*, thus leaving Jim out in the cold, and Walter's attempt in *Seen Dimly Before Dawn* to split Leonie off from Patrick.

Of the three central characters in *Simple Life*, Mendel is by far the most interesting. A fourteen-stone giant with rippling biceps, an unruly mop of yellow hair and marked Übermensch characteristics, he exerts an intimidating physical and psychological presence. Ruth, like many of Balchin's subsequent female characters, remains a placid, frustrating enigma in comparison with the two men. Devoid of strong opinions and bereft of a forceful personality, she is happy to acquiesce to Rufus's demands initially, whilst ultimately remaining in thrall to her long-time partner. In common with most of the love triangles in Balchin's work, one of the vertices therefore functions as an emotional doormat.

As Rufus's adventures in Wiltshire include sleeping with a girl in the village of Leaford as well as seducing Ruth, Balchin thought that *Simple Life* might be 'a possible book for the repressed spinsters who, apparantly [sic], are the mainstay of the libraries'. Hamilton disagreed, asking the author to tone down certain passages so as to avoid offending potential borrowers of the book. Balchin refused, and his publisher's fear was realized when Boots Booklovers Library (the subscription library run by the chemist chain) declined to stock *Simple Life*, considering it to be too racy for them. In a copy of the novel that he inscribed, Balchin lamented:

> One can only hope that no one seeking pornography will waste 7/6 on buying it.
> Was it for this that I took my contraceptive custom to Messrs Boots?

Published on 29 April 1935, *Simple Life* was more extensively reviewed than *No Sky* and in general the critics were very favourably inclined towards it. There was however a marked difference of opinion concerning which half of the novel was the more successful. Cyril Connolly,[29] writing in the *New Statesman and Nation*, described *Simple Life* as 'a graphic and interesting book' and came out firmly in favour of the second, 'philosophical', section ('I think it is where it really starts'). Contrarily, Doreen Wallace[30] in the *Sunday Times* preferred the first section, which according to her was 'funny and exhilarating', and she commented additionally that 'The advertising office is particularly well done'.

Critiquing the book for *John o'London's Weekly*, John Brophy[31] said that *Simple Life* was 'a double-barrelled satire, and hits both its targets fair and square.' L. P. Hartley[32] in the *Observer* felt that Balchin had 'fastened upon an interesting theme', while Iles,[33] reviewing a Balchin novel for the second time in the *Daily Telegraph*, praised the author's use of humour and described *Simple Life* as being 'a book which it is a great pleasure to read'.

Like *No Sky* before it, Balchin's second novel is badly handicapped by its excessive length. In particular, although the scenes in the advertising agency in Chapter II are great fun to read, they should perhaps have been excised as they delay the action and are out of sync with the second part of the book. Such material was commonplace at the time, C. E. Bechhofer Roberts[34] in the literary magazine *Time and Tide* remarking wearily that 'Mr. Nigel Balchin's Simple Life begins, like so many other modern novels, in an advertising agency'. (George Orwell, like Balchin a client of literary agents Christy & Moore, was writing *Keep the Aspidistra Flying* at the same time that *Simple Life* was being printed; it was also partly set in an advertising agency.) The book could just as well have opened on Salisbury Plain with Rufus striding purposefully towards Leaford because, as James commented, 'as soon as the hero breaks out into open country the story comes alive'.[35] It is also hard to disagree with James's observation that 'With the front shorn off and the rest trimmed of some of its commentary, *Simple Life* could still be an interesting novel'.

Relatively soon after the publication of *Simple Life*, Balchin began to obtain work with the BBC. At 9 pm on Sunday 25 August, as part of a feature entitled *Two Short Stories*, Balchin's 'The Service of Miss Eyles' was read out on the Regional Programme, alongside the H. E. Bates story 'Harvest Moon'. 'The Service of Miss Eyles' is a quiet, undramatic piece about the sixty-year-old woman of the title who is employed as companion and general dogsbody to the tyrannical Mrs Richardson, a rich widow. When Mrs Richardson dies, leaving her house and money to Miss Eyles, the new owner of Gravemont immediately places an advert for a 'refined Christian companion, willing to give help in house', thus already beginning to ape the erstwhile employer whom she had intensely despised. 'The Service of Miss Eyles' faintly resembles some of James Joyce's *Dubliners* stories but is very different from any of Balchin's better-known novels. Following the limited sales of *No Sky* and *Simple Life* and the pseudonymous publication of his second book, recognition for Balchin as a writer was not helped by the fact that the *Radio Times* spelt his name wrongly, printing it as 'Balcin'. His bank balance was not swelled appreciably either: the payment of £3 7s 6d (just under £200 today) that he received for the story being not much more than a quarter of his weekly wage.

Balchin would return to short-story writing much later on in his career but for now he directed his attention once more to writing books. *Business for Pleasure*, the sequel to *How to Run a Bassoon Factory*, was published on 17 October. As was the case with the book's predecessor, much of the material between its covers had already appeared in *Punch*[36] and its author was again identified as Mark Spade. The only review in a mainstream publication came in the *TLS*, and was contributed by one Charles Reginald Green.[37] Under the heading 'Christmas Humourists', Green considered Balchin's book alongside a handful of related volumes and seemed distinctly jaundiced by the nature of his task:

> There is evidently a publishers' conspiracy to produce as many humorous books as possible in time for Christmas.

(Anyone who has glanced at the tables in high street book stores in recent years during the run-up to the festive period and seen them groaning with books intended to be funny will note wistfully that the 1930s reader probably escaped comparatively lightly.) In spite of his general air of world-weariness, and the fact that he described Balchin's wit dismissively as 'the polite and sedate ragging which is the mainstay of our humorous journalist', Green was moderately enthusiastic about both the author and his book:

> "Business for Pleasure," by the entertaining author of "How to Run a Bassoon Factory," continues and expands the practical teaching of that work.

Business for Pleasure mirrors *How to Run a Bassoon Factory* very closely in terms of its style and the mirthfulness of its humour. Where the two books differ is that the later one deals more with general business principles than with the running of a hypothetical factory, and contains chapters entitled On Economic Principles, On Merging and Emerging, On Interviewing People, and Sales Promotion and Ideas Men amongst others. *Business for Pleasure* does not really stand comparison with *How to Run a Bassoon Factory* in terms of either its quality or joie de vivre and the author's idea of spoofing the business world had now started to flag.

On leaving the NIIP in early 1935, Balchin had hired office accommodation at 105 Blundell Street, N7, on the border between Camden and Islington. Balchin's office functioned as a peaceful retreat from the cries of his young daughter and here he was able to carry out some of his Rowntree's duties, as well as writing books and magazine articles as time allowed.

During the Second World War, Balchin claimed that he had become 'assistant to chairman of the Rowntree Group of Companies',[38] i.e. Seebohm Rowntree, when he left the NIIP, but it is unclear exactly what his duties amounted to in this capacity. For the next few years Balchin's work schedule seems to have been remarkably similar to that during his final days at the NIIP, revolving largely around the performance of chocolate tests, and he was closely involved in the consumer testing of a new confection that continues to flourish eighty years later.

Aero had been introduced in the north of England in 1935 using the slogan 'The New Chocolate' and proved so successful that it had spread to the rest of the country by the end of the year. Beginning in July 1935, when he showed that the public preferred The New Chocolate to Cadbury's Milk, Balchin performed a vast array of consumer tests on Aero for at least the next three years. He regularly sent samples of the product to a panel of testers and asked these guinea pigs to rate them against a Cadbury's competitor.

Two Rowntree's-related myths have clung to Balchin as surely as chocolate crumbs cling to the corners of the mouths of toddlers, namely that he invented Aero and came up with the name for the Kit Kat chocolate bar. These myths have been sustained in recent years by the gargantuan electronic rumour mill that constitutes the Internet but in-depth study at the Rowntree's Archive in York has furnished no evidence in support of either of them. Air bubbles occur naturally in chocolate bars during the manufacturing process and the moulds have to be shaken in order to disperse them. No one now knows who first turned this process on its head by deliberately bubbling air through chocolate to produce the distinctive aerated texture of Aero.

The name Kit Kat had been registered by Rowntree's as early as 1911—when Balchin was still a toddler himself—and used as nomenclature for a chocolate assortment that was defunct by the time that the company decided to rebrand its Chocolate Crisp bar in 1937. According to the unofficial history of J. Walter Thompson,[39] it was Donald Gillies, Group Head of the advertising agency, and not Balchin who thought of adding the prefix Kit Kat to produce the new name Kit Kat Chocolate Crisp, which was then truncated to the much more familiar Kit Kat after the Second World War.

In mid-November 1935, Balchin, Elisabeth and baby Prudence left their home in Portsdown Road, Maida Vale and moved into an apartment at Highpoint in Highgate. Highpoint was a futuristic housing project designed by the influential Russian modernist architect Berthold Lubetkin and one of the first high-rise developments to be built in England. Constructed from white concrete atop one of the highest vantage points in London, Highpoint commanded excellent views over the city. It had originally been commissioned by Sigmund Gestetner, head of the office equipment manufacturers, in order to house his workers. But the building was never used by Gestetner's employees; instead the bourgeoisie rapidly moved in and Highpoint became a superior residential development. Upon its completion in 1935, the Balchin family were among the very first tenants of the eight-storey apartment block. Balchin had gone up in the world, in more than one sense.

It was probably Balchin's newly acquired taste for elevated living that encouraged him to keep turning out books at a rapid pace as 1935 gave way to 1936, hoping that at some point his luck would change and his offerings would coincide lucratively with the tastes of the book-buying public. But his last two books for Hamish Hamilton did next to nothing to alleviate his financial situation and he must have relied heavily on his substantial Rowntree's salary—in 1936 they were paying him £1,032 a year[40] (£57,500 today)—in order to sustain his middle-class lifestyle.

Balchin's next book, *Fun and Games. How to Win at Almost Anything*, was published by Hamish Hamilton on 27 February. Released once again under the Mark Spade alias, this was another volume in the vein of *How to Run a Bassoon Factory* and *Business for Pleasure*, but this time the author turned his attention away from business matters and focused instead on sport. *Fun and Games* comprises twenty-four short chapters, each describing how to play a particular sport or pastime, such as cricket, football, rugby, golf, tennis, fishing and bridge. The title of the book was originally intended to be *The Sportsman's Vade Mecum* but it was altered before publication, perhaps in order not to mystify non-Latin scholars.

As with the other Mark Spade books, the comedy in *Fun and Games* has not worn well over time. It relies for its effect largely on humorous misunderstandings (such as thinking that water polo is played on horseback) or on listing the equipment required for playing a particular sport, one of the items being completely out of kilter with the others. The chapter on rowing is one of the best. Here is Spade giving advice to the novice oarsman:

> If you break an oar, throw yourself overboard immediately to lighten the boat. [...] If you throw yourself overboard *without* breaking your oar, swim after it and break it at once.

And the requirements for a good rowing coach are listed thus:

a   The ability to ride a bicycle along a narrow towpath keeping the eyes fixed on the crew, and carrying a megaphone, a revolver, a bell, a whistle, and a hunting horn.
b   A flow of descriptive images and arresting analogies.
c   Sympathy and leadership.
d   Optimism.
e   The ability to swim [necessary in case ability (a) fails].

Like a poorly drilled rowing crew, *Fun and Games* sank without trace. It was granted only one brief review, albeit a relatively complimentary one, with the anonymous critic[41] in the *TLS* observing that:

> If a good deal of it is chiefly verbal humour—the pun has had a noteworthy revival in these last few years—there are witticisms that occasionally go deeper.

Sales were sluggish, the book was never reprinted by Balchin's publisher and plans for an omnibus edition of the first three Mark Spade books were shelved; when a Mark Spade omnibus did finally appear in 1950, it did not include *Fun and Games*. Balchin was keen to keep his alias alive, pitching ideas to Jamie Hamilton in 1936 for two more comic works—a book entitled *Possible Professions* and 'a rag travel book'[42]—but both were turned down by the publisher.

Balchin concluded his six-book association with Hamish Hamilton with *Income and Outcome. A Study of Personal Finance*, which was published in November 1936. The book had a slightly unusual genesis. In the spring of that year, Balchin had written to his publisher seeking suggestions for the subject of his next work. The strain that family life in Highgate was putting on Balchin's finances is evident from his follow-up letter, the opening words of which were 'Very many thanks for your noble response to my appeal for funds'.[43] Jamie Hamilton had previously proposed that Balchin should write a book entitled *Industrial Britain*, which was to comprise an insight into a dozen leading British industries tackled with a light touch and along the lines already done for American industry by a native author. Balchin was enthused by Hamilton's suggestion but anticipated a number of difficulties with it. Within ten days, the author had come up with an idea of his own, a book on personal budgeting to be written with the layman in mind.

Balchin worked rapidly to produce *Income and Outcome*. By 9 August, less than four months after the inspiration for the book had first struck, he had completed the manuscript. Elisabeth was roped in to help with the donkey work required to produce her husband's first serious non-fiction book, as Balchin explained to Hamilton:

> Herewith Income and Outcome – produced in the time by the simple process of my wife and myself working on it until 1 a.m. for a few nights. I had no idea that the wretched thing would be so tough, but of course the figures took an immense time.[44]

Extremely accessible and written in an engaging way, *Income and Outcome* nevertheless represents a serious-minded enquiry into the subject of personal finance. Setting out to ascertain why people are always a lot poorer at the end of the month than they believe they should be, Balchin suggested that there is a great deal of 'casual expenditure' (much of it consisting of small items such as newspapers, bus fares, confectionery and cups of coffee) responsible for the shortfall between how much money is theoretically available for us to spend and what we actually have in our pockets. He attempted to instil some home truths about personal finance into his readership, and to demonstrate the advantages of budgeting, although he was keenly aware that in many cases the advice he was dispensing would fall on deaf ears.

Income and Outcome was accorded very few reviews. It did, however, receive a laudatory notice in the *New Statesman and Nation*, the anonymous reviewer[45] commenting with astonishment that 'This book performs the rare feat of living up to its publisher's blurb'. After praising Balchin's sagacity in filling the gap left by the refusal of the economists of the day to address financial issues likely to be of interest to the man in the street, such as 'How to Live an Upper-Middle-Class Life on a Lower-Middle-Class Income, or Why We Are All Broke At the End of the Month', the book critic concluded with an emphatic endorsement of *Income and Outcome*:

> It is a temptation to go on quoting indefinitely. It is that sort of book—need one say more? Only this; that Mr. Balchin has achieved a delectable blend of needful information, good

advice, sound psychology and first-rate entertainment which is the perfect antidote—even if not the sure preventive—for that recurring End-Of-The-Month Feeling.

Notwithstanding the fact that it represents something of a hidden gem within Balchin's oeuvre, *Income and Outcome*, as was the case with all of the author's books for Hamish Hamilton, was not a financial success. It was never reprinted and, just over a year after publication, Jamie Hamilton wrote to his client to tell him that:

> In spite of the "Daily Express"[46] (to say nothing of the excellence of the book), INCOME AND OUTCOME hasn't sold a copy for a long time now.[47]

Balchin's association with Hamish Hamilton had come to an end. The company had published six of his books in a little over two years but none of them had found the large and appreciative audience that both writer and publisher craved. If Jamie Hamilton still thought of Balchin as a writer of promise then his opinion was not being matched by the sales returns from the bookshops. Probably as a consequence of Balchin's unimpressive earning power, Hamilton decided at this point to sever his connection with his young protégé and set him loose. However, as Balchin's dream of 'a potential five figure sale' for *How to Run a Bassoon Factory* had not been matched by the harsh reality displayed on the sales curve then it might equally well have been the case that the writer was dissatisfied with the promotional efforts of his publisher and wished to try his luck elsewhere.

5

One Night in the West End

Nigel Balchin produced an enormous amount of written material during the 1930s. He also demonstrated admirable versatility by writing a mixture of novels, non-fiction books—both comical and serious—short stories and numerous articles, mostly of a light-hearted nature, for *Punch*, other national periodicals and some scientific journals. Yet amidst all this creative endeavour it is little known that Balchin also completed a number of stage plays, part of an ongoing quest to find the medium for which his writing talent was best suited.

Three plays written by Balchin in the 1930s were later reformatted by him for different media. *Carted Stag*, which is about a married couple who provide a safe haven for a man on the run, who is an old flame of the wife, ultimately became 'Among Friends', the final short story in the collection *Last Recollections of My Uncle Charles*. *Square Deal*, a piece about a couple of unlikely confidence tricksters, became 'Patience' in the same volume. Most notably, *The Highway Code*, probably written in 1935 and later described by its author as 'a rather bad play',[1] was cannibalized by Balchin more than fifteen years later and used as the basis for his novel *A Way Through the Wood*.

Four Balchin-scripted plays were performed in the London area in the space of three years, although only one reached the West End. The first production opened on 8 April 1935 at Croydon Repertory Theatre and ran for a week. It was called *Power*. The play was a political allegory inspired by the growing popularity of dictatorships on the Continent. Set in an unnamed country, it showed a political party firstly on the cusp of seizing the reins of government and later in power. Balchin claimed that his play was 'not propaganda but a study of human character'.[2] The anonymous dramatic critic[3] of the *Croydon Times and Surrey County Mail* agreed with this assessment, stating that the play was 'a thoughtful study of human reactions to certain circumstances'. But the reviewer went on to suggest that Balchin may have been swept away by the pace of events taking place across the Channel and that his characters merited a more in-depth psychological analysis—something that, as a novelist, Balchin would later also shy away from as a rule—to prevent them resembling thinly veiled versions of contemporary European political figures.

Balchin had written *Power* in his leisure hours over the course of a three-week period. Perhaps the lack of time he had devoted to crafting his play was responsible for a certain unevenness in the writing, as picked up on by the *Croydon Times and Surrey County Mail*: 'Some of the scenes are excellently written; others lack staying power in their dialogue.' Despite criticizing the 'too diffuse treatment of the theme', the reviewer did concede that *Power* 'possesses considerable merit and should not be allowed to pass into obscurity', which is precisely what did happen.

In the rival local newspaper, the *Croydon Advertiser and Surrey County Reporter*, another anonymous theatre reviewer[4] was kinder about the play, describing *Power* as having 'several points of unusual interest' and saying that it possessed 'real drama'. Although in retrospect the critic need not have been overly concerned about a potential West End audience's squeamishness towards the scenes of interrogation in the play, the review concluded with a positive recommendation:

> Everybody who is concerned about the future of humanity should see "Power".

As the script has not survived, perhaps the most interesting thing about this work, aside from Balchin's earnest engagement with the political issues of the day (which was only a feature of his writing in the 1930s), is the fact that he contributed a character sketch to the theatre programme.[5] Here we learn that he had 'played every English game except Polo', that he was currently working about seventy hours a week and that he 'Likes Bach, writing, motor-cars and speaking in public. Dislikes holidays and jolly social gatherings'. Given the title of the play that he had just written, it was appropriate that Balchin paid tribute to the power behind his particular throne:

> Inseparable from wife, red-haired Cambridge graduate, who, as he is wont to point out, "does all the work" connected with his writing.

Elisabeth served as Balchin's secretary in the mid-1930s.[6] She had left Newnham College in the summer of 1932 with a Second Class Honours degree in English, Archaeology and Anthropology. She then put her Cambridge education to good use by teaching English at a school in London before taking a break from full-time employment to give birth to her first child in the autumn of 1934. Between 1935 and the outbreak of World War Two she continued to work, parturition permitting. Almost certainly with a leg-up from her husband, she was given the opportunity to write radio commercials for the advertising agents J. Walter Thompson, which she did for nine months in 1937 before the birth of her second daughter. Elisabeth also experimented with creative writing, a hobby she would return to profitably after the war.

Balchin's follow-up to the modest critical success he had enjoyed with *Power*, *Peace in Our Time*, ran from 11 to 19 September 1936, also at Croydon Repertory Theatre. Balchin co-authored the piece with his father-in-law, Douglas Walshe; although primarily a writer of romantic and/or light comic novels, Walshe had also previously written a play. The plot of *Peace in Our Time*, in which three commercial magnates covet the business of a competitor, is similar to that of the Old Testament story of Naboth's vineyard. However, as with *Power*, the script produced by Balchin and Walshe had the virtue of topicality as it closely resembled events that had taken place the year before during the Abyssinian Crisis.

In addition to the *Croydon Advertiser and Surrey County Reporter*, whose unnamed critic[7] described *Peace in Our Time* as being 'an exceptional attraction' that was 'of special topical interest', the play was also reviewed in *The Times*, the first Balchin theatre production to receive this honour. The anonymous reviewer[8] praised the construction of the work:

> The allegorical argument is worked out with delightful ingenuity, completeness, and humour; and, though not all the hits are fair, they are all keen and shrewdly directed.

The two print journalists both honed in on the major weakness of Balchin's play. Whereas *Power* had featured an all-male cast, and thus an absence of romantic subplots, *Peace in Our Time* was encumbered by a love story involving the children of the main characters that, in the words of *The Times*, 'comes near to ruining the play'. It cannot just have been the influence of romantic novelist Walshe that was at work here because Balchin's two subsequent plays would attract opprobrium every bit as pungent as the parting shot from *The Times* ('the female characters are unnecessary, and make no impression') and Balchin would continue to be criticized for his lacklustre characterization of the fairer sex for much of the remainder of his writing career.

Miserable Sinners is perhaps the most important product of Balchin's short-lived and undistinguished career as a playwright. There are obvious reasons for this. Firstly, it was the only Balchin play ever to be performed in the West End, albeit for one night only (25 April 1937) at the Ambassadors Theatre in Covent Garden.[9] Secondly, it starred Balchin's old Cambridge friend James Mason (then struggling to make a name for himself on the London theatre circuit) and his wife-to-be Pamela Kellino and the play had been written specifically with the two young actors in mind. Reflecting on *Miserable Sinners* many decades later, Mason showed generosity towards his friend's endeavours, whilst simultaneously expressing doubts about Balchin's enduring worth as a playwright:

> He was to become an enormously skilful novelist but I don't think that he ever wrote a really good play let alone a successful one. Perhaps ours was the best of them.[10]

After incursions into the worlds of politics and big business in his two previous scripts, Balchin took a backward step when he wrote the lighter, frothier *Miserable Sinners*. Kellino played Nina Seward, who is discovered in flagrante delicto by her husband Richard (Mason). Nina and Richard quarrel, but then straighten things out and everything seems to have returned to normal until the couple's parents take a hand in the situation and proceed to make an unholy mess, bringing their children to the brink of divorce. Nina and Richard succeed in outwitting their parents before the curtain descends and all ends happily.

In general, *Miserable Sinners* was not well received in the press. It was again reviewed by *The Times*, whose unnamed theatre critic[11] thought it a 'silly play' and reserved particular vitriol for Kellino's Nina:

> An acid minx, a whining scrap of vanity, without that generosity of foolishness which is necessary to redeem the heroines of silly plays.

'R. B. M.'[12] in the *Era* could find only faint praise for Kellino, describing her performance as 'interesting'. The reviewer complained that the characters in the play were 'overdrawn' and that the playwright had failed to address his theme of parents meddling in their children's private lives 'in a particularly new or convincing way'. In contrast, an anonymous critic[13] in the *Stage* was rather more enthusiastic about the work, mentioning some 'bright, easy, dialogue' and claiming that 'It is all amusingly done'. On its first and last night, *Miserable Sinners* had apparently been 'heartily received, and the author was called'.

Before retiring from the business of playwriting for more than fifteen years, Balchin wrote one final script. *Profit and Loss* opened at the Embassy Theatre in Swiss Cottage on 3 May 1938 and ran for two weeks. Again the script remains elusive, but the reviewers' descriptions of the play suggest that, of all Balchin's theatrical work, *Profit and Loss* most nearly resembles the novels of his mature period. So when W. A. Darlington[14] wrote in the *Daily Telegraph* that 'Nigel Balchin has one of those themes that can generally be relied on to yield a certain amount of dramatic conflict—namely, the clash between business interests and domestic affections' he could almost have been describing the theme of *Sundry Creditors*.

Profit and Loss is set in the aircraft industry. Ronnie Goss, the daughter of an aeroplane manufacturer, marries one of her father's staff, who then goes to work for a rival firm. A merger with this company is suggested to Ronnie's father William, but he objects to the methods of his rivals and so holds out against them. Later, seeing that his order book is empty, Goss is forced to resort to desperate measures. He hires a thug to sabotage one of his rival's planes, which crashes with Goss's oldest friend on-board. As Darlington observed, with this promising set-up 'drama should occur' but the characters were largely unsympathetic and insufficiently finely drawn to carry conviction. The anonymous reviewer[15] in *The Times* was impressed by several of the individual performances but felt that these were 'not quite good enough to save a play which aims at many targets and hits none'.

They may not have done much to advance the critical standing of their author but Balchin's plays did provide employment for a collection of talented thespians who would later make their names both inside and outside the theatre. Apart from Mason and Kellino, the cast of *Miserable Sinners* also featured Esma Cannon, who appeared as a dotty old woman in several *Carry On* films, and the distinguished character actor Maurice Denham, who had previously taken a role in *Peace in Our Time* and would later feature in *Twenty-Three Paces to Baker Street*, a film for which Balchin wrote the screenplay. Alan Wheatley, best known for his performances as the doomed newspaperman Fred Hale in the Boulting brothers' film of Graham Greene's novel *Brighton Rock* and as the Sheriff of Nottingham in ITV's 1950s series *The Adventures of Robin Hood*, appeared in both *Power* and *Profit and Loss*. André Morell played Ronnie Goss's husband in *Profit and Loss* before launching a successful career on television (he starred as Professor Quatermass in *Quatermass and the Pit* for the BBC) and in film (where he appeared in classic British movies such as *Seven Days to Noon* and *The Bridge on the River Kwai* and had a minor role in the Balchin-scripted *The Man Who Never Was*). Leonard Sachs, later to serve as chairman of the long-running BBC variety series *The Good Old Days*, in which position he became famous for his lengthy alliterative introductions to the performers, filled one of the minor roles in *Power*.

Balchin's plays failed for a multitude of reasons. Judging by the remarks of the theatre critics who reviewed his work, he does not appear to have possessed an intuitive grasp of the medium for which he was writing; his ability to write brisk, realistic dialogue, although undoubtedly enhanced by his experiments in play-writing, had not yet attained the peak it would later scale so triumphantly in the 1940s and 1950s; Balchin devised strong dramatic themes for his plays but they were not matched by his storylines; his characterizations were generally thin and unreal; and he was particularly bad at writing parts for women. If he had stuck purely to what he knew best, namely the machinations of the business world that supplied the backbones for both *Peace in Our Time* and *Profit and Loss*, and ditched the trite romantic subplots, then perhaps he could have carved out a respectable niche for himself in the theatre. He might also have established himself as 'the playwright of work' in the 1930s before becoming similarly revered a decade later as 'the novelist of work'.

When Balchin returned to play-writing in the 1950s and 1960s with his self-confidence bolstered by the creation of a string of best-selling novels, his second round of plays for stage and television were also deemed to be critical failures. The one truly popular theatrical success to have emerged from a Balchin source was *Waiting for Gillian* and that was crafted in the 1950s by a much more experienced and adept playwright, Ronald Millar, from the raw material of Balchin's 'rather bad' 1935 play *The Highway Code*.

*

As documented on the last page of the book, Balchin completed work on his third novel, *Lightbody on Liberty*, on 26 September 1935. A few weeks later, on 2 November, the author sent a draft of it to Jamie Hamilton. After receiving a negative report from one of his manuscript readers, Hamilton declined to publish it. It took a long time for *Lightbody on Liberty* to make it into print, the volume finally reaching the bookstands more than a year after Balchin had finished writing it. In the meantime, he had moved publisher from Hamish Hamilton to William Collins. With the exception of *Income and Outcome*, which was published by Hamilton shortly after *Lightbody on Liberty* came out, all of Balchin's subsequent books appeared originally in Britain under the Collins colophon.

At around this time, and probably in 1936, Balchin severed his connection with his agent Leonard Moore at Christy & Moore and moved to Pearn, Pollinger & Higham, where he would be represented by one of the three partners, David Higham, for the next fourteen years of his career. Balchin would have been one of the agency's earliest clients as Pearn, Pollinger & Higham had only come into being in 1935. He joined a prestigious roster that included Edith Sitwell, her brothers Osbert and Sacheverell and the writer of detective stories Dorothy L. Sayers.

Several aspects of *Lightbody on Liberty* distinguish it as a real oddity amongst the author's works. Uniquely for Balchin, the central character, Alfred Lightbody, is working class. Lest the reader should be left in any doubt about this, Balchin has him consistently drop his aitches, which makes the dialogue look very different from that in most of the writer's other novels. The workplace is largely incidental to the action and there are no love triangles or serious romantic entanglements. But by far the most significant feature of *Lightbody on Liberty* is that it is the only purely comic novel in the Balchin canon. There may be pathos in these pages, together with satirical attacks on law

Lightbody on Liberty (1936)

·

Alfred Lightbody, owner of a small grocer's shop in North London, experiences several minor run-ins with the law in quick succession, the last of which coming when he is invited to overtake a police car and then promptly booked for speeding. Released on bail pending payment of a fine, Lightbody gives an interview to a newspaperman and the publicity generated by his maltreatment by the authorities awakens the interest of Sir Joseph Steers, a multimillionaire and political campaigner.

Sir Joseph uses Lightbody's experiences to launch the League of Free Britishers, a pressure group aiming to free the populace from needless petty infringements of their liberties or, to recast its intention in the grocer's vernacular, 'to sweep away all the tommy rot'. With the guidance of Perks, Sir Joseph's personal secretary, and on the back of some inspired suggestions from an advertising man called Haskell, the League quickly builds a membership of six million and holds a triumphal rally in the Albert Hall.

After the League of Free Britishers' candidate is humiliated in a London by-election, the movement for liberty is quietly dissolved by Sir Joseph. Lightbody protests, but to no avail. Perplexed and annoyed by Sir Joseph's decision, Lightbody sounds off in public about liberty, assaults a policeman and ends up in court again. He is fined and advised against getting into any further trouble. The book closes with him considering the possibility of inaugurating a campaign for liberty somewhere else in the Commonwealth, although, if he stays at home, there are the enticing prospects of seeing his first grandchild born and taking delivery of a new bacon slicer.

enforcement and the deceitfulness of advertising, but Balchin's primary intention throughout the book is to be funny and that is not the case with any of his other novels.

Lightly amusing throughout, *Lightbody on Liberty* never succeeds in attaining the pitch of hilarity one feels ought to have been possible given the characters and situations at the author's disposal. The story he tells—ordinary man caught up in extraordinary goings-on and surrounded by larger-than-life characters—has something of *Decline and Fall* and *Scoop* about it, but Balchin did not possess in his armoury the exuberance and comic gusto that Evelyn Waugh displayed so expertly in his 1930s novels. Balchin was too much of a realist (and too warmly enamoured of the loveable Mr Lightbody) to have written the sparkling comic fantasy that he perhaps envisaged when he first planned the structure of the book; as Clive James has observed, 'tripping the light fantastic was not something his mind could manage'.[16] The humour needed to be crueller, more vicious and perhaps more absurd to have been successful. It should though be mentioned in passing that several of the minor figures generate some amusement and that Lightbody's son Bert, a Communist Party member suffering from the ludicrous misapprehension that his father is a bourgeois parasite, is a notable comic creation.

Although the familiar Balchinesque theme of the book (a lone individual railing against the might of an organization, in this case the law) may be reminiscent of the plot of an Ealing Comedy, *Lightbody on Liberty* more closely resembles one of the Boulting brothers' 1950s/1960s satires on British institutions. It is not too much of a stretch to imagine Stanley Holloway as Lightbody, Irene Handl as his long-suffering wife Violet, Eric Barker as Perks, Richard Attenborough as Haskell and Alistair Sim as Sir Joseph. It is a great pity that Balchin, during his screenwriting period, didn't think of adapting his 1936 novel for the cinema. It would have made a cracking little film...

Lightbody on Liberty evoked a number of complimentary notices, with most of the critics remarking that the book was both enjoyable and entertaining. Writing in the *Observer*, Gerald Gould[17] (ironically the father of Balchin's love rival-in-waiting Michael Ayrton) described *Lightbody on Liberty* as both 'a gorgeous book' and an 'extremely readable and amusing work'. Ralph Straus[18] in the *Sunday Times* said that Balchin was 'good fun' and characterized the novel as 'a pawky satire on some of our odder legislation and that now elderly dame known as "Dora"[19]'. *The Times Literary Supplement* was also impressed by the book, although the praise issued by its splendidly named critic Eustratius Emmanuel Mavrogordato[20] was tempered by the opinion that Balchin's description of the League of Free Britishers' publicity machine was 'of the common stuff of the satirical writing of the day'.

For the remainder of the 1930s, Balchin placed increasing focus on the production of journalism. During his four-and-a-half-year stay at the National Institute of Industrial Psychology he had been responsible, in addition to the handful of articles he contributed to their in-house journal, for thirty-two humorous pieces for *Punch*. In the five and a half years after he left the Institute he wrote a further 132 magazine articles, all of which can be filed under the heading 'Humour', and this is perhaps one reason why he wrote only one novel during this period.

By the end of 1935 *Punch* had finished their serialization of *Business for Pleasure*, the third (and last) of Balchin's ten-part series for the magazine. Until he stopped writing for them in the spring of 1938, Balchin concentrated on the composition of stand-alone contributions, writing a further forty-three articles for the humorous weekly. These carried promising titles such as 'Programmes for Pachyderms', 'So Refreshing!', 'Visiting Mrs. Vestibule' and 'The Morbid Psychology of the Made-Up Tie', but the articles themselves did not maintain quite the same standard. Many of them were either ruminations on the political issues of the day or commentaries on items seen in newspapers (a number of pieces begin along the lines 'It has come to my attention that…').

There is thus little to commend these articles (none of which carried Balchin's byline incidentally). But no doubt they served a useful function for the struggling author by getting him into the habit of writing on a regular basis, and the frequent receipt of cheques from Messrs Bradbury Agnew & Co., the proprietors of *Punch*, would have been appreciated too.

One of the *Punch* articles is of some interest because it reveals, as hinted at in Chapter 2, which of his old Cambridge friends Balchin was still in touch with at the time. ''Little Fleas Have Lesser Fleas…'', published on 14 October 1936, starts like this:

> When I first knew John he was a rather shy, very handsome and completely charming undergraduate. That was eight years ago. John has now turned up again. He is still shy (in rather a different way), still very handsome (also in a different way) and completely charming (in the same way). But there has been a subtle alteration in the world's evaluation of John. Whereas in the old days his commercial value (like mine) was a rather large *minus* amount, I now understand that they pay him two hundred a week to be charming in films.

The dates and personal characteristics of 'John' reveal that he is none other than James Mason. Later in the article, Balchin records having watched him in two recent films, in one of which he had played an escaped convict.[21] Within about six months of being reunited with Balchin, Mason would star in *Miserable Sinners*.

Far more characteristic, impressive and more intrinsically enjoyable than Balchin's *Punch* contributions are the Pobottle articles. Between 19 August 1936 and 24 May 1940, Balchin contributed seventy-one humorous pieces of copy for an advertising campaign on behalf of High Duty Alloys (HDA) of Slough, a manufacturing company that produced high-strength aluminium alloys, such as 'Hiduminium', for the aerospace industry. These adverts, which appeared in the trade magazine *The Aeroplane*, were unusual in that they consisted of roughly 700 words of copy in the form of a magazine article. All of the adverts were beautifully illustrated with elegant Art Nouveau-style black-and-white line drawings by Beresford

Egan, who also contributed decorative matter to Balchin's *Income and Outcome*. The first article in the series was entitled 'Pobottle on Publicity'[22] and many of the subsequent articles also made mention of this eponymous character, who is described in one place as 'an obscure member of our staff. We have never been quite clear what he does, but he's on the pay-roll'.[23] Mr Pobottle was in fact a middle-aged bespectacled balding 'ideas man'.

The central conceit of the Pobottle articles is that HDA's advertising manager, in common with a number of his predecessors, has gone mad—'That's the eighth who's gone off the handle on us in the last two years'[24]—and left the company because selling aluminium alloys is too difficult a 'story'. A new copywriter is therefore hired (i.e. Balchin, although his name was never attached to any of the adverts) and this man, Pobottle's protégé, starts to write the advertising.

In order to write his Pobottle articles Balchin concocted a rough amalgam of the different forms of humour he had used in his (non-*Bassoon Factory*) *Punch* articles and the Mark Spade books. He borrowed some of the anecdotal 'News has reached us…' quality of the former and blended it with the whimsical flippancy of the latter. The Pobottle material is tighter and more focused than Balchin's previous attempts at comic journalism, and given his greater experience at this juncture it is also unsurprising to find that it is consistently wittier and more polished. The sheer exuberance of the writing suggests that Balchin thoroughly enjoyed composing his weekly article for *The Aeroplane*. Also, as the pieces were unattributed he was free to cannibalize some of his earlier work and so we find material from both his *Human Factor* articles and the Mark Spade books cropping up again in the guise of HDA advertising copy. Balchin didn't stop here either, because some of his Pobottle japery would later reappear almost word-for-word in novels as widely separated in time as *Darkness Falls from the Air* (1942) and *Seen Dimly Before Dawn* (1962).

A great deal of the humour in Pobottle arises from Balchin gleefully poking fun at himself. Thus in the article

'Despondency in Slough',[25] the suggestion is that the new copywriter has been fired:

> We have recently received a number of letters asking what has happened to the man who used to write our advertisements. Most of our correspondents expressed the view that whatever had happened to him he was darned lucky it wasn't worse.

In another piece, 'Subtle',[26] this theme is developed:

> We met a stranger the other day who congratulated us on our advertising. We found this very gratifying, because although we quite often meet strangers and they quite often mention our advertising, they usually do it rather in the sort of way that people ask after one's Epileptic Fits, i.e., with respectful sympathy.

Most of Balchin's advertisements were simply an excuse for him to say whatever he liked (and to be as funny as he could), and they often contained only the most tangential mentions of the wares that he was supposedly promoting. Quite what the directors of HDA thought about the Pobottle campaign is anyone's guess but they allowed it to run in much the same form for the best part of four years. As Britain rearmed in the mid-1930s to counter the threat of Hitler, sales of HDA's alloys were probably buoyed more by the need to defend the country's borders than by Balchin's quirky, idiosyncratic advertising.

During his Pobottle period, Balchin also had work published in two periodicals with greater literary cachet. *Time and Tide* was a political and literary magazine founded in 1920 by Lady Margaret Rhondda and originally intended to espouse feminist and left-wing views. The staff of *Time and Tide* were largely drawn from the upper echelons of society (when he acted as literary editor of the magazine in the 1950s, John Betjeman referred to it irreverently as '*Tame and Tade*') and those who wrote for it included intellectual heavyweights such as George Bernard Shaw, D. H. Lawrence, Virginia Woolf and

George Orwell. Balchin's article for the periodical, 'Keeping the Peace', appeared on 31 October 1936 and topically detailed an amusing variety of ways in which Blackshirt rallies could be broken up (a subject later discussed, in more sober and dramatic fashion, in *The Fall of the Sparrow*).

Night and Day, edited by Graham Greene, was a *New Yorker*-style weekly review of the arts that existed for a mere six months in 1937. In addition to Greene himself, it numbered among its contributors Betjeman, Cyril Connolly, Anthony Powell, Evelyn Waugh, Herbert Read, Elizabeth Bowen and Osbert Lancaster. Balchin supplied two pieces to the magazine in the summer of 1937.[27]

Balchin's labours on his magazine articles would have been briefly interrupted in November 1937. His second daughter, Penelope Jane, was born on the 19th in a private maternity clinic in Fitzjohns Avenue, Hampstead, not far from the family's dwelling in Highgate. By the time that Balchin had registered the birth, on 2 February 1938, the family had moved, this time to Robbery Bottom in Oaklands, a quiet suburb of Welwyn in Hertfordshire.

With war looming on the horizon, Balchin continued his dual quests to provide for his expanding family and to broaden the base of his writing operation with a view to bringing his work to the attention of the largest possible audience. To this latter end, the BBC was a godsend.

On 6 September 1937, Balchin had been approached by a Talks Producer at the BBC, Norman Luker,[28] who had read *Income and Outcome* 'with interest and amusement' and was of the opinion that its pages held the potential to contain 'some material for talking at the microphone'.[29] The two men met a week later, on which occasion Balchin made a good impression on his interviewer, who subsequently described the aspiring broadcaster enthusiastically to a colleague as 'a ready talker with quite a pleasant voice.' Balchin was therefore signed up for a new series of roundtable discussions on the National Programme under the umbrella heading *Men Talking*. The second of these (but the first to which Balchin contributed) went out at

8.40 pm on Thursday 14 October and oddly featured a woman in addition to Balchin and two other men. The subject was 'Family Budgets' and, not inappropriately given the nature of the book that had helped to secure Balchin his fee of five guineas (just under £300 today), the content of the debate overlapped to a significant extent with that of *Income and Outcome*.

One day before Penelope was born, Balchin made his second appearance on *Men Talking*. The script for the programme was not preserved, but its title, 'A Woman's Place is in the Home', gives a sizeable clue as to its content. For his third broadcast on the National Programme, Balchin retreated to less contentious ground. Developing the theme of his first contribution to the *Men Talking* strand, he spoke on the subject of 'Household Budgets' and this time he was on his own, with no panel to impede the flow of his argument. As detailed in the *Radio Times*,[30] Balchin's talk was:

> …addressed mainly to housewives and those who are just able to afford budgeting but still have to be very careful as to how they do it.

This lecture again drew heavily on *Income and Outcome* and Balchin dispensed sound common sense laced with his customary brand of urbane wit.

Balchin's final pre-war radio appearance occurred on 3 October 1938. This was another example of *Men Talking*, the programme being described by the *Radio Times*[31] as:

> …these now widely-known informal and impromptu discussions of topics of the moment by various groups of speakers.

The subject of this programme was 'Humour' and the rather rambling and inconclusive debate that went out over the airwaves proved that it was no easier in 1938 than it is today to define what is funny.

Not much more than a year after Luker had described

Balchin as 'a ready talker with quite a pleasant voice' he appears to have changed his mind about him. On 16 December the BBC man informed a colleague that he had detected 'Marked deterioration' in Balchin's October performance on *Men Talking* as a result of him having 'developed an affected and somewhat condescending voice'. Despite this deficiency, Luker did concede that the novelist's arguments were 'probably the best in the broadcast'. It is not known what prompted Luker's volte-face with regard to the timbre of the sounds emanating from Balchin's larynx but, in addition to his preoccupation with his war work, this is perhaps one reason why Balchin did no further broadcasting for the BBC for seven and a half years after his third and final participation in *Men Talking*.

During the winter of 1938–1939, Balchin returned to his family home in Wiltshire to be part of the congregation at his mother's funeral service, which was described by the *Wiltshire Gazette*[32] as being 'of a quiet and simple nature, there being no music'. Ada Balchin had died on 9 February from heart disease at the age of sixty-eight. Balchin's mother was characterized by the newspaper as a simple, homely soul who was well thought of in West Lavington.

In the wake of his bereavement, Balchin distanced himself from his remaining family. He was incredibly fond of Monica, and kept in touch with his sister for some years after the Second World War. But it was a different matter with his father and brother: despite regarding them with affection, Balchin had little in common with either of them and did not see them very often in the latter years of their lives (they died in 1958 and 1953, respectively).

Balchin never went so far as to disown his family and he was probably not ashamed of them, despite the fact that he enjoyed a standard of living that was far superior to that of his parents from the mid-1930s onwards. As soon as he left West Lavington for Cambridge in the autumn of 1927, Balchin began to move in social circles far removed from those of his family, with their endless round of church fetes and sports club dances, choosing instead something more sophisticated and metropolitan with which to amuse himself. Except on very rare occasions, such as family weddings and funerals, he showed no wish to pick up the threads of his simpler life back home in Wiltshire.

*

During the course of 1939, Balchin uprooted his family once more, moving them from Hertfordshire back to central London. With the imminent bombing of metropolitan areas widely forecast this was perhaps not the most sensible of house moves, but 51A Clanricarde Gardens in Bayswater was a convenient domestic base for Balchin and Elisabeth as they tried to fix themselves up with suitable employment in the early months of the war.

On 8 September, five days after the outbreak of hostilities, Balchin wrote a long letter to Frederick Fryer, Vice-Chairman of Rowntree's, setting out his qualifications and experiences that he believed would be of use to the company during the war with Germany. (Balchin was obviously very keen to perpetuate his association with Rowntree's because, according to Fryer, he had already turned down a number of other job offers.)

Balchin pinpointed his main virtues as 'imagination and ability to think fast',[33] adding that he also possessed the capacity to 'work ectremely [sic] hard and rather fast'. The two men agreed that Balchin could perhaps best be employed as a London-based liaison person for Rowntree's York headquarters. But Seebohm Rowntree, the company's Chairman, considered that such a role might well be a waste of Balchin's 'creative mind'. It was therefore probably Rowntree who was instrumental in Balchin performing a rather different job during the first year of the war.

Rowntree's evidently had a high opinion of Balchin. He had impressed them before the war with his work on Black Magic and his subsequent consumer testing and they expected great things of him in the years ahead. Fryer told Rowntree on 14 September that, in his opinion, Balchin had 'one of the best brains in the organisation' and he predicted that Balchin might 'in due course come to hold an important position in the organisation'. Fryer was eager for Balchin to view the war as an opportunity to broaden his range of experiences with his future prospects in the confectionery industry in mind. (This is akin to the way in which senior figures at the NIIP in the mid-1930s thought that Balchin possessed the ability to ascend as high as Director of the Institute if he so desired.) However, it is worth noting that George Harris, who succeeded Rowntree as Chairman of Rowntree's in 1941, remarked in 1947 that 'I consider Balchin to be an individualist who can only express himself as an individualist'. Balchin's career path, with its frequent changes of direction and his eventual concentration on the individualistic profession of authorship, bears out Harris's observation. Balchin's mid-period novels—and especially *Darkness Falls from the Air*, *The Small Back Room* and *Mine Own Executioner*—contain a number of characters who chuck in their jobs, often in acrimonious fashion after a bitter argument. Although Balchin only seems to have left one job in similarly convulsive circumstances, that at the Ministry of Food in 1941, he did accumulate quite a long history of quitting positions of employment.

In the letter he wrote to Fryer on 8 September 1939, Balchin commented that 'This is a very dull war so far.' It would not remain that way for much longer, at least not for Balchin.

6

Darkness Falls from the Air

"You couldn't get me in to your Ministry, I suppose? I've only got about a month to get fixed."

I said, "Why should I? You've never done me any harm."

"You all talk like that," he said quite snappily. "What wouldn't I give for your job!"

"Well, what would you? It's a lousy job. You work your head off, don't get paid, and get nothing done. You're welcome."

– Nigel Balchin, *Darkness Falls from the Air*

Darkness Falls from the Air, Balchin's fourth novel, is set in a government ministry, the workings of which are likely to have been based quite closely on those of the Ministry of Food, where Balchin was employed between July 1940 and May 1941. The ministerial environment characterized by vested interests, careerism, jockeying for position and Machiavellian intrigue that Balchin described in *Darkness Falls from the Air* via the mouthpiece of his narrator Bill Sarratt, one of whose typically world-weary utterances is reproduced above, was mirrored in a diluted form by the author's own experiences of working for (and in collaboration with) the Ministry of Food during the first eighteen months or so of the Second World War.[1]

In the summer of 1941, Balchin joined the army. On a form he completed on enrolment,[2] he described his most recent period of employment as having run 'From Sept. 1939 to May 1941' and that his responsibilities in this role had included being 'in charge of the allocation of Raw Materials in the Ministry of Food'. However, Balchin had been slightly economical with the truth when he filled in Army Form B199A because he had not joined the Ministry of Food as soon as the war began. Instead, he worked for the Manufacturing Confectioners Alliance (MCA) for approximately the first year of the conflict.

The MCA was 'the national organisation of the cocoa, chocolate and sugar confectionery manufacturing industry'.[3] It protected the interests of the trade, set prices for the industry and lobbied parliament whenever the state was poised to introduce legislation likely to damage the profits of the MCA's members, which included all the big industry players, such as Rowntree's, Cadbury's, Fry's, Terry's and Lyons. One of its Vice-Presidents in 1940 was Seebohm Rowntree and, as hinted in the previous chapter, it was probably the Rowntree's Chairman who considered that a job with the MCA would be a fitting use of Balchin's considerable administrative abilities. He would also have understood the importance of Balchin being in a position to look after the interests of Rowntree's in his capacity as Allocations Officer to the MCA.

Before the war, the MCA had formed a Defence Committee to work with the Board of Trade (the precursor of the Ministry of Food, which did not come into being until 4 September 1939). This committee was charged with collecting data on the consumption of raw materials by confectionery companies and coordinating deliveries and transport arrangements. Balchin, who was based in London, attended the fortnightly meetings of the MCA's Defence Committee once war had been declared. He acted as a link between the confectionery industry and the Ministry of Food and, beginning in December 1939 when food rationing first came into force, his department controlled the distribution of supplies of sugar, butter, fats and oils to manufacturers such as Rowntree's, Cadbury's and many other smaller producers of chocolate and associated products.

Elisabeth Balchin worked in a comparable realm to her husband during the early phase of the war. With her children entrusted to the care of a nanny, and sometimes temporarily evacuated out of London to stay with relatives when the threat of enemy bombing was at its height, she was free to work full-time to aid the war effort, something she was desperate to do. Probably with assistance from Balchin, she also found employment in the capital, in her case an administrative job as Chief Assistant to the Allocations Controller of the MCA's associated organization the Food Manufacturers' Federation.

Following the humiliating evacuation of British troops from the beaches of Dunkirk in May and June 1940 the country was put on a more warlike footing in expectation of a likely invasion, and a successful plank in this strategy was greater governmental control of industry in order that production of essential supplies could be prioritized. One long-term consequence of this policy was that chocolate assortments were viewed as luxury items and thus production of Black Magic (and other Rowntree's lines) was ceased for the duration in March 1941.

Balchin was an important player in the post-Dunkirk rationalization of the confectionery industry. On 19 June 1940, he told a meeting of the MCA's Defence Committee that he had been approached earlier that day by a representative from the Economics Division of the Ministry of Food asking his committee if it would consider devising a plan of rationalization for the chocolate industry. This plan would cover not just raw materials but manufactured goods as well. According to Balchin, this was the ministry's first attempt at central coordination.

Balchin's statement was somewhat disingenuous and cleverly glossed over his own involvement in the matter. In August, George Harris, Chairman of Rowntree's Executive Board, met with Balchin. In an aide-memoire he wrote soon after this meeting, Harris expressed severe displeasure with the origins of the rationalization scheme ('If we drew a line at that point I think I would have strong grounds for feeling thoroughly annoyed with the Ministry, with Balchin and with Cadburys'[4]). What had happened to make Harris so annoyed? In brief, a turf war had broken out between Balchin and John Cadbury, a junior director of Rowntree's great rival in the chocolate-making business. Cadbury was employed at the Ministry of Food and had taken to calling himself Director of Cocoa, Chocolate and Sugar Confectionery without, in Balchin's opinion, having any authority whatsoever to do so. Cadbury's duties overlapped to a large extent with those of Balchin, but the latter had only recently been made aware of this. A meeting was called to air Balchin's grievance at which a senior ministry official rejected Cadbury's claim to his grandiose title (he was only in fact Director of Cocoa Purchasing), stating instead that 'his job was to direct Raw Cocoa, and he had better get on with it'.

After he had left the MCA, Balchin argued successfully that if a rationalization scheme was necessary then it should be implemented under the auspices of the Economics Division of the Ministry of Food (of which he had recently become a member) and that Cadbury's department, which mostly dealt with ingredients, should not be involved. Harris was clear in his own mind that this squabbling between Balchin and Cadbury had been the spark that had ignited a far-reaching Ministry of Food proposal: 'I should not be surprised if this incident did not really fire the powder that later blazed into the Rationalisation scheme.' If one takes Harris's notes at face value then it can be seen that the proposal for rationalization of the confectionery industry had originated not from the Economics Division of the Ministry of Food, as Balchin had claimed two months earlier, but instead from Balchin himself:

> I am satisfied that the general statement that the Ministry was being sold hard that Industry wanted rationalisation, and that Industry was being sold hard that the Ministry of Food wanted rationalisation is justified and the one that caused this situation was unquestionably N.M.B.

On 5 July the MCA agreed to comply with a Ministry of Food request to consider some form of voluntary rationalization. Preliminary work in this direction had already been accomplished earlier in the year as Harris had entered into negotiations with Cadbury's to investigate ways in which the two companies could cooperate. Although Rowntree's and Cadbury's between them were responsible for 84% of the country's total chocolate output, the MCA's membership also contained a large number of much smaller producers and the voluntary rationalization scheme that was eventually put forward to the Ministry of Food in July was of limited value because the disparate nature of the MCA meant that it was impossible to include the entire membership in the same scheme. The voluntary scheme failed and this meant, inevitably, that compulsion was just around the corner.

In June the Ministry of Food was evacuated from London to Colwyn Bay in North Wales. A couple of weeks later, on 10 July, Balchin informed the MCA's Defence Committee that at 'very short notice'[5] he too had been asked to relocate to the seaside. The ministry had effectively decided to 'rebrand' Balchin's department: the MCA's Allocations Officer had been absorbed within the ministry's own bureaucracy, a new Allocations Branch of the ministry had been created within the Economics Division that would be headed by Balchin and he had become a temporary civil servant, like Sarratt in the forthcoming *Darkness Falls from the Air*. The MCA's Defence Committee expressed exasperation at the manner in which the governmental body had handled the change: 'it was felt that the Ministry should not have dealt with the matter in such a high-handed way.'

Balchin, Elisabeth and their two young daughters relocated to North Wales, finding accommodation in the Victorian seaside resort of Llandudno. Elisabeth, in common with her husband, continued to perform much the same role as she had in London, only she too now sheltered beneath the umbrella of the Ministry of Food. During the working week, Balchin was based at the Hotel Metropole, a short distance along the coast from Llandudno in Colwyn Bay.

As the rationalization row rumbled on, other personnel reshuffles were also taking place. At the meeting on 10 July at which Balchin had informed the MCA's Defence Committee that he was being transferred to the Ministry of Food, he had also hinted that the ministry was seeking to appoint a Director of Production to assume control of the confectionery trade. Lord Woolton—he who gave the famous vegetable-based Woolton Pie its name—had become Minister of Food on 3 April, and in

August he asked Rowntree's to release William Wallace[6] from their employ to act as a conduit between the ministry and the MCA as the result of a representation from the MCA's Defence Committee. Still based in London, the Defence Committee was concerned about the prospect of losing touch with the ministry given that Balchin had already taken up his duties in Colwyn Bay. Harris wrote to Wallace on 26 August recommending that he should take the position that was being offered to him:

> It is believed by the company to be desirable in the National interest and in the interests of the Industry and the Group that you should take this post.[7]

Wallace accepted, and by the end of August he had been appointed Trade Advisor for Cocoa, Chocolate and Sugar Confectionery. Wallace would obtain data on raw materials used by the industry from Balchin, and use that information to keep tabs on the trade. Working in consultation with Balchin, Wallace was now charged with developing a rationalization scheme that would be acceptable to the entire British chocolate industry.

There was still some faint hope that such a scheme could remain on a voluntary footing. In mid-July, Lord Woolton had stated that he welcomed schemes of voluntary cooperation and rationalization between food traders and industrialists. In September he reiterated this position when he stated that 'the Government could not control a trade as effectively as the trade itself'.[8] Balchin was also toeing his ministry's line: on 23 August he told the MCA's Defence Committee that 'there was no intention to thrust 'rationalization' down the throats of the trade' and that 'any scheme would have to be worked out in consultation with the industry'.

But very soon after his September pronouncement, his Lordship decisively changed his mind. Prefiguring a line from *Darkness Falls from the Air* in which Baxter, the minister, says that 'there are times when I feel a little happier if I have the law of the land behind me than all the goodwill in the world',

Lord Woolton now rotated his position through 180 degrees by stating that 'there was no prospect of the industry escaping state direction and enforced rationalisation'[9] and he proceeded to introduce an approved list of products for the confectionery industry to make. Although the details of this rationalization scheme would be thrashed out by the trade itself with the assistance of Wallace and Balchin, the ministry would enforce the resultant scheme. (This is a neat reversal of the situation in *Darkness Falls from the Air*, in which Baxter is initially in favour of compulsion but changes his mind in the course of a single meeting under pressure from industry representatives and ultimately permits the introduction of a voluntary scheme of area grouping for firms put out of action by enemy bombing, to the fury of Sarratt.)

During the remainder of his time at Colwyn Bay, Balchin appears to have performed similar duties to those he had undertaken in London. In addition to advising Wallace about the availability of sugar and other raw materials and working with him to bring about product rationalization,[10] Balchin's primary function still consisted of determining what supplies of foodstuffs were available and then issuing permits to food producers to allow them to purchase those materials to which they were entitled. In the years after 1945, Balchin did reveal some (relatively scanty) details about certain aspects of his wartime employments, either on the radio or in magazine and journal articles. The only comment to have surfaced so far about his days as a raw materials allocations officer concerns an 'atrocity story', which he defined as 'a complaint in the Press or in Parliament or to the department itself, which was true, as far as it went, but looked very different if one knew all the facts'.[11] The anecdote that Balchin related has a distinct flavour of *Darkness Falls from the Air*, detailing as it does the essential absurdity of some aspects of his working life during the first two years of the war:

> I, myself, once had to tell a man who wanted seven pounds
> of some substance of which the country was very short that
> I couldn't give him seven pounds, but that if he could show

a case for having fifty-six pounds I could arrange it. This sounds fantastic. But the simple and obvious explanation was that the stuff was in fifty-six-pound units and I had no means of breaking them.

A scheme for the classification of cocoa, chocolate and sugar confectionery products was finally agreed in January 1941. Four months later, Balchin severed his connection with the civil service, believing perhaps that his work there was now done and that the spark he had struck to launch the idea of product rationalization had finally found something it could set light to. But it is also apparent that Balchin was fed up with the backbiting and rancour that were endemic within the Ministry of Food and its associated bodies (as satirized so brilliantly in his forthcoming novel). In July, Harris, who had just succeeded Seebohm Rowntree as Chairman of Rowntree's, approached Balchin and asked him if he would return to the company fold and liaise with the Wartime Trades Association[12] and the Ministry of Food in order to implement a new scheme of consumer rationing. After two lengthy discussions on the subject, Balchin turned down this opportunity. Judging by the tone of a letter from Harris to Balchin written on 23 July, it is clear that Balchin had voiced his opposition to the new Chairman's plans in a very forceful manner:

> It became clear that you felt so strongly about the conduct of certain Ministry officials both as regards the treatment of the problems which are presently confronting the industry, and the treatment which you had received from them personally, that any contribution you might make could not but be so seriously coloured by your immediate past experiences as largely to lose its value. You felt, too, that until there were material changes in the personnel of the Ministry of Food probably by force of circumstances that the various problems of Consumer Rationing, Concentration of Production and Price Control were unlikely to be handled by the existing personnel at the Ministry in a satisfactory manner warranted by the

present needs of the National food economy. You agreed that necessarily there was a considerable merging of the personal and the impersonal aspects of this problem in your mind.[13]

At one of their meetings, Balchin told Harris that he had arranged to take a commission with the Army Psychological Department, which was then in the process of formation. There ensued a decidedly frosty series of written exchanges between the two men, the point at issue being whether Balchin had volunteered for the army *before* Harris had given him permission to do so. But then, at the end of July, Harris reluctantly agreed to release Balchin from his obligation to Rowntree's so that he could join the army.

The large drop in salary that Balchin incurred upon changing employers, from £1,400 with Rowntree's to £500 in the army (equivalent to about £57,000 and £20,000, respectively, today), was made more palatable when Harris agreed to pay him an additional £550 a year while he was serving in the military. This was clearly a 'golden handcuffs' payment designed to retain Balchin's services because Harris told his outgoing employee in writing that he was expecting him to return to Rowntree's after the war.

Balchin's desire to join the Army Psychological Department was thwarted. Instead, Brigadier K. G. McLean at the War Office assigned him to an associated organization, the Directorate of Selection of Personnel, that was also in the process of formation and on whose staff McLean served as Director. Balchin therefore returned to London from North Wales in the middle of 1941. He spent most of the rest of the war living with his family in an upper-storey flat, 9 Duke's Lodge, in well-heeled Holland Park.

*

Almost exactly eighteen months after Balchin had left the Ministry of Food, William Collins published 'the classic novel of the London Blitz'.[14] *Darkness Falls from the Air* was first displayed in the windows of Britain's booksellers on 9 November 1942. Initially, sales of the novel were not commensurate with the complimentary words employed by the nation's literary

Darkness Falls from the Air (1942)

Bill Sarratt is a temporary civil servant working in a government ministry in London during the Blitz of 1940. His wife Marcia is being permitted by her husband to have an affair with Stephen, a monstrously egotistical and totally unscrupulous poet. Sarratt hopes that the affair will fizzle out of its own accord, but, as this shows no signs of happening, he consents to Marcia leaving him temporarily to live with Stephen.

Sarratt's job at the ministry is generally a thankless one, but when he devises an Area Unit Scheme—a way in which manufacturers can cooperate if one of them is put out of action by bomb damage—he finds to his surprise that his proposal is backed not just by his immediate superior but also by the minister himself.

Marcia finally breaks off her liaison with Stephen and agrees to meet her husband for a celebratory meal. However, at a meeting held beforehand to ratify the Area Unit Scheme the minister agrees that it should remain voluntary rather than compulsory, a feature that to Sarratt renders his plan worse than useless. He walks out of the meeting in disgust, effectively kissing goodbye to his job.

Sarratt is sitting in a restaurant waiting for his wife to arrive when he is informed of a huge air raid in East London. As Marcia is working in Aldgate, Sarratt fears the worst and sets off to look for her. The casualty dressing station where she is employed has suffered a direct hit and Marcia is trapped beneath the rubble. Sarratt must try to rescue her before the building collapses.

critics to greet its appearance and there was an obvious reason for this, as Balchin elaborated twenty years later:

> I think there were about 5,000 copies and they all sold, but there wasn't any paper for a reprint.[15]

Despite the excellence of *Darkness Falls from the Air*, Balchin was still very much an unknown quantity as a novelist in 1942: his first two novels had sold in negligible quantities for Hamish Hamilton and the third had not done much better for his new publisher Collins, Clive James recording that 'Balchin's pre-war writings had small success, only the novel *Lightbody on Liberty* managing to sell in four figures'.[16] This may help to explain why the print run of *Darkness Falls from the Air* was restricted to a mere 5,000 copies. That, and the fact that paper was in such desperately short supply at the rough midpoint of the war when Balchin's fourth novel was sent to the printers. Although Collins were theoretically entitled to receive about 2,000 tons of paper per year throughout the conflict, far more than most other British publishers, and a second edition of *Darkness Falls from the Air* with the same print run as the first would have consumed little more than a single ton of paper, actually obtaining adequate supplies for printing books at that time was a different matter entirely.[17] It is perhaps partly because copies of *Darkness Falls from the Air* were so scarce during the 1940s that one of Balchin's finest novels remains undervalued and relatively little known even today.

Balchin's first three novels had been published over the course of a two-year span in the mid-1930s. A six-year hiatus then elapsed until the publication of *Darkness Falls from the Air*, which was not an untoward occurrence for the author ('I get periods like that'[18] as he put it). The long wait had been worthwhile. The book's terse, matter-of-fact opening sentence—'I stopped at about seven.'—has the immediacy and authority of a witness statement and the 1940s reader was left in no doubt that here was something very different from Balchin's previous fiction. Although the novel is almost exactly the same length as *No Sky* and *Simple Life*, crucially it *feels* shorter, and it is the writing style that is responsible for this. *No Sky* and *Simple Life* contain long descriptive passages, *Darkness Falls from the Air* has barely any, relying instead on dialogue to advance the story; sentences are shorter, more clipped in *Darkness Falls from the Air*; and the pace of the first two novels is that of a leisurely trot compared with the brisk canter of the wartime book.

Darkness Falls from the Air also evinces a significant structural difference from Balchin's earlier novels. Reviewing the book in the *New Statesman and Nation*, a young fellow writer, Philip Toynbee,[19] was quick to grasp this departure from Balchin's tyro efforts:

> There are three concentric themes to the book. In the centre is the Triangle of Sarratt, the Civil Servant, his wife Marcia and Stephen the poet. Round that is built the theme of Sarratt's work in the ministry, and his tragi-comic struggle with corruption and bureaucracy. The background to all this is the early days of the Blitz, culminating in the City fire.

No Sky, *Simple Life* and *Lightbody on Liberty* had all been concerned primarily with the work and home lives of their protagonists; to this blend, as Toynbee elucidated, Balchin had now added a magical third ingredient: the war.

World War Two exerted a dramatic and long-lasting effect on Balchin's novel-writing. As well as adding a fresh new stratum to what James has described as Balchin's 'layer-cake',[20] it also introduced the vital quality of urgency, a substance that hitherto had been badly lacking. When asked in 1962 to comment on whether *Darkness Falls from the Air* and *The Small Back Room* were better than his first three novels, Balchin gave an unequivocal reply:

> Oh, yes. They were both written under the great emotional pressure of the war. They were much less calm—in fact, not calm at all—and they were concerned with things I felt passionately about.[21]

During World War Two, Balchin experienced 'a burning need to say something' and he clearly felt that there was no time to waste. The war energized him and accelerated the pace of his writing, almost as if he was involved in a frantic race against time to commit his thoughts to paper before a bomb could be dropped on top of him.

Darkness Falls from the Air was more interesting, more proficient and more economically written than its three predecessors. It also possessed much greater contemporary relevance given that it concerned events of the immediate past, events fresh in the memory of anyone who had been bombed out of their home or had gazed in horror at the 'bright copper colour' of the City of London going up in flames. All the paraphernalia of wartime London is expertly corralled by Balchin in *Darkness Falls from the Air*: there are repeated descriptions of air raids; houses have their ends neatly sliced off by bombs so that each one resembles 'a doll's house with the front open'; incendiaries smoulder in Piccadilly; and prostitutes loiter in doorways as ARP wardens patrol the streets warning of the dangers of shrapnel and falling masonry. There is a running gag about a barrage balloon with a personality of its own ('like an elephant in a vile temper flapping its ears'), and Sarratt meditates on the decorative potential of this form of air defence on the very first page of the novel:

> Going up the street I looked at the balloons and still thought they looked like a shoal of silver fish, and that when the war was over it would be worth while to keep them as decoration.

These descriptions of life in London in autumn 1940 are incredibly vivid. But they acquire an even more remarkable quality when one is informed of the fact that their creator was in Colwyn Bay for most, if not all, of the time during which the Blitz was taking place and that he must therefore have relied largely on second-hand accounts of the bombing in order to write this material.

Unsurprisingly, *Darkness Falls from the Air* attracted a larger (and better) set of notices than any of Balchin's previous novels. It was very warmly greeted, and recognized as a significant leap forward on the part of its author. Among the book's most outspoken admirers was Elizabeth Bowen[22] in the *Tatler and Bystander*, who described it as 'one of the most remarkable novels I have struck this season'. She also praised *Darkness Falls from the Air* for its lifelike quality, stating that when she had closed its covers and laid it aside 'it left me feeling disturbed. I had become almost too much involved with the characters'.

Toynbee,[23] who had been the first Communist President of the Oxford Union in 1938, picked up on the anti-Jewish sentiments propagated by Sarratt and his acquaintances, insisting that 'a strong protest must be lodged against the use of anti-semitism as an aid to toughness'. Bewilderingly, amid a broadly complimentary review, L. P. Hartley[24] in the *Sketch*, who may well have been the first reviewer to draw an (inaccurate) parallel between Balchin's dialogue and that of Ernest Hemingway, was perturbed by how much alcohol Balchin's *characters* were consuming:

> As a study of emotional entanglements and maladjustments 'Darkness Falls From the Air' is very effective; it would be still more effective, I think, if the quality of emotion were not so febrile and so quickly affected by one drink more or less.

The final word on the novel's reception should be allotted to thriller writer Margery Allingham.[25] Reviewing the book for *Time and Tide*, she characterized it as 'a corking modern commentary' and observed additionally that 'I am not at all sure that the whole secret of the modern muddle about the equality of the sexes does not lie somewhere here'.

As well as being among the three best novels that Balchin wrote (and, in time, one of the best-selling[26]), the importance of *Darkness Falls from the Air* lies in the influence it had on his subsequent books. In 1949, Pamela Hansford Johnson[27] spoke somewhat dismissively of 'Mr. Balchin's formula' when reviewing his novel *A Sort of Traitors*, but by then the formula was already seven years old because with *Darkness Falls from the Air* Balchin had assembled the perfect blend of ingredients. He had written an exciting, relevant and genuinely popular novel, but one that also displayed a fierce intelligence and intense powers of observation. He had stirred into the mix a convincing love story, one that had been influenced by a real-life relationship, and had sprinkled enough humour and drama on the top of his confection to ensure its appeal to a wide readership. 'Balchin's formula' had come out just about right the first time it had been mixed but he would go on refining the recipe for at least the next decade.

7

Marital Discord 1: As Easy as EBCD

"As a person Stephen can be very attractive. It's only his methods that make you sick. Marcia doesn't compare us. She just compares what I do with what she knows she can expect of me, and what Stephen does with what she knows she can expect of him."
— Nigel Balchin, *Darkness Falls from the Air*

In the first few months of World War Two, Elisabeth Balchin had a brief love affair with Christian Darnton, an avant-garde composer three years older than her husband who was establishing a name for himself as an uncompromising figure in the classical music world and whose compositional style has been described as 'epigrammatic, strongly contrapuntal, and ruthlessly dissonant'.[1] The circumstances surrounding the first meeting between the two parties in this liaison are now obscure, but it would seem likely that Balchin met Darnton initially and then introduced him to his wife, as he was wont to do with 'interesting men' in general and in much the same way in which he would later disastrously (for him) introduce Elisabeth to Michael Ayrton. In the year after his divorce, Balchin raked over the ashes of his marital break-up and alighted on the year in which his relations with his wife had first soured: 'I should judge that by 1938 Elisabeth's attitude to me was highly ambivalent.'[2] Kicking up her heels with Darnton in the following year was one way in which she had made this ambivalence felt.

One wonders why Elisabeth chose to have an affair with Darnton. Perhaps the unreal, eerie atmosphere of London in the opening months of the war, with its pervasive 'We may all be killed tomorrow' attitude, may have had an effect on her. But it is much more likely that Balchin's desire that he and Elisabeth should enjoy an open marriage was largely responsible. Balchin's granddaughter Justine Hopkins has written that although Balchin 'thoroughly enjoyed going to bed with Elisabeth',[3] her grandfather was however 'frequently attracted to other women and saw no earthly reason why this should not be indulged'. (Balchin is known to have conducted several extramarital affairs, particularly while he was married to his second wife Yovanka. Those that I know of are mentioned later on in the text, but it is quite probable that a number of others, especially those that can be filed under the 'one-night stand' heading, have never come to light. In Yovanka's opinion, Balchin was 'a great picker-upper of people'[4] and when he was working in the film industry in the 1950s and early 1960s he was away from home for long periods at a time and would have had ample opportunity to pick up women.) Elisabeth was encouraged by Balchin to take advantage of the same level of marital freedom that he was determined to exploit himself. But she was cut from a different cloth, Penelope Leach characterizing her mother as 'not permissive exactly, just very devoted, interested, intelligent, warm'.[5] Elisabeth did not share her husband's taste for short-term sexual liaisons; instead, she developed, in the words of Hopkins, 'the awkward habit of falling positively in love with the men into whose arms Nigel's encouragement occasionally thrust her'.[6]

Darnton had married the painter Joan Bell towards the end of 1929 and was living in central London when the Second World War broke out. Joan and the Darntons' young son Nicholas were residing in a rented house at Jordans near Beaconsfield in Buckinghamshire.[7] Alone in London during the 'phoney war', it would have been natural for Darnton to have sought company in the form of Balchin and, through him, solace with Elisabeth to help him cope with the misery he was experiencing whilst living away from his wife and child.

By February 1940, Darnton's affair with Elisabeth had run its course and the composer used his bittersweet memories of the experience as inspiration for his second symphony, which he called *The Anagram*. This work, which he soon abandoned and never finished, employed the notes C+D (representing Darnton's initials) and E+B (those of Elisabeth) as a compositional motif and Darnton dedicated it to 'my memory of E.B.'.[8] A pianist friend of Darnton's who viewed it in its embryonic state divined an erotic interpretation of the score:

E.B. is always on top of C.D.—she must be a topping girl![9]

Darnton's biographer, Andrew Plant,[10] considers that *The Anagram* is not so much an affectionate evocation of Elisabeth but more an expression of the emotional turmoil that the relationship had caused its composer. As Darnton himself said about the symphony's opening: 'This movement must be played with the utmost intensity throughout'.[11]

Balchin's reaction to his wife's extramarital dalliance took a different artistic form but was also underpinned by very strong feelings. In his case though, the emotions evoked appear to have been anger and bitterness as opposed to the mournful poignancy expressed by Darnton. Balchin was deeply hurt by Elisabeth's fling with the composer and retaliated through the medium of his fiction, namely by poking fun at Darnton in at least three of the books he wrote over the course of the following decade. Written about two years after his wife had broken off her affair with the composer, Balchin's next novel, *Darkness Falls from the Air*, provides the first piece of evidence that he had yet to forgive Darnton for the part he had played in destabilizing and endangering his marriage.

Certain unflattering personal characteristics of the composer (who was delightfully described by Hopkins as a 'musician and self-dramatist'[12]) may have provided Balchin with the kernel from which he developed the figure of Stephen Ryle in the novel, the self-pitying poet whose work is stuck, his wife explains, because he finds the Blitz an unsympathetic milieu in which to create literature ("It's the war," said Peggy. "How can he speak beauty in a world like this?"). Although the poet is not a simulacrum of the composer, the sneering and supercilious attitude of Bill Sarratt, the narrator of the novel, towards his love rival may well be similar to that of Balchin towards Darnton while he was writing the book.

Speaking to Hopkins about fifty years after the affair had fizzled out, Elisabeth revealed that elements of Darnton's personality had, in her opinion, served to mould the character of Stephen.[13] Balchin had a marked and well-documented antipathy towards artists such as Stephen who pursue literature to the exclusion of any other form of employment ('I don't like literary gents'[14]), but the narrator's dislike of the poet is so pungent and vitriolic that it seems far more likely that Balchin, via the agency of Sarratt, is directing his ire towards a real and specific person as opposed to simply sending up a representative of the artistic profession in general.

In the opening chapter of the novel, when Stephen makes his first appearance, it is clear that if Balchin has caricature in mind then it is certainly going to be a wounding and mocking one ('Stephen was looking big and handsome and haunted and so like a creative artist that you wouldn't have thought he'd have the nerve to go around looking like that') and the poet's capacity for ham-acting and striking a pose is repeatedly emphasized:

Stephen was giving his impression of a man who has received a blow which has numbed him. (p. 50)

Stephen was sitting like a collapsed sack looking down at his plate in a tragic way. (p. 166)

One of the most unsympathetic principal characters to be found in any of Balchin's fiction, Stephen is afflicted by a fundamental lack of morality ("He's completely unscrupulous, completely unprincipled and completely unashamed of it"). At various points in *Darkness Falls from the Air* he is also revealed to be breathtakingly arrogant, rude, selfish, weak and self-obsessed ("he's got one interest and one interest only—his own precious ego"). L. P. Hartley[15] in the *Sketch* described him aptly as 'a good-looking emotion-monger and born maker of scenes'.

And although Philip Toynbee[16] in the *New Statesman and Nation* felt that 'Stephen is too heavily caricatured' he did concede that Balchin's caricature was plausible:

> Such emotional crooks certainly exist, shameless in their demands for pity, outrageously threatening and even committing suicide.

Intriguingly, Plant has suggested that, as well as supplying the outline for Ryle, certain aspects of Darnton's personality and experiences may also have fed into Balchin's creation of his character Adam Lucian in *Mine Own Executioner*. In a letter written to a friend in 1970, Darnton referred to this novel as 'Nigel Balchin's book about me'[17] but made no mention at all of *Darkness Falls from the Air*. He may have chosen to refer to *Mine Own Executioner* in preference to the earlier novel because Lucian, being a compassionate portrait of a man with severe psychological problems, is a much more sympathetic character than Ryle and because Balchin, through the vehicle of the central figure Felix Milne, clearly has much more affection for Lucian ("I liked him") than Sarratt does for Ryle ("Stephen's a louse").

Plant's forensic dissection of *Mine Own Executioner* divulged multiple clues that may help to explain why Darnton chose to identify himself more with Lucian than Ryle. The first of these concerns the name that the author chose for his schizophrenic patient. Balchin was not a novelist who demonstrably took elaborate care when it came to finding names for his characters. But as a moniker, Adam Lucian has less of a generic feel to it than the names of most of Milne's other patients (Lucas, Oakes, Whiteley and Harrison for example), and reference to a copy of *Brewer's Dictionary of Phrase and Fable* would have informed Balchin that the name Lucian means 'the impersonation of the follies and vices of the age metamorphosed into an ass', which may provide an indication that he was intending to satirize Darnton when he was engaged in constructing the character of Lucian.

There are also links between Darnton and Lucian as men in need of psychiatric help. In the years leading up to the Second

World War, Darnton sought psychiatric treatment from John Yerbury Dent, who specialized in treating individuals with acute anxiety, such as Darnton. Dent claimed to be able to alter the personality of his patients by administering high doses of the drug apomorphine in order to provoke severe vomiting; in a slightly similar fashion, Milne (temporarily) alters Lucian's state of consciousness by injecting him with the 'truth drug' sodium thiopental. Darnton must have had faith in Dent's methods because he submitted to the same treatment in 1952 when he wished to dredge a forgotten score from the depths of his memory, on which occasion it was successful.

In *Mine Own Executioner*, Lucian climbs to the top of a high building in London in order to commit suicide. During World War Two, and probably in 1943, Darnton was seriously injured when, whilst working in central London for the ARP Light Artillery Rescue, a branch of Civil Defence, he fell onto a metal bar and sustained both severe spinal damage and paralysis of his hands and feet. Plant believes that the composer had probably fallen a considerable distance and that, given a collision of problems in the private and professional spheres of his life at this juncture, his injuries may well have resulted from a botched suicide attempt. In two places in his novel, Balchin uses the musical/psychiatric term 'fugue'[18] in connection with Lucian, again suggesting a possible link with Darnton:

"But he left her five hours ago to come here, and he's in a pretty queer state. Might have gone off in a fugue or something." (p. 98)

If he had been a paranoid it would have been different. But a schizo of Lucian's type would be dead or wandering in a memoryless fugue. (p. 212)

Buried within the pages of Balchin's strangest book, *Lord, I Was Afraid*, is what appears to be another sideswipe at Darnton, implying that, some seven years after it had blown over, Elisabeth's affair was still rankling Balchin. There is a scene in which the playboy character Punch Hopkins is being tormented by a creature he believes at that moment to be the devil. He attempts to push this diabolical figure off the roof of the block of London flats on which they are both standing but the devil, instead of falling, simply flaps his wings vigorously, flies around and alights again on the roof. He then chastises Hopkins for his aggressive action:

> "You know, you oughtn't to have done that. For all you know
> I might have been killed. Or at least impaled on railings. I
> should hate to be impaled on railings."

This is uncomfortably close to what had happened to Darnton during the war, and surely too close to be a coincidence.

*

Balchin had used the love triangle plot as early as his second novel, *Simple Life*. The triangle presented in *Darkness Falls from the Air* is the first one to be found in a major Balchin novel and, as Clive James[19] has pointed out, it conforms to the following blueprint:

> The lady admires the competent man but loses her head over
> a charmer. The competent man looks on with resignation as
> the two irrational creatures waste each other's time.

(Although James also declared that this is 'the standard triangle of his novels', *A Way Through the Wood* is in fact the only other book apart from *Simple Life* in which Balchin deployed precisely the same form of three-cornered sexual relationship.) In *Darkness Falls from the Air*, Stephen is permitted by Sarratt to conduct an affair with Sarratt's wife Marcia because he believes that theirs is a romance of no great consequence that will soon fizzle out ("I've always been expecting it to die a natural death"). As Sarratt makes clear to Stephen:

> "I can see exactly why you attract her, and I think it's
> a second-rate sort of attraction. If it's stronger than her feeling
> for me, then her feeling for me is worth precisely nothing."

And yet Sarratt has underestimated the strength of his wife's attraction towards Stephen: Marcia still loves Sarratt but is loath to break the bonds that bind her to the charmer. When she does finally do so, the nature of her marriage has changed and she is much more distant from her husband than she was before Stephen's intervention.

The triangular relationship between the three principals in *Darkness Falls from the Air* seems to be based on the experience that befell Balchin during the opening months of World War Two. In terms of how he was regarded by women ('I am incurably serious-minded, & the thing that I enjoy most is discussion of & speculation about the fundamental problems of existence. To most women this is a hopeless bore'[20]), the practical, rational Balchin certainly answers to James's description of a 'competent man'. As such, he was highly vulnerable to approaches being made to his wife by pleasure-seeking men with a more irresponsible make-up. Balchin's wives may have loved and respected him but that didn't stop them from desiring an occasional break from their husband's seriousness and rationality. Because Balchin was in the habit of introducing Elisabeth to men that he thought she would find amusing, she often did not have far to look if she wanted to stray. It was Balchin's duty to stand patiently to one side and hope that his wife would return to him once the flames of the grand passion had burnt themselves out and her initial attraction towards the easy-going charmer had dissipated.

8

No More Square Pegs in Round Holes: Transforming Morale in the British Army During World War Two

In the spring of 1942, under the headline 'No More Army Misfits', the *Daily Telegraph* reported on a new scheme for personnel selection that had just been announced by Lieutenant-General Sir Ronald Adam, adjutant general in the British Army. Adam told the *Telegraph*'s reporter that the scheme:

> ...aimed at placing a recruit in the job for which he was most suited at the beginning of his career. In other words—no more square pegs in round holes.[1]

In a wholesale departure from prevailing practice up until this point in the war, recruits were to be enlisted in a new General Service Corps and then sent to a Primary Training Centre (PTC) for six weeks of basic training *before* being assigned to a specific regiment. In the understated language of the time, the newspaper concluded its report with a small measure of faint praise for this new development:

> It was emphasised that the scheme did not interfere with, or do away with, the old-established regimental system in any way. Actually the new scheme will be a help.

The column of text printed in the *Telegraph* described the end result of an enormous amount of hard work that had been undertaken during the previous year, work with which Nigel Balchin had been intimately involved.

Because he does not appear to have ever spoken publicly about this period of his wartime employment, Balchin's role in overhauling army personnel selection has been almost completely overlooked. Although only one calling point on his journey towards the uppermost rungs of the military ladder, the eighteen months or so that he spent working for the Directorate of Selection of Personnel (D.S.P.) represent a brief but important part of his life, and the reforms that Balchin and his colleagues were instrumental in bringing about undoubtedly helped to achieve a major upturn in the fortunes of the army during the concluding half of World War Two. This upturn was desperately needed: after Dunkirk, there was an urgent need to quickly build a large land army in order to repel the threat of a German invasion, and as the resources at the army's disposal were not being effectively utilized a change of tack was called for in terms of the strategies deployed for the selection and allocation of personnel.

Balchin's five years of distinguished service with the National Institute of Industrial Psychology (NIIP) between 1930 and 1935 probably facilitated his entry into the army given that a number of ex-NIIP staff were recruited by the military to work in personnel selection during the early years of the war. According to the official War Diary of D.S.P.,[2] civilians with psychological qualifications[3] were sought 'by Press Advertisements and other means'. In the case of Balchin, these 'other means' are likely to have involved the old boy network and it may well have been his Cambridge professor Frederic Bartlett, a member of the NIIP's Technical Advisory Board in 1941 and a man who had undertaken some pre-war work on personnel selection, who brought his name to the attention of the fledgling personnel selection unit that was beginning to coalesce in Whitehall during the spring of that year. Balchin had initially expressed a desire to work for the Army Psychological Department (see Chapter 6). As he was assigned instead to D.S.P., one cannot rule out the possibility that Bartlett may have been pulling strings behind the scenes.

In March 1941, a small committee of distinguished psychologists was appointed by the War Office to advise on the selection and allocation of army recruits. This committee recommended a radical overhaul of the existing procedure, including the establishment of D.S.P., the formation of which was approved by the Army Council—the service's premier administrative body—in June. D.S.P. was composed of three divisions, the most important of which, SP3, bore the title Technical Development. By 21 July, SP3 included on its strength Edgar Anstey, a man who, much later in life, wrote an invaluable account of his wartime work in the field of army personnel selection,[4] and four other psychologists who possessed some peacetime experience of working for the NIIP: Edith Mercer, Bernard Ungerson, Denis McMahon and Nigel Balchin.

During his first few weeks in the army following his departure from the Ministry of Food, Balchin would have had ample opportunity to observe the procedure for the training and assessment of new recruits that was extant before Adam made his announcement in May 1942. When Balchin joined up, an enlistee was sent initially to his arm or corps, regardless of whether he was likely to be suitable for it. This led to a plethora of 'appalling misfits',[5] i.e. 'pegs' that proved to be a poor fit for the army job (or 'hole') into which the military was attempting to insert them. The result was the generation of significant friction, followed by wasteful and time-consuming efforts to find a more appropriate fit for the peg.

Balchin arrived at the London District Reception Depot on being commissioned in the army's General List.[6] He was then posted to the Infantry Training Centre of the King's Own Yorkshire Light Infantry at Pontefract in Yorkshire. Here, in an echo of his first few months at Rowntree's in 1930, he displayed the ability to swiftly establish where improvements in efficiency could be made, allied to the gall required to bring any procedural deficiencies to the attention of his superiors. McMahon described how his SP3 colleague had been quick to make his mark:

> Within a week of arriving at the Training Centre, the instructor asked him to take over the instruction in chemical warfare; within a fortnight the commandant was seeking his advice on the running of his unit.[7]

On 2 August, Balchin (army serial number P/199427) was given the rank of acting captain and commenced his duties with D.S.P. In concert with Ungerson, he performed analyses of the entire gamut of tasks connected with the army's operation with, in Anstey's opinion, 'speed and efficiency'.[8] Within four months, the two men had completed their job analyses, working side by side with an assortment of troops at Bovington Camp in Dorset. The result of these efforts was a new classification of army jobs into seven broad categories known as Training Recommendations (TRs), which included skills such as driving, signalling and labouring. A suitable blend of TRs for individual army units was then decided upon. As an example, the infantry battalion to which Balchin had been temporarily posted on first being commissioned would have required about 60% general combatants and much smaller percentages of the other TRs.

The task of choosing a battery of selection tests was mainly devolved to Anstey, but Balchin and other SP3 staff also chipped in with ideas. Newly devised tests assessed attributes such as mechanical aptitude and physical agility. Such assessments were successful in identifying men of potential whose chances of career progression had hitherto been hindered by lack of opportunity. Anstey recalled how he had tested and interviewed a young recruit whose only previous position of responsibility had entailed looking after a petrol pump. His test results having revealed him to be in the top 3% of the population in terms of intelligence, he was recommended for promotion; three years later he made sergeant-major.

Balchin was involved in the selection and training of army officers capable of administering the new tests. A training course run by him and other psychologists produced 160 Personnel Selection Officers (PSOs) and 500 sergeant-testers, most of whom had been teachers before joining the army. In the early stages of their basic training, new recruits now took five written and three practical tests under the guidance of the sergeant-testers and were then interviewed by the PSOs. At the end of this process, each recruit was given three TRs, which were listed in descending order of each man's suitability for that particular task.

Balchin also made a vital contribution to the development of a technique that would enable the army's manpower requirements to be matched to the human raw material arriving daily at the PTCs. In the words of one observer, 'this proved to be the most difficult problem to solve'.[9] Balchin's solution was inspired, far-sighted and, crucially, practical. He reached back into his memory and recalled how the use of Hollerith punched cards had enabled effective sifting of the large amounts of data that had been generated during the market research programme he had coordinated before the launch of Black Magic in 1933. For each army recruit, a punched card was therefore prepared that held relevant information about him, such as personal details, test results and interviewer's comments.[10]

McMahon was present in a supporting capacity when Balchin demonstrated his punched-card sorting and allocation procedure in Cheltenham in the presence of thirty to forty senior army officers and, as he recalled, 'we were the only two without red on our collars'.[11] Seated towards the back of the hall were a handful of civilian experts in the sort of procedure that Balchin was proposing to introduce who had already found time to condemn the scheme and declare it to be unworkable. As Clive James has pointed out, McMahon's description of Balchin's performance at Cheltenham cannot help but remind us of a page taken from one of his forthcoming books and it is perhaps surprising that a fictionalized version of Balchin 'discrediting brass-hat opposition in just the sort of economically staged scene that crops up in his novels'[12] did not later find its way into either *The Small Back Room* or *The Fall of the Sparrow*.

McMahon explained the principle behind Balchin's scheme:

The manpower demands from the War Office branches would be mounted, fed into a central place, the cards on the intake would be sorted on qualitative criteria, and demands met by the sorting and allocation of the cards. Posting orders for the recruits at the end of their primary training would come stuttering out as print outs. [...] We knew that we had won when a major-general put up his hand like a schoolboy in class to suggest what we should do next to get out of a (previously planned) dilemma. As we left Nigel had a very senior officer on each side of him, both patting him on the back. (We tried to avoid the eyes of the experts at the back of the room.)[13]

In less than an hour, Balchin had got his proposal accepted and the Hollerith procedure was adopted by the army to help with the posting of recruits.

When he was photographed during his early days in uniform, Balchin may not have had red on his collar but, nevertheless, the neatly groomed junior officer exuded both intelligence and a serene confidence in his own ability, qualities that helped him to impress his superiors and make his mark during his time in the service. As James observed in connection with McMahon's admiring portrait of his army colleague:

...there can't be any doubt that Balchin was a gifted logistical thinker—a natural critical path analyst with a remarkable capacity for absorbing the detail of new fields.[14]

Following a small series of successful trials, the new personnel selection scheme that D.S.P. had devised was introduced in the army in July 1942. Enlistees were now allocated to the newly established General Service Corps (a sort of glorified transit camp), the institution of which was, in the words of Anstey, the 'first great achievement'[15] of D.S.P. Recruits took their intelligence and aptitude tests early on in their training schedule (before being sent to a PTC) and their Hollerith-generated postings then arrived at the PTC about three weeks later. The Hollerith machinery enabled army personnel to be assigned to units systematically, so that each unit received the correct mix of intelligence, experience and ability to enable it to perform efficiently in a battle situation.

The scheme was a triumphant success. During the first year in which it was operational, up to 12,500 men a fortnight were processed at PTCs up and down the country, and by the end of the war about 700,000 recruits had been screened in total, 6% of whom were earmarked as being of officer potential. In addition to the improvements in efficiency brought about by the work of D.S.P., Anstey also claimed that 'psychologists transformed morale in the British army from zero level in 1942'.

In parallel with the 'appalling misfits' problem that had previously been detected within the lower ranks, officer selection was also in crisis at the beginning of 1942. The old school tie was being accorded more weight as a marker of officer potential than more objective measures of ability and, in consequence, a high percentage of cadets were being 'returned to unit' owing to a lack of leadership attributes. More importantly, thousands of men who did possess officer qualities were being overlooked simply because they had not attended the right schools. Anstey crystallized the dire situation that confronted the service at this time:

> The expanding Army was thus faced with a serious shortfall of officers and in despair turned to the Directorate to introduce an entirely new system of officer selection.

The system introduced in the summer of 1942 by D.S.P. became known as the War Office Selection Boards (abbreviated to WOSBs, but always colloquially referred to by the nickname 'was-bees'). Although the army's psychiatrists played a greater role in setting up WOSBs than they had in the establishment of the General Service Corps, psychologists such as Balchin also had a crucial part to play. D.S.P. devised objective selection tests that would help to identify able candidates. These comprised a mix of leaderless group tests, outdoor practical tests, indoor discussions and interviews by two officers and a psychiatrist. Despite some initial resistance to their implementation, a noticeable drop in the proportion of unsuccessful candidates being returned to unit soon led to the widespread acceptance of WOSBs by the army.

The three-day residential WOSB procedure was the subject of a succinct and hilarious parody in 1956 by the Boulting brothers. In the film *Private's Progress*, the hapless conscript

Stanley Windrush (Ian Carmichael) reluctantly attends a WOSB because his solid middle-class background suggests that he is the officer type. His supportive father and more cynical sister debate the influence that his breeding is likely to have on his chances of passing the course:

"Well, he's a gentleman: that puts him halfway there."
"It's the other half Stanley has to worry about."

Windrush soon discovers the hard way that being a gentleman and having been to a good school count for nothing in the egalitarian world of the WOSBs: he trips over a guy-rope whilst attempting to erect a tent, causing the canvas to collapse on top of his colleagues, loses his undergarments in the process of negotiating an assault course and then comprehensively bamboozles the army psychiatrist (John Le Mesurier) during a word association test. As John and Roy Boulting were friends with Balchin (and had collaborated with him on the previous year's *Josephine and Men*), there is a distinct possibility that they consulted him for information about WOSBs before satirizing them on celluloid.

It was fortunate for Windrush that he did not have to face the horrific prospect of the 'barbed wire trench test', an idea dreamt up by the group containing Anstey and Balchin but which failed to get off the drawing board. In this hypothetical exercise, a trench was dug that tapered in width from twenty feet at one end to eight feet at the other. This channel was filled with barbed wire and the aspiring officer was invited to leap across it at the widest point he felt he could manage. It was conjectured that a timid candidate would choose a very narrow part of the trench and that an overconfident individual would choose the widest part, topple backwards onto the barbed wire and, in the dry phraseology of Anstey, 'eliminate himself'[16] from the selection process and thus be condemned to spend the rest of his WOSB weekend laid up in a hospital bed with spinal injuries.

McMahon only worked alongside Balchin in SP3 for less

than a year and yet the other man's personality, intellect and abilities made a deep and lasting impression on him:

> Nigel Balchin was the most intelligently effective *and* effectively intelligent man I have met. I have heard it said that he had a wit that was "blistering", "mordant". This was not true. His speed of reaction—and action—was phenomenal, his wit sharp, but his purpose was never to hurt. With a sideways grin he said once to a colleague who had suggested something: "There are ideas and there are good ideas; *this* is an idea." Everyone, particularly the recipient, would enjoy the occasion—and the recollection. And, in case it needs to be argued, he was once almost physically sick at the behaviour of a senior officer who indulged in flearing wit at the expense of a junior colleague.[17]

As well as impressing McMahon, Balchin also had a very positive effect on the men above him in the army's chain of command. In February 1942 he was made a deputy assistant adjutant general in SP3; three months later, partly as a result of his performance at Cheltenham, he was promoted to major.

By the end of 1942, with both the General Service Corps scheme and the WOSBs producing excellent results, there was little more that Balchin could do in terms of applying his industrial psychology skills to problems of personnel selection in the military; it was time for him to carve out another niche for himself in the army, this time in a scientific research environment.

*

Like her upwardly mobile husband, Elisabeth Balchin also spent the middle years of the Second World War performing useful work in the national interest. After working for the Food Manufacturers' Federation in London and the Ministry of Food in Colwyn Bay, she became a Senior Temporary Assistant in the Central Statistics Department of the Ministry of Supply in 1941 after Balchin volunteered for the army and she and her family therefore returned to the capital. The Ministry of

Supply—reputedly Britain's biggest wartime employer—was based at Shell Mex House in the Strand and its remit included supplying all three of the armed forces with equipment. As Balchin was also working close by at this point in the war, in Whitehall, and he and Elisabeth were often required to work late into the evenings, the couple rented a flat in a mansion block (Artillery Mansions in Victoria Street, Westminster) less than a mile away from their respective workplaces.

When she had been at the Ministry of Supply for about eighteen months, and had been promoted as far as Deputy Assistant Director, Elisabeth began to desire a change of scenery. Her husband therefore arranged for her to be interviewed by a colleague of his at D.S.P., Lieutenant-Colonel A. G. Sentance Tapp. Sentance Tapp recommended Elisabeth for a position with the Special Operations Executive (S.O.E.), the cloak-and-dagger outfit that had been formed in July 1940 to undertake sabotage operations in Occupied Europe or, in Winston Churchill's more evocative phrase, to 'set Europe ablaze'.

It took almost six months for S.O.E. to find a suitable position for Elisabeth, but in March 1943 she signed the Official Secrets Act and began work as one of 'Churchill's Secret Army' operating out of Baker Street (they were also known informally as the Baker Street Irregulars after Sherlock Holmes's gang of street urchins who helped with his cases).

On the application form she completed before joining S.O.E., Elisabeth proclaimed confidently that 'I am not afraid of responsibility; I am physically tougher than most women; and I can generally see fairly quickly how to tackle a new job'.[18] The new job she had set her sights on at the end of 1942 was that of an S.O.E. agent operating in France. As her daughter Penelope Leach points out, this aspiration was 'patently ridiculous since she was no more fluent [in French] than I am'.[19] Maurice Buckmaster, head of the French Section of S.O.E., turned down the request of the mother of two to train as an agent but, as Leach explains, he evidently admired her pluck and initiative and so offered her an alternative role in the organization: 'she was taken on to select and train other young women, which she did very successfully.' Until her work was brought to a halt by the birth of her third child at the end of 1944, Elisabeth therefore spent her time vetting potential agents for S.O.E. and organizing some of the office personnel in her role as Assistant Director of Female Staff.[20]

9

The Small Back Room

Colonel Holland: "Now then: the army's to have its own research section. The man in charge will have a free hand: equipment…"

Sammy Rice: "Personnel?"

Holland: "Anything: we want results. Of course you'll have to be in uniform, otherwise you'll never get anything. We'll make you a major or something."

— From the film of *The Small Back Room*

When Nigel Balchin started his new job in the army on 30 December 1942 he was promoted from major to lieutenant-colonel, given the title Assistant Director of Biological Research and put to work in the newly formed Directorate of Biological Research (D.B.R.). Unlike Sammy Rice at the end of the movie version of his imminent novel *The Small Back Room*, Balchin was not in charge of the army's research section, but he had now risen far enough in the military hierarchy as to be within touching distance of such an exalted position.

The primary remit of D.B.R. was 'inspiring biological research in the Army'.[1] As such, it was placed on an equal footing with another new department, that of the Scientific Adviser to the Army Council (S.A.A.C.). D.B.R. dealt with biological research problems while S.A.A.C. concerned itself with the physical sciences. Early in 1943, the secretary of the Military Personnel Research Committee communicated information about these developments to a colleague at the Medical Research Council. In slightly startled fashion, he conveyed essentially the same news that Colonel Holland breaks to Rice at the conclusion of the Powell and Pressburger film:

> It looks as if the Army is setting up a complete research organisation.[2]

D.B.R. was headed by Brigadier F. A. E. Crew. He said that when he had begun to collect his staff at the end of 1942 it had been:

> ...no easy matter, for I sought men of first class ability. In the fourth year of the war it was not to be expected that such were unoccupied. I am deeply indebted to D.S.P. and D.A.P.[3] for the great help they gave to me in allowing members of their staffs to join me.[4]

Balchin was one man of 'first class ability' who was released by the Directorate of Selection of Personnel (D.S.P.) as a result of it 'having been agreed by all concerned that his services could be best employed in the general field of research'.[5]

Whilst assigned to the staff of D.B.R., Balchin's work appears to have partly resembled that carried out by the backroom boys in *The Small Back Room*. He did not possess the requisite technical expertise to defuse bombs or report on new types of fuse but, like Rice, he was probably present at trials of experimental weapons. Professor Mair's research group in *The Small Back Room* is emphatically not part of the army and, until the latter part of the book when it is reconstituted under the auspices of the National Scientific Advisory Council, functions as an independent research organization that has work deposited on it by all and sundry: "We just tackle any job we're given". Although D.B.R. *was* part of the army, the manner in which its work was generated appears to have paralleled that of the fictional body, because Balchin reported in 1943 that he and his colleagues 'found their own problems for investigation, and in some cases had problems passed on to them'.[6]

During his first four months at D.B.R., Balchin did not

stray far from the sort of duties he had performed both at D.S.P. and, with due allowance for the change of scene, at the National Institute of Industrial Psychology (NIIP). He was predominantly employed in applying the techniques of industrial psychology to the military environment and a quintessential piece of work along these lines entailed carrying out time-and-motion studies of gun drills.

A cine-film analysis of the twenty-five-pounder gun in action gave rise to a comic anecdote that later became legendary in industrial psychology circles. Balchin's scrutinization of the firing procedure helped him to devise a new drill that could be used either to reduce fatigue, increase the rate of fire or reduce the crew in charge of the gun by one man, depending on whichever alternative the army deemed to be most desirable at the time. Details of these improvements in efficiency were related some years after the war had ended by the ergonomist Hywel Murrell:

> The drill was photographed and when the resulting moving picture was analyzed it was found that number six stood stiffly to attention at the back of the gun doing absolutely nothing. When enquiries were made as to what number six was supposed to be doing, no-one seemed to know. Number six had always been in the drill book as long as they could remember. Eventually an ancient Sergeant-Major was unearthed who said, "I know who number six was, he was the man who used to hold the horses".[7]

Balchin took charge of a study of accidents suffered by army vehicles whilst with D.B.R. and was principally responsible for proposing a new system of medical categorization.[8] The Directorate was also active in fields such as physiological and psychological aspects of warfare; fatigue and battle stress; and ensuring that weaponry developments took account of ergonomic factors and that military personnel received adequate training to enable them to handle their new weapons.[9]

Another investigation carried out by D.B.R. looked at causes of human 'wastage' among the intake at the Parachute

Training School, where wastage was defined as those who failed the course, in particular because of a refusal to throw themselves out of the aircraft. Information accrued during this study may have influenced *The Fall of the Sparrow*, in which Jason Pellew attends a parachute training course being run by his friend Henry Payne, and is later invited by Payne to point out deficiencies and anachronisms in the army's parachute training procedure.

At the end of 1943, Balchin and his colleagues were transferred en bloc to S.A.A.C. As the parallel organization was concerned with weapons, equipment and ways of making war it was felt that it would be more appropriate if D.B.R. were incorporated within it. On 9 December, Balchin took up his new position as a General Staff Officer (1st Grade) in the Science 2 section of S.A.A.C. based in Whitehall Court, retaining his rank of lieutenant-colonel.

Scant documentary evidence has survived concerning what Balchin did at S.A.A.C. during the rest of the war. He certainly spent some of his time observing troops in battle, and this was possibly an extension of a project he had undertaken at D.B.R. that involved the use of questionnaires to obtain factual information—as opposed to mere opinion or anecdote—from the front line. Balchin was in Paris when it was liberated from the Nazis during August 1944. During his stay he resided (along with other Allied officers) at the Hotel Raphael on Avenue Kléber close to the Arc de Triomphe, and this hotel would later become almost a home from home for him when he was writing film scripts in Paris in the 1950s. He also went to north-west Europe for a week with the Supreme Headquarters Allied Expeditionary Force in November as the Allied invasion of mainland Europe continued to push eastwards.

Like Rice in *The Small Back Room*, part of Balchin's duties whilst employed by D.B.R. and/or S.A.A.C. involved dealing with civilians who sought his opinion on new inventions likely to be of interest to the military. Balchin's journalistic career had been in almost total abeyance since just before he joined the Ministry of Food in Colwyn Bay, but two articles that relied for their content on details of his scientific work in the army were accepted in the mid-1940s by *Lilliput*, the pocket-sized magazine that began publishing in 1937 and comprised a blend of short stories, humorous articles and tasteful nude photographs of young women.

The first of Balchin's contributions to *Lilliput*, entitled 'An Inventory of Inventors', was published in the April 1944 edition. The author discussed the characteristics of five distinct types of inventor, among them The Bright-Idea-in-the-Bath School, a representative of which had evidently been in touch with him not long before he had written his article:

> A typical member of the school recently pointed out that if some means could be found by scientists for neutralising or suspending the force of gravity, it would be possible to employ airborne forces on a large scale without bothering the R.A.F. He thought it might be done, he added, by the use of large magnets.

Whilst remaining sceptical about the practicality or relevance of many of the inventions brought to his notice, Balchin appeared to regard the conveyor belt of cranks he had been subjected to with some affection, opining at one point that:

> The pouring of cold water on a man who comes glowing from the bath, having just invented a combined death ray and folding bicycle, is no fun for anybody—particularly him.

Balchin may well have been thinking about actual suggestions pitched to him in his capacity as Assistant Director of Biological Research when he wrote the Keystone Komics material for *The Small Back Room*, one of the funniest features of the book. The Komics are bright ideas sent in to Rice's team by members of the public with the aim of helping the Allies to win the war. Some of the brainwaves received include tanks that can tunnel beneath enemy lines, the transmission of bacterial infection via the medium of migrating birds and the training of dogs to carry explosive booby traps into enemy territory. Another externally submitted idea debated by the back-room boys is the use of poisoned barbed wire:

> "You scratch yourself on it and die in agony two hours later. Any bidders?"
>
> "What's the poison?" I said, "Curare?"
>
> "Oh, he doesn't go into *that*," said Joe. "He says he isn't a scientist himself. He just has ideas."
>
> "If I had ideas like that I'd see a doctor," I said.

Balchin's second piece for *Lilliput* ('Scientists in a Hurry') appeared in December 1947, long after he had been demobilized, and developed one of the themes of the Keystone Komics, being concerned with scientific con men. Balchin must have been writing from direct experience when he described some of the inventions that these tricksters had endeavoured to foist on him:

> There was a man who invented a means of making steel helmets magnetic. He had one with him, and picked up paper clips off my desk with it like one o'clock. When I asked him how the idea was to be applied, he said rather huffily that he was a scientist, not a practical man. There was his invention and it worked. The rest was up to the authorities.

Recognition for the work that Balchin had performed for D.B.R. and S.A.A.C. was forthcoming on 7 May 1945, one day before VE Day, when he was made Deputy Scientific Adviser to the Army Council. In this role he served as second-in-command to Charles Ellis, a physicist who had been appointed Scientific Adviser in 1943. After slightly less than four years in uniform, Balchin's vertiginous ascent through the army ranks since first arriving at the London District Reception Depot had finally terminated. In addition to a new job title, the rank of brigadier had also been bestowed on him at the extraordinarily young age of thirty-six. Balchin appears to have made only one public pronouncement concerning his final promotion within the War

Office. This came more than twenty years after the appointment had been made and was stereotypically self-effacing:

> "I was no great scientist, but I suppose I could administrate and that was what they needed: laying on return tickets to Woking and that sort of thing."[10]

Balchin excelled as an army officer because he tackled the tasks he was given both diligently and effectively but was also unafraid to make suggestions to his superiors if he felt that improvements could be made to the army's procedures. In addition, he possessed the mental flexibility to think outside the box, as for example when he persuaded the service to adopt the punched-card Hollerith method for sorting data on new recruits. In the words of Clive James, Balchin 'dealt in realities, the art of the possible. The test was relevance'.[11] With his country at war, Balchin knew that there was no time to waste on airy theorizing and so he concentrated instead on solving practical problems that would help to improve the efficiency and increase the fighting strength of the service. The army wanted results and Balchin gave them the results they wanted.

*

> In 1928 my foot was hurting all the time, so they took it off and gave me an aluminium one that only hurt about three-quarters of the time.
>
>   – Nigel Balchin, *The Small Back Room*

The Small Back Room was published on 6 December 1943, three days before Balchin left D.B.R to take up his new post at S.A.A.C. Fortuitously for him, his intelligence and organizational ability enabled him to gather the material he required to make his big breakthrough as a novelist from the sanctuary of a Whitehall office, as opposed to one of the more hazardous environments, such as the body of a tank or the gun turret of a heavy bomber, that other literary men were compelled to occupy during the conflict.

The Small Back Room improved upon *Darkness Falls from*

The Small Back Room (1943)

Sammy Rice is a scientific back-room boy working in London during the middle of World War Two for 'Professor Mair's research group', an autonomous outfit but one with strong connections to a government ministry. Rice, an amputee with an aluminium prosthetic foot, a drink problem and a lack of self-confidence, is romantically involved with Susan, the research group's secretary.

Rice's job entails evaluating new developments in military technology but he is offered a break from his usual round of weapons tests when he is asked to assist Captain Stuart, 'a young sapper officer' who is investigating a new type of Nazi weapon. Mysterious black cylinders, believed to have been dropped from enemy planes, have killed soldiers and civilians alike who have come into contact with them. In order to learn more about how they work, Rice and Stuart interview the bereaved mother of a bomb victim, as well as a badly wounded soldier who had the misfortune to touch one of the devices.

After quarrelling with Susan because he refuses to accept extra responsibility when Professor Mair is ousted as head of the section, Rice receives a telephone call from Stuart. Two of the booby-trap bombs have been found, intact, lying on a sandy beach. The army officer proposes to tackle one of them, with Rice detailed to have a crack at the other, should it prove necessary. When Rice steps off his train he is informed that Stuart is already dead, having failed to solve the deadly puzzle of the bomb's inner workings. In his own mind, Rice is now confronted by two possible alternatives: either he will blow himself to glory, as he would put it, or else he will succeed in defusing the remaining bomb and emerge from his ordeal as a hero.

the Air, extended the scope of the previous novel and received dual rewards in the form of complimentary remarks in the books pages of the newspapers and massive sales. In 1962, Balchin explained why he had been driven to write his best-known novel:

> "Somebody *had* to write *The Small Back Room*; to deal with the question of the treatment of scientists in the war. It was an important subject and, of course, I was in the business so I knew something about it and felt deeply about it—it was a natural for me and the subject was of general public interest at the time."[12]

Balchin was of the opinion that scientists had been undervalued and underused during World War Two and, when they had been used, a lack of central coordination of their activities sometimes meant that they had wastefully (if unwittingly) duplicated each other's efforts. This type of wire-crossing is satirized in *The Small Back Room* when the back-room boys clash with a rival research group regarding which of them should be conducting work on low-temperature lubrication.

The first noticeable difference between *Darkness Falls from the Air* and *The Small Back Room* concerns the central character of the later book. The limping scientist Sammy Rice is the first physically handicapped protagonist deployed by Balchin in his fiction (although more would follow). As Rice also has a love–hate relationship with whisky and throughout the novel is morose, grouchy and short-tempered, it can be swiftly appreciated that he is a very different type of person from the self-assured and slightly domineering Bill Sarratt from *Darkness Falls from the Air*. The extent to which Rice lets his personal problems overwhelm him is at the core of the novel, and is outlined by his girlfriend, Susan:

> "Look, Sammy—it's like this. You've got to make up your mind whether you want to spend your whole life being a person it's too bad about, or not."

This central dilemma is never fully resolved. Another of Rice's weaknesses, as identified by James,[13] is that he fails to seize the reins of power, even when they are offered to him more or less on a plate. In contrast to those people who are promoted beyond their ability, Rice is someone who undermines his own ambitions by sticking to what he knows he can do and refusing to stretch himself. James considered that, as a result of this theme of the shunning of responsibility, 'there can be few readers who have not been forced to take a long look at their own lives'.

With regard to the work background described in *The Small Back Room*, Balchin wrote about matters—bomb disposal and weapons testing—that the reading public would have been able to grasp with much less difficulty than some of the more nebulous concepts presented in *Darkness Falls from the Air*. Additionally, the war itself seems more dangerous, more warlike than it did in the preceding book. Instead of describing blackout curtains, windows falling out of their frames during air raids and the amusing characteristics of barrage balloons, *The Small Back Room* puts much greater emphasis on fundamental aspects of warfare such as soldiers and weapons: front line instead of home front. In *Darkness Falls from the Air*, unexploded bombs that have been dropped from aircraft are ridiculed and pitied ("I felt quite sorry for it in a way"); in *The Small Back Room* they have a nasty tendency to blow up unexpectedly and kill people. Both military personnel and civilians die at frequent intervals in *The Small Back Room* and the war is treated in deadly earnest, as tragedy instead of tragicomedy.

Balchin's reliance on dialogue as a means of conveying action and his use of short, incisive scenes helped to generate pace in the narrative of *The Small Back Room*. However, production of the high-quality literature that he was undoubtedly capable of may have been sacrificed in the process and several critics highlighted this deficiency in his armoury. J. D. Scott[14] for example, on the occasion in 1949 when he reviewed *A Sort of Traitors* for the *New Statesman and Nation*, exclaimed that it was 'a matter of real regret' that its author was 'not able to devote more of his time and energy to the pursuit of literature'. In an interview in 1962,

Balchin provided tantalizing evidence that, during 1943 at least, his wastepaper basket may have contained pages of the type of fine writing that the critics were anxious he should attempt to create:

> "I remember a chapter I had written for *The Small Back Room* of which, for a change, I felt rather proud. But when I came to read the first draft as a whole I found that the chapter added nothing to the story. It merely held up the action. It was like a pretty girl crossing the street; everything stopped to watch. Therefore, it had to come out."[15]

This streamlining, the excision of all extraneous matter, which sometimes worked to Balchin's detriment with regard to winning the plaudits of the literary set, was remarked upon by James: 'Pamela Hansford Johnson once said that the trouble with most Balchin novels is that everything in them is relevant.'[16] Balchin's early writing had often tended towards verbosity but, from *Darkness Falls from the Air* onwards, his novels were characterized, as Hansford Johnson correctly discerned, by the fact that they did tend to stick to the point.

The large number of reviews of *The Small Back Room* that were published, and the feature length of many of them, bore testament to the fact that this was Balchin's most important novel to date. Moreover, the intensity of praise that the book received greatly exceeded that for any previous Balchin novel. One of the most adulatory notices was printed in the *Sphere*, Vernon Fane[17] issuing the sort of encomium that must have been eagerly seized upon by the Publicity Department at William Collins because it was used to adorn the jackets of reissues of the book for decades to come:

> It is, emphatically, a book to be read, and it contains a sustained piece of action-writing near the end which, for sheer excitement, would beat most thrillers hollow.

Elsewhere in the press, Ralph Straus[18] in the *Sunday Times* described *The Small Back Room* as 'an uncommonly good novel' and L. P. Hartley[19] (*Sketch*) wrote that the closing scenes were 'almost unbearably exciting'.

Across the pond, *The Small Back Room* was the first of Balchin's novels to be reviewed by the *New York Times*. In its pages, Orville Prescott[20] pinpointed Balchin's talent as that of 'a shrewd and workmanlike craftsman' and called the book 'a blistering satire, witty, lacerating, furious' with a 'chilling climax'. An accurate portrait of the daily round in the small back room itself was provided in the form of a single memorable sentence:

> Stuffed shirts in high places, professional jealousies that make trespassing on somebody else's private scientific territory more dangerous than sabotage, departmental red tape, stupidity and complacency, sycophancy, opportunism, hypocrisy and duplicity, all are exposed in these pages like the slugs that come to view when a stone is lifted away.

(The jacket of the 1945 American edition of *The Small Back Room* informed its readers that Balchin's novel had been the first book purchased by General Montgomery when he returned to Britain from Italy at the end of 1943 to take command of Operation Overlord, the following year's Normandy landings.)

As had been the case with Balchin's previous book, *The Small Back Room* did not completely escape criticism, and some of the disapproving comments made about it had also been applied to its predecessor. Much of the reviewers' hostility was directed towards the style in which the book was written, with Philip Toynbee[21] in the *New Statesman and Nation* spearheading the charge in this regard by characterizing the language Balchin had used as 'flat exhausted slang'. He identified the 'fanatically undistinguished style' of the writing as that of 'the business world, of the public school fringe, of the provincial bar and the dubious major'.

Toynbee detected a clear parallel between the main characters in Balchin's brace of Second World War novels ('Rice, the hero, duplicates Sarrat [sic] as the decent, industrious, able man struggling rather less effectively than his predecessor, against corruption, conceit and stupidity'). But after noting that Balchin's theme was of 'intense and irresistible interest', he concluded his review with another compliment:

> ...Mr. Balchin is a writer of real skill, and he has a vivid perception of the artistic possibilities in technical information. He has established a firm monopoly on his peculiar but admirable territory.

James[22] revealed that *The Small Back Room* had sold 34,000 copies in hardback and more than 337,000 copies in paperback by the end of the 1950s. Subsequent reissues (such as the 1985 Oxford University Press and 2000 Cassell Military Paperbacks editions) will have pushed total sales of the book even higher, making *The Small Back Room* by some distance the best-selling of all Balchin's novels.

Most commentators—including this one—agree that *The Small Back Room* is the outstanding achievement of Balchin's writing career and one of the major reasons for this can be found within its final three chapters. The depiction of Rice's preparations before attempting to defuse the bomb and his subsequent disarming of the device itself represents the most captivating piece of prose to be found anywhere in Balchin's fourteen novels.[23] This memorable episode is intensely gripping and mesmeric and so naturalistic that one can almost hear the seagulls crying, smell the salty tang of the fresh early-morning sea air and feel the loose sand shifting beneath Rice's feet as he struggles to get his clamps around the shiny black body of the explosive device. The bomb disposal passage was written in one 'continuous take' and Balchin felt it unnecessary to change even a single word when he revised the manuscript.[24] With the exciting conclusion to *The Small Back Room* he had shifted up a gear: he had learned how to be a thriller writer and this was not a lesson that he was going to forget in a hurry.

10

Mine Own Executioner

Soon after the war was over, the Balchin family, now numbering five after the birth of Nigel and Elisabeth's third daughter, Freja Mary, on Boxing Day 1944, left their flat in Holland Park and moved to Kent. By February 1946 they were installed at Leigh Barton, a large half-timbered fifteenth century farmhouse about eight miles south of Canterbury, which served as a peaceful haven in which Balchin could turn out books. In 1947 he described his working routine:

> "I now spend a couple of days a week in London or elsewhere on industrial matters and write on most other mornings and late afternoons, but no longer at night except on rare occasions."[1]

The intense industry of Balchin's war work bled seamlessly into his time in Kent. In a little over four years, he wrote three full-length works of fiction, a monograph for the Ministry of Aircraft Production, some short stories and journalism and his first two film scripts. The works created beneath the ancient roof of Leigh Barton revealed Balchin to be at or near his apex as a writer, and in this brief period he produced books that were more creative and diverse than those that had gone before.

Leigh Barton was situated in a quiet lane about a mile away from the centre of Stelling Minnis, a village that was home to just a few hundred inhabitants. The house was attached to an extensive garden and surrounded by about twenty-five acres of land, which Balchin soon proceeded to turn into a fruit farm.

As his second wife Yovanka remarked, thinking in particular about their time together after Balchin had left Leigh Barton, her husband was 'passionate about growing fruit—in particular greengages, pears...',[2] adding on another occasion that 'We had to have peach trees if there was a wall anywhere—immediately there'd be an apricot or a peach planted; he loved fruit'.[3]

The first in a series of large and imposing properties that Balchin purchased, Leigh Barton represented a marked contrast to most of the dwellings that he and Elisabeth had occupied since their marriage. It may have been the case that, after more than seven years spent largely breathing the polluted air of central London, the couple wished to inhale the fresher pastoral aromas of the Kentish countryside. Or it could be that Balchin was in search of his lost youth, and seeking the same sort of space and rural isolation he had known in West Lavington and that he had abandoned when he had packed up his things and moved to London in 1930 to begin life as an industrial psychologist. It is most likely however that in the light of his new-found reputation as a successful novelist Balchin had sought a house that matched (or exceeded) his standing as a writer. When he bought Leigh Barton he acquired not just a large roof over his head, more room for his family and a place where he could write, he also acquired a status symbol. This pattern was to be repeated throughout the remainder of his writing career.

At Leigh Barton, Balchin had the opportunity to resume certain of his hobbies that would have been neglected owing to the suffocating time pressure of the war years. When he wasn't working on his fruit trees or carrying out other tasks in his garden he also indulged his fancy for woodcarving, one of the projects he accomplished whilst living in Kent being to reconfigure as a chest a broken and dismantled pulpit from which Daniel Defoe had once preached. He continued to play golf, telling Seebohm Rowntree in 1946 that he was working hard at lowering his handicap,[4] and he may have taken part in the occasional game of village cricket. The presence of a piano at Leigh Barton also allowed him to persist in hammering out the works of J. S. Bach, in the process 'sounding like a very bad player out of practice'.[5]

Nigel and Elisabeth gave occasional dinner parties in Stelling Minnis, and Alice McDine, wife of Brigadier Balchin's chauffeur and odd-job man Joe, assisted with the cooking and serving of meals. She recalled the Boulting brothers paying a visit, as well as possibly Margot Fonteyn and another writer who lived in the same county as Balchin:

> I remember Noël Coward coming one Christmas to dinner. He was wearing a frilly shirt with frilly cuffs. They went into the big drawing room after dinner [...] and he started playing carols. All of us stood round the piano singing carols, Joe and me too because they treated us like the family. Then they had a race, with Noël Coward and Nigel Balchin and the children racing round the piano and back again on hands and knees racing Lill their Alsatian dog.[6]

Balchin's waking hours at Leigh Barton were fully occupied with his writing and leisure-time activities, but what of Elisabeth? Her varied wartime employments had come with considerable responsibilities attached and had made her feel wanted. At one stage during the first half of the war she had, by her own admission, 'engaged & handled a staff of about thirty five women'[7] and latterly her work 'vetting potential agents for the espionage unit, SOE'[8] had made an important contribution to the success of Allied operations behind enemy lines in Europe.

But in Kent in peacetime, with one toddler to look after and two older daughters at school, domesticity beckoned for Elisabeth. Undoubtedly she would have liked to have continued working after the war, but Balchin now displayed a chauvinistic streak that was by no means atypical of the time and put his foot down. As his middle child Penelope recalled many years later, her father seems to have expected Elisabeth to become 'a country lady, caring for three children, breeding bees and playing the clarinet. You had to know her to see how comical this was—hopeless'.[9] The role that Balchin imagined Elisabeth adopting anticipates that which Jim Manning in

A Way Through the Wood thinks might have been suitable for his wife Jill:

> I said, "Well, you might have done what we agreed you should do when we came here—looked after the gardens. There was plenty to do there, and you just dropped it."
>
> "Oh, I know—I know. I've let you down about that. And I knew you thought so. But you don't know what it's like to be here all day, with nobody to talk to but the staff and—and then when you came back to find I'd forgotten about the—the bloody peaches or something, and that you were cross with me."

Within months of arriving in Kent, Elisabeth, in her granddaughter's opinion, was already 'chafing against the restrictions of her new life'.[10] With no job to go to each day, and no desire to spend as much time working in the gardens at Leigh Barton as Balchin had envisaged, Elisabeth turned to writing as a form of recreation that would usefully occupy some of the countless hours at her disposal. Before the war she had succeeded in having some poetry and magazine articles published; immediately after it she tried to build on this tentative beginning to her writing career. But Balchin was dismissive of her efforts—and perhaps disapproved of her attempt to muscle in on his own personal territory—and she quickly grew discouraged, and still more irritated by her predicament. Occasionally, she would take out her frustrations on those around her. Balchin's father lived at Leigh Barton for a time and carried out odd jobs in the house and garden in company with Joe McDine. Alice remembered how the two men used to hide in a shed whenever Elisabeth was on the warpath ('[she] used to chase them a bit'[11]). Although Balchin was always 'very friendly' towards Alice, she considered that Elisabeth was 'a more bossy type'.

By asking his wife to adopt the role of a country lady while they were living in Stelling Minnis, Balchin had supplied the perfect soil in which resentment would be able to flourish. Had he written them twenty years earlier then the following lines extracted from a 1966 newspaper interview would have seemed uncannily prescient:

> "What really kills marriage is slow-burning resentment—jealousy, in fact, though I'm a mile from meaning sexual jealousy."
>
> "I mean the sort of jealousy that afflicts a house-bound mother who resents what appears to be the more colourful life being led by her husband."[12]

When he purchased Leigh Barton and moved his family to the country, Balchin unwittingly sowed the seeds of his own personal downfall.

*

> There are too many Examples of men, that have been their own executioners, and that have made hard shrift to bee so; some have alwayes had poyson about them, in a hollow ring upon their fingers, and some in their Pen that they used to write with; some have beat out their braines at the wal of their prison, and some have eate the fire out of their chimneys; But I do nothing upon my selfe, and yet am mine owne Executioner.
>
> – John Donne, *Devotions Upon Emergent Occasions*

Balchin's next novel, the follow-up to *The Small Back Room*, was published in the autumn of 1945. It had been written in his spare time as his career in the army was drawing to an end:

> "I wrote *Mine Own Executioner* chiefly in the evenings and at week-ends, but I do not think it suffered particularly from being done while I had another absorbing job at the War Office."[13]

If *The Small Back Room* had represented a pinnacle in Balchin's career, then *Mine Own Executioner* found him resting on a plateau just below that summit. The fact that it burnished his reputation is attributable more to the book's subject matter than

Mine Own Executioner (1945)

Felix Milne is a London psychoanalyst. He has his own practice but also works at the Norris Pile Clinic, an establishment that provides free psychoanalytical treatment for those who cannot afford it. When the book opens, Milne is on the cusp of splitting up with his wife. This is partly because Patricia is clumsy and careless and Milne is irritated by her imperfections. But the psychoanalyst is also very taken with the bewitching, vampish Barbara Edge, one of Patricia's married friends, and makes repeated attempts to begin an affair with her.

Adam Lucian, a young Spitfire pilot shot down over Burma during the Second World War, represents a tough therapeutic challenge for Milne. Lucian is persuaded by his wife Molly to seek psychiatric treatment because he has made two recent attempts to murder her. Milne administers a hypnotic drug and is able to unearth the pilot's repressed memories of his brutal treatment at the hands of the Japanese soldiers who captured him following his crash landing.

Once he admits to Milne that he had divulged information to the Japanese under torture, Lucian believes that his mental 'boil' has been lanced and that he is now cured. He therefore declines to submit to further analysis and walks out of the practice, to the obvious disappointment of Milne.

Milne is once more in the process of trying to seduce Barbara when he is informed by Patricia that the police are anxious to speak to him. Lucian has fatally wounded Molly and then gone on the run. Milne ascends a fireman's ladder in an attempt to talk his patient down from a ledge atop a high building but Lucian shoots himself and dies. Milne is exonerated from blame at the ensuing inquest.

to any of its other qualities, admirable though many of those are. Without question however, *Mine Own Executioner* helped to consolidate the author's standing as one of the best young British novelists to have come to prominence during the war years.

Both *Darkness Falls from the Air* and *The Small Back Room* had been woven from the same three-ply yarn: the war plus the home and working lives of the central character. With *Mine Own Executioner*, Balchin removed the wartime backdrop that had featured so prominently in his previous two novels (and contributed so significantly to their success) and concentrated instead on the working practices of the psychoanalyst Felix Milne and his relationships with the two women in his life.

Although the events depicted in *Mine Own Executioner* occur in a post-war setting, one of Milne's patients supplies the missing element. In the third book of what can be thought of as Balchin's war trilogy, Adam Lucian is the war. By taking Lucian back in time under the influence of the 'truth drug' sodium thiopental, the author is able to crowbar the conflict (or at least that part of it that was conducted in the Far East) into his narrative. This is accomplished with real skill, and Lucian's description of his crash in the Burmese jungle, capture and torture by sadistic Japanese soldiers and subsequent escape from them is by some margin the most gripping passage of the book and a very strong contender for the most compelling piece of writing in the entire Balchin canon (only the bomb disposal climax of *The Small Back Room* exceeds it). In spite of this impressive highlight, *Mine Own Executioner* is somewhat denuded because the war does not loom over it and exert the same menacing presence that it had done in the two previous books.

As in *Darkness Falls from the Air*, the romantic subplot in *Mine Own Executioner* involves a love triangle. If at first sight this triangle looks different from that in the earlier novel, closer inspection reveals that only the vertices have been changed: all the angles remain the same. As Clive James adroitly deduced,[14] Balchin had merely switched the sexes around. In *Mine Own*

Executioner, Milne's wife Patricia is the 'decent chap' who waits patiently and with extreme stoicism until her husband has finished wasting his time flirting with an undeniably attractive competitor for his affections (Barbara), who was described in *The Times Literary Supplement* by Richard Charques[15] as 'a fatal female charmer, the vamp of a thousand and one Hollywood nights'. For Sarratt read Patricia, with Marcia and Stephen having been substituted by Felix and Barbara, respectively. There is therefore nothing new about this triangle plot, which is not nearly as well developed or finely nuanced as that in *Darkness Falls from the Air*.

(In passing, I think it is reasonable to assume that Elisabeth probably influenced some of the female characters that appeared in her husband's fiction during the 1940s. Eric St Johnston, one of Balchin's undergraduate friends, said that he could clearly recognize Elisabeth as a character in one of the films that were developed from a Balchin novel, and I imagine he must have been thinking of either Susan in *The Small Back Room* or Patricia in *Mine Own Executioner*.)

The inquest scene at the end of *Mine Own Executioner* is a condensed masterpiece of acute observation and withering satire. The coroner, a highly abrasive person, provides welcome comic relief, as witnessed by his caustic account of Milne trying to talk Lucian down from his precarious perch atop a high building:

"All you know is that Mr. Milne went up to make him see reason and he promptly shot himself."

The inquest also gave Balchin the opportunity to do something he was extremely good at and that he did repeatedly to great effect throughout his writing career, namely providing a vivid thumbnail sketch of a minor character with an amusing behavioural quirk. Thus Milne's solicitor, Mr Grandison, is imbued with the beguiling habit of inflating his cheeks and then bursting them with his hands ('Mr. Grandison blew himself into a paper bag and exploded himself'). Two other minor characters in Balchin's fiction who possess similar behavioural tics are the

Yugoslavian police chief from *In the Absence of Mrs Petersen* who repeats the last few words that his interviewee has spoken 'rather in the manner of the 'feed' man of a pair of comedians', and a naval commander in *The Fall of the Sparrow* whose utterances are preceded by a period of silence followed by a nod and then the apparent receipt of a 'message from his peculiar internal telephone exchange'.

Mine Own Executioner was much more widely reviewed than any previous book by the author, with press reaction bordering on the ecstatic. If one were to plot a graph of intensity of adulation evoked by Balchin's fiction against time then *Mine Own Executioner* represents a definite peak; thereafter the curve tails gently away, with only occasional spikes (such as that elicited by *The Fall of the Sparrow*) occurring as Balchin's career progressed.

L. P. Hartley[16] in the *Sketch* was in the vanguard when it came to bestowing plaudits on *Mine Own Executioner*:

> ...how brilliantly Colonel [sic] Balchin has presented his principal subject-matter, the psycho-analyst's routine.
>
> "Mine Own Executioner" is a triumphant success—the kind of success that makes one want to clap.

John Betjeman[17] in the *Daily Herald* said that *Mine Own Executioner* was 'an exceptionally good novel' and he earmarked Balchin as 'one of the hopes of British novel-writing'. Over in the *New Statesman and Nation*, Henry Reed[18] contended that *Mine Own Executioner* was 'so astonishingly simple in plot and design, so full of good scenes which seem to have fallen to the author merely for the asking, that one wonders why the book has not been written before'.

More than one critic maintained that the creator of *Mine Own Executioner* had been thinking about possible film adaptations of his novel whilst writing it. Although Balchin later denied doing any such thing ('it is a fatal mistake to design a novel with one eye on its film possibilities'[19]), he would continue to be dogged by similarly worded accusations for several years to come. The best remark along these lines issued in 1945 came from Daniel George[20] in the *Observer*. Having extolled the novel as 'feverish reading' and observed that the book's final chapters contained 'the thrill which admirers of Mr. Balchin have come to expect as their right', he concluded his review by posing a very pertinent question:

> Are these exercises in story-telling and character-stencilling by staccato dialogue, working up to a thriller situation, really what Mr. Balchin's talent is best fitted for?

This was a question that Balchin would attempt to answer with his next two works of fiction.

If one accepts that *Mine Own Executioner* is an inferior novel to both *Darkness Falls from the Air* and *The Small Back Room* then why did it attract so much attention in the press upon first publication? Clearly Balchin had generated significant momentum with his two previous books and as an emerging novelist whose stature had grown immeasurably during the course of the war he was now looked upon as 'one to watch'. There was also the fact that his military career had given him prestige and that he may have been seen as a more heroic figure among book reviewers having served in the army than if he had remained merely a temporary civil servant; from this point onwards, the title brigadier would periodically be attached to the front of Balchin's name when one of his novels was reviewed in the broadsheets. However, it was probably the topicality of psychoanalysis that proved to be the prime factor in ensuring the success of *Mine Own Executioner*. In 1945, the discipline was still regarded in the media as a new and exciting one, with public interest in it being stimulated and sustained by the movie industry. Hollywood had embarked on a lengthy series of feature films that dealt with psychological matters, with acclaimed examples of the genre including 1942's *Cat People* and *Now, Voyager* (the latter starring Bette Davis) and Hitchcock's *Spellbound*, released in the USA just a few months after *Mine Own Executioner* had been published in Britain. Balchin astutely tapped into the burgeoning appeal of psychiatry and it was this, allied to his readers' thirst for an intelligent presentation of the subject embedded within a stereotypically entertaining Balchin narrative, that generated very substantial sales.

In his comprehensive analysis of Balchin's work, James[21] stated that *Mine Own Executioner* had sold 54,000 copies in hardback (far more than *The Small Back Room*) and 250,000 copies in paperback by 1953, making it overall the best-selling of all his novels bar its immediate predecessor. Speaking in 1951, Balchin described *Mine Own Executioner* as 'the most successful book commercially that I ever wrote'[22,23] but, in 1967, he also said that the novel was 'the worst book I ever wrote'.[24] The reasons for Balchin's dissatisfaction were drip-fed to the media during the course of a series of interviews he gave on the subject over a period of almost fifteen years. In a radio discussion with the novelist Walter Allen in 1955, Balchin remarked that 'I don't really like my novels much because I think that I'm very good at getting very good ideas and I always have a feeling at the end that I've mucked them up'.[25] He then proceeded to describe the despair that had engulfed him on completion of *Mine Own Executioner*:

> Now when that book was finished I disliked it so much that I tried to tear it up but the typescript was too thick to tear – you know not being a man who can tear telephone directories in half – I just wrenched at it and then being furious with it I just threw it in the air and since the pages weren't numbered that made everything a bit difficult and my wife commented "I see exactly how you feel but I don't think I'd just throw it away". Now I always felt that that book was a perfect example of mucking up a good idea. It was done just well enough to make it difficult for somebody else to do it properly. But not done well enough […] to give me very much satisfaction.

In a 1969 newspaper profile, Balchin suggested that a second explanation for his dislike of the novel concerned his inability to bring the correct air of authenticity to the consulting room scenes:

> "I was trained as a psychologist and I wanted to say something about the psychiatrist-patient relationship. But it didn't come out as I wanted it too [sic]; I suppose you could say the book, as it were, took over."[26]

Balchin had been aware of this perceived flaw less than a year after publication when he said that, in connection with a proposed BBC radio adaptation of *Mine Own Executioner*, 'The real snag is that the relationship between a psychiatrist and his patient, which is what the book is about, develops slowly, and over a long period. If it is to be made credible, it needs more time than one can possibly give it in a play. Even in the book, where I had far more time, it is not done really satisfactorily.'[27]

A further source of Balchin's discontent with the novel stemmed from his self-confessed lack of familiarity with the discipline of psychoanalysis:

> "...it seemed to me throughout to be written with far too little real knowledge of the subject in hand—and that was based more on my experience of psychiatry during the war than on anything I learnt at Cambridge."[28]

Several critics alluded to Balchin's lack of psychoanalytical qualifications, chief among them being Reed[29] ('Mr. Balchin's knowledge of the technical aspects of psycho-analysis is no greater than that of most of us').

As previously mentioned in Chapter 2, Balchin had taken his first and second Bachelor of Medicine degrees whilst at Cambridge (as had Milne) and would therefore only have needed to do hospital training in order to have qualified as a doctor. He also claimed that he had practised as an abnormal psychologist during the 1930s, although both the extent of this work and the precise form it took remain unknown. But Balchin, like Milne, can be described as a quack psychiatrist and *Mine Own*

Executioner is thus given added resonance by the knowledge that Balchin would have empathized with the uncertain professional status of his central character.

So where did Balchin obtain the technical information he required in order to write *Mine Own Executioner*, inadequate as he considered it to have been? Apart from background reading on a subject that he had been very interested in since Cambridge, his knowledge probably derived from discussions with psychiatrists during his time in the army.

The Tavistock Clinic in London was founded in 1920 and was described in the 1960s as 'the headquarters of the eclectic psychotherapy which has found special favour in this country'.[30] It was one of the first clinics in Britain to offer free psychological treatment on an outpatient basis for 'adults and children suffering from hysteria, abnormal fears and obsessions, neurasthenia, and various disorders of conduct, who are unable to afford specialists' fees'. Initially, all the practitioners who offered their services were volunteers. A published account of the early history of the Tavistock Clinic suggests a parallel with Balchin's novel:

> ...there were great variations in the quality of the services offered by the pre-war Clinic. Among the 80 physicians who contributed six hours a week, many had little or no psychiatric training.[31]

In *Mine Own Executioner*, all of the staff at the Norris Pile Clinic with which Milne is associated give their time for nothing, and at least one of them, Paston ("He is an ignorant quack," said Tautz. "He knows nothing. He has no right here"), appears to have insufficient psychiatric training to perform this most demanding of jobs with the necessary competence.

Just before the Second World War broke out, the Medical Director of the Tavistock Clinic, John Rawlings Rees, was appointed Consultant Psychiatrist to the Army. Other psychiatrists from the Tavistock joined the Directorate of Army Psychiatry in 1941, a body that had strong links with the Directorate of Selection of Personnel (D.S.P.), Balchin's employers at the time. Records exist of at least one wartime meeting between D.S.P. and an Advisory Committee of Psychologists (including Frederic Bartlett and Charles Myers from the National Institute of Industrial Psychology) that helped to direct the use of psychology in the services during the war. Both Rees and Balchin were present on that occasion. Other psychiatrists from the 'Tavistock Group' in the army played a prominent role in the establishment of the War Office Selection Boards, with which Balchin was also connected via D.S.P. One member of the Tavistock Group was Eric Trist, later to become Chairman of the Tavistock Institute of Human Relations (the post-war successor to the Tavistock Clinic), who is known to have been a friend of Balchin's and may have met him at Cambridge in the 1920s, where their academic careers overlapped and where Trist, like Balchin, became interested in psychology and studied under Bartlett.

This body of evidence, despite its circumstantial nature, makes it reasonable to hypothesize that Balchin obtained the scientific details he needed to write *Mine Own Executioner* from speaking to some or all of Rees, Trist and other army psychiatrists and that the pre-war Tavistock Clinic probably gave Balchin the idea for the Norris Pile Clinic (although the latter had five, not eighty, psychiatrists on its staff).

*

By the end of 1945, Collins had published three Balchin novels in less than three years. *The Small Back Room* and *Mine Own Executioner* had sold in enormous quantities. All three books, including the first of the trio, *Darkness Falls from the Air*, had been granted very cordial receptions by the reviewers. As T. C. Worsley[32] observed in 1947, 'Mr. Nigel Balchin is a novelist whose last two books [*The Small Back Room* and *Mine Own Executioner*] have had a double success. They have been praised in serious terms, by writers whose good opinions are worth having, and they have also been chosen by the Book Society.' But Worsley was swift to warn Balchin that 'This may be the danger point for any novelist.' In the wake of *Mine Own Executioner*, the critic considered that Balchin ran the risk of repeating himself if he persisted in adhering to the constructional template that had helped him to win his spurs as a writer, after years of largely fruitless struggle. Mindful of the desirability of changing tack, Balchin's next work of fiction would prove to be such a shocking contrast to *Mine Own Executioner* that some of his admirers would be hard pressed to believe that the two books could possibly have emanated from the desk of the same writer. The new fiction would be a bold, brave departure from Balchin's carefully crafted formula, but would run the risk of losing him much of the critical esteem—and a substantial tranche of the loyal readership—that he had accumulated over the previous five years.

11

A Very Thorough Demobilization

> With peace, and the disintegration of national purpose,
> Balchin lost the opportunity of contributing to the nation
> as if the nation were a work of art. He had been demobilised
> more thoroughly than any front-line soldier. He was being
> asked to hide his own talent.
>
> — Clive James[1]

Almost six months after peace had been declared in Europe,
Balchin, despite James's assertion, had not completely lost his
opportunity to contribute to the nation. As an example, towards
the end of his time as Deputy Scientific Adviser to the Army
Council, Balchin played a role in Operation Backfire, a military
exercise that consisted of test-firing several V2 rockets in order
to master this facet of Nazi technology. This brought him into
conflict with acclaimed thriller writer Eric Ambler, a direct
contemporary and a novelist who also excelled in writing about
technical subjects.[2]

In the spring of 1945, as the Allied invasion of northern
Europe pressed on eastwards, a number of German personnel with
experience of the V2 rocket were captured. After consultations
that involved Balchin's boss Charles Ellis, Scientific Adviser to the
Army Council, it was decided that it would be desirable to assemble
and launch several of the projectiles. The original intention of
capturing a number of the rockets intact proved to be impossible
and instead parts were salvaged from fields, ditches, railway yards,
canals and factories and assembled by the German staff, under
British supervision. The site chosen for the test launches was the
Krupps gun-proving grounds near Cuxhaven, the location of

a former V1 factory on the German coast roughly sixty miles from both Bremen and Hamburg. From here, the rockets could be fired harmlessly into the North Sea.

Eric Ambler was born just a year after Balchin. There are many similarities between the two men: both came from humble backgrounds; both were highly intelligent schoolboys and were able to obtain good educations by virtue of scholarships; both failed as playwrights before succeeding as novelists; both held down jobs of a scientific or technical nature before concentrating on writing; both were involved with the advertising industry for a time; both devoted lengthy periods after the war to the writing of film scripts; and both became tax exiles as a consequence of their scriptwriting prowess. When the Second World War began, Ambler was indubitably more successful than Balchin as a novelist: he had already published five thrillers, four of them greatly accomplished.

Ambler joined the army in 1940 and was assigned to the Royal Artillery. In 1942 he transferred to the Army Film Unit, and went on to make almost a hundred training films for them. The most notable of these was *The Way Ahead*, starring David Niven, the proficiency of which enabled it to also achieve a cinema release. By October 1945, the month during which the V2 test firings took place, Ambler had risen to become Assistant Director of Army Kinematography, with the rank of lieutenant-colonel. Because Operation Backfire was being performed under War Office control, Ellis decided he wanted film records of a launch. Ambler was in charge of preserving Operation Backfire on celluloid but, as Balchin outranked him, the author of *The Small Back Room* was able to dictate to the writer of *The Mask of Dimitrios* how the filming should be organized. In an interview he gave to James in 1974,[3] Ambler took up the story:

'Balchin's boss said "Brigadier Balchin knows a very great deal about films, you know. He's under contract to Alexander Korda."[4] Well, so was every Hungarian refugee in England: it was no qualification. Balchin said that he wanted to see every foot of film shot. I had dozens of cameras shooting a ten-minute roll each at various distances, so as not to miss anything if the rocket misbehaved. Everything went off all right and we flew these miles of film back to England. Screening started at nine in the morning with a shot of the rocket about 200 metres away. The rocket stood there for about five minutes doing nothing and then silently went up. In the subsequent five minutes there was not even the rocket to look at. The next roll was the same thing from slightly nearer. And so on. At twelve o'clock Balchin said "Is it all like this?" If he hadn't climbed down it would have gone on for days.'

Perhaps slightly chastened having lost his battle of wills with Ambler, Balchin began to clear his desk at the War Office in readiness for his imminent demobilization. His last recorded duty whilst employed in the department of the Scientific Adviser to the Army Council entailed writing a report entitled 'Battle Study. Some Aspects of Psychological Warfare'.[5] This was one of a series of 'Battle Studies' designed to document factual information on various operational aspects of warfare.[6] The report is only of limited interest but it would not be a genuine Balchin work if it did not contain an occasional flash of his unique style:

To drop a pamphlet from an aeroplane has been reckoned as Psychological Warfare. But to drop a bomb has not; even though it may be realised that at least nine-tenths of the effect of the bomb is upon the enemy's morale and that the pamphlet and the bomb are in fact no more than different ways of representing the same argument to the enemy.[7]

Balchin was released from army service on 23 February 1946 and awarded the 1939/45 War Medal. This was a decoration issued as a matter of course to all individuals who had been a member of one of the armed forces for at least twenty-eight days. It was a meagre reward for someone who had placed his high intelligence and very considerable expertise at his country's disposal and made many telling contributions to the army's organization and operation. Balchin tended not to refer to his rank after the war unless writing to his coal or wine merchants, on which occasions he found that prefacing his name with the appellation brigadier sometimes helped to release scarce supplies of these commodities. When he left the army, Balchin apparently handed his uniform to a small boy in Stelling Minnis, who subsequently took great delight in parading through the village resplendent in the ill-fitting outfit.

Perhaps the magic word brigadier would also have helped Balchin to secure enough petrol to enable him to fill up the tank of his car and take the family out on a weekend jaunt into the country because he certainly undertook the long drive between Kent and Oxfordshire on a number of occasions in the immediate post-war period.

The marriage of Elisabeth Balchin's inseparable Newnham College friend Dorrie Jackson to Balchin's university pal and subsequent National Institute of Industrial Psychology (NIIP) colleague Alan Stewart had proved to be a short-lived one: as mentioned in Chapter 4, Dorrie had remarried in 1937, her second husband being the businessman Eric Stein, who was working for the Distillers Company when he first met Dorrie. The Steins had purchased a tumbledown farm a couple of miles to the south-west of Chipping Norton in 1940 as both an investment opportunity and a tranquil base for themselves and their children away from the dangers of wartime London. Jeremy Stewart, Dorrie's son by her first husband, had failed to see eye to eye with his stepmother when his father remarried after divorcing Dorrie. In 1942, aged eight, he had been entrusted to the care of his mother on a blacked-out Oxford railway station and taken by train to Kingham, and thence to nearby Conduit Farm, Churchill, which for him was a 'wonderful place where the war didn't exist'.[8] Stewart recalls Balchin turning up at Conduit Farm in 'a very smart Alvis Coupé'[9] during the period 1946–1947. Stewart's half-brother John also recollects these visits, on which occasions Balchin had 'smoked a lot with a fancy cigarette holder and drank quite a bit'.[10]

Balchin's promising career as a radio broadcaster had been put on hold in 1938 when a BBC employee had taken exception to his speaking voice and then suspended indefinitely upon the commencement of hostilities a year later. Once he had been officially released from army duty, Balchin wasted little time in wedging his foot once more in the BBC door that had swung open so invitingly for him after he had left the NIIP in 1935. On 8 April 1946 he appeared as a member of *The Brains Trust* on the Home Service, his first appearance on the radio for some seven and a half years. This was the only time that Balchin took part in the long-running 1940s forum of the air, but he did appear twice in the 1950s on *Any Questions?*, the similarly formatted programme that replaced *The Brains Trust* on the airwaves.

The Brains Trust was broadcast the day after being recorded. Exactly a week after its transmission, Balchin was back on the Home Service to give a talk entitled 'Sagas of Old Iceland'. The novelist was a fervent admirer of the Norse sagas—particularly those that emanated from Iceland—and expressed his admiration for them on a number of occasions across multiple different media. In the 1946 radio programme, he spoke about the saga of Burnt Njal, a tale he would later recite in much greater detail when it formed the basis for his contribution to the 1964 compendium *Fatal Fascination: A Choice of Crime*.[11]

The possibility of Balchin doing more work for the Corporation was discussed in the months that followed his two April appearances on the Home Service but did not amount to anything. A radio adaptation of *Mine Own Executioner* was one project that was mooted. A script was prepared for broadcast by a writer named Gilbert Thomas, but when it was sent to Balchin in July to gauge his opinion he was dissatisfied with it:

> It is essential to me that anything that is broadcast connected
> with my name shall show my work at its best, and frankly
> I cannot see how an adaptation of this book can do so.[12]

As hinted in the previous chapter, Balchin's disapproval of Thomas's adaptation centred mainly on the inadequate running time allotted to the play, which permitted insufficient scope for the psychoanalytical theme of the book to be satisfactorily developed. In a letter he sent to Val Gielgud, elder brother of John and, as Head of Productions at the BBC, in charge of all radio drama, Balchin elucidated further reasons why a radio version of *Mine Own Executioner* would do him no good, and might even adversely affect his reputation. He also made it clear that he was on shaky ground with regard to the theme of the play and could not afford any short cuts to be taken that would lay him open to ridicule by the psychoanalytical community:

> This is particularly awkward from my point of view, since it strikes at about the only two things that I have to offer as a writer—viz., that I write with reasonable accuracy about rather unusual and rather technical subjects, and construct my stories with some care. On this subject of psychiatry, for example, it is not enough for the thing to be good enough to get by with the layman. There are too many people writing books and films about psychiatric treatment who know nothing whatever about it. If I do that sort of thing I shall have my leg pulled by every psychiatrist in England.

The idea of *Mine Own Executioner* being transformed into a radio play was dropped and it would be another five years until an adaptation of Balchin's novel debuted on the BBC.[13]

Work was also coming in for Balchin from another pre-war source. For about a decade after leaving the army in 1946 he acted as an adviser on marketing strategy to Rowntree's (his job title was 'Advertising Consultant'), regularly attending board meetings in both London and York. By 1947, Balchin was being remunerated to the tune of £600 per year (about £19,000 per year today) for this work, but he succeeded in negotiating an additional annual payment of £400 as compensation for the train journeys he was required to take on Rowntree's business. He was also appointed to the Romary Board in June 1946.[14]

Another business interest of Balchin's at this time was his connection with the advertising agency J. Walter Thompson

(JWT), with whom of course he had been associated in the mid-1930s when the two parties had joined forces to assist with the launch of Black Magic. Post-war, Balchin served as a Creative Consultant to JWT, and one of his tasks in this role was to write the scripts for a series of cinema commercials for Horlicks.[15]

Balchin's accumulation of a varied portfolio of business interests was a deliberate strategy on the part of the former industrial psychologist. The aim, as he explained in 1947, was to improve his writing:

"I have always believed it important to retain my 'amateur status' as a writer. I combine business with authorship because I write better when doing other work. So I have a good many industrial interests to keep me in contact with everyday life, from which writing tends to cut me off."[16]

*

Similarly to the way in which he had flexed his financial muscle by purchasing Leigh Barton, Balchin demonstrated his intellectual credentials by entering the bookish environment of the Savile Club in 1945, joining on 3 October. As Balchin was required to attend JWT meetings in Berkeley Square, as well as Rowntree's meetings in both London and York, his new club served as a convenient base for him in the capital, and he would sometimes stay the night there before or after a business appointment.

Sequestered in the heart of Mayfair, the Savile Club had established a strong literary tradition in the years leading up to Balchin's election thanks largely to one man. Augustus Detlof ('A. D.') Peters started a literary agency in London in 1928 and was elected a Savile member in the same year. Under his influence, some of the cream of the pre-war writing fraternity— among them Evelyn Waugh, Cecil Day-Lewis, Hilaire Belloc and J. B. Priestley—would cross the threshold of the Club. Peters was one of a number of eminent Savilians (others included Stephen Potter and C. P. Snow) who supported Balchin's application for membership.

Balchin thoroughly enjoyed the evenings that he spent

in Mayfair, where he had the chance to play a few frames of snooker, pursue networking opportunities with potential business contacts in the arts world or just relax in the convivial atmosphere of London's clubland. His second wife Yovanka remembers that her husband knew a lot of people at the Savile Club but did not have any particular friends there. This may have been a consequence of Balchin's 'technique' when on the Brook Street premises, one that does not seem to have been designed to foster amity:

> Balchin had a powerful physical presence; latterly bearded, dark-haired, and bulky, which combined with more than a touch of shyness to make him rather an intimidating figure to those unable to pierce his daunting carapace. He generally avoided the larger convivial groups in the bar and Sandpit,[17] preferring to attach himself either to someone on his own or the less talkative ones when he would then sit brooding until, with a great show of carrying out a social duty, he would bark out a provoking comment on some remote subject on which, seemingly, he had been deeply pondering. If this produced a satisfactory response he would revert to silence and contented listening: if not, he would wander off in search of better fare.[18]

12

Socially Minded Donkeys and a Chinese Examination

> This country has many industrial problems at the present
> time—problems of equipment, method, organization
> and so on. But I do not think it will be denied that the
> overwhelmingly important one is the problem of incentives
> to effort. However well organized and equipped we may be,
> we cannot succeed industrially unless we are prepared to
> work hard; and we shall not work hard unless we find some
> kind of satisfaction in our work.
>
> – Nigel Balchin[1]

In autumn 1946, Nigel Balchin was certainly deriving some
kind of satisfaction from his work, which at that stage comprised
a mix of writing and business interests. Although he was working
hard—as he had done throughout his adult life—he was being well
rewarded for his efforts and was primarily engaged on work that
he enjoyed doing. In this respect, he can be said to have resembled
an acquaintance of his who 'claimed that he had never done
a day's work in his life, in the sense that he had never done anything
which he had not enjoyed and found supremely satisfactory'.

Most British people were not as lucky as Balchin and
his self-satisfied chum. Demobilized servicemen had been
returning home in dribs and drabs for eighteen months to
be confronted by a country that was broke, scarred by bomb
damage, drastically short of habitable houses and whose shops
were either empty or stocked only with limited quantities of
inferior-quality goods. Rations of bacon, poultry and eggs had
been reduced in February from their already low wartime levels
and bread—supplies of which had never been restricted during

the war—had gone on the ration in July.[2] One of the coldest, iciest winters of the century was just around the corner, with Siberian weather conditions set to exacerbate the deprivation and hardship faced by millions of Britons and to bring a genuinely snowy blizzard hard on the heels of the economic one. For the Man on the Clapham Omnibus, 1947 offered little prospect of an improvement in his material circumstances: the possibility of darkness falling on him from the air may have been banished for the foreseeable future, but in many other respects he was considerably worse off than he had been between 1939 and 1945.

One of the most serious problems facing the country was an urgent need to step up the production of commodities such as fuel and clothing that were in short supply. But the industries concerned, namely coal mining and the textiles trade, offered very unattractive working conditions for potential employees and were consequently failing to attract sufficient numbers of people through their gates. As he had done more than once during the war, it was time for Balchin to come to his country's aid yet again and to make another important contribution to the common good by applying his intellect and vision to the problem of incentives to effort.

Balchin's first direct engagement with the subject of incentives seems to have taken place on 16 October 1946 when he held a meeting on the topic with his erstwhile boss Seebohm Rowntree, who had retired as Rowntree's Chairman five years previously and was now Chairman of Balchin's former employers the National Institute of Industrial Psychology (NIIP). Rowntree had approached Balchin to seek his advice on how to obtain publicity for the NIIP. In a letter sent to a fellow member of the NIIP's Executive Committee six days earlier regarding this meeting, Rowntree had stated in connection with Balchin that 'I am not quite sure what he has been doing since he left the Works,[3] except writing novels, out of which I understand he is making several thousand pounds a year'.[4] (It is not known whether this figure[5] was factually accurate or simply a piece of uninformed gossip. But less than six months later, Rowntree's Chairman George Harris had formed the impression that

Balchin's gross annual income, based on sales of books and film rights, approximated to a five-figure sum.[6])

At their conference, Rowntree and Balchin did not speak much about publicity; instead, Balchin used the opportunity he had been presented with to climb onto his soapbox and attack the failings of the NIIP over the near-quarter century since it had come into being. He said that the precarious hand-to-mouth existence of the Institute had led it to take on work it was unfit to do, that its staff acted more like management consultants than psychologists and that it needed to start concerning itself with general principles rather than individual problems. Balchin suggested that the NIIP should engage in research work of value to industry as a whole, and in this regard he proposed that they ought to commission a large-scale, long-term investigation of incentives, thus showing leadership and establishing the Institute as the country's premier authority on this issue.

Rowntree was sufficiently enthused by Balchin's proposal that he invited him to address a meeting of the NIIP's Executive Committee so that Balchin could outline his scheme to a larger audience. There was a fair amount of enthusiasm on that occasion for a study of incentives, but Balchin's idea came under attack from someone well known to him. Frederic Bartlett, who had been the first to introduce Balchin to the discipline of psychology at Cambridge in 1930 and may also have helped his former student to secure positions with the NIIP and, during World War Two, with the army's Directorate of Selection of Personnel, took umbrage at the proposal that had been placed before the Committee. He felt that a general investigation of incentives would clash with a similar project already in progress under the aegis of the Medical Research Council (although Balchin made subsequent enquiries and established that no such overlap was in fact likely). Bartlett's counter-proposal involved a study of what he described as the 'unwanted industries', i.e. those in which workers were in short supply, with the aim of discovering how to make those unpopular professions more attractive to the labour market.

In a letter written to Rowntree two days after this meeting,

Balchin said that he was 'a little disappointed'[7] that his idea had been subjugated by that of Bartlett. Given the length of his letter, and the strong feelings embodied within it, it is more accurate to say that Balchin was quietly furious that Bartlett had waved aside his proposal in such a cavalier fashion, akin to a supercilious headmaster breezily dismissing a suggestion from a precocious pupil. As Balchin explained to Rowntree, the Institute's timorous nature had been exemplified by its response to his address to the Executive Committee:

> ...you asked me what I thought about the Institute, and I told you that in my opinion, its greatest weakness had always been its unwillingness to go boldly for the big, long term proposition. We could hardly have had a better demonstration of my meaning than the reaction to this proposal.

Despite Rowntree endeavouring to smooth Balchin's ruffled feathers by attempting to harmonize his proposal with that of Bartlett, it was the investigation of unpopular industries and not a broader study of incentives that received the green light from the NIIP's Executive Committee. The chosen industry was the cotton trade. The study then proceeded to become bogged down at committee level and, almost three years later, was still rumbling on having failed to generate any detailed report of its activities.

The rebuff that Balchin had suffered from both Bartlett and the Institute as a whole did not dissuade him from continuing to think about the theory of incentives and propounding his views on the matter. However, the clash of intellects and egos that had been enacted behind the walls of Aldwych House may well have precipitated the severance of links between Balchin and the NIIP. After renewing his acquaintanceship with the Institute after a break of nearly twelve years, Balchin would deliver just one more lecture on behalf of his old employers before permanently terminating his involvement with them.

Balchin's 'London Lecture', organized by the Institute, was delivered at the London School of Hygiene and Tropical

Medicine in Bloomsbury on 5 March 1947 and was the first of a series of talks, articles and broadcasts about incentives that he delivered over the course of the following eighteen months. It was entitled 'Satisfactions in Work',[8] was subsequently transcribed and published in several different journals and represents the finest crystallization of his original and invigorating ideas on the subject.

Balchin began by informing his audience that the most pressing problem facing British industry in 1947 was how to encourage people to work harder and be more productive, to hew out the coal that the country was desperately short of and to produce the manufactured goods destined for export. The welfare state and full employment had meant that the old incentive of 'work or starve' was no longer valid. In a letter to *The Times* written a few months later, on 29 August, Balchin supplied a vivid illustration of the previous system:

> The old type of incentive on which our economy was built was a simple affair of donkey and carrot. One hung the carrot of a higher standard of life in front of the donkey's nose, and whipped him behind with the prospect of unemployment and want—and the donkey went. The public conscience has removed the whip, and circumstances have removed the carrot. Why should the donkey go? Mr. Morrison[9] appears to think that he should go because he is a good, socially minded donkey.

Contrary to Herbert Morrison's opinion, Balchin argued in his lecture that he did not believe that people would work for 'an abstraction like society',[10] but only for some more tangible reward.

In places of work where piece rates were in operation, Balchin reported that it had been shown that the average employee worked well within his maximum capacity and would not overly exert himself to secure a higher standard of living, especially if the carrot being dangled was no more enticing than the prospect of a new wireless set or refrigerator. This philosophy was nicely illustrated by the story—a favourite anecdote of Balchin's, which he was to retell a number of times in the future—of the miner who was paraded before a visiting Cabinet Minister as a notorious absentee:

> The minister said, "They tell me you work four days a week. Why is that?" The miner replied, "Because I find I can't earn what I want in three."

So if a person had no need to work to avoid starvation and would not do so out of some sense of fulfilling a social duty or to attain a better standard of living, then what alternative was left?

Balchin's solution was to abolish work altogether, in the sense that it should no longer be viewed as something hard and unpleasant but instead should merge into those enjoyable pastimes that people indulged in during their leisure hours: 'A working man is one who spends his working life doing what he does not want to do. A non-working man is one whose productive efforts give him satisfaction.' Balchin cheerfully anticipated the 'complete annihilation' of the working man delineated by his definition. He proceeded to remind his audience that those industries that provided amusements and diversions for the populace had been forced to find out what their customers really wanted in order to entice them through their doors. Industry had not had to do this in the past because of the old work-or-starve ultimatum, but in the face of the recent change from a buyer's to a seller's market it was having to take steps—by way of advertising for instance—to attract labour into its factories and to make the work on offer more appealing. Research was needed, argued Balchin, to discover exactly what the attractive characteristics of popular entertainments such as concerts, cinema and the theatre consisted of, and then to determine how these might be incorporated into the work environment. It was clear to Balchin that because people were starved of pleasure and excitement from nine to five on weekdays they were compelled to seek these emotional elements in their social lives instead. As recorded in his novel *Sundry Creditors*, as soon as the factory hooter sounded at the end of the working day, the men and women employed at Lang's engineering works vacated the premises at high speed so that they could get ready to attend speedway meetings or go to the pictures.

The recommendations put forward by Balchin for making employment a more pleasurable activity included the use of brightly coloured clothing, organizing workers into teams and arranging competitions between them to see which team was the most productive, staging displays and exhibitions and introducing more variety within occupations. Although he was only too aware of the 'preparatory school joke possibilities' of the idea, Balchin also said that he had never yet heard of an industrialist who had appreciated the potential source of energy to be found in the relationships between his male and female employees. Balchin though had watched mixed-sex anti-aircraft batteries in action during the war and this had taught him that the sexual instinct ran far deeper than the more obvious manifestations utilized by the entertainment industry. In his view, a shift away from the traditional use of same-sex supervisors might have brought about an improvement in productivity:

> Would it be sacrilege to ask whether a man might sometimes get better results as overseer of a group of girls than a sour, elderly spinster?

Balchin's proposal to eradicate the traditional boundaries between work and leisure was radical and far-reaching. When 'Satisfactions in Work' was re-evaluated in 1993 by an occupational psychologist[11] it was suggested that Balchin's vision—especially with regard to the use of teamwork and the introduction of the emotional element into the workplace—had only begun to be realized some three to four decades after his 'London Lecture'. Anyone who has watched a catatonically bored young woman listlessly scanning barcodes at a supermarket checkout or studied the body language of a small group of bedraggled and despondent men sorting household recycling at the roadside on a wet winter's morning, and leaving a trail of wind-blown debris in their wake, will appreciate that a lot more work remains to be done in this area and that employers have still failed to take action on the majority of Balchin's suggestions almost seventy years after he first made them.

The substance of Balchin's NIIP lecture gave rise to a talk on the Home Service in December 1947 entitled 'Incentives: Why Work?'. This was followed by an address to the British Association for the Advancement of Science in Brighton the following September on the same subject. In the transcript of this second lecture, Balchin referred back to his BBC appearance:

> Some while ago I broadcast a talk in which I tried to put forward some of these rather woolly ideas. After it, I received a number of letters. One of them said, 'I am in charge of a number of men who collect sewage. I like your ideas and should like my men to enjoy their work. Will you please send me a copy of your system?' No letter could have expressed more simply the obvious criticism of all this. 'Come off it, and come down into the sewage pit amongst the—brass tacks.'[12]

Balchin succeeded in rising above this obvious criticism. In his talks and writings about incentives he was concerned more with establishing a theoretical foundation for the subject than with dealing with mere practicalities. In his opinion, it was the duty of the industrial psychologist to revolutionize industry and not to attempt to do the practical man's job for him, which is what Balchin felt that the NIIP had often been guilty of in the past. This was principally because its investigators had been forced to concentrate solely on the task in hand and had thus been denied the opportunity to construct theories pertaining to their work.

In his next significant piece of writing, published in May 1947, Balchin wrote briefly again about incentives but, as he stressed, there had been little real need for them in the British aircraft industry during the recent war:

> ...there was never much question about "what it was all for." To the normal British man or woman, with normal feelings

about the war and the flying services in it, the fundamental worth-whileness of work in aircraft production was never in doubt.

The Aircraft Builders. An Account of British Aircraft Production 1935–1945 was a ninety-six-page monograph about the wartime military aircraft industry issued by HMSO, and described by its author on the inside front cover as 'a story of Britain at its best and the British genius at its highest and most characteristic'. This resolutely jolly flag-waving tone—which acts as a corrective to the deeply cynical mood that pervades Balchin's next book, the fictional *Lord, I Was Afraid*—was maintained by Balchin throughout the entire text, unsurprisingly perhaps as the book had been prepared by the Central Office of Information on behalf of the Ministry of Aircraft Production.[13]

In three sections (The Challenge, The Achievement and The People), Balchin outlined the situation that the British aircraft industry had faced in 1935, when it was finally appreciated that there was an urgent need to rearm in order to counter the threat of Hitler, and how the industry had pulled together and ramped up aircraft production in response. The first section is by far the most readable and enjoyable, with frequent flourishes redolent of the familiar Balchin style; the remaining two sections are repetitious and bogged down by technicalities.

In his critical survey of Balchin's works, Clive James came out in favour of *The Aircraft Builders*, claiming that 'As a summary of a complicated matter it is quite outstanding in its plainness—Balchin had no equals at this kind of analysis'.[14] James was impressed above all else by Balchin's evocative account of the interchangeability of aircraft components produced by both established aircraft manufacturers ('parent companies') and the state-owned plants ('shadow factories') set up as a means of expanding production capacity that were operated by concerns with no expertise of building aircraft, but which did have relevant experience in a related field, i.e.

car manufacture, and that turned out products designed by one of the parent firms:

> The first shadow factory was finished in May 1937; the first shadow-produced set of components was delivered four months later; the first shadow-produced engine passed its tests in November. The acid test of complete interchangeability was made at an early stage. An engine from the parent company and one from the shadow industry were taken down to their smallest components. The parts were mixed, and two engines were reassembled from the mixed parts. The passing of their tests by both engines demonstrated the fundamental practicability of the shadow scheme.

*

The origins of Balchin's next work of fiction, *Lord, I Was Afraid*, can be traced back to a revue—not known ever to have been performed—that he wrote whilst living at Duke's Lodge in Holland Park. *Active Service* consisted of about fifteen comic songs and sketches that gently satirized certain facets of the Second World War. None of this material made it into the later work intact, but some of the ideas contained in *Active Service* were reworked for it.

Published on 25 August 1947, *Lord, I Was Afraid* differed markedly from the three accomplished and very well-received novels that Balchin had written during World War Two and it divided the nation's book critics to a greater extent than any other piece of Balchin fiction. Just for starters, there was a feisty semantic argument between them concerning exactly what type of book the author had written. Several reviewers felt that it was a play, whilst taking care to point out that it was not one that could have been performed on any theatre stage in existence at the time. For Stephen Potter[15] in the *News Chronicle*, 'The new book is vaguely like a film scenario, more precisely, in some of its scenes, like a radio script'. In the *Daily Mail*, Peter Quennell[16] called *Lord, I Was Afraid* 'an immense dramatic fantasy' and Harold Nicolson[17] in the *Daily Telegraph* contributed the observation that the scenes in the book 'can be likened to surrealistic paintings in which the characters have not only become animated, but also talk'. More than one critic drew a parallel between Balchin's book and Auden and Isherwood's 1935 play *The Dog Beneath the Skin*. Among them was T. C. Worsley[18] in the *New Statesman and Nation*, who came closer than anyone to establishing the true nature of the book, and in doing so simultaneously succeeded in skewering the evasion perpetrated by the Collins Publicity Department in the form of the blurb they had prepared for the inside of the dust jacket:

> *Lord I Was Afraid* is, to quote the publishers, "not a Nigel Balchin novel in the ordinary sense. In fact it cannot be described technically as a novel at all." In short it is not a novel. It is a sort of distended charade in some 23 scenes written in play form but not meant for performance, in which three men and women[19] of average, middle-class upbringing are conducted through a phantasmagoria of the problems of the inter-war generation.

(I concur with Worsley's assessment: *Lord, I Was Afraid* is a play, not a novel.)

As revealed on the dust jacket of *Lord, I Was Afraid*, we are told that the subject of the book is 'one on which the author has meditated and worked for ten years—the subject of his own generation, its nature, its faults, virtues, and direction if any'. The author's handling of his subject is more difficult to define. He had transmuted the cosy satirical mockery of his Mark Spade books and Pobottle articles of the mid-1930s into something much darker, more hard-edged, cynical and confrontational. Instead of just poking fun at industrial psychology, with *Lord, I Was Afraid* Balchin used his satirical wit as a blunt-edged weapon with which to attack the foibles and failings of those who, like him, had come to maturity between the two great wars of the twentieth century.

The format of *Lord, I Was Afraid* was totally different from those of *Darkness Falls from the Air, The Small Back Room* and *Mine Own Executioner*, but familiar Balchin preoccupations were still visible behind the new framework used to construct the book. In the scene in which Raymond and Sheila Murray pay a doctor to kill their son because he has taken away their freedom and happiness ('We feel that he has ruined our lives'), the anti-child sentiment propagated by Balchin is simply a more chilling and extreme version of that which was later aired in a provocative article published in the 1960s.[20] There are cracks about wartime bureaucracy and inefficiency—'A committee is a body formed to hinder a capable man in doing his job'—that would not be at all out of place in *Darkness Falls from the Air* or *The Small Back Room,* and a scene set in the assembly shop of a munitions works evokes both *Sundry Creditors* and *No Sky.* Relationships under tension (a perennial theme of Balchin's fiction from *Simple Life* onwards) are a prominent feature of *Lord, I Was Afraid,* and the account of the break-up of the union between Peter and Pamela Hargreaves shares some disconcerting similarities with Balchin's unpublished description of the disintegration of his own marriage.[21]

The principal emotions that the book engendered in the reviewing fraternity were confusion and puzzlement. Robert Lynd[22] in the *Observer* said that *Lord, I Was Afraid* appeared to have been designed to 'keep people like myself in a recurrent state of bewilderment' and he struck a blow for the average reader by confessing that 'I cannot speak with confidence of the meaning of the book in detail, for to me much of it is obscure'.

Pamela Hansford Johnson[23] in *John o'London's Weekly* complained that *Lord, I Was Afraid* was 'very dull' but did draw attention to the excellence of individual scenes: '*Lord, I Was Afraid* would not, however, be Mr. Balchin's work if it had not its occasional delights and brilliancies'. But there were only three commentators who seemed to derive satisfaction from *Lord, I Was Afraid* in its entirety. The thriller writer Julian Symons,[24] reviewing the book for the *Manchester Evening News,* described it as 'remarkable' and commended Balchin for his 'enviable power of comic invention' and 'brilliant flares of imagination'. Nicolson[25] characterized it as a 'strange, exciting book' and Quennell[26] expressed admiration for the novelist's willingness to 'throw his laurel wreath over the windmill', admitting, almost despite himself, that *Lord, I Was Afraid* was 'one of the most ambitious and remarkable performances of 1947'.

By far the best critical review of *Lord, I Was Afraid* was that penned by Worsley.[27] Correctly identifying that *The Small Back Room* and *Mine Own Executioner* had been uncomfortably alike as novels ('one about unpicking a dangerous bomb, the other about unpicking a dangerous person'), he felt that Balchin had arrived at a crossroads in his career. The author himself appreciated the temptation he had been exposed to after he had scored a hit with *The Small Back Room*, telling the *News Chronicle* in 1952 that 'The young writer with one success to his name will be asked to produce more books of the same kind, because his publisher and agent know that line will sell, and because his public will expect that line'.[28] Rather than gleefully freewheeling downhill in search of repeat success (and substantial royalties) with the same formula, Worsley[29] considered that Balchin, in the process of changing direction so drastically, had endeavoured to drive up a hill in a car encumbered by two flat tyres. Although he admired the courage that the novelist had displayed in attempting to escape from his typecasting, the critic's verdict was that this daring experiment, considered as a whole, had not come off:

> Mr. Balchin will be tired of being told by reviewers to forget this failure and return to his successes.

After he had climbed his hill on two flat tyres by writing *Lord, I Was Afraid*, Balchin found that the steep gradient he had laboriously ascended led nowhere more inviting than into a cul-de-sac. The experiments of language and form that marked the book out as a completely separate entity from his previous fiction were never to be repeated, and all of Balchin's post-1947 novels are 'conventional' works by comparison with *Lord, I Was Afraid*. When asked in a 1961 interview with the *Guardian*'s John Rosselli whether he would ever attempt anything along the same lines again, Balchin replied that he would be extremely wary of doing so unless he was sure he had enough to say:

> "It's terribly easy for a book of that sort to be a fake—for the manner to be used to cover up a lack of matter. And I do very much dislike that kind of fake."[30]

As Balchin explained to Rosselli, he had crammed everything he could think of into his strangest book:

> "Lord, I was afraid" he now thinks, was "a very uneven book... writing it was something of a Chinese examination. You know, in a Chinese examination you had to put down everything you knew."

Balchin had emptied his brain onto the printed page, filling the book with ideas, allusions, quotations and 'all that one knew about the use of one's own language'. In spite of the intermittent incomprehensibility of the product he had created, the result of his labours was a tour de force: among his many books, *Lord, I Was Afraid* was, in Yovanka's opinion, the one that her husband 'was most proud of',[31] and he valued it above all the others.

When Francis Bacon's first major painting, the striking and horrific *Three Studies for Figures at the Base of a Crucifixion*, was exhibited at the Lefevre Gallery in London in April 1945 it 'shocked a British public unused to the subject or its handling'.[32] Like Bacon's writhing and tormented forms, which provoke feelings of queasiness and revulsion in some people, *Lord, I Was Afraid* never fails to leave an indelible impression on the mind of any intrepid soul who succeeds in reading all 320 of its difficult, but ultimately rewarding, pages. However, the unusual form of *Lord, I Was Afraid*, allied to its dependence on symbolism and the inclusion between its covers of some subject matter that would have remained obscure to all but the best-educated classicists, initially frustrated and bamboozled a reading public that had derived so much satisfaction from the much more straightforward *The Small Back Room* and *Mine*

Own Executioner. After the huge commercial success of his two previous works, Balchin experienced a precipitous drop in sales with *Lord, I Was Afraid*: the book sold a mere 11,000 copies in hardback[33] and was never issued in paperback.

Balchin's seemingly unperformable play was not quite as unsuitable for theatrical presentation as the book critics had imagined.[34] Anthony Burgess must have read *Lord, I Was Afraid* soon after publication because, sometime between 1948 and 1950, he adapted it for the stage whilst working as a lecturer in Speech and Drama at Bamber Bridge Emergency Training College near Preston in Lancashire, where he was responsible for transforming ex-servicemen returned from the war into qualified teachers. The genesis of this singular spectacle has been described by Burgess's biographer Andrew Biswell:

> Anthony Burgess read *Lord, I Was Afraid* and wrote to Nigel Balchin and said "I want to adapt this for the stage" and the author wrote back and he said "I can't imagine how this could possibly be done but if you're willing to try it, go ahead with my blessing."[35]

(In addition to writing the script, Burgess doubled up as director of the Bamber Bridge production of *Lord, I Was Afraid*.)

When he reviewed Balchin's *Seen Dimly Before Dawn* in 1962, Burgess[36] decried its lack of any real 'literary' quality, comparing it negatively with *Lord, I Was Afraid*, which he referred to as 'an epic closet-drama whose real hero was Mr. Balchin as a Flaubertian virtuoso'. Another twentieth century colossus of English literature, J. G. Ballard, was also very fond of the book from which Burgess developed his stage play ('I loved [...] Nigel Balchin's experimental novel *Lord, I Was Afraid*'[37]).

*

Two months after the release of *Lord, I Was Afraid*, Balchin wrote a two-part article for the literary magazine *Time and Tide*, his first appearance in its pages since 1936. In the opening part of his contribution he showed that, although he had not worked as an industrial psychologist since 1935, he continued to think like one.

On arrival at a well-known London railway terminus, Balchin had used his extensive 1930s experience of factory transportation procedures to express dismay at the inefficient and illogical management of the taxi queue as practised by the porters:

I came out of Charing Cross Station one morning recently in a hurry. There were twenty-four taxis waiting in the station yard and others were arriving rapidly. Seventeen of us wanted taxis. We were marshalled into a queue by two porters and the taxis were brought up one at a time. When I reached the head of the queue (now reduced to eight) I said to one of the porters, "It would really be quicker, wouldn't it, if we didn't have a queue? There are more taxis than people." He shouted very loudly, "We do things proper here. Everyone has to take his turn *whoever* he is. Now then—who's next?"

I said, "Well, as a matter of fact, I am."

He was puzzled and said, "Then what're you fussing about?"

I said, "But, you see, some of these other people may be in a hurry."

"Well, that's for them to worry about, isn't it? You've waited your turn. Here you are."[38]

13

Finding the Key to the Film World

> Writing for pictures is not just highly paid hackwork in an
> inferior medium. If you sell the film rights of your novel you
> must either be prepared to cut your brainchild to ribbons
> to suit the new medium or hand it over to a professional
> scriptwriter—if you cannot be your own executioner.
>   – Nigel Balchin[1]

Balchin's long association with the movie-making business had
begun as early as June 1944, while he was still working at the War
Office, when he had been put under contract by MGM British
Studios. That arrangement ultimately came to nothing because
the company, formed by a merger between MGM and Hungarian
émigré Alexander Korda's London Films, soon fell apart having
made only one movie, and it was not until July 1946 that Balchin
completed his first screenplay and handed it over to his new
employers at Charter Films, the Boulting brothers. The Boultings
had enjoyed some critical success during the war with films such
as *Pastor Hall* and *Thunder Rock*. When they first collaborated
with Balchin, the moviemaking twins (they tended to alternate as
producer and director) were engaged, as film guru Leslie Halliwell
put it, in the task of 'raising the sights of British films'.[2]

It is unclear exactly how Balchin came to be acquainted
with the Boultings. A member of the Army Film Unit from
1942 onwards, Roy Boulting spent a certain amount of time
at the War Office in the later years of the conflict and may
conceivably have bumped into Balchin in those Whitehall
corridors on occasions. But as Boulting was a Savilian (having
become a member in February 1944, about eighteen months

before Balchin) there is also a strong possibility that the two men met at the Savile Club and that, with his war work behind him, Balchin was asked by Boulting to write a script for a film that the twin was intending to direct in the near future.

For his initial venture into the world of screenwriting, Balchin had chosen not to wield the axe on one of his own brainchildren but instead to manipulate the work of another popular novelist. The book that he had been contracted to adapt was *Fame is the Spur*, the fourth novel by Welsh author Howard Spring. It was an account of the life of Hamer Radshaw (Michael Redgrave), a Labour politician who drags himself out of a childhood of grinding poverty in a Manchester slum to become Prime Minister (although, in the film version, we only see him as a Cabinet Minister in the 1930s coalition National Government). The central character is generally assumed to have been based on a former Labour Prime Minister, and Roy Boulting observed many years after the film was made that Radshaw 'was clearly inspired by the fate of the late Ramsay MacDonald'.[3] However, Rosamund John, who played Radshaw's wife Ann in the film, spoke to Spring on set and was informed that the protagonist was 'based on *any* chap who had feet of clay, and he'd taken bits from various people'. MacDonald is referred to once or twice by Radshaw in the film and so clearly exists offstage as a separate character. It is more useful therefore to think of the picture's main theme—political idealism being gradually eroded by realism and self-interest once a politician assumes power—as having been inspired by MacDonald's career trajectory.

Understandably, Balchin was forced to grossly simplify a 670-page novel that covered more than sixty-five years of British history in order to produce a filmable script. The work that resulted had an episodic structure, centring on the deterioration over time of the relationship between Radshaw and his boyhood friend Arnold Ryerson (a fine, sensitive performance from the underrated Hugh Burden), a fellow Labour MP who, unlike the pragmatic Radshaw, refuses to compromise his principles in exchange for political advancement.

Fame is the Spur is sincere and well made, with a

commanding central performance from the screenwriter's Cambridge contemporary Redgrave, and Balchin's script is functional and literate. But despite the dramatization of some memorable incidents (a recreation of the Peterloo massacre; Radshaw inciting a riot at a coal mine; Ann being force-fed in a prison cell, whence she has been sent because of her activities as a suffragette) the film is, in the words of 'A Special Correspondent'[4] in the *Observer*, 'very serious and rather long'. The same critic added meaningfully that "Power corrupts!' is the message; and one's only complaint is that it corrupts so slowly'.

Sadly for both the Boultings and Balchin, *Fame is the Spur* did poor business at the box office, with one latter-day observer noting that 'It was not a popular success: critics generally praised its seriousness of purpose, but it failed to find large audiences'.[5] It was not assisted at all by the fact that it could be interpreted as a veiled attack on the Attlee government, which had swept to power on the back of a landslide election victory little more than two years previously and was still deemed by many to be practically immune from criticism. More significantly though, the film was not a hit with the cinema-going public because it failed to give them what they wanted in the dreary post-war world of bomb-sites and rationing. As Roy Boulting explained:

> ...after five years of death, destruction and austerity, it was far too grim for an audience now seeking escapism and peace. It flopped.[6]

Balchin's second screenwriting project brought him much closer to home. When the London Films' production of *Mine Own Executioner* premiered at the Empire, Leicester Square in November 1947, Freda Bruce Lockhart[7] in *Time and Tide* observed, almost with incredulity, that Balchin had been 'allowed to undertake the extraordinary experiment of writing the screen play of his own novel'. An unknown critic[8] in the *Monthly Film Bulletin* detailed the advantages that this had conferred on the moviegoer:

Probably the fact that the author of the book also wrote the script goes a long way to make the film ring true and the tale stick to the point.

Described by his fellow director Michael Powell as 'A useful work-horse'[9] and by Dulcie Gray, who played Patricia in the film, as 'a very positive man',[10] the producer and director of *Mine Own Executioner*, Anthony Kimmins, had cut his teeth in cinema before the war at Ealing Studios; working almost exclusively in the genre of light comedy, he had directed a number of George Formby's most successful pictures. In the words of Powell, 'Tony Kimmins was one of those men whose great charm made people suspect his talent. But he knew exactly what he could do and he did it very well.'[11] With *Mine Own Executioner*, Kimmins would not seem to have interfered much with Balchin's script because the picture that resulted from their collaboration is very faithful to the book.

In the tradition of the 1940s, an American actor was parachuted in to play the starring role of psychoanalyst Felix Milne. According to Gray, the only reason that Burgess Meredith came to England at all was because his wife, Paulette Goddard, was already in the country to film Korda's version of Oscar Wilde's *An Ideal Husband*: 'their marriage was on the rocks and finished immediately afterwards'.[12] In his memoirs, Meredith does not allude to any marital problems that may have been troubling him on set, but he does admit to having sought professional psychiatric advice when he wasn't required to be in front of the camera:

> …during the filming I had long talks with the British analyst who was our technical adviser for the picture.[13] I told him I thought I was on the way to some sort of breakdown or collapse and I needed advice. What should I do?
>
> In his clipped, British way, the doctor suggested, "Why don't you have children? Sometimes that helps."[14]

Meredith's unstable personal life probably helped him to get to grips with his character: Milne is on the verge of splitting up with his wife when the film opens and their relationship remains brittle and uncomfortable throughout.

Meredith's performance in *Mine Own Executioner* is sensitive and nuanced and he displays the correct amalgam of professional wisdom and care towards his patients and ill-focused annoyance towards his clumsy, scatterbrained wife. Gray is less of a success as Patricia but this is scarcely her fault given that Balchin's character-drawing in this area is not wholly credible. The actress appreciated the challenge of inhabiting the role. Her remark on the work she had felt impelled to perform regarding the construction of a back story for Patricia provides an eloquent commentary on Balchin's inability, at this stage in his career, to write convincing roles for women in either book, play or movie formats:

> I found her rather upsetting to play; she needn't have been so awfully inadequate. She was so in awe of her husband that I had to invent a background for her[15] to be able to play her. Why does she put up with his having all these affairs? I think she knew she was inadequate but it wasn't ever explained, because he was rather cruel to her even though he was going through trouble himself.[16]

In the other significant female roles, the luminously beautiful Barbara White, in the few minutes of screen time she was permitted, contributed a very fair impersonation of Molly Lucian. Christine Norden's performance as Barbara divided the critics. William Whitebait[17] (real name George Stonier) in the *New Statesman and Nation* described her as 'convincing', whereas the *News Chronicle*'s Richard Winnington[18] felt that Norden's role (and that of Gray) had been 'suburbanised and simplified into nonentity'.

In 1947, Kieron Moore (Adam Lucian) was an actor who seemed to have the film world at his feet. Just twenty-two when *Mine Own Executioner* was shot, he had been awarded a seven-year contract by Korda, and Kimmins's movie was only the third he had appeared in, following on from *A Man About the House* earlier in the same year, for which he had won high praise. As demanded of him in his role as a schizophrenic, Moore alternates adeptly in *Mine Own Executioner* between withdrawn sullenness and over-bright enthusiasm, but although his performance is a touching and memorable one it did not serve as the springboard for attaining the stardom he had seemed certain to achieve.

The playing of the minor roles is solid rather than spectacular, with a few outstanding exceptions. Mr Lefage the coroner is exquisitely brought to life by Lawrence Hanray, who died only a few days after the film opened in cinemas. His performance sparkles with wit and intelligence, as does that of John Laurie (permitted to deviate from frequent typecasting as a dour Scot) as Milne's colleague Garsten. Elsewhere, Michael Shepley is enjoyable as Barbara's buffoonish husband Peter and the ever-reliable Walter Fitzgerald offers a sound interpretation of the put-upon clinic chief Norris Pile. In what is likely to have been a joke cooked up on set between Kimmins and Balchin, the latter appears (uncredited) in a walk-on role as a guest at a party who utters a mere five words to his host ("Thank you sir, very much") before departing the scene.

For print journalists, the film of *Mine Own Executioner* proved to be even more praiseworthy than the book. Winnington was especially enthusiastic, referring to 'a fascinating and faithful translation of an arresting contemporary novel' and lauding the movie as 'the fourth notable British post-war film', after *Great Expectations*, *Brief Encounter* and *Odd Man Out*. This could perhaps be taken as a damning indictment of the post-war British film industry, but Winnington's praise was so effusive and wide-ranging that it is clear he was not just using Balchin as a stick with which to beat the rest of the home-grown cinematic profession.

Whitebait[19] admitted that '*Mine Own Executioner* is the first film I have seen that both deals with human beings and successfully makes drama out of psycho-analysis', and Winnington[20] agreed with him, describing Kimmins's movie as 'the first psycho-analytical film that a grown-up person can sit through without squirming'. In the *Daily Telegraph*, Campbell Dixon[21] was impressed by Milne's attempted rescue of Lucian from the top of a high building ('one of the most hair-raising sequences I have ever seen') and hailed *Mine Own Executioner* as a 'subtle, brilliant film'.

Writing in the film magazine *Sight and Sound*, a little after most of the above-mentioned reviews had appeared, Arthur Vesselo[22] sounded the only discordant note among the loud trumpet blasts of adulation that had accompanied the release of the picture. He wrote that *Mine Own Executioner* 'does not seem to deserve all the fanfares with which it has been welcomed' and he felt that its success was attributable more to a 'feeling of contrast with the usual trite Hollywood nonsense about psychiatry' than to any intrinsic merit of the work itself.

The rapturous critical reception accorded *Mine Own Executioner* did not translate into financial returns, but the film still performed creditably at the box office, grossing £158,734, about average for a first feature of the period. By comparison, *The Courtneys of Curzon Street*, the most successful British film of 1947–1948, grossed £317,836 and the Boulting brothers' impressive *Brighton Rock* took £190,147. (Takings for *Mine Own Executioner* may have been adversely affected by the fact that the film did not open in British cinemas until 9 February 1948, more than two months after most of the appreciative notices had been published.)[23]

Mine Own Executioner is an important Balchin artefact, and not just because it ranks as one of the best British films of the late 1940s. It is also significant because it is the first time that Balchin (or anyone else for that matter) had tried to transform one of his works into a different format. This initial attempt would soon be followed by many more adaptations of Balchin's novels and stories for radio, television and even the stage; talking in 1955 about his 1951 novel *A Way Through the Wood*, which had by then already appeared in four or five different guises, Balchin joked that 'the only thing it hasn't been yet, as far as I know, is an opera'.[24]

In spite of its limitations (it is, as Bruce Lockhart[25] observed, 'too word-bound', as well as being cinematically unadventurous), *Mine Own Executioner* remains a fascinating movie and

Whitebait[26] was right to say that 'Mr. Balchin has gone into films—into one film; at least—without being swallowed up'. In 1950, the poet, journalist and long-time editor of the *London Magazine*, Alan Ross, put a more positive spin on the importance of Balchin's second screenplay, venturing the contention that the novelist had 'found the key to the film world with Mine Own Executioner'.[27]

Balchin may have found the key to the film world, but pushing open the door to Hollywood was still proving troublesome. In the first few days of 1948 he appended his signature to an agreement with MGM's American operation. He had been asked to write a treatment for a movie provisionally entitled *Carnival in Venice*, which was to be based upon the centuries-old mask-based festival still held to this day in the floating city each winter. In the company of Elisabeth, Balchin undertook a first-class all-expenses-paid trip to Venice in January to allow him to collect material and absorb the authentic Venetian atmosphere. The pair then sailed from Southampton to New York on the Queen Elizabeth on 4 February and from there travelled to MGM's headquarters in Culver City, California for script conferences. Whilst in America, Balchin completed his treatment for *Carnival in Venice*, for which he pocketed $5,000 (about £30,000 today). Had the film been made (which it wasn't), he would have received an additional $75,000, but Balchin probably considered that even a mere $5,000 was adequate recompense for a few weeks' work in California and a free holiday in Italy with his wife, which turned out to be almost the last he took with her.

*

"It began in a curious way. My wife and I went to a wartime revue. I think it was called *Sweet and Low*.[28] There was an item in it about the Borgias including the lines:

> *Oh the Borgias are having an orgy;*
> *There's a Borgia orgy tonight.*

It was great fun but I remarked to my wife during the interval that it was a pity that everyone thinks of the Borgias as though they did nothing else but go around poisoning people.[29] In fact, they are extraordinarily interesting people and there is no real evidence that Cesare Borgia ever poisoned anyone."

– Nigel Balchin[30]

Following on from his first two screenplays (for *Fame is the Spur* and *Mine Own Executioner*), Balchin's next major writing project saw him branch out into another form of new territory. Published on 19 July 1948, his historical novel *The Borgia Testament*, an account of the life of Cesare Borgia (1476–1507) told in the first person in novelistic form, originated in a specific incident, as relayed (above) by the author during the course of a magazine interview in 1962. Balchin evidently commenced work on the book very soon after seeing *Sweet and Low* because in the same piece he informed his interviewer that 'I worked for four or five years pretty solidly on the research and, whatever else may be said about the book, I can claim that it is as factually accurate as I could make it'. The author admitted that, although he had enjoyed writing *The Borgia Testament*, it had been 'a long, complicated job'.

When he finally put down his pencil on 11 July 1947, having completed the manuscript of his latest work, what sort of book had Balchin written? As Walter Allen[31] was swift to point out in his review in the *New Statesman and Nation*, *The Borgia Testament* is 'only dubiously a novel'. It is in fact a fictionalized 'celebrity' autobiography, something that, in these days of David Peace's *The Damned United* and Joyce Carol Oates's *Blonde*, is no longer seen as groundbreaking or unusual, but it must have seemed a strange proposition in the summer of 1948 to admirers of Balchin's writing weaned on *The Small Back Room* and *Mine Own Executioner*. The fact that the book was written in language more redolent of the 1940s than the fifteenth century in which the events described were principally set contributed an additional layer of oddness.

Appearing in print a year after *Lord, I Was Afraid*, *The Borgia Testament* was another attempt by Balchin to sidestep critical expectations after his three great triumphs of the mid-1940s

The Borgia Testament (1948)

The story begins in 1504. Cesare Borgia has been imprisoned in Rome by his long-term adversary Della Rovere, who has just been elected Pope Julius II. Unsure how much time he has before his usefulness to the new Pontiff is exhausted and he is thus disposed of, Cesare begins to write his memoirs.

As a young man, Cesare is groomed for a life as a churchman and is made Bishop of Valencia on the same day in 1492 on which his father, Rodrigo, is elected Pope. But Cesare's unsuitability for a life clothed in clerical vestments soon becomes apparent and he is thus defrocked.

Following the murder of his brother Giovanni (a crime for which he denies responsibility), Cesare travels to France. Here he succeeds in raising an army and then initiates his grand plan to create a unified Italy, which involves forging alliances with rival powers, particularly the French, conducting military campaigns and murdering anyone who attempts to get in his way.

Cesare has made good progress in conquering the Romagna region of northern Italy and bringing it under papal control when he falls ill and is confined to bed for a lengthy period, during which time his father passes away. Della Rovere is elected Pope, Cesare is arrested and the story is brought full circle. An epilogue then tells how the prisoner is released from his confinement by Della Rovere, arrested by the Spanish and shipped to Spain, imprisoned in a fortress from which he escapes three years later and is then murdered by the French.

but, like its predecessor, probably had the undesired effect of discombobulating a substantial proportion of his audience. Unlike *Lord, I Was Afraid*, *The Borgia Testament* is written in the form of a straightforward (predominantly linear) narrative and does not present such a forbidding intellectual challenge to potential readers. But it is still very different from Balchin's fine trio of war novels, and George Malcolm Thomson[32] in the *Evening Standard* gave a very fair impression of what it is like to read when he described it as 'a novel that compels respect and exacts fatigue'. One or two other critics noted that, for all its descriptions of fighting, political machinations and bloodshed, the book possessed a deadening, stodgy quality. However, the writing is at least consistently embroidered with Balchin's characteristic dry wit. Approached more as gentle education than literary entertainment, *The Borgia Testament* is a complex and subtle novel that rewards the discerning reader, even if it does offer up its treasures at a leisurely pace.

The book attracted much the same range of muted responses from Britain's literary critics as had *Lord, I Was Afraid*. Julian Symons[33] in the *Manchester Evening News* was perhaps its most passionate advocate. Symons branded *The Borgia Testament* 'very remarkable' and felt that Balchin's talents had 'never been more finely displayed'. The verdict of Peter Quennell[34] in the *Daily Mail* was that *The Borgia Testament* was 'an extremely fascinating narrative' and 'undoubtedly one of the most interesting historical novels to emerge since Robert Graves, who shares Balchin's gift of making historical personages credible and understandable, began his 'Claudius' series'.

Balchin's use of what L. P. Hartley[35] in *Time and Tide* referred to as 'a racy modern idiom' in order to recount his story left him vulnerable to critical attack. Anthony Powell[36] in *The Times Literary Supplement* was especially scathing, accusing Balchin's version of Cesare Borgia of being possessed of 'a modesty and breadth of mind which would be surprising in a contemporary politician' and adding that there was no escaping the fact that Balchin had imposed on him 'a personality that at moments suggests an intelligent Civil servant expounding world affairs in a railway carriage'.

Only a small handful of reviewers picked up on the fact that what Balchin had written was not an exciting adventure story or an invigorating historical novel but a psychological case study of the development of a megalomaniac over a prolonged period. This was an approach that the author would adopt again, seven years later, when he recorded the life of another disturbed individual, the neurotic kleptomaniac Jason Pellew, over a similar time span in his novel *The Fall of the Sparrow*. Hartley[37] did understand that Balchin's 'chief interest in re-telling the story is psychological and philosophical', and Elizabeth Bowen[38] in the *Tatler and Bystander* observed that 'what Mr. Balchin has been concerned to do, and has done, is to open a door straight into the inside room of Cesare Borgia's mentality'.

In his exhaustive and thought-provoking analysis of Balchin's novels,[39] Clive James drew parallels between the characters that Balchin wrote about during his 'experimental period' of the late 1940s and their creator's personal situation. With specific reference to *The Borgia Testament*, he considered that Balchin's fascination with Cesare Borgia was indicative of the author's own mindset at the time and that he had introduced 'a sharp personal focus' into his fiction by writing the book. He referred to this passage from the closing pages, in which Cesare declares that:

> ...if I haven't been reasonable enough myself, I have expected too much reason from the men of my day. I could never believe that my father was right, and that these barbaric, superstitious, shadowy legends [i.e. the mysteries associated with the Roman Catholic faith] have a real meaning and value for them.

In James's view, 'It is not just permissible but obligatory, I think, to assume that in such passages Balchin is looking into himself, and half-perceiving that his own rationality might be a limitation'. It was his belief that Balchin, via the agency of characters such as Bill Sarratt, Felix Milne, Cesare Borgia and many others in his later novels, was continually questioning whether his practical, logical persona was debarring him from experiencing 'the full possibilities of emotion' and that 'he can't put this question in a way that will oblige him to try answering it'. It is impossible to take issue with another of James's contentions, namely the fact that 'Cesare's unsentimental appreciation of what needed to be *done* in given circumstances was exactly the power which Balchin had good reason to think he possessed to an unusual degree' and which he had repeatedly demonstrated with aplomb during his recently terminated wartime work for the army.

Cesare Borgia was missing from the contents list of *The Anatomy of Villainy*, a series of thirteen essays about famous villains, when it was published in November 1950. This volume, which one can view in some ways as a more wide-ranging factual counterpoint to *The Borgia Testament*, holds the unique distinction of being the only example of a serious work of book-length non-fiction within the Balchin canon (although *Income and Outcome. A Study of Personal Finance* is non-fictional, it is not wholly serious). Six weeks after publication, *The Anatomy of Villainy* was reviewed by Penelope Houston[40] in the *Sunday Times*. Better known today as a film critic (she reviewed the Balchin-scripted *Suspect* in 1960), Houston helpfully summarized the content of Balchin's book:

> He calls thirteen curiously assorted prisoners to the bar, examines them in brief sketches, finds, or fails to find, extenuating circumstances, and pronounces sentence.

Although Houston conceded that 'The rogues gallery is shrewdly and readably presented', in her opinion *The Anatomy of Villainy* comprised 'a piece of book-making rather than a serious investigation'. Balchin would have been dismayed to read such a statement because this sort of 'book-making' was something he generally deplored, and he uttered a comment to this effect in 1962:

> "The dangerous thing is when you reach the stage where you say, 'I must write another book. What shall it be about?'

Book-writing, then, is just a habit—and a bad one.

I like to think that every book tries to have some particular impact, to have something definite to say."[41]

Balchin's cast of villains in *The Anatomy of Villainy* is a real ragbag. Some, such as Richard III, Guy Fawkes, Rasputin and Judas Iscariot, are very well known. Others, including Richard Parker (instigator of a naval mutiny in 1797), Titus Oates (disseminator of the Popish Plot of 1678 and described here by Balchin as 'completely unprincipled, a bare-faced liar and a heartless rogue') and Matthew Hopkins (the seventeenth century Witchfinder General) are more obscure, confirming Balchin's statement in his Introduction that 'this is a book for those whose interest in history exceeds their knowledge of it'. In the case of Daniel Dunglas Home, a Victorian medium accused of charlatanism and whose antics seem to have given Balchin some ideas for his short story 'Mrs Sludge' in *Last Recollections of My Uncle Charles*, the label 'villain' seems scarcely appropriate, as the author himself readily admitted in the book.

The original hardback edition of *The Anatomy of Villainy* is unattractively presented: Michael Ayrton created a series of illustrations for it but they were not used, and the publishers were obliged to rely instead on just a handful of photographs and line drawings to break up the lengthy blocks of text. The book must have presented a stern challenge to the Marketing Department at Collins and a more engaging and accessible structure might have boosted sales. There are a few good jokes scattered amongst these pages and an occasional flash of the familiar Balchin style, but on the whole the book lacks the wit, liveliness and page-turning readability that one associates with his better novels and makes for a rather dry and intimidating read. It is among the least appealing of all his many works and, despite the author's noble aspiration, does not make a very deep impact on the reader. This is perhaps no surprise given that Balchin's personal life was in the process of unravelling as he was writing the book, and when in 1952 he referred to the fact that he had 'done some poorish work'[42] over the course of the previous three years, *The Anatomy of Villainy* may have been one of the projects he had in mind.

Pamela Hansford Johnson[43] prefaced her review of *The Borgia Testament* for *John o'London's Weekly* by stating that 'Mr. Nigel Balchin is still in his experimental period' but he was also in the midst of his 'historical period'. In addition to the historical themes of *The Borgia Testament* and *The Anatomy of Villainy*, 1947's *Lord, I Was Afraid* had featured a modern reworking of the Battle of Lake Regillus. Much later in his career, Balchin authored an essay for the true-crime compendium *Fatal Fascination*[44] that drew on his long-standing love of the Norse sagas—a subject that he spoke about on both radio and television—and he also supplied a preface to Joan Haslip's book *Lucrezia Borgia. A Study*.[45]

There are thus strong historical threads running through Balchin's bibliography, of which *The Borgia Testament* is undoubtedly the most important and *The Anatomy of Villainy* the least important. Speaking to Allen on BBC radio in 1955, Balchin said that 'I love writing non-fiction but nobody will ever let me',[46] the reason being presumably that his publishers were well aware that it didn't sell. With *The Borgia Testament*, Balchin had the opportunity to write vividly about a non-fiction subject, skilfully disguise his work as a novel and still be assured of doing good business (40,000 copies of the hardback were shifted according to James's figures[47]). *The Anatomy of Villainy*, by contrast, appeared without any fanfare whatsoever and proceeded to sell no more than about 4,000 copies in hardback. With the exception of his contribution to *Fatal Fascination*, the 1950 experiment of writing long essay-style works of non-fiction was not to be repeated and, as far as books were concerned, nothing but fiction would issue from Balchin's study for the rest of his career.

14

Mr. Balchin's Formula:
Too Much the Mixture as Before?

> Mr. Balchin, after adventures into history and new
> techniques, has returned to his formula: a struggle of
> conscience, based upon some psychological insecurity, solved
> by a "chase" in the wisest cinematic tradition. It is a good
> formula, and so long as it enables this writer to produce
> novels of such wonderful readability, there is no reason why
> anyone should ask more of him.
>
> – Pamela Hansford Johnson[1]

Towards the end of an intense period of writing activity whilst he
was living at Leigh Barton in Kent, *A Sort of Traitors*, Balchin's
third work of fiction in less than two years, was published on
20 June 1949 and this 'scientific' novel represented a return
to the type of material with which he had made his name. In
terms of books completed, he was now roughly halfway through
his novel-writing career and, appropriately enough, *A Sort of
Traitors* is very much the median Balchin novel in terms of
quality. It is a tempting 'pick-and-mix' selection of some of his
greatest attributes as a novelist, but although he bolted it together
expertly from an array of tantalizing component parts it is
simply a collection of brilliant scenes suspended in a substandard
narrative and therefore remains a frustrating enigma.

The episodic structure of *A Sort of Traitors* did suit Balchin
though: he had been polishing this facet of his fiction since
Darkness Falls from the Air and it gleams brightly both here and
in the slightly later *Sundry Creditors*, which represents the zenith
of this approach. Another link with *Sundry Creditors* concerns
the novel's point of view. Balchin had written novels in the

A Sort of Traitors (1949)

The novel is set in the Haughton Laboratory, a biological research facility in central London, and when it opens Professor Sewell, the leader of the research team, is on the verge of announcing some important results concerning the control of epidemics. But before he is able to do so, the laboratory is advised by the government not to publish its work in case it is used by foreign powers for nefarious, non-altruistic means, i.e. as the basis of a biological weapon. Sewell is outraged by the decision, but in the eyes of one of his juniors—young, naive, idealistic Bob Marriott—does little to rectify the situation.

Marriott's colleague Lucy Byrne acts as live-in carer for a man called Ivor Gates, an embittered double-amputee whose arms were blown off during the war. Marriott starts going out with Lucy and through her meets Ivor. The trio discuss the fact that the Haughton is being gagged and prevented from publishing its research. Ivor then introduces Marriott to an acquaintance of his, Bill Brown, who spins a yarn about a body called the International Scientific Exchange that "exists for the private exchange of information between scientists" and might therefore be willing to publish the work clandestinely.

The Haughton staff have been placed under surveillance by MI5, whose employee Mr Prince identifies Ivor as a security risk. When Prince attempts to interview Ivor he discovers that he has committed suicide, having by his own assertion 'scuppered' Marriott by introducing him to Brown, who in turn is well known to MI5. Marriott removes the research paper from the laboratory, intending to give it to Brown. But the security forces are now hot on his trail...

third person before: in addition to his first three books, *Mine Own Executioner* was also constructed in that way. But with *A Sort of Traitors* he broke away from his previous style. Written throughout in the third person, the perspectives of a number of different characters are presented, with the young biologist Bob Marriott being the most prominent figure. The novel loses its focus in the absence of a single strong central character; *Sundry Creditors* suffers from the same defect.

By way of compensation for the lack of a compelling protagonist, *A Sort of Traitors* does contain, in the shape of the bumbling, world-weary MI5 agent Mr Prince, one of Balchin's best-drawn minor characters:

> "Now, as you both know, some time back we were told to keep an eye on the Haughton Laboratory. It was one of these 'no trouble' jobs. We weren't to *do* anything, of course. We were just to see that nothing leaked from a place which wasn't under proper security control, which was part of another building, which might be open all hours of the day and night—and so on. Just one of those little jobs that make us go away and shoot ourselves."

In spite of its limitations, *A Sort of Traitors* is the most beautifully written of all Balchin's novels. It is also one of the funniest books that he wrote. The humour is resolutely dry and mocking throughout but does not have quite the same satiric intention as it did in the wartime novels: the comedy is still dark, but not as black as before.

In his 1974 article on Balchin, Clive James[2] stated that *A Sort of Traitors* was originally due to be published in 1945, before the actual appearance of *Mine Own Executioner*. If this is correct—and when he was researching his article, James had access to Collins material which is unfortunately no longer available—then there would be a certain logic behind this order of publication. *Darkness Falls from the Air*, *The Small Back Room* and *A Sort of Traitors* would have formed quite a coherent wartime trilogy looking at the effects of the conflict on three different groups of workers of a scientific or administrative bent: the officials of a government ministry, weapons scientists and biological research workers, respectively. It is not known why *A Sort of Traitors* was not published until the summer of 1949.

As was the case with *Mine Own Executioner*, the technical material that the author deployed in *A Sort of Traitors* was not accumulated during his day-to-day working life: Balchin had no more experience of biological research laboratories than he did psychoanalysts' consulting rooms. However, the descriptions of the scientific routines contained in *A Sort of Traitors* are completely authentic, and J. D. Scott[3] in the *New Statesman and Nation* was impressed with the author's 'understanding of scientific research, with its excitement, its repetitive tedium, and its awful hours of low grade clerical work'. This is yet more evidence of Balchin's extraordinary ability to appear far more knowledgeable about scientific and technical matters than he actually was (*The Aircraft Builders* constituting just one example). When she reviewed *A Sort of Traitors* in the *Daily Telegraph*, Pamela Hansford Johnson[4] referred to 'Mr. Balchin's own brand of ubiquitous authority' and marvelled at his apparent omniscience: 'one feels there is nothing he doesn't know about, no back room into which he has not been admitted'.

Notices for *A Sort of Traitors*, most of them favourable, started to appear in the second half of June. P. H. Newby[5] in the *Listener* supplied a beguiling image to illustrate the impression that Balchin's prose technique had made on him:

...he has a brisk confidence in the telling of the story that is very stimulating; between each chapter one feels one really ought to be taking sharp trots round the garden.

For Cyril Ray[6] (*Sunday Chronicle*) the truth to nature of Balchin's work was its standout quality:

[*A Sort of Traitors*] is peopled by real men and women, who love and work and talk more convincingly than the creations of almost any other living novelist. No English writer since

Kipling has had such a gift for making the technicalities of a job fascinatingly plausible, its jargon so readable.

For the second Balchin novel in succession, Anthony Powell[7] wrote a sniffy review for *The Times Literary Supplement*. Having dismantled *The Borgia Testament*, he opined this time that the new book, despite resembling *The Small Back Room*, 'does not carry the same degree of conviction'. And in the *Sketch*, Rupert Croft-Cooke,[8] in the course of one of the most negative reviews of a Balchin book ever printed, took aim at the novelist's reputation:

> I have never been able to see in Mr. Balchin much more than a highly competent novelist whose themes combine inner conflict in the minds of his characters with somewhat melodramatic events in their lives.

Croft-Cooke also accused Balchin of writing with cinematic adaptation in mind: 'it is all rather like a good film—and no doubt it will make one'.

C. P. Snow[9] in the *Sunday Times* found much in Balchin's novel that pleased him, characterizing it as 'a very good story, told with streamlined efficiency'. However, he articulated the concern that Balchin was in grave danger of repeating himself: 'It begins to look as though his vein despite the brilliant use he has made of it, is a shallow one'. On this point, Hansford Johnson[10] agreed with her husband-to-be (she married Snow a year later). She headlined her review 'Mr. Balchin's Formula' and observed that the author of *A Sort of Traitors* 'tells a story gloriously, and if it is usually the same story, it remains a good one'. K. John[11] in the *Illustrated London News* also wondered whether Balchin was now guilty of writing to order, although this proviso did not prevent the book critic from warmly extolling the virtues of *A Sort of Traitors*:

> Too much the mixture as before? I can't deny it, or deny that all these embittered cripples are rather much of a good

thing. But what a mixture! It has so much wit, brilliance, penetration and sheer enjoyableness that I should go on reading it for ever, if it went on for ever.

Only a month after *A Sort of Traitors* was published, a screen version was due to go into production at Shepperton Studios.[12] Like *Mine Own Executioner* before it, the film was to be made under the London Films banner, with Anthony Kimmins as director. In the starring role, Richard Attenborough had been lined up to play Marriott. However, the shoot was cancelled, possibly because Attenborough, who was under contract to the Boulting brothers, was required instead for one of their projects. It was to be another eleven years until the movie (retitled *Suspect*) was released into British cinemas as a superior-quality supporting feature and so *A Sort of Traitors* did make a good film, eventually.

*

At about the same time that he was correcting the galley proofs of *A Sort of Traitors*, Balchin, after penning several film scripts of his own in the previous couple of years, had the opportunity to settle back in a padded cinema seat and admire the efforts of a fellow screenwriter, in this case the distinguished Hungarian Emeric Pressburger, who had written the script for the second of Balchin's novels to be adapted for the screen. It is a tribute to the excellence of Balchin's dialogue—a feature of his writing that secured him scriptwriting work off and on over a fifteen-year period—that Pressburger lifted large chunks of it from the book, and used them in the film either verbatim or with only very minor amendments.

The Small Back Room is by far the best film ever to have been produced from a Balchin source, and much of the credit for this triumph must be given to Michael Powell in recognition of the brilliance of his direction. As well as being a long-standing fan of Balchin's writing in general ('I thought that Nigel Balchin was one of the best writers, and certainly one of the best stylists, to come out of the war years'[13]), the director happened to be especially fond of *The Small Back Room*. Despite Alexander

Korda[14] pestering him to remake *The Scarlet Pimpernel* with David Niven ('a project which filled me with boredom'[15]), Powell chose instead to concentrate his creative energies on translating Balchin's finest hour as a novelist into moving pictures. The resultant film, whilst not quite a classic, is continuously absorbing and almost every scene benefits from a light dusting of Powell magic, which lifts it above the level of the humdrum and differentiates it from the plainer, more workmanlike *Mine Own Executioner*, which was directed by a skilled craftsman (Anthony Kimmins) as opposed to an acclaimed auteur.

The first sequence to be filmed for *The Small Back Room*, in the spring of 1948, was the unpicking of the bomb. The evocative setting that Powell chose for this was Chesil Bank in Dorset, which is overlooked by St Catherine's Chapel, the place where Sammy Rice first meets Colonel Strang in the movie version. According to the film's male lead, David Farrar, 'It was a long and difficult sequence, most of it shot at about 5 am in early March with, as I remember, a biting east wind coming in off the sea'.[16] Powell had high hopes for this dramatic passage, wishing it to become, in time, a cinematic pièce de résistance to rival the famous Odessa Steps sequence in *The Battleship Potemkin*. The relative obscurity of *The Small Back Room* prevented his ambition from being realized, but he had succeeded in making a compelling and heart-stopping piece of cinema nonetheless. If one includes the preliminary scene in which Rice listens to the transcript of Captain Stuart's notes, read to him by Renée Asherson's A.T.S. girl, the entire sequence lasts approximately seventeen minutes. For Powell, this temporal measure was 'the longest time that an audience can hold its breath'.[17]

The way in which the bomb disposal sequence was presented on film led to the occurrence of two noteworthy deviations from the novel during the movie's final minutes. The first of these is that Rice manages to wrench the second cap off the booby-trap bomb himself, rather than relying on Strang to loosen it for him. The legacy of this change is that Rice's status is automatically upgraded from that of heroic failure to outright hero, as reflected in the film's catchpenny American title *Hour of*

Glory. Secondly, in its closing scenes, *The Small Back Room* parts company with the book entirely. On his return to London from Dorset, Rice is summoned to the War Office, where Colonel Holland offers him a post heading a new army research section, which he promptly accepts. Rice is then reunited with Susan, who had walked out on him earlier. She hugs her returned hero, offers him a (non-prescription) painkiller for his phantom foot—"Have a drink Sammy!"—and as stirring music swells in the background we are led to believe that the couple are now happily reconciled. This is a significant departure from the characteristically unresolved ending that Balchin had written for his novel. In the film, all the loose ends left dangling in the book are neatly plaited together: Rice successfully defuses the bomb on his own, gets the girl and lands himself a new job into the bargain. Powell and Pressburger's decision to graft a happy ending onto their movie was apparently approved of by Balchin, as mentioned by Paul Dehn[18] in his *Sunday Chronicle* review of *The Small Back Room*: 'Mr. Balchin, who chose the book's ending, has himself chosen the film's'.

With the possible exception of the direction, the greatest strength of *The Small Back Room* is the excellence of its cast, and this is another area in which the film surpasses *Mine Own Executioner*. Powell selected his actors extremely carefully ('I hand-picked every man on the squad'[19]) and it paid handsome dividends. Jack Hawkins conveys quite a lot of the odiousness and self-seeking nature required of him as Rice's direct superior Waring, and Powell considered that the role of Stuart was 'brilliantly, and nervously, played by Michael Gough'. Leslie Banks gives a memorable performance as Holland, managing to imbue the character with the requisite layer of blimpishness but also hinting successfully at the sound professional soldier residing just beneath the blustering facade. There is a fine array of cameos, among them Anthony Bushell as Strang, the army officer whose outwardly conventional military bearing conceals a core of decency and compassion; Milton Rosmer as the vague, distracted 'Grand Old Man of Science' Professor Mair; and Cyril Cusack, in a superb early screen performance, as the stammering, careworn fuse expert Corporal Taylor, a man who is driven halfway round the bend because his foreign wife disports herself like a tart. Bryan Forbes made his feature film debut as 'The Dying Gunner' (and later wrote about the experience of working with Powell warmly and hilariously in his memoirs[20]) and Patrick Macnee also had a non-speaking role during the Reeves Gun conference. In his 'dark and heavy way', as M. T. McGregor[21] in *Time and Tide* put it, Farrar is adequate as Rice although he is too virile and handsome to be truly convincing in the scenes in which he is called upon to be pathetic.

But the real star of the film is undoubtedly Kathleen Byron, reunited with Farrar having played opposite him in 1947's *Black Narcissus*, which was also made by Powell and Pressburger. Byron performs wonders as Susan, despite working from what amounted to virtually a blank canvas. Speaking about the role, she said that 'I enjoyed playing that un-neurotic character because I thought she had a nice lot of strength and quality'.[22] Using little more than subtle changes in her facial expression and tone of voice, she invests Susan with a realism and solidity that is not apparent on the printed page.

The Small Back Room opened in London on 21 February 1949. It attracted widespread critical acclaim, the reviews being almost as ecstatic as those for *Mine Own Executioner* at the end of 1947. Virginia Graham[23] in the *Spectator* was one of the most ardent admirers of the picture, praising it for possessing 'humour, courage, pathos, suspense and a lively understanding of the English character'. Writing in the *New Statesman and Nation*, William Whitebait[24] adjudicated that *The Small Back Room* 'is a better novel than *Mine Own Executioner*, and it has made a better film', a notable accolade from a critic who had heaped fulsome praise on the earlier movie.

It was the performances in *The Small Back Room* that brought forth the greatest volume of compliments from the film critics' typewriters, Freda Bruce Lockhart[25] in the *Tatler and Bystander* remarking that Powell and Pressburger's film was 'the best-acted British picture I can remember'. Byron's impersonation of Susan found widespread favour: A. E. Wilson[26] in the *Star* applauded her 'delicate and understanding performance' and Bruce Lockhart observed that she functioned as 'a nice next-best' to the incomparable Celia Johnson.

The small amount of critical comment that the film attracted mostly centred on the expressionistic hallucination sequence in which Farrar is menaced by a teetering over-sized whisky bottle and tormented by a rapidly multiplying array of ticking clocks. This infamous scene generated almost unanimous scorn from the movie critics, being variously described as 'hideous', 'exasperating', 'regrettable', 'inexcusable' and 'exaggerated to the point of absurdity'.[27]

The Small Back Room did not do very good business for Korda and London Films. Powell said that his movie was 'a failure'[28], although, considered purely in terms of its earning power, that assessment is not strictly accurate. The film grossed a modest £129,732,[29] which was roughly average for a British film of the period but almost £30,000 less than the inferior *Mine Own Executioner* had taken in the previous year. Powell, however, in his customarily forthright way, was adamant that *The Small Back Room* had been badly received by British moviegoers:

The public stayed away in droves. They refused to accept that it was a love story. It was a war film. And war films were out—O-U-T.[30]

Released into cinemas less than four years after the cessation of hostilities, *The Small Back Room*, with its eerie backdrop of wartime London, was anathema to an audience that had seen enough of wartime London to last a lifetime. Like *Fame is the Spur* before it, the film suffered at the box office because it was too serious and gloomy and lacked appeal to a public seeking something more straightforwardly enjoyable (Ealing Studios alone chalked up three financial triumphs in the same year that *The Small Back Room* was released with lighter non-war-related fare in the shape of *Whisky Galore, Passport to Pimlico* and *Kind Hearts and Coronets*). Powell and Pressburger's picture does however remain one of the most interesting and best-made British movies of the late 1940s and was deservedly nominated for a 1950 British Film Academy award as 'Best British Film', although it lost out in the face of stiff competition from the likes of *The Third Man* (the winner) and the Ealing triumvirate detailed above.

While Powell was shooting his famous bomb disposal sequence in Dorset, a radio version of Balchin's most celebrated book was being rehearsed. The BBC Third Programme transmitted *The Small Back Room* (the first of the author's novels to be adapted for radio) in April 1948, roughly eighteen months after the same station had binned a version of *Mine Own Executioner* following a complaint from its author. This launched a flotilla of BBC radio and television adaptations of Balchin's fiction—but mostly of *The Small Back Room* and *Mine Own Executioner*—that persisted up to and beyond his death.[31]

Two of the most well-received television adaptations were shown on the BBC in 1959. Both were scripted by Balchin's son-in-law, John Hopkins, who was married at the time to the novelist's eldest daughter, Prudence, and was soon to receive recognition as a screenwriter by virtue of his work on the popular BBC police series *Z-Cars*.

The first of Hopkins's scripts to reach the small screen was *The Small Back Room* in April. Starring John Gregson ('unfaultably right' in the view of the *Daily Telegraph*'s 'K. Y.'[32]) as Rice, this BBC version was described as 'exemplary' by an unnamed reviewer[33] in *The Times*. Maurice Richardson[34] in the *Observer* agreed, stating that the book used for the adaptation ('one of the most obsessively readable novels of the past twenty-five years') had triumphantly survived its transition into the visual medium: 'I could not have looked away'.

The Hopkins version of *Mine Own Executioner* was broadcast in late summer. Writing again in the *Daily Telegraph*, 'K. Y.'[35] cast aspersions on Balchin's psychiatric knowledge—'his predigested Freud does scant justice to the subtlety and integrity of that great man. Or to psychiatry in general'—but did admit that the play was 'unflaggingly entertaining'. In another part of Fleet Street, an anonymous contributor[36] to *The Times* chose to treat the fourteen-year-old *Mine Own Executioner* as something of a museum piece ('it is beginning to gather dust'), but applauded 'a beautifully composed study by Mr. Michael Gwynn [as Felix Milne] of the characteristic Balchin hero— a good, intelligent man despairingly obsessed by one private failing'. The critic supplied a pithy summary of a key feature of Balchin's work during the 1940s:

> The appeal of Mr. Nigel Balchin's novels—which is considerable—depends largely on their accurate reflection of their decade. No one was quite so expert as Mr. Balchin in catching the uprooted and jittery attitudes of the not-so-young generation just after the war, and packaging them into a sleek narrative skin.

Other 1950s BBC versions of Balchin stories included a radio broadcast of *A Sort of Traitors* and both radio and television adaptations of *A Way Through the Wood* (in the guise of Ronald Millar's *Waiting for Gillian*). In 1960, Hopkins adapted the first of his father-in-law's great novels, *Darkness Falls from the Air*, with a view to it being presented as a Sunday night television play the following year, but the work never made it onto the air. It is astonishing to think that a book as seemingly telegenic as *Darkness Falls from the Air* has never made the transition even to *radio*, let alone television. Given British television's ongoing love affair with dramas set during World War Two, this seems like one high-class serial that will have to be made eventually.

*

Balchin's successes as a screenwriter, together with his continuing fame as a novelist and broadcaster, led to a series of speaking engagements in the late 1940s. He turned down several of the opportunities presented to him, sometimes because he was hard at work crafting his latest novel or screenplay, but did address the Writers' Circle Summer School held at Swanwick, Derbyshire in August 1949 and, two months later, gave a talk on the subject of 'The Novel and the Film' at the Cheltenham Festival of

Contemporary Literature. This was a busy period for Balchin's voice because, in the week after he had appeared at Cheltenham, he spoke to a club in Cambridge, the Heretics Society, that was devoted to discussion of religious matters and 'provided a forum for many of the advanced thinkers of the day'.[37] Before addressing the students, Balchin looked in on his old tutor Paul Vellacott, who had by this time ascended to the position of Master of Peterhouse. No doubt Vellacott would have been impressed by the achievements notched up by his former charge since he had left Cambridge, and pleased that the prediction he had issued about Balchin's future almost exactly twenty years previously ('I think he is a man who will go a long way'[38]) had now been emphatically fulfilled.

Balchin's fame had also spread across the Atlantic.[39] On 1 September he was sent an invitation to partake of a midday glass of sherry in London. His invitee was Blanche Knopf, a colourful and formidable woman who, in partnership with her husband, ran the long-established American publishing firm of Alfred A. Knopf, Inc. Put in charge of the European side of the business at the end of World War Two, Mrs Knopf travelled frequently to the continent both to meet with her existing authors and to woo potential new clients. During her 1949 European trip she was tipped off by Carol Brandt, then International Story Editor of MGM but later to become a leading New York literary agent, that Balchin was due to leave his American publishers Houghton Mifflin—he had been with them since the publication in the USA of his second book, *How to Run a Bassoon Factory*, in 1936—after the stateside publication of *The Borgia Testament*. In Brandt's opinion, Balchin had a brilliant future ahead of him.

The meeting between Balchin and his prospective new American publisher took place on 6 September, and Blanche wrote a letter to her husband at their New York office reporting on it the next day. She was clearly impressed by what she had seen of Balchin, describing him as 'about as fine a character as I have met over here' and adding that 'he seems everything in the way of a person that we should have on our list'. However, when she had flourished a contract and asked Balchin to sign up with

Alfred A. Knopf, Inc. he had demurred, proffering the excuse that he ought to check with his American agent before agreeing to anything. After they had exchanged words with the writer's British and American agents (David Higham and Mike Watkins, respectively), the two Knopfs concluded that skulduggery was afoot and that Balchin did not in fact intend to leave Houghton Mifflin in the near future. Alfred confessed that 'I don't like the smell of any part of this situation' and Blanche responded in kind ('Dirty work going on'). Alfred had been led to believe by Watkins that Balchin's prevarication when confronted by the Knopf contract did not in fact stem from his being 'an honourable man' but was merely his way of 'evading any commitment to you at all'. The Knopfs were unwilling to precipitate a bidding war for the author's services and withdrew from the contest at this point, Blanche remarking that 'In the circumstances I will have nothing to do with BALCHIN. If he ever does leave Houghton Mifflin I expect to have first offer of his book.' Balchin remained with Houghton Mifflin for at least another five years, and Blanche's original assessment of her quarry's character was perhaps tainted by her attempt to conduct business with him.

Two codicils should be appended to this transatlantic squabble. Firstly, Balchin told Blanche that his next novel, which he planned to finish within a year, would be entitled *Mind of Nicholas Hurst*. Like *A Way Through the Wood*, which instead became Balchin's next work of fiction when it was published in 1951, the 'Nicholas Hurst' project was one that adopted an array of guises before eventually being abandoned, unpublished, by its creator in the mid-1960s (see Chapter 22 for more details). Secondly, Balchin was probably not trying to be difficult or underhand when he refused to sign on the dotted line. It may just have been that so much traumatic upheaval was taking place in his private life in September 1949 that his head was in a whirl and he was therefore unable to give his full attention to what may have appeared to him to be comparatively trivial business matters. Set against the collapse of his fifteen-year marriage, they were.

1. Balchin in 1952, when he was close to the peak of his post-war fame.

2. Balchin pictured as an infant: 'Rather a splendid chap I must say – what a pity it couldn't last.'

3. Balchin as an undergraduate student at Peterhouse, Cambridge.

4. 'Down at the boats': Balchin's friend James Mason pictured as part of the Peterhouse 2 rowing eight in 1929.

5. *A 1934 newspaper advertisement for Black Magic extolling the virtue of the 'simple sophisticated black box' designed for Rowntree's by Balchin.*

6. *Balchin in army uniform during the Second World War.*

7. *Elisabeth Balchin and her four-year-old daughter Penelope in London in 1942.*

8. *In a scene reminiscent of* The Small Back Room, *Balchin attempts to control an ungainly piece of experimental weaponry during World War Two.*

9. Christian Darnton.

10. Michael Ayrton.

*11. Yovanka Tomich photographed aged eighteen in the late 1940s,
shortly before she first met Balchin.*

12. *In the film of* Mine Own Executioner, *Burgess Meredith (as Felix Milne) prepares to inject Kieron Moore (Adam Lucian) with a hypnotic drug that will unlock Lucian's repressed memories of his experiences in the Far East during World War Two.*

13. *David Farrar (as Sammy Rice) struggles to remove the crucial second cap from the bomb in Powell and Pressburger's superb film adaptation of* The Small Back Room.

14. Clifton Webb (right) as Ewen Montagu and Robert Flemyng bandy words from Balchin's BAFTA-winning screenplay for The Man Who Never Was.

15. Emily Watson and Tom Wilkinson in a scene from Separate Lies, *the most recent film to have been made from a Balchin novel* (A Way Through the Wood).

16. *The weary scriptwriter: Balchin crossing the USA by train on film company business in the mid-1950s.*

17. *Balchin with son Charles in Italy towards the end of the 1950s.*

18. *In the last few years of his life, Balchin generally sported a beard: 'with a face like mine almost any change is an improvement'.*

15

Marital Discord 2: 'People Do What They Want To'

> I don't know how to be good. I don't know how to be kind. I
> don't know how to help the people I love. I only know that it
> is far harder & more complicated than I once believed.
> — Nigel Balchin[1]

At first glance, the sentences above may resemble the sort of
self-pitying words that Balchin was in the habit of putting into
the mouths of one of his deeply troubled fictional characters,
a Sammy Rice or Ivor Gates or Jason Pellew perhaps. But they
are not. These words were written by Nigel Balchin *about*
Nigel Balchin. Over the course of the preceding few years his
personal situation had become as convoluted and distressing
as that of any of his novelistic creations. So on a summer's day
in 1952, Balchin sat down at his desk to perform an audit of
his professional and personal lives in an attempt to 'clarify my
mind about where I go from here'. How had he ended up in such
a trough of despondency? To find the answer to that question
one needs to rewind the Balchin story a few years to the end of
the 1940s…

*

The artist Michael Ayrton had been a member of the Savile Club
since turning twenty-one in February 1942.[2] Balchin became
a Savilian in October 1945 and at some point thereafter the
paths of the two men crossed within the walls of the Club, with
the most important meeting probably taking place towards the
end of 1947. On that occasion, Ayrton upbraided Balchin for
having had the temerity to misquote Thomas Nashe's poem 'In
Time of Pestilence' in the epigraph (and title) that Balchin had

chosen for his novel *Darkness Falls from the Air*. In Balchin's version, the epigraph ran:

> Darkness falls from the air,
> Queens have died young and fair,
> Dust hath closed Helen's eye...

When she reviewed the novel in 1942, Pamela Hansford Johnson[3] explained the error:

> Mr. Balchin doubtless knows that it was brightness, and not darkness, that fell from the air when queens died young and fair; but he should have noted the fact.

Balchin did not note the fact in the book[4] but he knew what he was doing. Instead of absentmindedly misquoting Nashe (as in fact, in precisely the same way, Stephen Dedalus does in James Joyce's *A Portrait of the Artist as a Young Man*) he had deliberately amended the first word of the extract to suit his own purpose. Despite the ear-bashing that the author of *Darkness Falls from the Air* received that night at the Savile Club, Balchin and Ayrton were drawn together by a mutual love of English literature, among many other things, and a long-lasting friendship had begun.

The wide-ranging erudition of the polymathic and largely self-educated Ayrton—he had left school at the age of fourteen after sleeping with the French mistress—was displayed in the 1940s both in public forums such as the BBC's *Brains Trust* and in the more intimate setting of the Savile Club. As part of a biographical sketch of his friend, the publisher and art critic Tom Rosenthal provided an exhaustive list of Ayrton's areas of professional expertise, which exceeded even those of Balchin:

> For more than three decades Ayrton practised as a painter, sculptor, draughtsman, engraver, portraitist, stage designer, book illustrator, novelist, short-story writer, essayist, critic, art historian, radio and television broadcaster, and cinema and television film-maker.[5]

Ayrton's mother, Barbara Bodichon Ayrton Gould, was a suffragette who became a Labour MP in 1945 and his father, Gerald Gould, was a poet and left-wing journalist who reviewed Balchin's novel *Lightbody on Liberty* in favourable terms for the *Observer* less than six weeks before his death in 1936. It was Gould who, relieved that his son had displayed hetero- and not homosexual tendencies at his public school, had removed him from the educational system. Ayrton cut an imposing and distinctive figure and can hardly have failed to make a strong impression on Balchin:

> ...his handsome head with long, straight, swept-back hair and full beard, the powerful torso of the sculptor, and the mellifluous voice of a born teacher and conversationalist were compellingly attractive.

The enjoyment that both men derived from their initial discussion at the Savile led to further contact, and before much more time had elapsed Ayrton was invited to spend the weekend with Balchin and his wife in Kent. On that occasion, Ayrton appears to have been immediately drawn to the 'attractive, auburn-haired'[6] Elisabeth, having swiftly discerned 'both her intelligence and her passionate nature'. More meetings of the trio followed during the course of 1948 and soon three became four, Ayrton's partner Joan joining the others for social gatherings either in London or at Leigh Barton. Joan Ayrton—she changed her surname from Walsh by deed poll upon falling in love with the artist but was never married to him—had been living with Ayrton for about five years at his house in All Souls' Place in central London when the ménage à quatre began to take shape. Balchin experienced a strong attraction towards Ayrton's personable lover, who was more than ten years Balchin's junior, and his daughter Penelope Leach believes that it was her father who initiated the ménage:

> ...he started that foursome: it was Nigel who wanted Joan. He suggested the swap. It was just very bad luck for him that it went the other way.[7]

By the spring of 1949, the four-cornered relationship was starting to go 'the other way' and to resemble firstly one of the eternal triangles familiar from Balchin's fiction and then just a straight line from which the novelist had been cruelly excluded. In February, the four friends spent a blissful week in Paris, sight-seeing by day and eating, drinking and talking in the evenings. The two original partnerships had now been irreversibly shuffled. Ayrton and Elisabeth indulged their mutual love of architecture by exploring the great Parisian buildings together. Balchin revelled in the opportunity to lavish money on Joan in a way that Elisabeth had not really enjoyed, one of his expensive purchases for her being a fur coat, thus mimicking the action of Felix Milne in *Mine Own Executioner*, who buys one for his wife Patricia. Although the relationship between Balchin and Joan seems to have been of a light-hearted and frivolous nature, that between Ayrton and Elisabeth had deepened into something much more serious by the time the four of them returned from Paris. Elisabeth had fallen decisively in love with the artist, and as he was on the verge of breaking up with Joan a strong bond now united the pair. Another foreign jaunt was swiftly proposed, with Italy the intended destination, but Joan saw which way the chips were likely to fall and backed out of the arrangement at this point, preferring to stay at home in London instead of flying to Rome with her three friends.

Balchin therefore undertook to play gooseberry as he accompanied Ayrton and Elisabeth on a miniaturized 'Grand Tour' which, after their stay in Rome, also took in Florence and Venice. In Ayrton's opinion, Balchin was content for the majority of his Italian sojourn ('except for spasms, Nigel seems happy'[8]), and when the three of them arrived back in London they were joined by Joan for a weekend in Stelling Minnis. A volatile situation then rapidly deteriorated: Elisabeth and Ayrton spent a few days, sans Balchin, in Dublin. On her return, Elisabeth intercepted her husband as he returned home from one of his Rowntree's meetings and Ayrton predicted that the heart to heart would have an unhappy denouement:

E is seeing Nigel on his way back from York on Saturday afternoon and we shall see what happens. It all looks rather gloomy.

Ayrton had read the runes correctly. Joan moved out of All Souls' Place a matter of weeks after the Dublin trip; the Balchins hung on at Leigh Barton for a few more months until they had found a buyer for the house, but by mid-September they had left Kent for good and moved back to London.

Domiciled in the capital for the first time in almost four years, the Balchin family settled in at 140 Hamilton Terrace in St John's Wood which, perhaps not coincidentally, was the same street in which Ayrton had lived as a child. For Balchin, one of the principal aims of moving to London was to escape from Leigh Barton, scene of many of the events that had stretched his marriage to breaking point, and to try to make a fresh start with Elisabeth in new surroundings. But this attempt at repairing the marriage was destined to end in failure and within a short while the couple had separated and were no longer living under the same roof. Balchin went to a service flat in Dolphin Square in Pimlico while Elisabeth took the couple's three children to live with her in a maisonette in Marylebone High Street.

Shortly after the Balchins had moved to Hamilton Terrace an extra layer of complexity had been added to their already complicated domestic arrangements. Yovanka Zorana Tomich was a nineteen-year-old Yugoslav who had arrived at Balchin's house one morning as a temporary agency typist charged with the taxing duty of converting his almost illegible manuscript pages—which were often scribbled rapidly in blunt pencil— into immaculate typescript.

Born in Belgrade, Yovanka's early life had been peripatetic. Her father, Zoran, was a member of the Yugoslav Foreign Service and Yovanka and her mother, Vera, had travelled extensively throughout Europe with him during the 1930s, spending time in Sofia and Istanbul before arriving in Paris in 1940. The Tomichs left the Vichy region of France in 1942 when the Nazis were poised to invade it, travelling via Spain, Portugal and Ireland before arriving in England towards the end of that year. When the war was over, Zoran returned to Paris, scene of his last diplomatic posting, and found work there, whilst his wife and daughter stayed behind in England, Vera eking out a living as best she could.

What sort of young woman was it who turned up for the first time on Balchin's doorstep in September 1949? She was a diplomat's daughter whose family had enjoyed both status and wealth before war and the political upheavals of 1945 had turned their homeland upside down. As Yovanka explains, her paternal grandfather had served as tutor to the King of Yugoslavia and her mother's father had been an eminent doctor:

> We were a highly positioned family: my father had the position; my mother had the money. She came from landed people and they owned a tremendous amount of land in the middle of Serbia.[9]

After arriving in England, Yovanka had successfully integrated herself into post-war London society. In common with her Yugoslav girlfriends, she had turned her back on her old way of life by refusing to be groomed for marriage with one of the two brothers of the exiled King Peter of Yugoslavia living in London: 'not for us shades of past glories, we just wanted to get on in the present which, of course, our parents and their contemporaries found impossible to do'.[10]

In her own words, Yovanka was 'young, pretty and knew how to dress'. She instantly caught the eye of her employer, and also made a strong impression on his daughter Penelope:

> …Jane[11] was a phenomenon. […] I'd never seen anybody like Jane. Nobody wore clothes like that and lipstick like that and talked like that. […] Nigel must have fallen very heavily for her but he paid a hell of a price I think.[12]

Yovanka's visits to Hamilton Terrace on secretarial duty alerted Balchin to the fact that she was a potential candidate to fill the gap in his life created by his estrangement from Elisabeth.

Yovanka recalls the exact moment at which their relationship became less about business and more about romance:

> All I can remember of this period is that at some point Nigel was in bed with a cold and that I went into his bedroom to deliver the pages I had been typing and that Nigel put out a hand to take mine and that was the start of it all.[13]

The liaison between the forty-year-old writer and the nineteen-year-old typist blossomed very quickly. Only a couple of months after their first meeting the pair were already travelling in Italy together, on which occasion Balchin delighted in being able to demonstrate his knowledge of art and architecture to a companion eager to profit from his prodigiously stocked mind: 'the moment I met him I started to learn. [...] And that's what attracted me'.[14]

Further overseas trips, first to France and then again to Italy, followed during 1950. Then, in May 1951, the couple travelled to Florence, a city that was to assume increasing importance in their lives as the decade progressed. On the 15th, Yovanka's twenty-first birthday, they watched a performance of the opera Macbeth in the company of Una Troubridge, a sculptor who had lived for many years in England as the partner of the female writer Radclyffe Hall, author of lesbian classic *The Well of Loneliness*, before emigrating to Italy after Hall's death in 1943. Even in her mid-sixties, Troubridge, wearing a tuxedo and smoking a cigar, had cast admiring glances in Yovanka's direction:

> Nigel and his girl there, she *very* pretty, a lady, & only 21.[15]

Back in England, the opening months of the 1950s were a makeshift period during which the domestic arrangements of all the people—both adults and children—affected by the splintering of the Balchins' marriage were largely unsatisfactory. Perhaps only Yovanka (who, with financial help from Balchin, acquired a flat of her own in Bayswater during 1950, at which point she considered herself to be 'officially Nigel's mistress'[16]) experienced anything like contentment, aided by a phlegmatic approach to her new role:

> As Nigel's mistress, I don't always have an easy time—Nigel obviously going through an emotional period—but basically I am there for him. I was very good at being someone's mistress as I did not feel the need to make any demands and took the days as they came.

Elisabeth paid frequent visits to All Souls' Place to see Ayrton and would undoubtedly have liked to move in there with her children, but Balchin forbade it. He considered that it would not be appropriate for his offspring to be brought up in a household in which the adults were unmarried, especially as Ayrton had a long-standing reputation for enjoying a bohemian lifestyle in which alcohol flowed freely. For Leach, a piece of dissemblance in this regard that was propagated by Balchin, and faithfully adhered to by Elisabeth for a number of years, led to resentment of her father:

> I was told that the divorce court judge had said that I was not to reside in a house where my mother and stepfather-to-be were together. That this was a moral issue [...] Actually that was all a deception: it was my father who had said "You're not having her in the house." And actually I think it's true to say I never forgave him for that.[17]

Prevented from living in the same house as Ayrton, Prudence and Penelope remained with their mother in Marylebone High Street while they became 'established at a respected day school nearby'.[18] Ayrton and the Balchins thus continued to pursue their lives in interconnected ways from three separate London addresses: Dolphin Square, Marylebone High Street and All Souls' Place. This uneasy situation persisted for about six months, with the children paying occasional visits to their father, until the pieces in the human jigsaw were jumbled once more.

The catalyst for what soon began to look like a decisive

rearrangement was Prudence. Demonstrating both intelligence and precocity, Balchin's eldest daughter had passed her school certificate at the age of fourteen and then revealed a desire to become an actress, winning a place at the London Academy of Music & Dramatic Art and leaving her sister Penelope at the school in proximity to Marylebone High Street that she detested. Balchin insisted that, rather than acceding to Elisabeth's request that her middle daughter should now be allowed to live with her and Ayrton, she must instead be transferred to a boarding school in Malvern, which she proceeded to dislike even more than her previous place of education, informing Sue Lawley on BBC Radio Four's *Desert Island Discs* in 1992 that 'I really cannot tell you how much I hated it'.[19]

Opposed to her daughter's banishment, Elisabeth retaliated in spring 1950 by moving into All Souls' Place with five-year-old Freja in tow. Penelope was finally incorporated into the Ayrton household when she contracted pneumonia at school and was later sent home in order to recuperate; Balchin realized that he could not cope with an invalid and so reluctantly allowed his daughter to be cared for by Elisabeth. Even as late as June 1952, when his children had been living under Ayrton's roof for about two years, Balchin still considered that they were growing up in an environment that was less than ideal ('The lives the children now lead, & some of the influences to which they are subjected, are unsatisfactory in many ways'[20]) but by that time there was really nothing he could do about it. Balchin may have been mollified a little when he learnt, slightly later that summer, that Ayrton and Elisabeth had purchased a large property in the country and were planning to relocate before the end of the year. Bradfields, a 'ramshackle farmhouse'[21] in Toppesfield, a small village located in a very unspoilt corner of north Essex, would have been viewed by Balchin as a much more appropriate place in which to bring up children than Ayrton's home in the heart of London. But, from the point of view of the future of his children, an event that would have mollified Balchin in a much more profound way was the marriage of Elisabeth to Ayrton, which took place on 28 November 1952, just a few days before the couple moved to Bradfields.

Some insight into Balchin's mindset in the early months of 1950, as the emotional gulf between himself and Elisabeth continued to widen, is provided by a significant upheaval in his professional life. David Higham at Pearn, Pollinger & Higham had been his literary agent for close to fifteen years, from around the time of Balchin's third novel, *Lightbody on Liberty*. On 1 February Higham wrote to his American counterpart, Mike Watkins, to inform him that 'He [Balchin] has dropped a bit of a bombshell on us'.[22] Higham's client wished to terminate their lengthy association and move his business to A. D. Peters, the leading literary agent of his day, responsible for the affairs of, among many others, Evelyn Waugh, J. B. Priestley, Terence Rattigan, C. S. Forester and an emerging female novelist who was soon to become a good friend of Balchin's, Elizabeth Jane Howard. Despite the fact that Balchin and Higham had 'the friendliest of talks' about the matter, the former insisted that the time was right for a change of agent. In the view of Higham, Balchin put forward 'no very convincing reason for wanting to go' although he did say that he was a long-standing friend of Peters (in his letter to Watkins, Higham pointedly amended this designation to 'old acquaintance'; Balchin would have had more than four years in which to become acquainted with Peters at the Savile Club but it is not known how deep their friendship ran).

Similarly to the way in which Balchin had contemplated changing his American publisher less than six months earlier, his decision to leave Pearn, Pollinger & Higham may well have been influenced by his emotional condition at the time. When he wrote to Watkins, Higham drew attention to the 'complete upset of his [i.e. Balchin's] private life which has resulted in him and Elizabeth [sic] parting. It is certainly true that Nigel was personally in a considerable state and the end isn't yet.' Only a month elapsed between Balchin dropping his bombshell on Higham and moving to A. D. Peters, who assumed control of the novelist's affairs on 1 March and remained his agent until Balchin's death.

After just over a year of residing and working exclusively in London, Balchin came to the conclusion that he could write best in a rural environment, telling an American newspaper in October that 'I prefer to live (and certainly to write) in the country, in an old Sussex cottage, descending on civilization (i.e. London) for about one day a week'.[23] The new dwelling he had found himself was located in the village of Sempstead, near Robertsbridge. As its name suggests, Oast Cottage had been converted from an oast house—the writer's study being located in the former hop-drying kiln itself—and was an attractive old building with round rooms and low wooden beams, which Balchin quickly became very fond of, despite the considerable financial outlay it necessitated: 'The cottage is extremely pleasant, if a big item of expenditure'.[24] As his London base, Balchin upgraded from Dolphin Square to a top-floor apartment at 15 Portman Square, which afforded fine views northwards over Marylebone towards Regent's Park.

In July, Balchin had informed the American magazine the *Saturday Evening Post* how he envisaged life in Sussex working out:

> "I have just bought a place in the country [...] The family, the pony, the dog, the staff and I will move in shortly."[25]

This statement completely obscures the depth of Balchin's feelings for Yovanka, and if he was including Elisabeth in his vision of the immediate future then he was deluding himself, as she was by now comfortably ensconced with her lover in All Souls' Place. It is exceedingly unlikely that Elisabeth would have wanted to uproot herself again and move with her husband back to the country, given that she had been so unhappy living with him in bucolic isolation in Kent.

And yet, incredibly, this is what came to pass, albeit temporarily. Before Balchin had fully settled in at his new country residence, Elisabeth had reappeared at Oast Cottage. It was twelve-year-old Penelope who accidentally initiated this doomed attempt to restore domestic harmony:

> ...I got up the courage to say that I didn't want to hurt daddy's feelings but I was very used to doing everything with

235

mummy [...] I did miss her very much and, to my horror, Nigel said "Well I tell you what we'd better do: you'd better come back where you belong" to my mother [...] and I knew that was hopeless. It wasn't what I'd meant, it wasn't what I was asking for... But she did, she came back for a week...[26]

The short-lived Oast Cottage experiment was brought to an end on 15 October when Ayrton telephoned Elisabeth to inform her that his mother had died. She rushed to be with him and never lived with Balchin again.

The failure of this last desperate throw of the dice brought home to Balchin the fact that his marriage, after almost eighteen years, had now finally run its course:

> It never was very successful, & such success as it appeared to have depended on a great deal of effort from both of us. Once one of us felt that that effort was no longer worth while, there could be only one end. I do not think my verdict on Elisabeth, or hers on me, is in the least likely to change now, nor can I see any possible advantage to either of us in our trying to live together.[27]

At the end of 1950, when in Balchin's words he had 'at last realized that the break up of my marriage was inevitable', divorce proceedings were initiated, with Ayrton named as co-respondent. With a heavy irony that a master of black humour such as Balchin might have appreciated, even during one of the bleakest phases of his life, his decree nisi was issued by the High Court of Justice on 14 February 1951. Six weeks later, on 30 March, he received the decree absolute and his marriage, which had given the impression of being an insoluble problem for about three years, had now officially been dissolved.

What did Elisabeth see in Ayrton that led her to ultimately choose him as her life partner in preference to her husband? Whereas Balchin, by the late 1940s, was perhaps viewing Elisabeth more as his wife and the mother of his children than as a person in her own right, Ayrton treated her as an individual and enabled a woman distinguished, in her granddaughter's opinion, by 'shyness and lack of self-confidence'[28] to emerge from her shell. He was also prepared to entertain the Newnham graduate as his intellectual equal, and even deferred to her at times on subjects such as poetry and archaeology. Ayrton functioned as a benevolent pedagogue, educating Elisabeth in areas in which her knowledge was deficient. The relationship between the pair thus paralleled that between Balchin and Yovanka, although in this case it was a younger man who was imparting information to an older woman. When Yovanka stated vis-à-vis Balchin that 'the moment I met him I started to learn'[29] one could have transferred the same form of words into Elisabeth's mouth and they would have applied equally well to Ayrton.

The artist's easy-going nature (what Balchin referred to pejoratively as his 'completely irresponsible hedonism'[30]) would also have come as a welcome change to Elisabeth after the more overbearing personality of her serious-minded husband. Balchin almost admitted as much in 1952 when he explained that, before Ayrton drove a wedge between himself and Elisabeth, 'I *had* allowed my life to become grey & stodgy. I *had* lost my zest, & I *had* fallen back on a sort of dull, cold goodness with mighty little in it of real love or warmth.'

In addition to making Elisabeth happy, Ayrton also encouraged her to write. At Leigh Barton she had begun to craft short stories and poems but Balchin had not been convinced of their quality ('he did not consider her a good writer'[31]) and so she had become disheartened. In the 1950s, with help from Ayrton, her stories were published in magazines such as *Vogue* and some of her poems were broadcast on the BBC's Third Programme. Under Ayrton's benign patronage, Elisabeth's writing flourished and she proceeded to construct four novels and a handful of cookery books, some of which, like 1958's *Good Simple Cookery*, remain classic texts.

Incompatibility in the bedroom is another possible reason why Elisabeth chose to leave her husband. Among some of his papers that were deposited at the British Film Institute after his death, I discovered an undated fragment written in Balchin's hand in which the author, despite using the third person, appears to be describing his own personal situation (although it must be pointed out that it is by no means certain that he was). Writing I would imagine in the 1960s, Balchin analyses why he had suffered so badly from loneliness during his life and alights on one plausible reason: 'The breakdown of a first marriage in which he felt himself to be sexually unacceptable'.[32] No indication is given by Balchin of what form this sexual unacceptability took and nor is it clear how much of a bearing it had on the collapse of his marriage. However, as Leach posits, 'if somebody [i.e. Elisabeth] has an affair that then turns into a lifelong passionate marriage it's reasonable to assume that Nigel and Lis's sex life wasn't wonderful'.[33]

It was therefore a cocktail of many different factors that led to the dissolution of Balchin's marriage, another one being that Elisabeth wanted to have a fourth child soon after the move to Leigh Barton but Balchin said no. In his opinion, his existing offspring had already damaged relations with his wife, as Leach makes clear: 'He believed that children ruined everything. He thought [they] ruined his marriage with Elisabeth'.

Speaking in 1992, Leach also remarked that, 'despite the very considerable unhappiness of that three or four years',[34] she was 'glad the divorce happened'. Elisabeth soon made the discovery that she was happier living with Ayrton than she had been with Balchin and it is Leach's view that her mother ultimately benefitted from all the upheavals that had taken place in her life between 1948 and 1951:

It was really because he [Ayrton] loved her so much actually. She became a completely different person and it was very exciting to see. She began to write, she began to giggle.

The same could not be said about her father, at least not in the short term:

I think in every marriage break-up there's always a loser and I'm afraid in this one he was the loser.[35]

The dismantling of Balchin and Elisabeth's union had been a painful and protracted affair. Both parties had made repeated efforts to patch up their differences and had tried on several occasions to continue cohabiting, almost as if Ayrton's intervention into their lives had happened to some other couple. Balchin had used the unhappiness of his children as a lever to try to persuade his wife to 'come back where she belonged'. Elisabeth, in her turn, was unwilling to snap all of the bonds with her former husband and wanted to stay on good terms with him, as indeed she did for the rest of his days. After they married, Ayrton and Elisabeth remained close friends with Balchin and continued to be concerned for him.

In the notes that Balchin penned about his personal affairs in the summer of 1952, he gave an impression of what the preceding few years had been like for him:

> The vital fact is that the material harm Elisabeth did me, in breaking up my family life, my home & so on, was of much less importance than the mental, moral & emotional confusion into which I was thrown by the whole matter. I never found anything very surprising or shocking in the fact that she fell in love with Michael. These things do happen; & had she left me, as I wanted her to do, in the Spring of 1948 I might have been surprised, hurt & angry. But at least I should have known where I was. In the event, she never had the courage to do me an ordinary honest piece of dirt and take the consequences, but went on for nearly three years protesting that she loved me & could not live without me, whilst always refusing, when it came to the point, to co-operate in my efforts to bring us together.[36]

16

Finding a Way Through the Wood

I think he had a perfectly horrible second half of his life. I can't imagine how horrible it can have been.

– Penelope Leach[1]

Published in June 1951, just over two months after he had received his decree absolute, *A Way Through the Wood*, which was originally entitled *Nothing That is Mine*,[2] was Balchin's attempt to make sense of the calamitous recent events in his private life through the medium of his fiction. Reviewing the book in the *Daily Telegraph*, John Betjeman[3] was the only critic who came close to appreciating the significant torment that Balchin had endured before committing his thoughts to paper: 'He writes like someone who knows what it is to love and to be hurt'. The book's prologue, although attributed to the narrator and central character, Jim Manning, could easily have been signed by Balchin himself:

But though it is all over now I am still desperately confused; and I am tired of confusion. There is still a great deal about the whole business that I don't understand, and it is very important to me that I should understand it; for not to do so is not to understand people – how they will think and feel and act. Until this happened, I thought I understood people tolerably well. Now I am in the dark wood, in which it seems that anything might happen. I know that there must be a logic – a justice – even an inevitability, about what has happened to me in the past year; and Heaven knows, it is a thing that happens to plenty of people. But knowing that there is sense in it somewhere, I still can't see it or feel it.

So I shall write it all down, hoping that as I do so, some pattern will emerge, and I shall see the shape of my dark wood, and how it came to be planted – and even perhaps a way through it.

Clive James observed that *A Way Through the Wood* has been 'generally thought of as Balchin's response to the collapse of his marriage'.[4] Other commentators have characterized *A Way Through the Wood* as being among the most autobiographical of all Balchin's novels, but to what extent is this true? In one particular at least, not at all. The police investigation that forms one of the two major strands of the story was extracted by Balchin from the pages of the play *The Highway Code* that he had written in about 1935 and was certainly not based on a contemporary real-life experience. But it was only this police procedural plot line and the moral dilemma at the heart of the novel ("Should we tell the authorities about the car accident or hush it up?") that were derived from the earlier work. The love triangle that ensnares the three central characters (Jim and Jill Manning and Bill Bule) was added later by Balchin after his own marriage had broken down.

It is to the middle and final thirds of *A Way Through the Wood* that one must look for parallels with Balchin's personal life. Penelope Leach described what had taken place as her father's marriage began to unravel:

> The three of them—he and Michael and Elisabeth—kind of chased round Europe weeping as far as I can see. They were always meeting up to have another drama in Paris or Venice or somewhere.[5]

(The central section of the novel contains a couple of summits between the Mannings in Paris and, sandwiched between these two meetings, Jim talks over his marital predicament with an old female friend in Venice.)

Immediately after the Mannings and Bule return to Sussex from Paris there is another sequence that is hauntingly realistic. This is the part of the book in which Manning finally realizes

A Way Through the Wood (1951)

When Joe Pearce is knocked off his bike in rural Sussex in a hit-and-run accident and subsequently dies from a head injury, Jim Manning suspects that the driver of the car that struck the man a glancing blow was local aristocrat Bill Bule, a friend of his and his wife Jill. His hunch proves to be almost correct: Jim discovers that it was Bule's car that hit Joe but, crucially, Jill reveals not just that she was driving but also that she has been having an affair with Bule. Unaware that she had hit the cyclist, Jill had not stopped the car. In order to prevent Jill from going to jail, the Mannings and Bule decide to keep their mouths shut.

P. C. Eddie Cator, the brother of Joe's widow, Elsie, begins to investigate the case. He hones in on Bule as the prime suspect for Joe's manslaughter, aided by an anonymous poison pen letter written by Bule's chauffeur. Jim therefore deploys a prefabricated alibi, trusting that his standing as a magistrate will raise him above suspicion in the eyes of the police.

The Mannings split up so that Jill and Bule can live together. One evening Bule tells Jim that he has argued with Jill and that she has walked out in a huff. Jim suspects that she has gone to confess to Elsie that she was responsible for Joe's death. Jim and Bule drive at high speed from London to Sussex, hoping to reach Elsie's cottage before Jill does. When they arrive, Jill is already installed at Elsie's and has sent for P. C. Cator because she has something important to tell him…

that his marriage is unworkable, initiates divorce proceedings and puts his house on the market. The descriptions of a heartbroken man moping around at his London club and at his home in the country seem too true to life not to have been based at least partly on Balchin's own experience. In addition, a factual account of the writer's departure from his Kentish home Leigh Barton, which he gave to the *Saturday Evening Post* in 1950, eerily parallels the fictional version presented in *A Way Through the Wood*.

A Way Through the Wood is therefore not that much more autobiographical than earlier Balchin novels such as *No Sky*, *Darkness Falls from the Air* or *The Small Back Room* and large expanses of the narrative did not have a basis in fact. The 1951 novel is however an important illustration of what Balchin highlighted as one of the key tenets of the writer's creed: 'whatever happens to you can be turned to advantage'.[6]

A Way Through the Wood saw the introduction into Balchin's novels of a new sort of character. Jim Manning is morally superior, condescending towards women, supercilious, rather priggish and determined to be in control of every situation. James noted a clear resemblance between this character type and the man who had created it:

> Balchin's pride in his own real-life competence is easily detected as a projection in his novels. There is always a character, usually a major one and often enough the holder of the main viewpoint, who knows how things ought to be done.[7]

Balchin himself, when he analysed the fallout from his broken marriage in 1952, admitted that a self-righteous streak had existed in his psychological make-up before his wife had taken up with Michael Ayrton (see Chapter 15) but considered that it had diminished following his entanglement in a three-cornered relationship:

> I can even feel that some of the over-caution, some of the self-righteousness, & some of the dull bitterness about life

have disappeared as the result of this experience, & to that extent it has been salutary.[8]

Armed with a knowledge of the participants in the Balchin–Ayrton ménage, the disastrous outcome of which was still obsessing Balchin when he sat down to write *A Way Through the Wood*, should one approach the novel with the assumption that Bule is a representation of Ayrton, Jill a version of Elisabeth and Jim an avatar for Balchin? Although Leach agrees that her father answered the description of a man 'who knows how things ought to be done' ('That was Nigel'[9]), her answer to this question is an emphatic no:

> None of the characters match the characters; what matches is the protagonist's attitude to them. Actually Michael Ayrton was nothing like Bule, but the way Nigel felt about him and talked of him and talked to him and talked to Elisabeth about him was so like what's in the book that it's really quite painful to read.

Two points should be made in this connection. The first is that, although Balchin admitted in the same year that *A Way Through the Wood* was published that 'Nobody in his senses puts portraits of his friends in books; there is no point in doing so',[10] he wouldn't have been feeling especially friendly towards Ayrton when he was drafting the novel and he did take the trouble to explain that his fictional characters were inevitably influenced by people he had encountered:

> …it must always be remembered that an author isn't God; he can't create people. He can only synthesise them from bits and pieces of the reality which he has experienced.

The second point to note is that, towards the end of the book, Balchin takes a favourite expression of Ayrton's and places it in the mouth of Bule. When the aristocrat is lying in his hospital bed with TB and utters the words 'People do what they want to' we are only a short syntactical hop away from a phrase that Balchin claimed to have frequently heard being emitted from Ayrton's lips:

"Everybody" as Michael so often assured me "Does what he wants to, really."[11]

So although Bule should not be thought of as a mere impersonation of Ayrton, the two characters do share some personal characteristics, at least in relation to how they speak.

The comprehensive reconstitution of 'Balchin's formula' represented by *A Way Through the Wood* did not find universal favour with the literary critics, but the mood in which the book was received was nevertheless broadly positive. Two of the most complimentary reviews were contributed by George Malcolm Thomson[12] in the *Evening Standard* and Peter Quennell[13] in the *Daily Mail*, both of whom awarded *A Way Through the Wood* the accolade of being their 'Book of the Month'. Norman Shrapnel[14] in the *Manchester Guardian* was also very impressed by *A Way Through the Wood*, describing it as 'a quite dazzling example of the Nigel Balchin technique—not a word out of place, not a situation mishandled'. Writing in the *Sunday Times*, C. P. Snow[15] observed contrastingly that, of all Balchin's novels, *A Way Through the Wood* was 'the most moving and the most faulty'. The reviewer also complained that Balchin, in attempting to generate pace in his narrative, had sacrificed too much: 'a novel can become so streamlined that there is nothing left'.

In the most thought-provoking review generated by *A Way Through the Wood*, John Raymond[16] in the *New Statesman and Nation* opined that 'As a novel about adultery, this book must be rated a failure. Wife-stealing, like any other anti-social activity, is a moral subject and demands a moral treatment.' Raymond suggested that Balchin would be well advised to stop dabbling in affairs of the heart and return to writing about what he knew best:

Mr. Balchin's dynamic is elbow-grease and the sooner he realises that this is a necessary and not a shameful limitation, the better.

Like other critics before him, Raymond had sampled the new recipe for 'Balchin's formula' but had decided that he preferred the regular flavour. If Balchin read reviews of his own novels then this type of criticism must surely have driven him to distraction by now. Previously, he had been informed that, with his 'men at work' novels of the mid-1940s, he had fallen into a rut and needed to change his style in order to extricate himself from it and thus avoid typecasting. Balchin had tried to do this, firstly with *Lord, I Was Afraid* and then with *The Borgia Testament*, but neither of those experiments in fiction-writing had met with widespread critical approval. He had then reverted to his 'formula' for *A Sort of Traitors*, as advised by a number of book reviewers, and this had prompted renewed objections on the literary pages that he had a tendency to repeat himself. Now Balchin had changed again, by writing a cross between a detective story and a harrowing romantic novel, and a prominent critic duly advised him to go back to doing what he had previously been lambasted for doing too often! Whether or not he was goaded into doing so by the press reaction to *A Way Through the Wood*, Balchin would indeed return to his elbow-grease dynamic for his next piece of fiction, *Sundry Creditors*.

A Way Through the Wood represents a welcome departure from the succession of work-based novels with which Balchin had established himself during the previous decade, the world of employment being entirely absent from its pages. Perhaps the book would have been more successful had it been *either* a story about a marriage falling apart *or* an account of a police investigation, but the material that Balchin imported from *The Highway Code* was harmoniously pleached with the romantic elements, with no suggestion that it had been bolted on in any way. An intelligent and compassionate love story with a heart-breaking conclusion, *A Way Through the Wood* is a singular entity within Balchin's bibliography.

*

As he sat in his Sussex cottage on 13 June 1952, mulling over his personal affairs and committing the results of the exercise to paper, Balchin alighted on an ongoing deficiency in his domestic arrangements:

> ...the only missing bit in the organisation is somebody to run the cottage for me if I wish to be here by myself. Until I have that, then I am *materially* (as opposed to emotionally) dependent on Yovanka, & I think it is a gap in the organisation that must be filled.[17]

When Balchin first moved into Oast Cottage he had taken on a housekeeper to look after him, but the arrangement had not worked out and so she had left. By the middle of 1952 he had therefore been reduced to living on his own when in Sussex, but the thought of continuing to do so filled him with dread:

> ...to accept the inevitability of loneliness, & to live alone instead of merely mentally alone, is a terrifying prospect, unless one can organise it far better than I have been able to do so far.

If Yovanka had agreed to keep house for Balchin would this have been a possible solution to his predicament? He seemed to think not, the sticking point being that she was becoming 'more & more trained for a highly specialized job which nobody is going to let her do permanently'. Not much more than a year after being granted his divorce, Balchin was not yet considering tying the knot with the young woman: 'There is no possible excuse for a man of 43 to entangle a girl of 22, whom he does not intend to marry, in his life & his affairs'. Within a few months Balchin would perform an about-turn on this decision, appreciating that, if not the perfect solution to his dilemma, Yovanka would at least be capable of filling the gap in his organization. More importantly, she might also be able to help lead him out of the dark wood, in the depths of which he had lost his way.

17

A Return to Elbow Grease

I shall write probably from about half past nine to half past twelve every day, seven days a week, and then again, if the thing's going well, from about five o'clock for another hour and a half or so. While doing this I shall smoke all the time; at least, I shall constantly take out cigarettes and light them, put them down in an ash tray and let them burn and then stub them out and light another cigarette. I think the point there is that the actual motion of taking out a cigarette and a box of matches and lighting a cigarette gives me just the pause that I need in which to think.

– Nigel Balchin[1]

Balchin's writing routine was related in a televised talk entitled *Speaking Personally* that he gave in August 1951 as he limbered up to write the novel that eventually became *Sundry Creditors*. The programme was broadcast at 9.30 pm on a Saturday, and it shows how much the medium has changed in the course of the last six decades that a novelist reading a prepared script about the mechanics of his art could command a fifteen-minute primetime slot on national television.

In *Speaking Personally*, Balchin described his eccentric approach to the writing of novels. He explained that the ideas on which they were based generally took a very long while to bring to fruition—ten to twelve years was by no means an atypical time lag—and that when he was in the process of beginning a book he would scribble down a number of 'rather odd, slightly mysterious notes on paper', which he would then proceed to either lose or fail to understand the meaning of at some later date. One of the oddest ones he had come across read simply 'Italians can't tango'. Once a new book was under way, Balchin said that he found the writing process 'a comparatively peaceful affair' but he felt it was probably necessary for a degree of agitation to precede a spell of writing in order to prevent the finished book from being too orderly:

> ...unfortunately I find that if one's approach to the whole job is brisk and businesslike, the results tend to read as though they were a trifle brisk and businesslike, and if no emotional flap of any kind goes in, then no emotion of any kind comes out.

For a novelist whose writing was often accused of being too brisk and businesslike this was an illuminating admission but, as Balchin conceded, the results might have been 'even worse' had he not got into a flap before picking up his pencil.

Balchin's fame as a novelist, which peaked in the late 1940s and early 1950s, led to a further spate of television appearances in the aftermath of *Speaking Personally* as he cashed in on the burgeoning popularity of this new form of entertainment (the number of television licence-holders soared from 1.45 million in 1952 to 3.25 million in 1954[2]). In 1952 he read a *Saturday-Night Short Story*, 'Major Cole's Third Shot', before appearing in an edition of *Snapshot* ('The fourth of a series of six programmes in which every picture tells a story'[3]) the following year. Then in 1954 he used the experience of having written *The Anatomy of Villainy* to take part in *The Balloon Game*, a show in which viewers were 'invited to join a studio jury in passing judgment on three famous characters in history'.[4] Balchin was sufficiently well known to the viewing public to be able to appear as a mystery guest on *What's My Line?* in 1956; this represents the pinnacle of his career as a television personality, although he did make several more appearances in the mid-1960s.

*

Anyone who has worked in a factory will read *Sundry Creditors* with delighted recognition.

– Walter Allen[5]

Sundry Creditors, the tenth Balchin novel, was published on 4 May 1953. The title appears to have been changed at a very late stage because the book was still being referred to as *Heir and Heiress* when serialization of an abridged version began in *Woman's Own* on 19 March.

After he had completed *Sundry Creditors*, Balchin said that he had been 'wanting to write a novel about industry for at least twenty years'.[6] In addition to his first excursion into this territory, his 1934 debut novel *No Sky*, Balchin had also written a novel about industrial matters in about 1937. However, in the author's own opinion that book was 'unbelievably bad and I threw it away'. *Sundry Creditors* was thus a chance for him to make amends for the earlier failure and also to improve upon *No Sky*, which can be viewed as something of a preliminary draft of the 1953 book. Balchin was aware that, in the face of indifference from his fellow writers, he had set himself no easy task:

> Novelists, as a race, know very little about industry. They regard the subject as fundamentally dull.

There is nothing dull about *Sundry Creditors*. Although it has been undeservedly neglected ever since it first rolled off the printing presses—UK sales were less than half those for *A Sort of Traitors*, the most recent comparable volume in the canon—it demands to be considered as among the greatest achievements of Balchin's lengthy (and intermittently illustrious) career as a novelist. Writing about *Sundry Creditors*, Clive James said that 'As a novel about business decisions this book is right out on its own'.[7]

Sundry Creditors is important for two main reasons. With the exception of Balchin's final book, *Kings of Infinite Space* (which is very feeble fare by comparison), it represents the last example of a genuine 'men at work' novel in his portfolio. With its short interleaved scenes and terse, economical prose (a resurrection of that used to construct the wartime novels), *Sundry Creditors* is also the apotheosis of a style of writing that Balchin had been honing for more than ten years. Most of the action is conveyed by means of dialogue and many scenes open in a stylized fashion—'He could have rung up to make sure she was coming, but he wasn't going to run about after any little bitch, and certainly not Lang's daughter.'—that is almost jarringly abrupt. Balchin would not write another novel in the same manner, but then how could he improve on the effect he had achieved with it in *Sundry Creditors*?

Balchin's third attempt at writing a factory novel is notable too for its cast of characters, which is one of the finest he ever assembled and also one of the widest ranging, with everyone from shop-floor workers to directors playing an important role in the narrative. Although the engineering works in which the story is set is perhaps the real star of the novel, two of the human protagonists in *Sundry Creditors* are especially worthy of mention.

In the shape of the nubile eighteen-year-old Rosamund Lang, daughter of the megalomaniac Managing Director of Lang's, Walter, a girl who is neglected by her father and asked to adopt the role of his surrogate wife following the death of her mother, Balchin created an unforgettable portrait of a bored and desperately lonely young woman who is being groomed for a life of domesticity when all she really wants to do is to enjoy herself. This thirst for excitement leads her to begin an unlikely relationship with Jack Partridge, one of her father's junior staff. Inevitably all turns out wrong in the end, as the course of true love never does run smooth in a Balchin novel, but by creating Rosamund the author succeeded in climbing inside the head of a privileged but depressed teenager. Upon publication of *Sundry Creditors*, Julian Maclaren-Ross[8] in *The Times Literary Supplement* suggested that Balchin, despite his 'expert knowledge of the world of men', had 'rarely drawn a credible woman'. This was true, but Rosamund is the first of a handful of convincingly drawn female characters that enhance Balchin's later novels.

First glimpsed as a glowering presence in the shadow of his press, refusing to use the safety guard designed to protect his hands from being crushed because 'it gets in the way slightly', Rosamund's boyfriend Partridge is a powerful, intimidating and significant minor character. He can be seen as a prototype of the Angry Young Men who would come to dominate British fiction in the years immediately after *Sundry Creditors* was published. With his class consciousness and contempt for his bosses, his determination to improve the lot of his shop-floor colleagues via his position on the Works Council and his head-turning dalliance with Rosamund (initiated originally as a means of winning a bet with a friend worth Twenty Players Weights), Partridge is every bit as angry, chippy and confrontational as the likes of Jim Dixon, Joe Lampton or Arthur Seaton. Regrettably, the Partridge–Rosamund romance comprises little more than an extended subplot of *Sundry Creditors*. Had it been made more prominent, and had Partridge himself narrated the story, Balchin might have had a smash-hit on his hands. His book predated exemplars of the Angry Young Man genre such as Kingsley Amis's *Lucky Jim* and, by five months, John Wain's *Hurry on Down*, which is generally considered to have been the first of the 'Angries'. Alan Sillitoe's *Saturday Night and Sunday Morning*, in which Seaton, the hero, is a lathe-operator in a Midlands factory, was not published until five years after *Sundry Creditors*.

With his 1953 novel, Balchin took a few broadly affectionate potshots at a family of famous industrialists, one of whose members he was very well acquainted with. Gustavus Lang, Chairman of the company and benevolent half-brother of the tyrannical Walter, is a kindly old soul who believes in treating the workers like human beings: "I don't think I've ever heard anybody who can put nineteenth-century paternalism more beautifully in a nutshell". Many of the enlightened reforms that we are told that Gustavus was instrumental in having introduced at Lang's overlap with a list of achievements attributable to 'liberal and progressive industrial thought'[9] that Balchin reeled off in a lecture he gave in the same year that *Sundry Creditors* was published:

> ...seeing that people at work were warm, that workshops were light and clean, that fatigue should be reduced, that there should be hot water in the cloakrooms and so on.

Sundry Creditors (1953)

At the annual Works Party of Midlands engineering firm Lang's, Rosamund Lang, attractive eighteen-year-old daughter of the Managing Director Walter, dances with a young press-shop worker named Jack Partridge. The Chairman of the company, Gustavus Lang, collapses and dies as soon as he arrives home from the party. Walter realizes that he can now become the principal shareholder in Lang's if he can get his hands on the shares that his half-brother was holding. But when he makes an offer for them he is swiftly rebuffed by the trustees, to his considerable annoyance.

The head of a rival concern, Sir Francis Proudfoot, a man who also happens to be a friend of Henry Spellman, a director of Lang's, expresses an interest in buying Gustavus's shares. The trustees agree to the transaction, but when Walter later visits Proudfoot, the latter springs a surprise, telling Walter that Henry is thinking of retiring and is likely to sell his shares to his friend. Outmanoeuvred, Walter sees that if Proudfoot buys the shares then he, not Lang, will be the majority shareholder and will be able to absorb Lang's into his own combine.

Unbeknown to Walter, Jack has been carrying on with Rosamund ever since the Works Party. Walter drives to the South Coast, finds his daughter holidaying with Jack and confronts him. In the ensuing scuffle, Walter falls, hits his head and is knocked unconscious. After a spell in a sanatorium, the businessman returns home.

Several days later, Walter wakes up at seven feeling much better and decides to go to his office in case there is still time to prevent Henry from selling his shares to Proudfoot. But he has slept the clock around and it is in fact evening not morning. The novel concludes with Walter lurking in the shadows of his beloved press-shop, but is he alive or dead?

Some aspects of Gustavus's personality were probably based on those of Seebohm Rowntree, the social reformer, sociologist, founder member of the National Institute of Industrial Psychology and Chairman of Rowntree's between 1923 and 1941 whom Balchin worked for throughout most of the 1930s. In tandem with his father Joseph, Seebohm brought in many improvements for the staff at the York Cocoa Works during the first half of the twentieth century, among which can be numbered wage increases, a shorter working day and a pension scheme. As a young man, Seebohm is known to have been an enthusiastic attender of Rowntree's staff socials, a penchant he shares with Gustavus in the fictional work. However, as mentioned in one of the Notes to Chapter 3, Gustavus's love of pigs, which is referred to obliquely in *Sundry Creditors*, was almost certainly inspired by Balchin's familiarity with Oscar Rowntree, Seebohm's brother, who was a pig farmer and short-lived member of the Rowntree's Board.

Balchin's familiarity with the business methods and personal foibles of George Harris, Rowntree's Chairman between 1941 and 1952, may have provided him with useful source material for his portrait of Walter Lang. As detailed in Chapter 6, Balchin had clashed with Harris as early as 1940 (and again the following year) and it may have been the case that he wished to exact revenge by caricaturing Harris in the form of Walter. If that is what Balchin had in mind when he began planning the form of *Sundry Creditors* then it would have been akin to the way in which he had caricatured Christian Darnton in *Darkness Falls from the Air*, and to a lesser extent in *Mine Own Executioner* and *Lord, I Was Afraid*. A published account of the modus operandi of Harris whilst he was Chairman of Rowntree's reveals certain personality traits that he shared with Lang:

> Harris was always producing product ideas, and his impatient wish to seize entrepreneurial opportunities was both feared and respected. He demanded the highest level of commitment from his staff—he was himself a 'workaholic'—and, although always willing to praise staff

when appropriate, he was capable of bawling at those who failed him. Harris' behaviour and methods were well known and established, but the pressures of work and his illness made him seem erratic—perhaps increasingly erratic—to many at the company.[10]

Balchin was probably working on *Sundry Creditors* when he was made aware that Harris had been removed as Rowntree's Chairman in something of a boardroom coup and replaced by another of Balchin's old sparring partners from his Ministry of Food days, William Wallace. In January 1952, Harris committed a trifling road traffic offence in the centre of York and, faced with prosecution, unwisely chose to defend himself. There was concern among some Rowntree's directors that if Harris were to be involved in court proceedings then it would generate bad publicity for the company. It has also been suggested that Harris had undermined Peter Rowntree, son of Seebohm and a member of the Rowntree's Board, by stripping him of his managerial responsibilities. Balchin and Peter Rowntree served together on several post-war Rowntree's marketing committees and Balchin may well have resented any attempt by Harris to destabilize his colleague. When word reached Seebohm of Harris's intentions towards his son he 'mobilised major family, close associates and family trust shareholdings to force the board to request Harris's resignation'.[11] The way in which Harris was outmanoeuvred and eventually ousted by his colleagues is thus reminiscent of the way in which Walter is defeated—like so many other central Balchin characters of the 1940s and 1950s—and emasculated by the combined forces of Sir Francis Proudfoot and an alliance of hostile parties on the Board of Lang's. A description of the precise moment of Harris's overthrow exudes a distinct odour of the closing pages of *Sundry Creditors*, wherein Walter realizes that he has overslept and is thus too late to regain control of Lang's:

On the 15th of January [1952], Harris travelled to a Rowntree board meeting at the Cocoa Works, but, told of the growing concern about him, Harris felt unable to continue as chairman. The way to his office being barred, he wrote his resignation and completed some business in his car. At the board meeting, Wallace, as vice-chairman, presided, and officially reported Harris' awaited resignation.[12]

As a coda to this story, it should be pointed out that the Rowntree's constitution contained a clause that required any director to resign if requested to do so by all the other members of the Board. It is more accurate therefore to say that Harris was forced to resign—not politely invited to do so—and the official Rowntree's line about the traffic offence may simply have been a smokescreen designed to conceal the somewhat underhand means by which Harris's downfall had been brought about.

Most reviewers were bright and positive about *Sundry Creditors*. Following on from *A Way Through the Wood*, George Malcolm Thomson[13] in the *Evening Standard* once again made a Balchin novel his 'Book of the Month', rhapsodizing about the latest achievement of an 'able if wayward novelist':

> Sundry Creditors is literature, at least in the sense of being immediately and lastingly readable. Balchin has the rare magnetic power that draws the human eye from one sentence to the next. His second virtue is that he plainly knows what he is talking about.

John Raymond,[14] who had been critical of *A Way Through the Wood*, made *Sundry Creditors* the subject of a fifteen-minute essay transmitted on the BBC Home Service. He described Balchin as 'In our own day the outstanding novelist to deal with work', praised his 'unchallenged ability to render the poetry of work' and perceptively crystallized one of his greatest gifts:

> Balchin has an uncanny knack of at once getting inside any kind of organization—whether it's industry, business, medicine or simply Whitehall. He can always be relied on to give us the set-up magnificently.

Two of Balchin's fellow writers drew attention to an obvious failing of *Sundry Creditors* that they had identified in its closing pages. In the *Daily Telegraph*, John Betjeman[15] stated that 'The end of this readable and clever book flags', and Marghanita Laski[16] in the *Observer* elaborated on this theme in a very perceptive manner:

> ...it is only when the book is finished that one feels that it all rather faded away, each little tale dying out, and that what was dramatically needed to complete this kind of good story-telling was a resounding climax uniting the separate human parts.

In the *Daily Express*, the vituperative and scatterbrained Nancy Spain[17] fired the first shot in what was to be a short, but very sharp and personal, mid-1950s broadside against Balchin. Spain was described by Evelyn Waugh's biographer Christopher Sykes as 'a 'general stunt' columnist, who on some Beaverbrook whim had been appointed the paper's principal literary critic'[18] and he also explained her journalistic technique:

> She was an iconoclast who hoped to reduce certain reputations which in her crude opinion were over-valued.

Spain[19] tagged *Sundry Creditors* as 'quite innocuous— a very weak cup of tea indeed'. Reviewing Balchin's latest work alongside the new novel by his technocratic contemporary Nevil Shute, she concluded that the general public was to blame for the type of fiction that emerged from the studies of the two authors:

> Such is our neurotic necessity for our weekend drug of Shute or Balchin that we goad these writers into producing sad little works of fiction like "In the Wet" or "Sundry Creditors".
>
> But for goodness sake don't let any of us go around pretending that they are literature.

Balchin's honeymoon period of the 1940s was now well behind him, his novels were attracting increasing amounts of criticism (both of the hot-tempered Spain type as well as calmer, more thoughtful appraisals of his perceived shortcomings) and there was a general feeling in the literary columns that he was not making the most of the considerable talents at his disposal. The *Bookseller*'s diarist, 'Henry Puffmore', used the press reaction to *Sundry Creditors* to anticipate what lay in store for Balchin the next time he published a novel:

> ...it is fairly certain that reviewers will say of it one of these three things: it displays his gifts of nonchalant story-telling; its terseness of style suggests that he had easy film-adaptation in mind; it is written to a pattern which is clearly recognisable in his earlier novels. His reviewers also follow a pattern clearly recognisable. They welcome the appearance of a new Balchin; they recognise a serious intent behind an easy style; they then mention at least one of the three points given above; and end up by regretting that he hasn't done as well as we have been accustomed to expect. With *Sundry Creditors* (Collins) everybody has behaved according to expectation. It is all slightly boring; we shall never get people talking like this.[20]

*

When he was not occupied with his writing or required to be in a television studio in the opening half of the 1950s, Balchin used his leisure hours productively. As well as spending time with Yovanka, Elisabeth and his three children from his first marriage, there were the gardens at Oast Cottage to attend to, his boxer dog William to exercise and long-established hobbies ranging from woodcarving to making music, playing golf and the collecting of paintings and oriental rugs to provide diversions for him. A passion from his youth, the playing of cricket, which had necessarily remained dormant during the wartime period, was reactivated in the late 1940s and persisted after his divorce. Balchin's publishers, William Collins, played a match against their authors at Marlow in Buckinghamshire every summer and Balchin took part on several occasions. There is a photograph in the *Bookseller* of the two teams who contested the 1948 game, with Balchin attired in pads, suggesting that he was about to open the authors' innings in concert with his captain and fellow writer, Sidney Rogerson.[21] Balchin was also present on the occasion of the 1951 contest, when spectators included his fellow Collins author Agatha Christie.

Less than a month later, Rogerson was required to pull on whites again when Balchin put together a team of friends and acquaintances to take on Tenterden Cricket Club as part of a festival held at Tenterden in Kent in late summer. 'Mr. Nigel Balchin's XI', which Balchin captained, contained the likes of his publisher William 'Billy' Collins, his wartime colleague Bernard Ungerson, the critic Lionel Hale and the actor Ronald Simpson, who had played a small role in *Mine Own Executioner*. Philip Snow, younger brother of C. P. 'Charles' Snow, was also on Balchin's side and contributed a brief reminiscence of the occasion to a biography of his more famous sibling. After the game, Philip, Charles and the rest of Balchin's team repaired about ten miles across the county border to Oast Cottage for refreshments. The conjunction of C. P. Snow's ample frame and the restricted internal dimensions of the converted oast house had a painful outcome for the author of the *Strangers and Brothers* novel sequence, with Balchin's venerable cottage exacting revenge on Snow for some of the uncomplimentary things he had said about *A Way Through the Wood* a few weeks earlier:

> Its low roof, in combination with Charles's somatic awkwardness, made it a safe bet that he would bang his head on a beam. Duly plastered, he spent the rest of the evening in abstruse conversation…[22]

To an unwitting observer, it may have looked as if the best-selling author of *The Small Back Room* and *Mine Own Executioner* had recovered from the unpleasant experience of his marital break-up and was now looking confidently to the future. After all, Balchin had the run of impressive and attractive residences in both city and country, 'a charming mistress'[23] of whom he was very fond, a range of business activities that kept him busy, supplied him with ideas for his fiction and supplemented the money brought in by his writing and his literary stock, despite a dip whilst he had been going through his protracted separation from Elisabeth and had by his own account 'done some poorish work', was on the rise again, presaging a brief golden period in the mid-1950s. But a rose-tinted view of Balchin's personal situation in 1952 would have been a false one. The novelist may have made the necessary practical adjustments to his new circumstances but he was still struggling to come to terms with the damage inflicted on his psyche by Elisabeth's preference for Michael Ayrton. In the company of his friends he could put on a convincing impression of a competent and supremely successful novelist and businessman, but in private—as revealed by some of his writings from the early 1950s—he remained a vulnerable, shell-shocked individual painstakingly putting his world back together piece by piece in the wake of his divorce.

In his June 1952 analysis of his private life, Balchin was clear that, when it came to his dealings with women, their needs and desires were out of sync with his own:

> ...I have a great capacity for giving women the things they don't want, but no capacity at all for giving them the things they do. In my view, the things that women like best are things which, on the whole, they can get much more easily from somebody else; whereas the things that I regard as characteristic & valuable – the things which I regard as being me at my best – they do not rate very highly, & often positively dislike.

By Balchin's own admission, the things that he could offer women included loyalty, honesty and commitment. As previously mentioned in Chapter 7, he also enjoyed 'discussion of & speculation about the fundamental problems of existence. To most women this is a hopeless bore.' When his women desired something less intellectually taxing, more frivolous, they were required to seek it elsewhere and occasionally they found what they were looking for in company with the likes of Ayrton or Christian Darnton.

Even though Balchin realized that his quest to find a new female companion might well end in disappointment ('I start by accepting that I cannot be a satisfactory partner, & therefore cannot find one who will be satisfactory to me'), he had not given up all hope of becoming close to a woman who was in possession of 'more intellectual capacity & interest than she [i.e. Elisabeth] had'. Yovanka was disqualified from serious consideration as a long-term partner at this point owing to her extreme youth, but during 1952 an intriguing new candidate appeared on Balchin's radar.

The novelist Elizabeth Jane Howard (author of the *Cazalet Chronicle* among many works of fiction) met Balchin through Ayrton, a mutual friend. After socializing with Balchin for a while, Howard began to feel that she was perhaps being viewed as a potential replacement for his recently departed wife:

> …I'd had a vague impression that Nigel was sort of sounding me out as a possible successor to Elisabeth and he never attracted me at all.[24]

If Balchin experienced strong feelings for Howard, a striking and extremely desirable woman in her late twenties with one published novel—*The Beautiful Visit*—already under her belt, these were emphatically not reciprocated and marriage bells did not so much as even distantly tinkle, the relationship between the two writers remaining strictly platonic.

For Howard, the chief emotions evoked by her fellow novelist while she was getting to know him were mostly negative ones, with pity being towards the top of the list:

> I don't think I realized how unhappy he was. […] I thought he was interesting; I thought he was neurotic; I felt sorry for him.

Another of Howard's first impressions of Balchin is revealing:

> He was a very curious mixture. I think he was a very unbalanced person: very grown-up in some ways and

absolutely not in others. And I think he was very, very unsure of himself sexually as a man. I think he had very low self-esteem in that way and I think Elisabeth smashed what there was of it really.

Howard also put forward the contention that one of Balchin's most glaring weaknesses as a novelist—'generally speaking, I don't think he was good at women'—was attributable to a combination of fear and bewilderment on his part where women were concerned:

He's afraid of them. He doesn't know who they are. [...] I really don't think he did understand women. I think they were something of a frightening mystery and I think probably he thought he did understand Elisabeth and he found that he hadn't and that sort of put everything out of joint.

Yovanka had been surprised to discover a few years earlier that Balchin's wartime achievements, and the fame that attended him in the late 1940s as he continued to add to a series of acclaimed novels, had not been matched by recruitment of a large circle of admirers: 'By the time I knew him, he was very friendless. [...] He was singularly without friends.'[25] Howard quickly spotted the same deficiency:

...the other thing I think was very noticeable about him was, except for Michael [Ayrton], I don't recall him having any men friends at all. [...] He never introduced me to another writer or indeed anybody. [...] I think he was very shy.[26]

Balchin's lack of male companions may have been partly attributable to his strait-laced bearing, but another trait that Howard discerned would not have improved his popularity:

He was like a little boy in a gang who wasn't the gang leader a lot of the time. I remember taking him to have a drink with somebody I was going out with who was very successful and having a good life. He [Balchin] started boasting: "Oh you've got a kelim carpet. It's not a very good one. I collect them; I know about these things; I've got a great many of them at home."

Balchin's tendency to boast and take excessive pride in his own accomplishments, which was perhaps a continuation of a character facet identified at Peterhouse in the late 1920s by his tutor Paul Vellacott ('He was at one time perhaps a little trying through over-exuberance about his own interests; this was very natural considering his antecedents and earlier circumstances'[27]), was also observed by Yovanka when her partner landed himself a lucrative screenwriting contract:

...when he made this deal with Twentieth Century Fox he used to brag about it. And I know that people at the Savile— because I had feedback—were awfully fed up with it. [...] He just wanted to be bubbly about it and for people to say "Aren't you a clever chap?" Well it kind of went down like a lead balloon.[28]

At around the time that he first met Howard, and before he signed up with Twentieth Century Fox in the mid-1950s, Balchin was briefly associated with Ealing Studios. After a break of almost five years, during which time he had concentrated on writing books and supervising the necessary rearrangement of his domestic affairs, the third Balchin-scripted movie to reach the screen was released in the UK in August 1952. Directed by Alexander MacKendrick, in the year after he had made *The Man in the White Suit*, Balchin's only screenwriting credit whilst employed by Ealing was attached to a small-scale but very moving picture, and one that is the antithesis of the famous comedies that the studio is better known for. MacKendrick had worked at the J. Walter Thompson (JWT) advertising agency as an art director in the 1930s and his path may have crossed with that of Balchin when the latter was in and out of JWT's

Aldwych offices in connection with his Black Magic box design. Both men later worked on Horlicks commercials for JWT (MacKendrick as art director, Balchin as scriptwriter), although not necessarily at the same time.[29]

The first draft screenplay for MacKendrick's film *Mandy* had been written by Jack Whittingham, an Ealing staff writer.[30] Whittingham developed his script from a novel entitled *The Day is Ours* by Hilda Lewis, but only the opening chapters of Lewis's work were cannibalized to construct the screenplay. As the film writer Philip Kemp observed: 'Of all MacKendrick's films, *Mandy* owes the least to its source material.'[31] The director was unhappy with Whittingham's original script because in his words it contained 'no conflict, no third-act climax' and so turned to his former JWT colleague for assistance. If MacKendrick was looking for the insightful gaze of the psychologist when he gave Whittingham's script to Balchin then that is precisely what he got.

Mandy tells the story of a young girl with congenital deafness who is therefore also unable to speak. She is enrolled at a school for deaf and dumb children at the instigation of her mother and this causes a schism between her parents. Balchin's key interpolation into Whittingham's script was the character of Dick Searle, headmaster of the special school represented in the film by the Royal Residential Schools for the Deaf in Manchester. Still mute having failed to settle in at the establishment as a boarder, Mandy returns to the home of her paternal grandparents in London. But when the school allows her to attend as a day pupil on condition that her mother lives nearby, Christine Garland walks out on her husband and takes a flat in Manchester. With the help of extra tuition in the evenings from Searle, Mandy begins to make real progress towards conquering her speechlessness. Using his knowledge of the concept of transference, which was familiar to him from his interest in psychoanalysis and is mentioned on several occasions in *Mine Own Executioner*, Balchin introduced the idea that Christine might (subconsciously) fall in love with Searle as he began working with her daughter, in comparable fashion to the way in which some of Felix Milne's patients in the novel had become spellbound by the psychoanalyst.

Phyllis Calvert is convincing as Christine and Jack Hawkins (who had enjoyed a small role as Waring in *The Small Back Room* and would take a much more substantial one in the Balchin-scripted *Malta Story*, released the year after *Mandy*) is ideal as Searle, the tetchy headmaster who becomes more equable as he gains the trust of both Mandy and her mother. Speaking about the role that he played, Hawkins said that 'It is rare to find a part with such depth of character'.[32] It was a momentous performance for the actor because it led providentially and directly to him being awarded the role of Commander Ericson in his next Ealing film, 1953's *The Cruel Sea*, which made him a star, and Hawkins considered that '*Mandy* was undoubtedly the turning point in my career as a film actor'.

In the role that gave the film its name, child actress Mandy Miller—seven years old when the movie was shot—is exceptional, Dilys Powell[33] in the *Sunday Times* remarking that 'it is barely possible to believe that she is acting a part and is not in fact stone-deaf'. Miller had featured fleetingly in *The Man in the White Suit* but MacKendrick had thought that she would be 'much too tough'[34] to take on the lead role in *Mandy*. Producer Leslie Norman (father of film critic Barry) considered otherwise and a test scene with Australian actress Dorothy Alison—superb as a conscientious, persevering teacher—in which the deaf and dumb girl produces her first sounds proved him right. Miller's sad eyes and mournful demeanour lend her performance, described as 'astonishingly brilliant' by an unnamed film reviewer[35] in *The Times*, a degree of soulfulness not usually achieved by a child actor. She has to carry the film for long stretches at a time but in her hands it never tips over into mawkish sentimentality, a real danger given the theme of the piece.

Lit up by the performances of Miller and Hawkins, *Mandy* is an engrossing human interest story and one of the very best pictures that Balchin was involved with. Nominated for five British Film Academy awards (although it failed to win any), it was deservedly hailed as 'An extremely touching film' by Powell[36] and as 'a work of art' by *The Times*.[37]

Balchin's next screenwriting project saw him dip his toes into a genre with which he was to retain an acquaintance for much of the remainder of the decade. The British film industry's enthusiasm in the 1950s for wartime stories depicting the pluck of Allied forces was nearing its zenith when Balchin worked on *Malta Story*, this time for GFD/British Film Makers. As with *Mandy*, Balchin was brought in to improve upon an existing script, in this case the work of William Fairchild, a writer who was responsible for scripting two commendable films in the early 1950s—*Morning Departure* and *The Gift Horse*—that depicted bravery on the briny.

Malta Story records the heroic (and strategically important) role played by the tiny Mediterranean island during the 1939–1945 conflict, which led to it being awarded the George Cross by King George VI in 1942. The film starred Alec Guinness, Muriel Pavlow and Jack Hawkins and was described by Leslie Halliwell as a 'Glib propaganda piece which is not very excitingly written or characterized, and fails to convince on any but the most elementary level'.[38] This is a harsh and not entirely fair assessment, but *Malta Story* is a lacklustre piece of film-making (enlivened only by some action sequences and a few characteristic Balchin touches in the dialogue) that retains the ability to quell an outbreak of boredom on a wet Sunday afternoon but otherwise has little to commend it.

*

Towards the end of 1952, Balchin finally took belated steps to resolve his domestic situation. As he put it himself, his ongoing liaison with Yovanka allowed him to enjoy the best of both worlds ('I am alone when I want to be & have a charming mistress when I don't'[39]). Typically though for the compassionate and unselfish Balchin, he was worried about the effect of the blossoming partnership on its female half:

> ...this happy state of affairs [...] is achieved at Yovanka's expense; & whereas that may have been all right as a more or less accidental arrangement in an emergency, it simply won't do now that the emergency is over.

Yovanka, by contrast, saw no need for any alteration in their arrangements:

> ...I went into this relationship with eyes wide open, was in love with Nigel and content to be with him. I was the perfect mistress material, young enough not to be worried about my future and perfectly content to carry on as we were.[40]

Balchin faced an awkward dichotomy: he had embroiled his girlfriend in his life during 'a period of complete desperation & as an act of pure self-preservation'[41] but did not propose to marry her. However, as we saw in the previous chapter, there remained 'a gap in the organisation that must be filled', namely someone to run Oast Cottage for him whilst he was in Sussex.

The novelist wrestled with his dilemma for months until, in January 1953, whilst under the influence, he changed his mind about getting married for a second time and proposed to Yovanka. She was uncertain whether her partner was doing the right thing:

> ...I gave him every opportunity the next day to withdraw; he was certainly not sober when he asked me and I thought it only fair to let him change his mind. He didn't...[42]

With hindsight, Yovanka considers that Balchin's protracted attempt to find a way out of his dark wood had culminated in him taking a wrong turning:

> Marrying me was certainly the worst thing that Nigel could have done. As his mistress, I had no claims on him and enjoyed a relaxed and satisfying relationship. As his wife, overnight I needed shows of loyalty that Nigel did not give naturally.

This reluctance to show loyalty to a single person, and Balchin's continued attachment to Elisabeth and their children, would be ever-present, complicating factors in the early years of his second marriage, and would threaten to tear it apart almost before the last scraps of confetti had been swept off the steps of the registry office.

Balchin's second wedding, almost exactly twenty years to the day after his first, took place in London on 5 February 1953. The bride and bridegroom wished to marry in a church in Sussex close to Oast Cottage, but as Balchin was a divorcee the vicar forbade their nuptials, which were hosted instead by the Marylebone Registry Office, followed by a religious service at the Serbian Orthodox Church in Notting Hill. The fact that no photographic record was made of the ceremony gives an indication of what Yovanka's parents thought about the match:

> ...my parents were horrified with my marrying Nigel, absolutely horrified. It was the last thing that they had envisaged for me...[43]

Their opposition was largely a result of the disparity in age between the two parties: 'I think it was just the shock of my marrying somebody much older than myself, which somehow wasn't really done.' Zoran, Yovanka's father, was also incensed that Balchin had not formally approached him, in the conventional way, to ask for his daughter's hand in marriage. He and his wife Vera provided a reception for the newly-weds at their flat in Kensington and the wedding supper, attended by Howard amongst many others and which Yovanka 'didn't much enjoy',[44] was held at Boulestin, a classic French restaurant in Covent Garden, and paid for by Balchin. In lieu of a honeymoon, the couple holidayed in Yugoslavia in July. Balchin was unable to take off for foreign climes immediately after the wedding because he had to attend a Rowntree's meeting, as jokingly alluded to by Yovanka: 'Nigel next day had to go to York: I've never forgiven him!'.

18

Before Hollywood

Balchin's second marriage began to go wrong almost from the start. The union was less than a year old when divorce was first being spoken about, and before the couple had even celebrated their second wedding anniversary they had chosen to live apart for a six-month period. To help trace the development of the fault lines in the marriage it is instructive to first assess the psychological make-ups of the two parties at the time of their wedding.

When Balchin married Yovanka he was forty-four, a very successful novelist, an emerging screenwriter and a man whose frequent appearances on radio and television had seen him achieve public recognition in his native country: in a more vulgar age, he would have been thought of as a minor celebrity. This should perhaps have given Balchin confidence and a feeling of comfort in his own skin but, as mentioned in the previous chapter, this was not the case. His self-esteem had been eroded by the experience of losing his wife to Michael Ayrton, the impact of that loss being made clear by Yovanka: 'I only see now how easily his confidence could be shattered, and [...] the break-up of his marriage shattered it for ever.'[1] Once his relationship with Elisabeth had ended, Balchin began to look for a new partner who could offer him the support he craved, and that was essential to someone engaged in a profession as lonely and frustrating as that of authorship. As Yovanka now realizes, her husband made an unwise choice:

> Shattered from his divorce from Elisabeth, Nigel was looking for someone he could mould and impress—and who was young enough to go along with this. Sadly for him, he mistook me for that person.

269

Yovanka's sophisticated appearance and air of self-possession also cloaked a personality riddled with insecurity. During the war years she had lost her country and her social standing. After her parents had separated, she and her mother had found themselves desperately short of money and the post-war establishment of a Communist government in Yugoslavia had thwarted Yovanka's expectation of one day being able to inherit her grandparents' fortune, a situation later dramatized by Balchin in his novel *In the Absence of Mrs Petersen*.

Shortly before meeting Balchin, Yovanka had also experienced personal tragedy. At the end of 1948 she had met and fallen in love with an American army officer whom she soon planned to marry. But he was then killed in an aeroplane crash just days after getting her pregnant. Vera Tomich had to sell the family silver in order to pay for her daughter to undergo an abortion, an action for which, in Yovanka's words, 'she never forgave me'.[2] Yovanka had also resigned from a much-cherished job with the Rank Organization when her pregnancy had become apparent to her colleagues, which is why she was temping for a secretarial agency in 1949 and was paired with Balchin when he required the services of a secretary after parting from Elisabeth. In the aftermath of this very dark period in her life in the months leading up to her first meeting with Balchin it comes as little surprise to learn that Yovanka was 'not the most confident of persons [...] I needed more support from Nigel than he could realize'. Both halves of the relationship needed mothering but, to use a favourite Balchin expression, the maternal instinct was not a commodity that either of them 'had in the shop', as Yovanka explains:

I realize now that Nigel was just as insecure as I was and that neither could give the other the support they needed.

Balchin's determination to remain friends with Elisabeth quickly became a source of friction between him and his second wife. In fact, Yovanka took exception to her husband's perceived lack of loyalty towards her even before he had formally become her husband:

A couple of days before our wedding, Nigel writes Elisabeth a letter which I am not supposed to read but do. 55 years later, I can't remember the exact words—and maybe I made too much of it—but I know I was very hurt by them. I think Nigel was apologizing for trying to find some happiness and it was probably a typical Nigel letter—not wanting to hurt anyone he had loved in the past—but I took it as a betrayal, a lack of loyalty towards me. And loyalty was what I needed in a big way.

If Balchin's first marriage had been childless then perhaps a cleaner break could have been made between him and his first wife and his second attempt at matrimony might have got off to a happier start. But although they were now firmly and officially attached to new partners, both Balchin and Elisabeth were still keen to spend time in one another's company, almost as if they were hankering after the rosier days of their early married life.

In 1953, Balchin and Yovanka were invited to stay with Michael and Elisabeth at Bradfields, the Essex farmhouse that the Ayrtons had moved to shortly after their marriage at the end of the previous year. There was a pond in the garden and someone made the suggestion that the four individuals might like to bathe au naturel. Yovanka refused because she was 'just not ready for this: to go swimming naked with his former wife!!'. So it was a mere trio of intrepid swimmers that instead took the plunge into the cold water: 'they went swimming anyway and then Nigel and I had a row. A pattern was set.' This pattern consisted of Balchin socializing with old friends or lovers, more or less forgetting that his new wife was also in his presence and acting as if the clock had been turned back to 1948 or earlier. Balchin would sometimes fail to stick up for Yovanka in front of his friends and a conflagration would be the inevitable result, as she recalls:

I never trusted Nigel [...] He was not willing publicly—which is when I needed it—to be on my side. And therefore I was very hurt and then would react to being hurt...[3]

Balchin's heavy drinking—a feature of his life that had worsened in the years leading up to his marriage to Yovanka (see Chapter 24)—could also lead to the occurrence of flashpoints, and being reunited with his old family was something that was almost guaranteed to induce overindulgence: 'Nigel would get very drunk and then I would get very upset that he'd got very drunk and it used to be very unpleasant.'

Another pattern that persisted after Balchin married for the second time was his predilection for partner-swapping, following on from his dalliance with Joan Ayrton at the end of the 1940s. As with his desire to remain in close touch with Elisabeth, coveting other men's wives was one more way in which Balchin insisted on clinging onto parts of his old life, to the detriment of his new one. Yovanka remembers an occasion at the end of 1953 when she and her husband met up with an old friend of Balchin's, Major [this was his forename, not his military rank] Lester, with whom he had worked at the Ministry of Food in Colwyn Bay during World War Two: 'Major had married Beryl who, as befits the daughter of a vicar, was very prone to sexual games and in particular the great fashion of the time, wife swapping.'[4] The Lesters were responsible for precipitating another ruction between the Balchins. The two couples dined together one evening, large quantities of alcohol were imbibed and a partner-swapping session was proposed. Yovanka stormed off to bed in disgust and left the other three to their own devices ('I've no idea what they did do'). Balchin had failed to appreciate that his wife might possess firm moral standards on subjects that to him were just a bit of harmless fun ('I don't think Nigel ever understood that I minded'). For her part, Yovanka was beginning to realize that she had married not just an insecure novelist but, crucially, his past as well.

After the couple had discussed the possibility of divorce at the end of 1953, Balchin's reaction to his wife's unhappiness was to seek advice from the medical profession in the following year. Yovanka was dispatched first to a Harley Street psychiatrist and later to Professor Linford Rees, father of *Poldark* actress Angharad, who was 'an eminent psychiatrist and academic'.[5] The take-home message that Balchin teased out of the psychiatric reports was that, in order to help his wife feel more secure, he should stop seeing Elisabeth quite so often and Yovanka should have a child.

By October 1954, the relationship between the Balchins had become so strained that they had agreed to a trial separation. In December, Yovanka travelled to Yugoslavia to begin work there. During her six-month absence from Oast Cottage, Balchin used his time wisely. He continued to work on his next novel, the follow-up to *Sundry Creditors*, and maintained his business connections with Rowntree's and J. Walter Thompson. He also put in a number of lengthy shifts at Broadcasting House. The first of several radio appearances came on *Desert Island Discs*[6] in October.

Before unveiling the eight records that he would choose to have with him if he were to be marooned on an imaginary desert island, Balchin expressed consternation at the archaic nature of most of his selections:

> …of the things I've chosen, the things I really mind about, practically all seem to have been written before the death of Mozart…

His pieces of music included compositions by Purcell, Berlioz and Haydn, and he confessed that if he had been permitted just a solitary choice then it would have been Bach's choral prelude 'Sleepers Wake!'. Balchin suggested to Roy Plomley that the isolation he would experience on the island, although deeply unpleasant to him, would nevertheless provide an opportunity to do some serious thinking:

> …I intensely dislike being lonely but it might have one point, for me as a writer, and that is that one would at least be able to sit down and think really carefully about things that had happened in the past without their being confused all the time by the present and the future.

There would have been plenty of events in Balchin's recent past that would have given him food for thought had he really been shipwrecked.

Balchin transferred from the Home Service to the Light Programme for his next outing behind the microphone. He had made his debut on *Any Questions?* in March, the topical debate show coming on that occasion from an RAF station at Hullavington in Wiltshire, little more than fifteen miles from his place of birth. He then served on the panel for the spin-off programme *Sporting Questions* in July, before making his way to another unprepossessing location, this time the factory canteen of an electrical motor business at Yate, near Bristol on 10 December. The novelist was able to draw on his knowledge of the business world and his wartime experiences to answer questions about a recent rise in the price of tea and the annual expenditure of the Foreign Service, but it was a much less politically loaded question ('Does the team agree that a single act of adultery should be grounds for divorce?') that enabled him to make a reply freighted with personal significance and to win favour with his audience by doing so:

> I would never accept that any single act of any kind should be grounds for divorce. I believe that people should stay married as long as they love one another and wish to stay married. I do not like the idea that one catches out the other member of the partnership (VOICE: hear, hear) through any single action of any kind whatsoever. (applause)[7]

Balchin's final radio appearance for the time being saw him in conversation with fellow 'factory novelist' Walter Allen on 7 April 1955. As part of a series called *We Write Novels*,[8] he discussed his 'approach to the novel', talking in particular about his way of working and restating the way in which he had been influenced by the Norse sagas:

> ...ideally, I would like to write quite objectively; tell people what was said and what was done and make the inferences of that in themselves sufficient to tell you what was going on in a person's mind.

In Balchin's opinion this was a satisfactory response to Allen's observation that reviewers had accused him of not being morally committed in his novels. Balchin agreed that the accusation was 'a fair statement' and felt that it arose from a combination of two things, one good, one bad:

> ...the bad one of course is sheer cowardice on my own part—unwillingness to commit myself; the good one is that I don't happen to see either people or moral issues in black and white terms. Thinking, probably conceitedly, that I know to some extent why people behave in the way they do—I find it very difficult to label them heroes and villains.

Tellingly, Balchin also revealed that, despite deriving 'tremendous satisfaction out of making anything up', the writing of fiction was not an activity that gave him much pleasure:

> I've never really liked writing novels and I don't like it to this day. It's appallingly hard work—much harder work than writing anything else at all.

Yovanka has suggested a potential alternative career that might have suited her husband rather better:

> Nigel should have been a don at Cambridge with no children and having fun with the pretty girl students. That would have been what he would have loved. [...] He knew he could make money out of it [writing] and he enjoyed the fame that came along with it—and I think that was very essential to him because it gave him a position in society—but he didn't really like it.[9]

Balchin could not resist the temptation to use the platform afforded him by *We Write Novels* to stress his antipathy towards men of letters and to underscore the importance, in his own case, of possessing some other form of employment that could serve the dual purpose of both informing his fiction and providing a welcome distraction from the chore of producing literature:

> ...I have no ambition at all to be a literary gent. I don't like literary gents and I don't think being a literary gent makes for very good novels. I think that you have to live a fairly complicated life for say seven-tenths of your time in order to write for the other three-tenths.[10]

Balchin would soon be living the complicated life of a Hollywood scriptwriter, but the stress of the occupation would leave him bereft of the energy required to produce novels in his spare time.

While she was working in Belgrade, Yovanka met a Bosnian Serb in his early thirties called Jovan Milicevic who, as well as being a talented classical actor, was also 'devastatingly good-looking, a charmer, highly intelligent and great fun. Just what a girl needed.'[11] A brief fling ensued, but when Yovanka was ready to terminate the romance, Jovan revealed that he had fallen in love with her. A succession of telephone calls kept Balchin fully informed about what was happening in Yugoslavia, but in his wife's opinion he did not seem unduly concerned about her infidelity ('we giggle about it and he knows it means nothing'). Yovanka left Yugoslavia once she had finally succeeded in freeing herself from Jovan's clutches and was reunited with her husband in Italy in March 1955. Further correspondence between Balchin and Yovanka flowed backwards and forwards on the subjects of divorce and separation, but neither party had the heart to go as far as to begin legal proceedings and so they agreed instead to get back together again. The couple's first child was conceived at the end of March, in line with the psychiatric advice they had received the previous year and echoing the suggestion made to Burgess Meredith by a psychiatrist on the set of *Mine Own Executioner* in 1947.

*

One of the most striking aspects of Balchin's career during the 1950s was his willingness to explore the possibility of transmuting his work into different media and obtaining full value—both artistic and financial—from his ideas. His 1951 novel *A Way Through the Wood* had started life as a play, *The Highway Code*, in the mid-1930s; in 1954 it was converted back into theatrical form by Ronald Millar. Best known nowadays for having written Margaret Thatcher's "You turn if you want to. The lady's not for turning" address to the 1980 Conservative Party Conference, Millar began as an actor before establishing himself as a playwright. He then spent six years in Hollywood after the Second World War writing film scripts for MGM. The very first thing he did on returning to Britain from America was to have lunch with Balchin, during the course of which he asked permission to adapt *A Way Through the Wood* for the stage. Balchin consented, and later also gave his blessing to Millar's script for the new work.[12]

Millar's play, *Waiting for Gillian*, ran for a total of 101 performances at the St James's Theatre in London between 21 April and 17 July 1954. If one overlooks some inevitable simplification, the piece stuck quite faithfully to the original text. The one significant change that Millar introduced was to have Jill Manning convicted for manslaughter and condemned to languish in prison for a year before returning to the embrace of her husband. In the two leading roles, husband-and-wife pairing John McCallum and Googie Withers appeared together on the West End stage for the first time.[13]

Waiting for Gillian attracted an array of mostly tepid reviews. Ivor Brown[14] in the *Observer* was one of the greatest enthusiasts for the play, which he referred to as 'well put together and extremely well performed'. Elsewhere though, T. C. Worsley[15] in the *New Statesman and Nation* would only commit himself so far as to say that *Waiting for Gillian* was 'good of its type', Ronald Barker[16] in *Plays and Players* suggested that it would provide 'a pleasant evening's entertainment' and the *Spectator*'s Anthony Hartley[17] described the piece piquantly as a 'goodish middlebrow drama of the 'what would you do, chum?' variety'.

Waiting for Gillian proved to be popular with the public, if not with all of the critics, and the West End run that it enjoyed spawned a BBC television adaptation that won the *Daily Mail* award for best drama of the year. This may have led Balchin to ponder the fact that, despite his multiple failures as a playwright during the concluding half of the 1930s, his ideas were at home in a theatrical setting. Perhaps spurred by the success of *Waiting for Gillian*, Balchin soon constructed a play of his own. *The Leader of the House* was one of only three Balchin-authored original television plays that made it onto the small screen in his lifetime. This project is another example of the same concept being manipulated by its creator to suit multiple media: the play started life as a radio piece—starring Wilfred Hyde-White in the title role—in August 1955, transferred to television that same autumn and was then performed on stage at the Liverpool Playhouse in 1960.

The Leader of the House, a political farce of dubious merit, was not treated kindly by the television critics. Maurice Richardson[18] in the *Observer*, for example, described Balchin's first attempt at writing for television as 'An hour and a half of pretty solid disappointment' and intimated that watching *The Leader of the House* being performed live on 13 November 1955 when it aired as part of the Corporation's Sunday-Night Theatre strand must have been a painful experience for the viewer:

> ...the cast acted—both under and over—like fiends; forgetting lines, mumbling into fists, banging on tables, threatening to have strokes.

*

Balchin's next book took him into virgin territory again, his first (and only) collection of short stories being published by Collins in November 1954. Most of the pieces had already received an airing in various newspapers and magazines, but Balchin appears to have written a few new ones specifically for this volume. Sadly, two of the best short stories he ever wrote—'Dover Incident'[19] and 'The Salamander'[20]—were not included between the pale orange covers of his compendium *Last Recollections of My Uncle Charles*.

The volume comprises a set of seventeen linked stories. The connection between them is that they are all recounted by the same character, namely the eponymous Uncle Charles (an imaginary relative of the author and one of his finest fictional creations). A born raconteur, Charles is an amiable sponger—or 'professional guest' in Balchin's words—of advanced years who uses his charm to wheedle his way into the affairs of his acquaintances and extended family, witnessing some extraordinary goings-on as a result. He then relates his experiences to his cousin, the narrator.

The quality of the tales varies, and several of them are distinctly mediocre. The pick of the collection is 'Among Friends' and concerns another of Balchin's beloved love triangles. Charles's niece, Josephine, has become engaged to Carl Stockman, a handsome businessman with good prospects. Stockman introduces his fiancée to a friend of his, a struggling playwright called David Hewer who is an altogether feebler specimen. Josephine, in the memorable words of an anonymous reviewer in *The Times*, is 'a born helper of lame dogs over stiles'[21] and as Hewer can emphatically be filed under the 'lame dog' heading she duly recants her earlier decision and ends up marrying the playwright instead of the businessman.

Some years later, Charles is staying with Hewer and Josephine at their cottage in the New Forest when Stockman turns up unannounced, soaked to the skin and on the run from the law having become embroiled in some shady financial dealings. The closing scenes, which involve an anxious wait for a decisive piece of action, could quite easily have been slotted into one of the post-war novels, for example *A Sort of Traitors* or *A Way Through the Wood*, and the story resolves itself satisfyingly by way of a tight, tense, minutely observed psychological study in the author's finest manner.

Despite the excellence of at least half a dozen of Balchin's stories, *Last Recollections of My Uncle Charles* only sold somewhere in the region of 10,000 copies. Although William Collins informed the writer on 30 November that 'The first edition of 8,000 is just about sold out, and we have already put on a reprint',[22] printing of the second edition was delayed, and despite 'a super-human effort'[23] from the Collins factory in Glasgow and the publisher himself arranging for the books to be 'sent down specially by passenger train to get them into the bookshops', they only became available for purchase a week before Christmas, fatally stalling sales and perhaps preventing some potential readers from obtaining a little light fireside reading to enjoy over the festive period. Clive James stated that Balchin's foray into this new genre 'proved, among other things, that collections of short stories don't make it as merchandise'.[24]

While William Collins was frantically trying to keep booksellers topped up with copies of *Last Recollections of My Uncle Charles* in the run-up to Christmas, the author of the book was busy making his own plans for the forthcoming holiday season. On 10 December, during his second appearance on *Any Questions?*, he gave the following reply in response to the enquiry 'How do the team propose to spend Christmas Day?':

> I propose to spend Christmas Day in a farm in the Cotswolds with some very old friends of mine of whom I'm extremely fond, who have five children, one of whom is my godson,[25] and I don't doubt that we shall be swarmed over by children the whole time, and I can only tell you that I heard from the lady who will be my hostess, this morning, and she said: "We are all delighted that you are coming except Rickie." Rickie is one of her small sons, and he said: "Bother, now I shall have to buy another Christmas present."[26]

The old friends in question were Eric and Dorrie Stein and 'Rickie', then just approaching his eighth birthday, was their youngest son Rick, who would become well known long after Balchin had died as a chef, restaurateur and television personality. He recalls that, on the occasions when his family were visited by Balchin, the novelist 'always wore nice suits and had long, very intellectual conversations with my mother'[27] and that 'He was always extremely nice to me and I found him amusing and very intelligent'.

Reviews of *Last Recollections of My Uncle Charles* appeared throughout November. Their tenor was mostly approving, and Nigel Nicolson[28] in the *Daily Dispatch* accorded the book almost unreserved praise: 'The stories are beautifully contrived [...] and they run in Mr. Balchin's easy dialogue as if fixed on casters'.

The Times was the only newspaper that expressed an outright dislike for the book:

> Mr. Nigel Balchin could not be boring if he tried, but in his Last Recollections of My Uncle Charles he is a great deal below his usual standard.

Their anonymous reviewer[29] claimed, not without some justification, that Uncle Charles's stories 'command attention at the outset but almost without exception disappoint at the end'. When reviewing *Last Recollections of My Uncle Charles*, several critics made comparisons between Balchin and Somerset Maugham, but it was only in *The Times* that the connection was used pejoratively:

> They [the stories] are all worldly reminiscences of the Somerset Maugham genre but entirely lacking the master's ability to turn the dross of trivial experience into the gold of literature.

Elizabeth Bowen[30] in the *Tatler and Bystander* described Balchin as 'a master story-teller' and said that 'Uncle Charles's narrations become spellbinders'. She also pointed out that Balchin was in a position to obtain additional mileage from some of the stories in his collection if he chose to do so:

> One must, however, admit that the finest tales, the masterpieces, are those most nearly told in the Balchin manner: "The Bars of the Cage", "The Forgetful Man" and "Among Friends" could each of them, had the author liked, been expanded into full-length novels.

Bowen's observation was a perspicacious one but she had plumped for the wrong medium: Balchin duly expanded 'Among Friends' into a film instead of a novel, which premiered in London in November 1955, about a year after copies of the first edition of *Last Recollections of My Uncle Charles* had been unpacked by the country's booksellers. Both the storyline of 'Among Friends'—namely the harbouring of a wanted man by a married couple, the female half of which was previously engaged to the runaway—and the central moral dilemma (is loyalty to an old friend more important than one's own convenience and morally upstanding nature?) were borrowed from Balchin's 1930s play *Carted Stag*.

In order to convert his idea into movie format, Balchin teamed up with the Boulting brothers once more, agreeing to write the screenplay for the last film that the siblings made before embarking on the series of celebrated comedies satirizing British institutions that began with *Private's Progress*, and subsequently gave us such screen gems as *Lucky Jim* and *I'm All Right Jack*. Despite additional contributions from Roy Boulting and Frank Harvey,[31] the eventual shooting script for *Josephine and Men* was neither fish nor fowl, as discerned by an anonymous reviewer[32] in *The Times*, who observed that the picture 'havers between two styles, two conceptions'. What the critic meant was that Balchin's script constituted an uneasy blend of farce and psychological case study:

> Certainly the lines and the "business" ask for, and get, occasional laughs, but the characters, becalmed in an old-world cottage, seem to be waiting for something side-splittingly funny to happen, for someone to lose his trousers, for instance. Instead, the psychiatrist, who is always whispering into Mr. Balchin's ear, threatens to take charge and turn the whole thing into a clinical examination of the egos of the people involved. This does not happen either, and *Josephine and Men* remains untidy, unresolved, amusing and entertaining in fits and starts...

'Among Friends' was emphatically not a farce and whoever chose to turn it into one for the screen made a catastrophically poor decision. Padded out to way beyond its natural length, and conceived more as a comedy than the taut psychological drama it could and should have been, *Josephine and Men* travestied Balchin's original story.

Despite the weighty presence of Peter Finch and Donald Sinden as Hewer and Stockman, respectively, and Glynis Johns as the titular heroine condemned to impersonate another of Balchin's too-good-to-be-true 'dream girls', it is Jack Buchanan as Uncle Charles who, as Elspeth Grant[33] in the *Tatler and Bystander* remarked adroitly, 'gives a trivial comedy its one touch of sophistication'. If *Josephine and Men* served no other purpose, it did establish that Buchanan, with his immaculately groomed appearance, mellifluous voice, urbanity and gently cajoling manner, was the living embodiment of Uncle Charles.

Fred Majdalany[34] in *Time and Tide* was the only journalist who seemed to like *Josephine and Men*, which he categorized as 'a pleasant little English comedy' with the 'quality of beguiling readability which is a feature of Nigel Balchin's novels'. Other film critics were nowhere near as complimentary about Balchin and the Boultings, ruthlessly dismantling their handiwork in the British newspapers and literary magazines.

Josephine and Men represents a definite nadir in Balchin's career as a film scriptwriter but he would soon follow this flop with one of his greatest triumphs.

*

BALCHIN: …usually novels which I write take place within a comparatively short period and on a comparatively concentrated canvas. This takes place over a period of—oh— nearly thirty years so there's a change in that respect [...]
ALLEN: There'd have to be a technical change to accompany that.
BALCHIN: Yes I don't know whether I can do it or not.
  – Balchin in conversation with Walter Allen, on the
BBC Radio programme *We Write Novels*[35]

After the variable quality of the stories in *Last Recollections of My Uncle Charles*, Balchin returned to his best form for his next novel, *The Fall of the Sparrow*, a book that must have been written principally during that productive period when Yovanka had been estranged from him in Yugoslavia. Pleasingly for both Balchin and William Collins, the new book sold about three times as many copies in hardback as the short-story compendium had the year before.

The Fall of the Sparrow, a roman-fleuve concerning an infuriating yet endearing central character called Jason Pellew, was published in September 1955. With its elongated time span and mellower tone, the novel was very different from anything the author had attempted to write before and it was received with great warmth by book reviewers, most of whom seemed to appreciate a welcome change in the scenery. K. John[36] in the *Illustrated London News* expressed this sentiment better than most when he said that 'there is no denying that he [Balchin] had worn sardonic anguish rather too hard'. Balchin had now succeeded in sanding down some of the rough edges that had been apparent in his fiction of a decade earlier; *The Fall of the Sparrow* is therefore a cosier, more enveloping read than certain of its predecessors and represents a high-water mark in his career as a storyteller.

One way of approaching *The Fall of the Sparrow* is to regard it as a ruthlessly condensed version of Anthony Powell's twelve-novel sequence *A Dance to the Music of Time*. It contains a much smaller cast of predominantly middle-class characters and the book does not run the same time course as Powell's masterpiece, describing as it does Jason's life between the ages of seven and thirty-six, but there is the same progression from school through university to working life, the war occupies a substantial portion of the narrative and characters keep bumping into each other by coincidence.

The Fall of the Sparrow can also be viewed as a kind of synthesis of some of the author's greatest successes as a novelist up until this point. It contains intriguing echoes of all three of the excellent novels that Balchin wrote during the Second World War: the narrator Henry Payne's work in a wartime physiological research outfit faintly recalls *The Small Back Room*; the evocation of London during the Blitz, and particularly a scene at a party, is heavily reminiscent of *Darkness Falls from the Air*; and when Jason is advised by Payne to consult a 'trick cyclist' and undergoes the preliminary stages of psychoanalysis the reader is transported temporarily to the setting of *Mine Own Executioner*.

If there is a problem with *The Fall of the Sparrow* then it lies with the maddening 'little man' himself. Despite Balchin's best efforts to make Jason as lifelike as possible he did not quite succeed, as Julian Symons[37] in *The Times Literary Supplement* correctly discerned:

> The trouble is that at the end of the book Pellew himself has still not come to life either as a character or as the symbolic social misfit Mr. Balchin evidently sees in him.

Jason is often either surrounded by colourful friends or dwarfed by whatever fresh catastrophe he is engulfed in at the time; he is defined by these other characters and situations and his own personality steadfastly refuses to emerge. As an unnamed obituarist in the *Guardian* observed in 1970, *The Fall of the Sparrow* 'attempts a difficult subject—a sympathetic yet objective understanding of the mind of a psychopath—and fails only because such a person is essentially unknowable'.[38] When we encounter Jason he is often withdrawn, sullen, dissembling or playing his cards too close to his chest to allow any significant personal disclosures to seep out. Balchin offers little hope for his protagonist and no explanation for his antisocial behaviour as an adult beyond that attributable to a difficult childhood blighted by the opposing poles of parental discipline represented by an insanely strict father and a limp dishrag of a mother. 'They fuck you up, your Mum and Dad' would be a suitable epitaph for Jason.

Jason may not fully 'come to life', but James remarked perceptively that 'Balchin has allowed his imaginative charmer an independent personality, one that can't be fully reproduced on a punched card'[39] and this would be because he was based on a real person. The inspiration for the character was a good friend of Yovanka's whom she had known in the years leading up to her initial meeting with Balchin and whom she last heard of when he was endeavouring to sell Scotch whisky to the South

Africans. Jason's girlfriend Leah is also far more realistic (i.e. less like a china doll) than many of the women who appear in the earlier novels and Balchin may have been influenced here by elements of his new wife's personality.

Two of Balchin's longest-standing supporters were very well disposed towards his new novel. Peter Quennell[40] in the *Daily Mail* said that the book was 'among the best that he has yet published' and, in the *Tatler and Bystander*, Bowen[41] wrote that the creator of *The Fall of the Sparrow* 'never lets the reader down'. The author of *The Heat of the Day* added that 'Mr. Balchin not merely retains his level: this time, he has risen to a peak'. The question of Jason's verisimilitude divided the critics, but Bowen offered a corrective to Symons's opinion, stating that Balchin's central character was for her 'so over-poweringly real, so living, that one cannot believe he is not in the room with one'. She wrapped up her review by revealing that '*The Fall of the Sparrow* is a somewhat heartbreaking novel: indeed, it haunts me.'

John Connell,[42] writing in the *Evening News*, also confessed that the story had got under his skin:

> I believe this to be Mr. Balchin's best book since "The Small Back Room"—but that may be because its theme is to me as haunting as it is apt.

In Connell's opinion, the account of Jason's vicissitudes constituted 'a brilliant, perplexing, distressing story' and one which 'strikes home to the heart with extreme sharpness again and again'.

John Davenport[43] began his review in the *Observer* with an unequivocal recommendation:

> Mr. Balchin's book should be bought openly by aspiring novelists: there is no more efficient practitioner in the business.

Davenport admired a book that was 'well constructed, economically written, serious, amusing, a miracle of competence'.

He did admit however, somewhat incongruously, that he had nevertheless found *The Fall of the Sparrow* to be 'curiously disappointing'.

After stunning Balchin with a low blow in 1953, on which occasion she had corralled him with Nevil Shute as a purveyor of 'sad little works of fiction'[44] whilst reviewing *Sundry Creditors*, Nancy Spain returned to the attack in 1955, hoping this time perhaps to land a knockout punch.

The controversial 'stunt columnist' had found herself in trouble a few months previously when she had contributed two pieces to a sequence of articles in the *Daily Express* entitled 'A Cool Look at the Loved Ones'. This was a series intended by the Beaverbrook paper to reappraise the careers of prominent figures in the arts world, such as J. B. Priestley, Laurence Olivier and his wife Vivien Leigh and Sir Malcolm Sargent. As her two 'targets', Spain selected the Poet Laureate John Masefield and Evelyn Waugh, and when she doorstepped the latter at his home near Stroud in June it initiated a chain of events that ended with Waugh successfully suing the *Express* for libel in 1956 to the tune of £5,000 (roughly £100,000 today), the main bone of contention being that Spain had dared to suggest that Waugh's books sold in smaller quantities than those of his brother Alec.[45]

Like Waugh, Balchin was a novelist whom Spain claimed to have enjoyed reading in her younger days. But in her opinion, Balchin had gone off the boil after writing the 'supremely moving and honest'[46] *Darkness Falls from the Air*, thereafter producing novels that resembled 'faint rubber stamp impressions deriving from this prototype'.

Spain's 'review' of *The Fall of the Sparrow* was entitled 'My grouse against Nigel Balchin'.[47] She dismissed the novel in four scanty paragraphs, reserving the remaining three-quarters of her weekly books column in the *Express* for a lengthy fulminating condemnation of both Balchin the man and Balchin the novelist, which began with the provocative statement 'For some years now I have wanted to complain about Nigel Balchin' and continued with a litany of factual errors. The tone of the piece can be intuited from scrutiny of the only critical comment of direct relevance to the book she was supposed to be reviewing:

> ...Jason was condemned right from the start to become one day one of Mr. Balchin's poor mixed-up kids, one of Mr. Balchin's favourite psychopathic heroes. Which seems to me the most depressing fate that can befall anyone.

There were some grains of wheat among Spain's bruising fusillade of chaff. One of her barbs that was broadly true may have wounded Balchin although it would surely have been familiar to her victim from reviews of his books from the mid-1940s onwards:

> Balchin as a novelist is an excellent psychologist and a fine reporter. He writes novels that skim over the surface of human emotions all right, but he never (as an artist should) produces any *depth* of emotion. Nor does he offer any solution for his characters.

Spain concluded that 'It is better by far to be inarticulate and to have something to say than to say nothing at all as smoothly as Mr. Balchin says it.'

Just what was it about Balchin that had so inflamed Nancy Spain? In her two 1950s reviews of his novels, the critic gave no indication that she had ever encountered the object of her derision in person, but Elizabeth Jane Howard, a friend of Spain's at about this time, considered that they probably did know each other to some extent ('I should think it's very likely that they met[48]) and that a social gathering may have provided a plausible venue for such a meeting: 'There were far more literary parties then than there are now'. Howard also suggested that Balchin's female characters might have caused the lesbian journalist to wrinkle her nose in disgust:

> If she liked you she would be very loyal. She must have had it in for him from somewhere. Maybe she just very much disliked how he wrote about women.

The Fall of the Sparrow (1955)

The book begins with Henry Payne, the narrator, receiving news that an old friend of his has got into trouble with the police. Jason Pellew is being held in prison, awaiting trial. We are then taken back in time to find out why Jason turned out the way he did...

Payne first meets Jason in the mid-1920s when they are both small boys. Jason's father, a retired sapper general, is an irascible martinet who treats his son as if he were a recalcitrant junior officer instead of a close blood relative, and Jason in consequence is terrified of him. A few years later, Jason joins Payne at his public school and soon makes himself very unpopular with prefects and teachers alike. Shortly after receiving a 'house beating' for acting like a "swanky little tick", Jason is informed that his father has died in a lunatic asylum. Upon returning to school after a period of mourning, Jason endears himself to staff and fellow pupils alike in a new guise as a loveable eccentric.

The two principal characters are reunited at Cambridge and also meet on several occasions during the Second World War. Jason disports himself with reckless gallantry at Dunkirk and wins the Military Cross for his part in a cloak-and-dagger operation in Italy. But he then starts to unravel, and becomes even more psychologically unstable when he learns that his girlfriend has been killed whilst employed on a clandestine mission for the navy. Following a breakdown, Jason is invalided out of the army.

Jason adapts badly to England in peacetime: he struggles to find work, and after an inadvisable marriage to a rich socialite disintegrates he turns to crime as a possible solution to a shortage of funds. We are then back to where we came in, with the judge poised to deliver his verdict.

Unlike Evelyn Waugh, Balchin chose not to react publicly to Spain's bilious attack on him. But as Yovanka admits, her husband was certainly aware of the unwarranted assault on his reputation and was hurt by it: 'unfortunately, a lot of it was true. Which actually at the time was exactly what Nigel didn't want'.[49] Perhaps wisely then, after finishing the superb *The Fall of the Sparrow*, Balchin wrote no more novels for seven years. Instead, he focused all of his creative energy on writing screenplays, and in so doing escaped the poisonous tentacles of ill-tempered book reviewers such as Nancy Spain.

19

The Man Who Never Was

In view of the mediocre quality of his last two film projects (*Malta Story* and *Josephine and Men*) and the fact that he had written only a brace of truly outstanding scripts (for *Mine Own Executioner* and *Mandy*) in almost a decade of screenwriting, it is surprising that Hollywood, in the shape of Twentieth Century Fox, came calling for Balchin in the mid-1950s and made him a lucrative offer to write scripts for them for the next few years. Yet this is exactly what happened, Yovanka recalling that her husband struck a deal with Fox that saw him placed under contract to script 'three films a year for three years'.[1] In return for his services, Balchin was offered a salary of '£30,000 a year' (about £600,000 a year today). Elizabeth Jane Howard also confirmed that Balchin was paid considerable sums of money by Fox:

> He had a retainer of $5,000 a week [about £30,000 a week today] from Hollywood, whether he worked or not. And that was a lot of money in those days, as a retainer.[2]

Before taking up his new position with Fox, Balchin wrote a script in England for Sumar Films, a Fox affiliate. *The Man Who Never Was* describes the design, execution and aftermath of Operation Mincemeat, a World War Two confidence trick dreamt up and perpetrated by Naval Intelligence. The mechanics of Operation Mincemeat were outlined in a review of the film penned by an anonymous contributor[3] to *The Times*:

> The man who never was is, of course, the dead body dressed in the uniform of an officer of the Royal Marines which

was launched off a submarine to drift on to the shores of the Spanish peninsula. On the body were documents and a letter, signed by Mountbatten, written to suggest that the main allied attack would be on Greece, not Sicily.[4] The odds against the series of events which would result in the Germans acting on the information seemed great, but the gamble came off.

As portrayed in the film, the plan was envisaged by Commander Ewen Montagu (Clifton Webb) and allowed to proceed only after it had gained the grudging approval of his chief:

> "In over thirty years of intelligence work I've never heard of anything like it. [...] It's the most outrageous, disgusting, preposterous (not to say barbaric) idea. But work out full details and be on hand at the War Cabinet offices at four-thirty tomorrow afternoon."

Campbell Dixon[5] in the *Sunday Telegraph* shrewdly observed that the best feature of the movie was the implementation of the deception scheme: 'So long as it sticks to facts, the story of the plan is fascinating'. The flaws are to be found elsewhere, with Leslie Halliwell[6] pinpointing the main one when he spoke of the film being 'marred by an emotional romantic sub-plot'. This is largely the fault of Gloria Grahame (on loan from Hollywood), who is unconvincing as a librarian whose tears for her dead pilot boyfriend are mistaken by the Nazi spy checking up on the bona fides of 'William Martin'—the name given to the corpse used in the operation—as grief for the body washed up on the beach. Webb's accent veers freely between both sides of the Atlantic but the actor reins in the more irritating of his mannerisms, whilst retaining flashes of the amusing irascibility with which he had made his name as a cantankerous journalist in *Laura*. The investigations of Stephen Boyd as the Nazi agent from the Emerald Isle, which were bolted onto the true story by Balchin, have an air of falsity about them despite their watchability.

And yet the positives far outweigh the negatives. The

playing of the minor parts is of a uniformly high standard, with stalwart British character actors such as Laurence Naismith, André Morrell, Geoffrey Keen and Michael Hordern all turning in above-par performances. The picture is very well constructed, Balchin's dialogue is sharp and direct and Ronald Neame's assured direction keeps the action moving in a smooth, swift rush. Of all the movies for which Balchin contributed the screenplay, *The Man Who Never Was* is the most satisfying, and also the most cinematic. Modern-day viewers will probably agree with the verdict of Dixon,[7] who confessed that 'despite its perfunctory love story, the film held me enthralled'.

The success of *The Man Who Never Was* must have partly stemmed from the fact that its scriptwriter would have felt very much at home in the world that he was asked to write about, the screenplay containing many Balchinesque elements familiar from his novels of the 1940s and 1950s. These include a scene depicting testing of military equipment, descriptions of high-level Whitehall conferences, a scientific plot thread, a death-bed sequence and the inclusion in the cast of two actresses, Grahame and Josephine Griffin, who adopt the stereotypical Balchin female roles of a vamp and a not very realistic maternal girl, respectively. In addition, what Halliwell[8] called the 'fictitious spy hunt which cheers up the last half hour' is very much in the vein of that to be found in *A Sort of Traitors*.

An advertising wheeze cooked up by Fox to promote *The Man Who Never Was* led to security being tightened at naval establishments in Portsmouth in the spring of 1956. Cinema attendances in the mid-1950s were in sharp decline in the face of intense competition from the newer medium of television, and therefore, as one social historian has recorded, 'cinemas under threat were resorting to all sorts of gimmicks and promotions to try to retain their once loyal audiences'.[9] On the day before the charity premiere of *The Man Who Never Was* in London on 14 March, *The Times* reported that about a thousand fake identity cards, all bearing the name William Martin and depicting the outline of a face into which blank space an unscrupulous type could have pasted their photograph, had been issued by a Portsmouth cinema that was due to screen the film the following week. It is not known how many different William Martins attempted to hoodwink naval security checks but clearly the service was taking no chances, as the secretary to the Commander-in-Chief at Portsmouth informed the newspaper that:

"At a quick glance one of these cards might be mistaken for a proper identity card, and all sentries are being instructed to examine the identity cards of any officers whom they do not recognize personally."[10]

Assisted by this inspired piece of publicity, *The Man Who Never Was* proceeded to do brisk business at the box office.[11]

Balchin flew to Los Angeles on 16 June 1955 to begin work for Fox. The first book dropped into his in-basket for adaptation was *The Nursemaid Who Disappeared*, a 1938 novel by Philip MacDonald, an accomplished British writer of detective thrillers.

Balchin's screenplay was entitled *Twenty-Three Paces to Baker Street*. Phillip, a blind playwright, overhears a conversation in a pub that suggests to him that he is witnessing the formulation of a kidnap plot. The police feel that there is insufficient evidence to go on, leaving the playwright with no choice but to play detective himself, with the help of his manservant and his ex-fiancée, and the scene is thus set for an enjoyable race against time as the trio of amateur sleuths strain every sinew to try to prevent a serious crime from being committed.

Like Burgess Meredith (*Mine Own Executioner*) and Clifton Webb (*The Man Who Never Was*) before him, American actor Van Johnson was dispatched to England to star in *Twenty-Three Paces to Baker Street*. Johnson's performance was a distractingly mannered one, consisting of frequent agonized twitches and bouts of face-pulling. His character also possesses a mournful self-loathing streak, and an unnamed film reviewer[12] in *The Times* identified who had embellished him with this unattractive personality trait, observing that the playwright is 'embittered by blindness and makes no bones about it (the part is a bore, a weakness in the film for which Mr. MacDonald is not responsible)'. Phillip is of course another of Balchin's psychological studies of physically damaged men (following on from Sammy Rice in *The Small Back Room* and Ivor Gates in *A Sort of Traitors*) and one of his least successful ones. The way was therefore open for the actor playing the manservant to steal the show. As *The Times* pointed out, he displayed 'all the massive suavity, the mournful impressiveness, with which Mr. Cecil Parker can endow a part'.

Halliwell[13] wrote that *Twenty-Three Paces to Baker Street* was a 'Sufficiently engrossing murder mystery'. *The Times*[14] rightly asserted that 'the direction of Mr. Henry Hathaway needs tightening here and there', whilst also remarking that *Twenty-Three Paces to Baker Street* 'does not let the audience down and is, of its type and class, an admirable film'. Balchin himself thought otherwise, telling Yovanka in a letter home that '23 Paces is awful. But awful'.[15]

After completing his screenplay for the film in the early autumn of 1955, Balchin, in company with Yovanka, walked up the gangplank of an iconic oceangoing liner so that he could return to his homeland for a while. So famous had Balchin become by now that even this comparatively humdrum occurrence was reported on by one of London's evening newspapers, the *Evening News*:

> Homeward bound in the Queen Mary from America to-day so that the baby they are expecting in December will be born English are the novelist Nigel Balchin and his wife Yovanka.[16]

The paper also informed its readers that Balchin was hoping to 'find a house in London for the birth but he will probably return to Hollywood afterwards'.

The couple did not succeed in finding a house in time and so were forced to settle instead for a mere pair of luxury flats. Their old friend Eric Stein had now risen to become a director of the Distillers Company and the firm had acquired an entire row of Georgian houses, Connaught Place, just around the corner from Marble Arch. The lower floors were converted into offices for Distillers. The upper floors—complete with enticing views of Hyde Park—were divided into flats and let to friends of the owners. The Balchins claimed two of these apartments: one for themselves and the other being held in reserve for use as a nursery, Yovanka later commenting that this demonstration of extravagance, which would characterize most of the couple's married life, had been 'utterly ridiculous'.[17] She also recalled that her husband, ever sexually aware, had joked that the proximity of the flats to Hyde Park (a popular stomping ground for prostitutes) meant that 'if you ever needed a tart all you had to do was to lower a bucket in front of the house and bring her up!'.

Balchin's only male heir, Charles Zoran Marlin, was born in London at the very end of 1955. Celebrating the birth a few months later, *Woman's Own* sketched in some background for its readers:

> Just before he was born his mother finished watching her favourite TV show and then went to hospital—which seems to be a way with modern mothers![18]

The show in question ('TV's most popular panel game'[19]) was *What's My Line?*, the guessing game in which a small band of celebrities had to ask questions in order to establish the occupations of a number of famous guests. The edition that Yovanka watched aired at 9 pm on Boxing Day, on which occasion those doing the guessing included Lady Isobel Barnett and Kenneth Horne. (Just under a year later, on 25 November 1956, Balchin was one of the guests that the panel, made up of Gilbert Harding, Bob Monkhouse and Isobel Barnett again, had to attempt to identify.)

Yovanka experienced contractions soon after her favourite programme had finished and was whisked by taxi the short distance to St Mary's Hospital in Paddington. Baby Charles was delivered by Caesarean section in the private Lindo Wing of the hospital (where both Princess Diana and the Duchess of Cambridge would subsequently give birth) during the early hours of 27 December. *Woman's Own* gushed that 'we'll make a little bet right now, that when he looked at his new baby son and his lovely wife, his worldly successes faded and Mr. Balchin knew the happiest and most satisfying moment of his whole life'.[20] If this was so then Balchin did not have much time to enjoy the company of the new addition to his family: by the middle of January 1956 he was installed in the Beverly Hills Hotel in Hollywood and had reported for work on the Fox lot again.

*

...I found a great deal of fear among people in Hollywood— fear of not succeeding, and fear of succeeding but then losing the success. I've often said that it was a pitiless place, full of insecure people, men and women who had nervous breakdowns, or who were alcoholics or had other crippling problems. The unhappiness out there was like the smog—it covered everything.

– Grace Kelly[21]

Grace Kelly only worked in Hollywood for about five years in the 1950s. After making *High Society* in 1956 she left the smog-ridden atmosphere of Los Angeles behind her in order to marry Prince Rainier. The actress claimed not to have enjoyed the time she had spent working in the Californian film industry ('I never really liked Hollywood'). Kelly's abiding impressions of Hollywood would later have resonated with Balchin had the pulchritudinous star with the 'ice maiden' looks been in a position to exchange notes with the tall, dapper English scriptwriter who began working in Los Angeles at almost exactly the same time that Kelly was adjusting to her new life in the Principality of Monaco:

...I found it unreal—unreal and full of men and women whose lives were confused and full of pain. To outsiders, it looked like a glamorous life, but it really was not.

Balchin's view of Hollywood, forged after six years there, on and off, was more concise and matter of fact and couched in

297

less melodramatic language, but the underlying sentiment was broadly in line with that of Kelly:

> …Hollywood is a dull place where you come to do a job and go away again as quickly as you can.[22]

If Kelly's life in Hollywood was unglamorous, then that of Balchin, positioned several crucial links further down the movie-making food chain, contained even less sparkle. Yovanka considers that it was principally the tedium of the scriptwriting process ('it was boring'[23]) that led to Balchin soon becoming unhappy with his work in the Fox offices and she is also of the opinion that her husband had combatted his unhappiness with bouts of heavy drinking. Writing in a small cubicle, with a secretary positioned on the other side of a partition, Balchin was labouring within the same sort of soul-sapping environment he had endeavoured to ameliorate for the menial workers of British industry in the early 1930s, as his widow makes clear:

> You go into the studio [at] nine o'clock in the morning and you stay there 'til five and you're given a book to script. It was not a creative existence.[24]

In an interview printed in the *Daily Mail* at the beginning of 1962 and wanly entitled 'What they did to me in Hollywood',[25] Balchin elaborated on the demoralizing experience of having operated for a while as a small and relatively insignificant component of the vast American cinema enterprise:

> "It is immensely hard and difficult work. But I wanted to find the answer to a question that obsessed me—whether it is possible finally to see on the screen something approximating to what you intended.
>
> I now know the answer. It is possible. It is also possible to win the football pools."

Part of Balchin's dissatisfaction with screenwriting was attributable to the involvement of so many other parties in the film-making process ('it is bound to be one-fiftieth yourself and 49-fiftieths other people'). However, his low expectations when he had first entered the profession meant that at least he had not suffered the deflating experience of having all his idealism knocked out of him:

> "Yet I have not been disillusioned about film-writing, for I was never illusioned.
>
> There is a type who flirts briefly with Hollywood, then runs away clutching his skirts about him, as if an indecent suggestion had been made, and writes articles about how his integrity was nearly ravished.
>
> I haven't rushed off clutching my skirts. It was an experiment that I wanted to make that I have now made."

*

The rifts between Balchin and Yovanka, which had become apparent within a year of their union being made official in the confines of the Marylebone Registry Office, were not sealed by the birth of their first child; if anything, Charles's arrival caused them to widen. The fragile harmony of the relationship was undoubtedly undermined by the scriptwriter's globetrotting: during his 'Hollywood years' he estimated that he had clocked up either 120,000, 150,000 or half a million miles of air travel, depending on which newspaper report one prefers to believe, as he crisscrossed the planet on film company business.[26] In the first couple of years of Charles's life, Yovanka divided her time between London and whichever part of the world her husband happened to be working in. This inevitably led to a pattern of intimacy being gradually re-established after an enforced lull, only for a period of separation to then intervene and weaken the bonds between the couple, as Yovanka explained in a letter to her husband written at the end of 1957:

> To say that I miss you would be an understatement; you always go away just when I fall in love with you all over

again. And then I stay alone, get resentful and by the time you get back (usually by the fastest route) I could kill you.[27]

The oscillating fortunes of the Balchins' marriage are encapsulated by events that unfolded during 1956. In January, the scriptwriter wrote his wife what she referred to as 'a loving letter'[28] from Hollywood, but the mood then quickly darkened because on 15 March he sent her 'another "Nigel" letter', meaning that he was responding, calmly and logically, to a communication from her in which she had suggested that they should split up. In June there was a further exchange of letters discussing a possible parting of the ways, but, the following month, Yovanka and Charles flew to America and the Balchins rented a house for the summer at Belfast Drive in Beverly Hills. By October, Yovanka was installed again in England having, by her own admission, 'been horrid to Nigel', and in November the heightened tension in the marriage was preoccupying the pair to such an extent that Balchin felt the need to write what Yovanka described as 'a very loving letter, a desperate one but loving nevertheless'.

When he reviewed a new production of Noël Coward's *Private Lives* in 2012, *Daily Telegraph* theatre critic Charles Spencer[29] characterized the two lovers at the heart of that play, Elyot and Amanda, as a couple who 'can't live together and can't live apart'. Reading that description, one is acutely reminded of Balchin and Yovanka, particularly when Spencer outlined the attributes required of any actors who attempt to fill the leading roles in *Private Lives*:

> You really need to feel that this is a pair that have great sex together but drive each other mad when they aren't in bed. Perhaps that's precisely why the sex is so good.

Yovanka could almost have been referring to Elyot and Amanda, and not to herself and her husband, when she described sex as the glue that had held their delicate relationship in one piece, albeit precariously at times, for the best part of twenty years:

I honestly think that the reason we boxed and coxed so much about being together, parting, being together again was that when we did get together sex was so great that it kept us afloat until the next breakdown of communication.[30]

*

Soon after the top rate of tax had been established at 97.5% following Labour Chancellor Hugh Gaitskell's budget in April 1951,[31] Balchin had expressed the opinion that being subject to this 'Supertax' would be likely to hinder his development as a novelist:

"The writer no longer has freedom of action. I cannot save up and give myself a year to try new work I think important."[32]

In the wake of that pronouncement, Balchin wrote just two more novels—*Sundry Creditors* and *The Fall of the Sparrow*— before turning his back on fiction-writing for a prolonged period in preference to working for the film industry, where he was asked to adapt other people's writing (and was handsomely remunerated for doing so) and was not required to generate his own ideas for stories at his own expense. Over the course of 1956 he pondered the best way to make the most of the vast, but very possibly short-lived, wealth he was accruing from the film business. His solution was to stop commuting between London and Hollywood and instead to live solely outside the UK. In some notes he wrote for his own benefit in 1959,[33] Balchin explained the reasoning behind his decision to become a tax exile:

Our original object in this whole operation was to create a cushion of capital for me, and this is obviously still desirable. One of the chief objects for which the capital cushion was required was to insure the proper maintenance and education of my children, and this obligation still exists. But another main object was to make proper provision for my wife at my death or at the time when I cease to earn. She is twenty-two years younger than I and it is a reasonable assumption that had we remained together[34] I should have predeceased her by many years.

Balchin's new life as a refugee from the British taxation system began in the first few days of 1957, when he flew to Los Angeles after a Christmas break in England to resume work for Fox. As a consequence of his screenwriting peripateticism, he would barely set foot on the soil of his native country again until autumn 1961. From Hollywood, Balchin's travels took him to Paris, where he hired a room at the Hotel Raphael in February for use as an office, remembering his liking for the place when he had stayed there in 1944 to observe the liberation of the city by the Allies. He worked first on a screenplay entitled *Destruction Test*. The film that was subsequently developed from Balchin's script took almost four years to lumber its way through the Hollywood machine and when it was finally threaded onto cinema projectors it had changed its name to *Circle of Deception*.

The last Balchin-scripted film to appear under the Twentieth Century Fox banner was a wartime 'mission' movie with a psychological theme that thus played to one of the screenwriter's principal strengths. In outline, the plot of *Circle of Deception* is very similar to that of *The Man Who Never Was*. In place of a corpse laden with false information, the central character of *Circle of Deception*, Paul Raine, is a live agent parachuted into occupied France in 1944, captured by the Germans, tortured by the SS and made to reveal details of which communications channels the French Resistance are required to destroy in order to assist the imminent Allied invasion. The twist in this tale is that although Raine has been primed with false information that will serve to divert German resources from the true Resistance targets, he does not *know* that it is phoney. Therefore, when he breaks down under torture his shame is genuine and this convinces his interrogators that he is telling the truth.

With regard to its atmosphere (and much of its material), *Circle of Deception* is the most Balchinesque of the many film scripts that the novelist wrote. It contains depictions of the interviews and psychological assessments that Raine submits to before he is identified as being in possession of the required combination of temperamental instabilities that should enable him to succeed in his mission. Much of the early part of the film is set in London, there is a scene that takes place during an air raid that is reminiscent of *Darkness Falls from the Air* or *The Fall of the Sparrow* and, before his departure for France, Raine falls in love, in time-honoured Balchin fashion, with one of his female colleagues. Raine (like Sammy Rice and Felix Milne) is an archetypal Balchin character haunted by the prospect of failure and driven by a burning need to prove himself ("I never know whether I've got any guts until I try something").

Halliwell[35] described *Circle of Deception* as 'Depressing' and this is a very fair summation of a relentlessly downbeat movie composed of dark subject matter and disfigured by an ugly torture sequence as it approaches its finale. When it was released in Britain on 30 January 1961, Penelope Houston[36] in the *Monthly Film Bulletin* was also unimpressed with *Circle of Deception*, stating that 'There is a striking story here, and the disappointment is that the film has left it unexplored'.

The undoubted highlight of Balchin's career as a film scriptwriter came in February 1957, while he was striving to finish his script for *Destruction Test*, when he was informed that he had won that year's British Film Academy award for Best British Screenplay for the work he had carried out two years previously on *The Man Who Never Was*. Balchin had faced tough competition in the shape of *Reach for the Sky*, the Nevil Shute-derived *A Town Like Alice* and three films scripted by erstwhile collaborators of his—the Boulting brothers' *Private's Progress*, *Smiley* (co-authored by Anthony Kimmins) and Powell and Pressburger's *The Battle of the River Plate*—but he emerged from the contest victorious.[37] Becoming a British Film Academy award winner burnished Balchin's reputation in Hollywood and increased his market value when he became a free agent again in 1959 on completion of his final assignment for Fox.

20

'A Very Destructive Period': Florence 1957–1962

The trips that Balchin had taken to Italy after the war, first with Elisabeth and later with Yovanka, had left him with an abiding love of the Mediterranean country. Tired of working in a Parisian hotel room, he sought greater permanence in his domestic arrangements and so, in the late summer of 1957, Yovanka began the search for a new home for her family somewhere else in Europe. The south of France was toyed with—but quickly rejected—and following a house-hunting expedition in Florence, she settled for a rented villa a few miles outside the Tuscan capital, in the small hillside community of Fiesole. Balchin's wife and child and the family dog William were installed at 3 Via delle Coste by October. It would however be another couple of months before Balchin himself would be able to enjoy the comforts of his plush new residence in the land that Percy Bysshe Shelley had appropriately called 'a paradise of exiles'. This was because in November he boarded a plane to Japan in response to a plea for help from his good friend John Huston, the celebrated American director of *The Maltese Falcon*, *Moby Dick* and *The African Queen*.

Huston was directing *The Barbarian and the Geisha*, a vehicle for John Wayne, for Twentieth Century Fox. Dissatisfied with the labours of the original screenwriter, Huston sent for Balchin and, in Yovanka's words, asked him to 'do a rescue job'[1] on the script. But it proved to be incapable of salvage, leaving the director to remark that '*The Barbarian and the Geisha* turned out to be a bad picture'.[2] Balchin's name was missing from the credits and it is uncertain what the scale of his contribution was to a stilted and dreary film reputed to be the only Wayne movie not to have made a profit.

Even though he now had a home in Italy, 1958 was another nomadic year for Balchin, which saw him dividing his working hours between Hollywood, Paris, Greece and also the south of France, where he met his old wartime boss Winston Churchill with a view to writing a film dramatization of the great statesman's early life for MGM, although this idea failed to get off the drawing board. Leisure time was split between Rome, Florence and Dubrovnik, and it was in the vicinity of the 'pearl of the Adriatic' that a romance was enacted that would again endanger the Balchins' fragile marriage.

With her husband occupied with his film work, Yovanka spent the summer of 1958 with Charles and her Yugoslavian relatives at the seaside in what is now Croatia. Her mother Vera hired a villa for them in Mlini, near Dubrovnik, and Balchin came over for a brief visit. Yovanka can remember Balchin and Vera—who were of a similar age—ganging up against her on some long-forgotten pretext and how she had been desperately upset that Balchin had sided with his mother-in-law and not his wife. Lingering resentment of her husband's perceived disloyalty may have been the spark that found readily combustible tinder on a beach on the Dalmatian coast. Here Yovanka met Steven Dedijer, who in her eyes resembled 'a Jugoslav intellectual copy of Nigel',[3] and as Balchin had now left Mlini to resume his Fox-sponsored globetrotting, the way was open for a relationship to develop.

Yovanka's new acquaintance, a forty-seven-year-old writer, academic and visiting professor at the University of Zagreb, immediately impressed her as being both 'very gregarious' and 'huge fun' and the rapprochement between the two Yugoslavs soon turned into rather more than just a carefree holiday romance. Yovanka stayed with Steven in Zagreb that summer, and after she and Charles had returned to Fiesole she remained in close touch with him.

During the winter of 1958–1959, while Balchin worked on his final batch of Fox assignments in Hollywood, Yovanka—now installed in another villa outside Florence that she and

Balchin had chosen for themselves—was torn between her husband and her new boyfriend and agonized over her future. Steven presented a proposal to her. He intended to obtain a chair in either Sweden or the USA and suggested that Yovanka and Charles should come and live with him in one of those two countries. Over in California, Balchin was perturbed by this development, not wishing to lose contact with his son, and so he intervened in the tug-of-war that was taking place for possession of Yovanka's heart, as she explains:

> He writes the most incredibly generous and WISE letters (having been there before with Elisabeth). I send Steven's letters to Nigel. Nigel warns me that Steven might not have my interests totally at heart; Steven senses that *my* heart might still really belong to Nigel. Nigel sits and waits. I don't know what I really, really want.

Unlike the case of his wife's earlier affair with Jovan Milicevic (see Chapter 18), which Balchin seems to have treated more or less as a joke, this latest alliance struck him as being far more serious. On 2 May he took a break from working on his first draft script for the film *Cleopatra* in order to write some lengthy notes analysing his financial position in what he took to be the likely event that he would soon be without a wife.[4] In these, he considered making a one-off payment to Yovanka of $30,000 (about £150,000 today), which would considerably lessen 'the sum which it would be necessary for me to leave at death', and debated where he would go to live if he became forcibly single again, the options on the table including remaining in the USA, returning either to England or Europe or residing instead 'somewhere like the West Indies or Bermuda where English is spoken but which will not upset my taxation situation'.

While Balchin waited and Yovanka assessed the pros and cons of the two men in her life, Steven took decisive action to ensure his future happiness. He arranged a meeting with Yovanka in Ljubljana and, as she recalls, informed her that he was calling time on their affair:

> He then tells me that whereas he has loved me and always
> will, he senses that I will never totally belong to him and that
> he has decided to live with someone else who was prepared to
> be totally his. Nigel did warn me![5]

'Devastated', but at the same time 'hugely relieved' to be released from her commitment to Steven, Yovanka flew to Los Angeles to be with her husband and the next month that they spent together in California, after a heavy emotional weight had been lifted off their shoulders, was in her opinion 'probably one of the happiest periods of our lives'.

*

Speaking of the three years that the Balchins spent at the third of three Tuscan villas that they inhabited, the beautiful Villa di Tizzano, which was perched in the hills above Florence overlooking the Chianti region and came complete with 'an 80-mile view to the sea',[6] Yovanka remarked that 'In many ways it should have been the most idyllic of existences'.[7] In reality, it proved to be very different. Of the four family members who moved into the Florentine villa in August 1959, only one, three-year-old Charles, subsequently found the experience to be an enriching and memorable one. William, the couple's much-loved boxer who had been an important part of their lives since the Portman Square days that had preceded their marriage, lasted only a matter of weeks in the hot Tuscan sun before expiring from heart failure. Balchin returned to England two years later with the manuscript of a sparkling new novel tucked under his arm, but otherwise all he had to show for his Italian sojourn was an extensively ulcerated stomach.

As touched on briefly in Chapter 1, the fifteenth century Villa di Tizzano belonged to Count Pandolfini but was vacated in a hurry after the younger of the Count's two sons accidentally shot and killed the elder whilst cleaning guns after a shoot, the Contessa refusing to have anything to do with the place from that point onwards. When the lease on their second Italian home ran out and they were unable to renew it, the Balchins could not believe their luck when

Tizzano unexpectedly became available to rent.

The villa, which was ringed by an estate comprising twenty or more farms, was for Yovanka 'an absolutely fabulous house with the most glorious panoramic views towards Florence'. Staff were on hand to attend to the Balchins' every need, with the retinue of servants including a butler, and Yovanka's duties extended only as far as informing the cook in the morning what food they wanted to eat that day. The 'lovely Italian garden, full of vistas and paths and cypresses and huge stone urns' was also not a space in which she could exercise any creative flair because 'the gardener kept it all in trim'. Even the care of her child had been entrusted to someone else: 'Charles basically lived in a world of his own, surrounded by doting peasants and his beloved Julianna [an Italian nanny]'. With time weighing heavy on her hands, Yovanka 'was bored and sulked' and her life in Italy acquired a listless quality: 'There was nothing to *do*. You just sat and looked out of your window'.[8] Apart from lunching on occasions with the famous aesthete Harold Acton at his nearby villa and swimming in the pool of the American Club in Florence during the warmer months, Yovanka had little in the way of company and grew discontented with the Tuscan lifestyle: 'I hated it, Nigel loved it'.

What was it about his Florentine abode that Balchin found so convivial? Unlike Yovanka, for whom familiarity rapidly bred contempt, the scriptwriter did not spend all his time at home but continued to travel extensively at the behest of a number of movie companies. Once he had stopped working for Fox at the beginning of 1960 he had no need to commute to Hollywood any longer and was able to do his scriptwriting primarily within Europe. But he still spent a lot of his time travelling and could thus view Tizzano with fresh eyes every time he returned home, exhausted, after a scriptwriting conference or a meeting about a potential new film project. There was also a plentiful supply of alcohol for Balchin to enjoy in the bowels of the house. When the Pandolfinis had abandoned the villa they had left behind them, as Yovanka recalls, 'a huge cellar full of the Count's wine'[9] and her husband wasted no time in sampling the multifarious vintages, with predictably damaging consequences:

> He just sat, looked at the Chianti hills, drank an awful lot because the wine was down in the cellar [...] He enjoyed it; he liked it like that. But it was very destructive.[10]

The decline in the quality of Balchin's writing that became apparent during the 1960s—the only time in his career when he was a full-time writer of books—partly had its roots in the life of indolence and lethargy that he had lived in Florence. The city that had provided Shelley, Byron, Robert and Elizabeth Barrett Browning, Henry James, E. M. Forster and many others with bountiful inspiration failed to work a similar magic on Balchin, who in Yovanka's opinion found the prospect of following in the footsteps of such distinguished company too daunting:

> ...as he himself said, everything had been written about Florence—there was nothing there to inspire you. So he had no experience—nothing was happening to him.

Balchin, a former Minor Counties cricketer in his youth and who had entered his forties as a man who still took part in the odd game of cricket or played an occasional round of golf, had now sunk irrevocably into a sedentary existence. With the exception of a frame or two of snooker at the Savile Club when he was back in London, the playing of sport would be firmly off the agenda for the rest of his life. He continued to practise one of his favourite pastimes, woodcarving, a half-ton cabinet being just one of the carpentry projects he accomplished whilst living in Florence, but another hobby now occupied much of his free time. Perhaps all the hours Balchin had spent on film sets during the previous decade had instilled a passion for cinematography because in the late 1950s he indulged his love of gadgetry—tape-recorders and cameras were among his favourite electrical playthings—by buying a Bell & Howell cine camera. He used this new toy extensively over the course of the next few years to record his family's travels in Europe and America and also to document his children growing up. Many of these silent home movies have survived and there are some brief clips, presumably shot by Yovanka, that depict Balchin playing with Charles in Italy. As he instructs his son in the rudiments of bows and arrows or leaps out of a hedge in the course of a game of hide and seek, to the delight of the small boy, Balchin demonstrates that he was more than willing to spend time with his children whenever the demands of a film scriptwriter's life allowed. In the footage that he shot of the gardens and surrounding countryside at Tizzano, which was captured more than half a century ago, the colour palette of the Tuscan scenery still seems remarkably bright and vivid and the vibrant images shimmer with the intense heat of an Italian summer.

The heat of central Italy may have helped Balchin to conjure up the feel of Egypt and Rome, two of the principal settings for *Cleopatra*, his last film project for Fox. After scripting an ill-advised updated version of *The Blue Angel*, that 'masterwork of late twenties German grotesquerie'[11] that had made an international star out of Marlene Dietrich, Balchin commenced work on *Cleopatra* at the start of 1959, using as his template the script of a 1917 silent movie version that had been prised out of the Fox vaults. He produced three draft screenplays over the course of the next year. By the time it finally received its premiere in New York's Times Square in June 1963, Balchin's work had been abandoned and thus his input predictably went unmentioned in the credits. In the interim, numerous other writers—including the novelist Lawrence Durrell—had attempted to produce a workable script, two script consultants had been employed, the original director had been fired and replaced by another who insisted on writing his own script from scratch and the film had mushroomed in length to a bloated and indigestible 243 minutes, although it had been trimmed to a more palatable 192 minutes when the picture went on general release. The tortuous writing process gave Balchin ample scope to make merry quips in the newspapers about his early role in the debacle, telling the *Daily Mail* at the start of 1962 that he had written 'the first folio edition of *Cleopatra*'[12] and explaining to the *Evening Standard* the previous autumn that his initial labours had later been diluted by the involvement of so many others:

> "In Hollywood I was involved in the First Folio stage of Cleopatra—though everyone on this earth has had a share in it by now."[13]

Yovanka considers that her husband's script for the movie was subsequently rewritten and dumbed down in order to make it acceptable to the average cinemagoer ('he did a beautiful script [...] but it was too highbrow'[14]).

At the time the most expensive film ever made, the final cost of *Cleopatra* ran to an estimated $44 million (about £220 million today), Elizabeth Taylor's share of this gargantuan figure being a cool $7 million. (A record $1 million had been allocated from the budget to tempt her to take on the titular role but her earnings then swelled seven-fold as the movie's protracted shooting schedule wore on and she was required to spend many more weeks on set than originally envisaged.) Farcically, the picture's original producer, Walter Wanger, attempted to recreate the look and feel of ancient Egypt on an outdoor stage at Pinewood Studios 'only to discover belatedly that English skies stayed stubbornly grey, the buildings were constantly soaked in un-Egyptian rain, and the supposedly nilotic [sic] background looked like a Thameside suburb when transferred to the screen'.[15]

After Rouben Mamoulin had been supplanted as director by Taylor's choice, Joseph L. Mankiewicz, the set then shifted southwards from London to Rome in search of both drier conditions for filming and a warmer climate that would be more acceptable to the female star given her delicate health (she was still frail after a bout of pneumonia contracted on the damp Pinewood set had brought filming to a lengthy and expensive standstill). The film finally clawed back the astronomical sum it had cost to make, accumulating a profit of more than $5 million and becoming one of the ten greatest box-office successes of all time when it had completed its initial run, but not before it had come close to bankrupting the studio that had green-lit the project and had caused heads to roll within the Fox hierarchy.

Taylor paid a visit to Villa di Tizzano at the beginning of the 1960s to discuss aspects of the *Cleopatra* script with Balchin. In readiness for the star's overnight stay the Balchins went to the trouble of converting a quantity of the attic space of the Pandolfinis' villa into a bedroom and en suite bathroom. As Yovanka points out, this was 'Fine for the Pandolfinis, who at our huge expense acquire a gorgeous new bathroom, but pretty stupid for the Balchins. An expensive one-night stand.'[16] Fresh from the set of the most lavish and wanton film ever made, on which one of Taylor's many costume changes had seen her pull on a dress woven from twenty-four-carat gold, it is unlikely that the star of *Cleopatra* would have fully appreciated the financial outlay that Balchin and his wife had incurred just to ensure her comfort, a gesture that represents further evidence of their spendthrift nature.

The next script that Balchin wrote after finishing work on *Cleopatra* saw him reunited with a pair of old friends for a film that would prove to be far less time-consuming, difficult and expensive to make than the Egyptian epic. Eleven years on from publication of *A Sort of Traitors* and after an attempt by London Films to make a film of the book had been abandoned in that same year, Balchin re-engineered his novel for the screen and the resultant movie was the last of his works to be adapted for the cinema during his lifetime. It opened in London on 13 November 1960 under the title *Suspect* (in America the film was retitled *The Risk*, its working title in Britain). *Suspect* was made by the Boulting brothers at the British Lion studios at Shepperton, with filming lasting a mere seventeen days. In the Boultings' own words, *Suspect* represented 'an experiment in raising the level of the supporting feature',[17] without a commensurate hike in the budget. Patrick Gibbs[18] in the *Daily Telegraph* speculated that the picture had probably cost less than £25,000 to make (slightly under £500,000 today), a tiny drop in the Nile compared with *Cleopatra*'s budget.

The best feature of *Suspect* is its cast. Peter Cushing, Kenneth

Griffith, Donald Pleasence, Ian Bannen, Thorley Walters, Raymond Huntley, Spike Milligan: this would have been a starry line-up for a major British film of the period, let alone a B-movie that cost peanuts to make. Following on from Kathleen Byron in *The Small Back Room*, it is one of the lesser lights, Virginia Maskell, who again stands out though, skilfully conveying the boredom and frustration of a young woman (Lucy Byrne) trapped in a job she doesn't enjoy, whilst also being saddled with the responsibility of caring for her invalid boyfriend. As the double amputee Ivor (here renamed Alan Andrews), Bannen gives what Elspeth Grant[19] in the *Tatler and Bystander* hailed as 'a remarkable and shattering performance'. Tony Britton is a disappointment as Marriott, largely because, at the age of thirty-six, he was too old to impersonate the immature twenty-four-year-old delineated in Balchin's novel. How much better the film might have been had the 1949 shoot gone ahead and Richard Attenborough—fresh from playing a pair of teenagers in two consecutive Boulting brothers' productions: Pinkie Brown in *Brighton Rock* and Jack Read in *The Guinea Pig*—had taken the leading role. Cushing is well-cast as the ageing, prickly, ineffective Professor Sewell and Pleasence, in a very early film role, is superb as Bill Brown: in a few short scenes he expertly sketches in his portrait of a scheming, traitorous coward. Huntley is believable as the hard-headed Cabinet Minister Gatling and only Milligan, in a pure comic turn as Arthur the lab assistant, looks seriously out of place, being guilty of perpetrating what W. John Morgan[20] in the *New Statesman and Nation* termed 'An idle piece of facetiousness' at the movie's end.

A few caveats notwithstanding, *Suspect* generated largely positive notices. The *Daily Herald* led the way, an anonymous reviewer[21] contributing the opinion, beneath the headline 'TRIUMPHANT EXPERIMENT', that the film was 'a second feature so first rate that many a main feature might support it'. Alan Dent[22] in the *Illustrated London News* earmarked the movie as 'a highly intelligent little drama' and Morgan[23] remarked that 'The acting is altogether excellent, the pace swift'.

Not everyone was quite so complimentary. Reviewing

the film for the Left-leaning literary magazine *Time and Tide*, young American controversialist Clancy Sigal[24] referred to it as 'one of the most pernicious political films I have ever seen'. In a view shared by a number of other critics, he bitterly attacked the Boultings' excessive reverence for authority, describing *Suspect* as 'an apologia for officialdom' because the scientists portrayed in the film allow their work to be obstructed by the government. Penelope Houston[25] in the *Monthly Film Bulletin* was also critical of the siblings' experiment, but for a different reason. To her it resembled 'nothing so much as a prestige TV play' and she suggested that the Boultings were going about the business of raising the quality of B-pictures in the wrong way:

> A better standard of low budget film-making is badly needed, but the way to do it is not by making pictures which look as though they have strayed from television.

Houston also drew attention, quite rightly, to *Suspect*'s unimaginative 'pistols and fisticuffs climax'. But despite this botched ending and what Dilys Powell[26] in the *Sunday Times* correctly pinpointed as the film's 'Workaday narrative style', *Suspect* is compulsively watchable, very faithful to its source material and vastly superior to the unmitigated hash that the Boultings and Balchin had made of the latter's story 'Among Friends' five years earlier in the guise of *Josephine and Men*.

*

As the end of 1959 approached, Balchin's desire to write screenplays for a living was beginning to wane and he had turned his attention back towards writing novels. On 9 December he replied to a letter from William Collins in which his publisher requested him to send 'some good news'[27] with regard to the 'prospect of a new novel'. Balchin dispatched an encouraging response from his Florentine base:

> Regarding my plans, I have two books that I want to write. The question is how and when to do them. As you probably gather, I have a definite policy over this film business, and

particularly want to get clear of all film committments [sic] before I settle down to books again. Much depends here upon what happens in the next few weeks.[28]

What happened in the next few weeks was that the Collins author became immersed in the business of writing yet another film script and all thoughts of starting on a novel were ushered to the back of his mind as the new movie project monopolized his time and creativity.

Audrey Erskine Lindop's novel *The Singer Not the Song* describes a small village in 1920s Mexico under the yoke of a vicious bandit named Anacleto. A new priest, Father Keogh, arrives in Quantana and, despite attempts on his life, tries to bring Anacleto into the church's fold but is distracted from his task by the romantic attentions of the beautiful daughter of a local landowner. Rank acquired the rights to the story and detailed Roy Ward Baker to direct it.

Baker had made two excellent films in succession for Rank in the late 1950s: *The One That Got Away* having been closely followed by *A Night to Remember*, the classic black-and-white account of the sinking of the Titanic. After more than twelve months of wrangling with his bosses over the identity of his next film, Baker was told that he would have to direct *The Singer Not the Song*, to his evident dismay:

> There was not one single element in this story which appealed to me. I was not interested in any way and the situation of the girl falling in love with the priest had been done to death, as it has again since.[29]

The role of Anacleto had been assigned to the (Rank-contracted) Dirk Bogarde at an early stage, Peter John Dyer[30] in the *Monthly Film Bulletin* later observing that Bogarde's 'aptness for a part requiring Marlon Brando [was] approximately nil'. Scouring Hollywood for suitable talent to play the part of Keogh, Baker approached Hugh French, Balchin's film agent, to enquire about Richard Burton's availability. During their discussion,

French put forward Balchin's name as a candidate to write the script. The novelist was at a loose end, having in Baker's words 'recently extricated himself from the complications of *Cleopatra* and several other writers and directors'.[31] Balchin wrote his screenplay for *The Singer Not the Song* at Villa di Tizzano over the course of the 1959–1960 winter. Baker took several trips to Tuscany to discuss the work with him ('Certainly, that was no hardship') and the pair met up with Bogarde in Rome to 'talk over script, which went happily enough', although the star later waspishly derided Balchin's input, saying that he had written 'a terrible script'[32] for the movie. (In fairness to Balchin, he had been given a pretty wretched book to adapt and had done a very fair job of distilling it down to its essential elements and focusing the viewer's attention on the few dramatic passages to be found in Erskine Lindop's original text.)

Burton meanwhile, in common with several other actors, had turned down the chance to play the Irish priest, telling Baker, in words that were reaching his ears with monotonous regularity: 'No thank you, but I'd like to play the bandit'.[33] Burton was signed up instead by Fox and flown to the set of *Cleopatra*, where he replaced Peter Finch in the role of Mark Antony and played opposite Taylor, with well-known romantic ramifications.

When John Mills was eventually cast as Keogh, Bogarde took great exception, as Baker recollected:

> ...when I told Dirk that Johnny had agreed to appear, Dirk declared, 'I promise you, if Johnny plays the priest I will make life unbearable for everyone concerned.'
>
> Well, he was as good as his word and he succeeded.[34]

Even as late as 2006, when he introduced *The Singer Not the Song* on the DVD version of the film, Baker was still unaware of the origin of Bogarde's dislike of Mills:

> What I didn't understand (and still don't) is that there was some extraordinary enmity between John Mills and Dirk Bogarde. Neither of them ever would explain...[35,36]

Successfully overcoming Bogarde's opposition to his appearance in *The Singer Not the Song*, Mills served up a typically solid and professional performance as Keogh that prevented a ramshackle amusement from collapsing into total chaos and confusion. Bogarde in contrast, if not actually intending to sabotage the film, certainly tried to subvert it. He found a tailor in Rome who made him some skin-tight black leather trousers and proceeded to feminize his performance accordingly ('I did the whole thing for camp and nobody had any idea what was happening!'[37]).

The Singer Not the Song displays some familiar Balchin preoccupations, being essentially a 'psychological' piece of cinema, and much of the psychodrama enacted between the priest and the bandit was Balchin's handiwork and not that of Erskine Lindop. On one level, the film is about the tussle for control of Quantana between Keogh and Anacleto. But there is also the question of the struggle for possession of Anacleto's soul: will it go to the Devil or will Keogh succeed in securing it for the church? Keogh appears to be making some headway when Anacleto moves in with the priest in order to take religious instruction from him. At this point the theme that gives the movie its title grinds into gear: is Anacleto being beguiled by the church (The Song) or is he captivated merely by the priest (The Singer)? Finally, the intertwined emotions of the three principal characters (Anacleto, Keogh and the girl Locha) provide Balchin with the opportunity to give a bold new twist to his treasured love triangle plot device. The variation here is that one can construct a plausible case for all three of the vertices being in love in some way or other with the other two.

Almost forty years after the film was released, Baker declared that the reviewers who attended the press showings in early 1961 had enjoyed 'a field day. They tore the picture to pieces, every one of them',[38] but this is not entirely accurate. The *Daily Telegraph*'s Eric Shorter,[39] amid a mixed notice, did find some compliments to bestow on *The Singer Not the Song*, referring to the film's 'good colourful Mexican backgrounds[40] and good colourful English acting' and reporting that it dealt effectively with 'the subject of religious conversion and the sources of spiritual power'. Dyer,[41] despite complaining about the acting, the direction and Balchin's script, seemed to like the picture, which he said was 'strangely compelling' and Alexander Walker[42] in the *Evening Standard* felt that the performances were 'endurable and often enjoyable'. However, the opinions of other film critics were broadly in line with Baker's summary. As an exemplar, an anonymous reviewer[43] in *The Times* highlighted 'parts simplified to the point of nonentity' and spoke of the 'slightly lunatic mood of the piece'.

In spite of the panning administered by the British press corps, *The Singer Not the Song* proceeded to enjoy great popularity in selected pockets of the world; these predictably included countries such as Mexico with a large Roman Catholic community, but also parts of Europe, notably France and Germany. Twenty-three years after its release, the film went into profit. But the director of *The Singer Not the Song* has never softened his attitude towards a movie that caused him so much heartache to make, remarking in 2000 that 'I loathe it'.[44]

When his work on *The Singer Not the Song* came to an end, Balchin moved seamlessly onto his next script. Dino de Laurentiis stayed at Villa di Tizzano to discuss his latest film project, *Barabbas*, with the novelist-in-exile. The Italian film producer spoke little English and Balchin's knowledge of Italian was very limited. Yovanka's ability to interpret for the pair proved invaluable on this occasion ('If ever I earned my keep, I earned it during those two days'[45]). Balchin was awarded the job of scripting *Barabbas* and worked on his screenplay during the spring and summer of 1960. *Barabbas* was the last of Balchin's screenplays to be filmed, although his work had again been augmented by that of other scriptwriters by the time that shooting began.[46]

Barabbas proved to be an inauspicious choice as the first picture to be shown at the new Odeon cinema in Haymarket on 4 June 1962. Adapted from a novel by the Swedish writer Pär Lagerkvist, it was yet another entry in what Dyer[47] in the *Monthly Film Bulletin* wearily described as 'the current and apparently endless cycle of Biblical films', trailing behind much more commercially successful examples of the genre such as 1951's *Quo Vadis*, Cecil B. DeMille's *The Ten Commandments* from 1956 and another Charlton Heston vehicle, 1959's *Ben Hur*. The de Laurentiis film imagines the subsequent life story of the criminal cut down from the cross in a show of clemency by the Romans at the time of Christ's crucifixion. Barabbas is forced to work as a slave in a hellish silver mine before converting to Christianity and finally achieving fame as a fearless gladiator. The film is noteworthy for an overpowering larger-than-life performance from Anthony Quinn as the freed criminal and for the lurid shades of the Technicolor palette, but for little else. With a running time of 144 minutes, *Barabbas* is overlong, bedevilled by what Dyer referred to as its 'ponderous and eclectic' approach and founders on its episodic construction and the presence of numerous languorous passages that try the patience of its audience. The film is also marred by a nasty undercurrent of gore and violence, so much so that Leslie Halliwell[48] dismissed it as 'a gaudy display of carnage'. Dyer[49] went further in condemning the unwholesome nature of this 'depressing chronicle', dubbing it 'unacceptable in its pain-preoccupation and its religiosity'.

Balchin's 'horrified fascination for the film business'[50] had by now worn very thin. For the rest of his life he was spared any further association with movies of such limited merit as *Barabbas* and could concentrate instead largely on writing novels, with the odd television play thrown in for good measure. Although his friend Elizabeth Jane Howard affirmed that Balchin 'had got a flair'[51] for scriptwriting and that he appealed to the movie moguls because 'He knew how to write dramatic, pared-down dialogue', his work in the medium was almost as uneven as that accomplished during his more illustrious novel-writing career. Of the numerous screenplays he wrote—and he may have scripted as many as twenty-five films—only three (*Mine Own Executioner*, *Mandy* and *The Man Who Never Was*) subsequently resulted in first-rate movies. It is telling that this trio of pictures were all made in Britain relatively soon after the novelist began working in the film industry. Balchin produced his best scripts either when the book he was asked to adapt was one of his own (*Suspect* being another example of one of his better screenplays) or when his services were actively sought by a film company with a project in mind that dovetailed with his interests and experience (*The Man Who Never Was* for instance). Especially during the embryonic phase of his scriptwriting career, when he was not under contract to any one studio and was only accepting occasional movie projects, Balchin could afford to cherry-pick the best of the assignments offered to him and turn down any he disliked the look of.

Balchin wrote a very effective script (for *The Man Who Never Was*) shortly before he went to Hollywood in 1955. But as soon as he was put under contract by Twentieth Century Fox, the quality of his screenwriting declined, for two reasons. Firstly, Fox wanted the Englishman to become a jack-of-all-trades, someone who could adapt whichever book was presented to him, regardless of whether it suited his skill set. Secondly, Balchin's handiwork was interfered with far more in Hollywood than it had been in Britain, where he had worked with sympathetic collaborators—some of whom were also close personal friends of his—such as Alexander MacKendrick and the Boulting brothers. When Jim Petersen, on the second page of Balchin's novel *In the Absence of Mrs Petersen*, refers to 'the really heart-breaking part of a scriptwriter's work', the list of irritations he recites must surely have tallied with Balchin's own experience of toiling in Hollywood:

> ...the meetings with the Front Office, the gradual tearing away of all distinction from what one has written, the fatuous suggestions which have to be treated politely and respectfully, and the eventual realization that you are talking a completely different language...

21

All These Bloody Things

Nigel Balchin was bored with dying. After a year in hospital with a haemorrhaged ulcer, peritonitis, and pneumonia in rapid succession the author of *The Small Back Room* and *Mine Own Executioner* gave an ultimatum to the London Clinic doctor.

"Let us come to a clear arrangement about this," he said. "I will now get better or I will snuff out."

It was mutually agreed that he should get better.[1]

Balchin's health began to deteriorate in the first few days of 1961. On 4 January, whilst at Villa di Tizzano, he suffered a haemorrhaged gastric ulcer. Yovanka recalls that the dramatic prelude to a long period of indifferent health on the part of her husband came when 'I heard him thumping on the floor in the bathroom and he was bleeding like a pig'.[2] Balchin received medical attention at the emergency department of a local hospital and then returned to Tizzano for a while before continuing his rehabilitation in a flat in Florence overlooking the Ponte Vecchio. On 15 February, whilst installed in this pied-a-terre, Balchin and Yovanka witnessed a total eclipse of the sun ('All the bats flew out. V. eerie' reads the entry in the latter's scrapbook), the same eclipse that the camera crew working on the set of *Barabbas* in Nice successfully captured to form the dramatic opening sequence of that film.

Balchin felt strong enough to be able to resume work by the time that spring arrived in Tuscany. Released at last from his film commitments, he made rapid progress on a novel that he would later entitle *Seen Dimly Before Dawn*, the writing of which he said 'took about four months, working on it more or less full time'.[3] Still troubled by his ulcer over the summer, which had failed to heal with drug treatment alone, Balchin's Italian doctor decided that it was necessary for his patient to undergo surgery. Balchin chose to have this operation in England, not Italy, and soon after he had completed the manuscript of his twelfth novel he boarded a flight to London. He and Yovanka had also decided that, after one final winter in Italy, they would return to England permanently in the spring of 1962.

By 29 September, the day on which filming of the Mankiewicz version of *Cleopatra* began in Rome, Balchin was convalescing at the Hyde Park Hotel after surviving an operation at University College Hospital, during which the surgeon found—and repaired—a total of five ulcers. Yovanka then rented a flat in Hyde Park Gardens so that her husband could recuperate preparatory to the return flight to Italy. This interlude did not pass off uneventfully, as she remembers: 'he was having a bath in that flat when the thing erupted again'.[4] Intense abdominal pain was a sign that Balchin was suffering from peritonitis, a frequent sequela of a gastric ulcer. After repair of the perforation at what his wife described as the 'horrid, dirty'[5] St James's Hospital, he was admitted to the private London Clinic (the same institution that Elizabeth Taylor had been taken to in the spring after going down with pneumonia while shooting *Cleopatra*) at the end of October for further treatment.

When he was not under anaesthetic, Balchin used his period in England in the autumn of 1961 to conduct a sequence of press interviews, some of them presumably from his hospital bed. While *Seen Dimly Before Dawn* was being typeset by Collins, Balchin spoke to the *Guardian*, *Sunday Times* and *Evening Standard*, and longer feature-length pieces about him later appeared in the *Daily Mail* and the literary magazine *Books and Bookmen* to coincide with the publication of the novel in January 1962. After almost thirty years of novel-writing this was the first time that Balchin had participated in any sort of concerted promotional activity, but then authors of his generation did not tend to talk to the press very often (if at all). The publicity drive for *Seen Dimly Before Dawn* must have been instigated by A. D. Peters and/or William Collins, who would have impressed upon Balchin the importance of reintroducing himself to the British book-buying public after more than six years had gone by without the appearance of a new novel. This promotional effort paid off because *Seen Dimly Before Dawn* topped the *Evening Standard*'s best-sellers' chart for two weeks at the start of 1962, and as late as 4 March it was still occupying the Number Two slot in a similar list printed in *The Times*.

In the course of one of his newspaper interviews, Balchin intimated that he was thinking of resuming his original occupation ('He will look for a post as an industrial psychologist'[6]). It is uncertain how serious he was about this or how hard he looked for such a position, but he never worked as an industrial psychologist after 1935, and his three-year stint in Hollywood in the employ of Twentieth Century Fox in the 1950s represents the last full-time office-based job he held down. When he spoke to the *Daily Mail*, Balchin said that the long period during which he had concentrated on writing film scripts had proved fertile in terms of generating ideas for novels—'In these seven years four plots have been slowly cooking and are ready for serving'[7]—but at most two of these ideas (for *Seen Dimly Before Dawn* and *In the Absence of Mrs Petersen*) would appear to have been dished up before he died.

Balchin stayed at the London Clinic throughout most of November and December. He contracted pneumonia there, necessitating further medical attention. In addition to the financial toll exacted by this lengthy period of hospitalization (whilst at the London Clinic he racked up fees totalling £164, equivalent to about £3,000 today), Balchin's appearance was also ravaged. On 1 December he wrote to Yovanka, informing her that 'I continue to run a slight temperature and the stuff continues to drain. [...] I weigh 11 st. 5 lb. and look like a cross between Sammy Davis, Jnr. and a two-tone [sic] sloth.'[8] Balchin lost a total of three stone in weight during the course of 1961, as well as a sizeable quantity of his intestinal tract, the inevitable consequence of multiple surgical repairs in the abdominal region. Yovanka recognizes that 1961 was a watershed year with regard to her husband's health. In her opinion, he was never physically strong again from this point onwards, his frailty not being helped by his tendency to prioritize consumption of alcohol over ingestion of food:

> He just never ate enough and he just got weaker and weaker, and with the alcohol…[9]

(When Balchin began to be troubled by stomach ulcers in the early 1960s, it was believed that they were caused by a range of lifestyle factors that would have been relevant in his case, namely smoking, drinking and exposure to stress. Twenty-first century medical opinion no longer agrees with this hypothesis, infection with the bacterium *Helicobacter pylori* now being considered to be the culprit. However, it is thought that certain lifestyle factors may exacerbate the symptoms of stomach ulcers.)

While he was connected up to drainage tubes and running a fever, Balchin could probably have done without the need for serious contemplation of the uncertain state of his marriage, and in his letter to Yovanka he admitted that he currently possessed 'an excuse for not trying to think about things much'.[10] But the receipt of letters from his wife suggesting that it might be for the best if the two of them were to split up had forced him to at least entertain the 'rather frightening' prospect of thinking about their future:

> I will try to do as you ask and not just send a letter saying that everything is finished. But there is no doubt about it that the only way in which we can avoid an absolutely major mess for all concerned is if we can arrive at some sort of agreement as to what we are both going to do, and that I shall have to write to you about as soon as I feel rather less like a rachitic kitten.
>
> Tell Charles that I love him, and try and get yourself well, so that we can look at all these bloody things like sane human beings.

The misery of a long hospital confinement may have made Balchin unduly pessimistic regarding the prospects for the continuance of his marriage. He and Yovanka had of course accumulated considerable experience over the previous eight years at patching up their differences and the beginning of a more stable phase in their relationship was in fact only a few months away.

Balchin was discharged from the London Clinic in time for Christmas, which he spent with the Steins at their home in Cornwall. By February 1962, he had recovered sufficiently to be able to fly back to Italy with Yovanka and begin the process of packing up the family's belongings and shutting down Villa di Tizzano in readiness for the relocation to England.

After a year in which it had appeared at times as if the Balchin family were likely to lose a member to illness, their numerical strength was instead about to be increased by one. In the midst of his many days of ill health during the previous autumn Balchin had succeeded in summoning the energy required to conceive his fifth child and so Yovanka was now six months pregnant. As Charles, in her opinion, had been endlessly fawned on and fussed over by the Italian staff at their Florentine residences, Balchin's wife insisted that they should return home so that her second offspring would be born and raised in England: 'I wasn't going to have another child spoilt by the Italians'.[11] Cassandra Marlin Balchin was therefore born, like her brother before her, in the Lindo Wing of St Mary's Hospital, Paddington on 24 May 1962. Eight days later, the Balchins took possession of the sprawling seventeenth century Sussex farmhouse that Yovanka had discovered at the end of the previous winter while Balchin had been recuperating in London.

Tufton Place, situated about a mile south-west of the village of Northiam, was the first in a small series of capacious properties that Balchin and Yovanka owned during the 1960s. They had lived in imposing houses before, particularly in Italy and California, but they had only rented them and this vast house near Rye was their first real status-symbol purchase, the sort of home that Balchin must have thought would be a suitably luxurious abode for a famous novelist and celebrated scriptwriter to live in. As Yovanka now appreciates, the act of purchasing properties such as Tufton Place was a way in which her partner had sought to bolster his self-confidence by demonstrating the depth of his wealth:

> I think Nigel had a lack of confidence [...] and I think everything he did was trying [...] to give himself a confidence that he'd not possessed through possessions.

Balchin's lack of self-confidence presumably stemmed originally from his humble upbringing, but would have been further undermined by Elisabeth's rejection of him, which in Elizabeth Jane Howard's opinion destroyed what remained of his self-esteem.

As soon as Balchin clapped eyes on the estate agent's particulars for the Sussex house he knew it was the right place for him, as Yovanka remembers:

> ...I found Tufton Place. I came back, it was the snip of the century, and I said to Nigel: "This is a fantastic place but we can't possibly live there." Well, he took one look at all the things it had and fell for it.

'The things it had' take a while to recite. The house alone contained twenty rooms, including five bedrooms, four bathrooms and a nursery. The extensive grounds in which it stood encompassed seventy-six acres of woodland, a ninety-three-acre farm, paddocks, gardens and a pond. For good measure, the very reasonable asking price of £19,000 (only about £330,000 today) also included two oasts, a dairy, stables and garages. Lack of space looked unlikely to be a problem for the Balchins whilst they were living at Tufton Place.

*

When Balchin had spoken to John Rosselli of the *Guardian* in the autumn of 1961 the journalist had revealed that the author of the forthcoming novel *Seen Dimly Before Dawn* had experienced a sense of creative liberation having finally snapped his ties with the movie industry:

> …after spending some time on film scripts—and inevitably "feeding into a machine which then takes over"—he has done in the novel exactly what he wanted to do.[12]

What he seems to have wanted to do was to get away from the sort of book he was best known for and to write something altogether different, in this case a warmly nostalgic story located in the Kent countryside in the late 1920s. *Seen Dimly Before Dawn* stands out among Balchin's novels because it is set in the past, the world of work has no significant part to play in the narrative, much of the action takes place out of doors and the central character, instead of being one of the middle-aged professional men from whose ranks Balchin customarily plucked his heroes, is a gauche teenager.

The closest relative to *Seen Dimly Before Dawn* in the Balchin catalogue is *Simple Life*, his second novel, which was also set primarily in the open air and was concerned more with recreational activities than work. Like *Simple Life*, *Seen Dimly Before Dawn* contains a love triangle at its core; it is of a different nature to that in the earlier novel and is also at variance with the more familiar examples in *Darkness Falls from the Air* and *A Way Through the Wood* (in both of which the protagonists are all of a similar age). But, when reduced to its constituent elements, the triangle in *Seen Dimly Before Dawn* still consists of two men fighting over the same woman. This at least, in his innocent and deluded way, is what fifteen-year-old Walter Parrish thinks he is doing after he learns that his 'Aunt' Leonie is unmarried and, in consequence, enacts a plan to prise her away from his Uncle Patrick. As Balchin's granddaughter Justine Hopkins has illustrated, *Simple Life* and *Seen Dimly Before Dawn* are also connected because they both 'revolve around the attempts of a naïve and bewildered protagonist to understand women who are erratic, incomprehensible and ultimately unreliable'.[13] However, this is also of course a feature of other examples of

Balchin's fiction, most notably *A Way Through the Wood*.

Balchin displayed immense natural ability by writing his novel from the perspective of a teenage boy, and Anthony Curtis[14] in the *Sunday Telegraph* was correct when he said that 'the adolescent's callow, earnest, egocentric tone is brilliantly caught and sustained for the whole length of the narrative'. The author captured with uncanny accuracy the wild optimism of youth and the sense that, unbounded by the normal demands of rationality, anything is possible in the mind of a child. In Walter's *Looking Glass* world, a schoolboy can attempt to spirit a beautiful and sensual twenty-six-year-old woman away from his father's brother and see nothing intrinsically absurd in this.

Described by Balchin in the novel as being both 'deeply religious' and 'a monumental prig', Walter shares sufficient personal characteristics with the author as a young man for the reader to be led inexorably to the conclusion that Balchin's youthful hero was partly based on a certain Dauntsey's schoolboy of a 1920s vintage. Scattered amongst the early chapters of *Seen Dimly Before Dawn* is the information that the scholastically advanced Walter has a parental home on the Wiltshire downs, is tall, physically well developed and 'a good cricketer', looks older than he is, loves poetry, is an infrequent cinemagoer and a devotee of classical music whose tastes encompass 'a great deal of Mozart, Bach and Handel'.

As she has no obvious counterpoint in real life, Leonie would appear to have arisen predominantly from Balchin's imagination but, naturally enough, the woman he was living with at the time may have had some input into his portrait, as Yovanka admits:

> ...Leonie certainly at times says things that are very me. All the critical things about Leonie will be the critical things about me.[15]

Leonie is the most well-rounded female character to be found anywhere within the pages of Balchin's fourteen novels. Rosamund in *Sundry Creditors* and Leah in *The Fall of the Sparrow* are rivals of a sort but they are only minor characters, whereas Leonie, the moody, vivacious, passionate and utterly captivating creature that gives the book its soul, is a far more substantial figure.

In his review of *Seen Dimly Before Dawn*, Curtis[16] lamented Balchin's unwillingness to use his novel as a vehicle to depict the 1960s in the same way in which he had previously documented the 1940s:

> After seven years of silence as a novelist one might have hoped that he had come to terms with the modern world and was going to do for it what he did for the world of wartime boffinry in "The Small Back Room."

Upon publication of *Seen Dimly Before Dawn*, Balchin revealed that his reticence to write about the modern world arose from an awareness that he did not feel truly at home in it. His comment referred specifically to *The Fall of the Sparrow*, but it applied just as aptly to the later novel:

> I found the war years, and the few years immediately afterwards, extremely stimulating. They brought to the surface an awful lot of problems and views of people which I hadn't noticed before. When I wrote *The Fall of the Sparrow*, the last novel of mine to be published, I felt that I'd said all I wanted to about those particular years. At the same time I hadn't settled sufficiently in the post-war period to find anything that I particularly wanted to say about people then. It was a time when I was observing, asking questions, rather than having any comment to offer myself.[17]

When he began writing his new novel at Villa di Tizzano in the spring of 1961 Balchin had of course spent almost all of the preceding six years outside his native land. It was therefore only prudent of him not to have attempted a 'state-of-the-nation' address from the detachment of his Florentine villa.

Seen Dimly Before Dawn may have been set in the 1920s, not the 1960s, but it did reflect contemporary mores by displaying much greater frankness about sexual matters than any previous Balchin novel. Walter and Leonie are constantly kissing and cuddling each other, a young girl of Leonie's acquaintance complains to her mother that Walter has made improper advances towards her, there is a scene in which Walter performs an intensive examination of Leonie's naked form whilst she is taking a bath and the book concludes with the most graphic scene to be found anywhere in Balchin's fiction. It is Walter's lustful pursuit of Leonie that gives *Seen Dimly Before Dawn* both a dynamic tension and a modern feel, despite the fact that it is set in 1928. Balchin's two subsequent novels—both of which were written at the height of the Swinging Sixties—would also see him responding to the changing moral climate, not perhaps by taking us all the way through the bedroom door but at least by leaving it tantalizingly ajar.

Published on 18 January 1962, *Seen Dimly Before Dawn* received glowing notices in the literary columns of British newspapers as the peripatetic screenwriter was welcomed back with something approaching open arms. Curtis[18] made the book the subject of a feature-length review in the *Sunday Telegraph*. He described how Balchin 'does not miss a trick in playing out his classic hand' and referred to the 'notable lack of wastage in this finely constructed and enjoyable novel'. The *Guardian*'s Norman Shrapnel[19] said that Balchin had deployed 'all his usual lucidity, vigour, and devilish readability' and Jeremy Brooks[20] in the *Sunday Times* also spoke in reverent terms about 'Nigel Balchin's excellent new novel'.

Almost the only dissenting voice among the critics belonged to Anthony Burgess,[21] orating on this occasion from the appropriately sceptical environment of *The Times Literary Supplement*. He characterized Balchin disparagingly as 'a general practitioner, producing well-made and highly readable novels which any competent craftsman could have written'. Burgess detected a familiar quality about much of the material from which Balchin had constructed *Seen Dimly Before Dawn* ('one feels uneasily that one has met a good deal of it before') and claimed that the author's purpose seemed to be 'to titillate,

Seen Dimly Before Dawn (1962)

Walter Parrish, a fifteen-year-old schoolboy, is sent to stay with his Uncle Patrick and Aunt Leonie in rural Kent for the summer holidays. As Patrick, an invalid, is confined to bed for lengthy stretches, Walter spends much of his time in the company of his aunt. Leonie, aged twenty-six, is much younger than Patrick and, in Walter's view, constitutes 'a strikingly beautiful woman'. The schoolboy soon falls hopelessly in love with her. When Leonie informs Walter that she is not actually married to Patrick it quickly becomes apparent to Walter that he is free from any moral impediments that would have prevented him from making advances towards her had she in fact been related to him.

Colonel Masters, a neighbouring farmer, is convinced that Leonie's Alsatian Remus has been worrying his sheep, and tells her that if he catches him amongst the flock then he will put a bullet in him. Leonie retorts in kind: "If you ever dared put a bullet in Remus, I'd put one in you." The dog is soon caught running the sheep and is shot and killed by one of the Colonel's farmhands.

Leonie agrees to become engaged to Walter but only if he will help her to kill the Colonel. He refuses but, in jest, unveils a plan that might allow Leonie to murder Masters and get away with it. Walter wakes a few days later to discover that Leonie has gone out armed with a pistol. He hurries off to the nearby copse that Leonie had selected for her assassination attempt, climbs a tall tree and is just in time to observe the woman point the gun at Masters as the farmer takes an early-morning stroll through the woodland.

in a popular novelist's manner, with an isolated hunk of over-simplified experience'. For Burgess, Balchin's most prominent virtue was not necessarily a good thing:

> His novel is, of course, most readable. We can gobble it like porridge, but porridge, one was always told, goes quickly through the system.

*

> "I feel I need some other work. There is a danger of becoming a "literary gent", the sort of person who is in contact only with other people who write. This is too limited a range of contacts for a novelist.
>
> Now in the film business you are constantly seeing strange places and meeting even stranger people. There is no danger of sinking into literary isolation, no shortage of human material."
>
> – Nigel Balchin[22]

The 'human material' that Balchin came into contact with whilst employed by the National Institute of Industrial Psychology in the 1930s helped to produce two novels about industry (*No Sky* and *Sundry Creditors*), the opening section of another novel (*Simple Life*) and two satirical works of non-fiction (*How to Run a Bassoon Factory* and *Business for Pleasure*). One year at the Ministry of Food and four years in the army during World War Two saw Balchin gather sufficient material to write two of his very best novels (*Darkness Falls from the Air* and *The Small Back Room*) and receive the inspiration for a third (*Mine Own Executioner*). In contrast, almost twenty years of sporadic contact with the world of movie-making, including a six-year stretch when his sole occupation was as a film screenwriter, generated practically nothing in the way of books. When asked by *Books and Bookmen* in 1962 if he had ever contemplated the possibility of writing a *Bassoon Factory*-style satire on the inner workings of the film business, Balchin was struck by the novelty of the idea and his reply suggested that it was deserving of serious consideration:

"What a brilliant idea." *(Long pause while he chews over the possibility.)* "No, I can't honestly say that it has occurred to me but it's worth thinking about."

Any subsequent thought that Balchin may have undertaken on the subject did not lead to a book and all his wide experience of the film world, with its strange places and even stranger people, culminated in just two pieces of written work: the opening two chapters of the novel *In the Absence of Mrs Petersen* and one television play, transmitted in the summer of 1962.

Balchin's 'first original play for television'[23] was called *The Hatchet Man*. It was broadcast by the BBC on 15 June and awarded a prominent place in the schedule: 9.25 on a Friday evening. (In Hollywood parlance, a hatchet man is an 'executioner' employed by a film studio to fire movie personnel deemed surplus to requirements and thus save the studio boss from getting his hands dirty should it later be necessary to employ someone previously given their marching orders.) The play, which according to the *Observer*'s Maurice Richardson[24] possessed 'plenty of viewability and a neat circular story', starred Donald Pleasence—who had acted so admirably in the Balchin-scripted film *Suspect* eighteen months previously—in the title role. Pleasence's character is made to view the Hollywood system through the other end of the telescope when he produces a movie as a starring vehicle for his actress girlfriend and finds himself getting the brush-off from the new hatchet man at the studios where he used to perform the same role.

The Hatchet Man was not preserved by the BBC and so one has to rely on newspaper reviews from the 1960s to discover what Balchin's play was like. Philip Purser[25] in the *Sunday Telegraph*, despite bemoaning the absence of an authentic American feel, said that *The Hatchet Man* was 'a good solid melodrama' and that it contained 'lots of wry details obviously inspired by the author's own experiences in Hollywood'. Richardson[26] concurred with the latter comment ('you could see the expert knowledge sticking out all over the place') and reported that *The Hatchet Man* had kept him 'happily entertained for 90 minutes', even though 'the hand of the zombie lay heavily upon it at times'. In the *Daily Telegraph*, Lyn Lockwood[27] singled out 'a bitterly amusing reconstruction of a script conference' as 'one of a number of excellent scenes' and summed up Balchin's work as 'a taut, dispassionate and economically written play'.

The relative warmth of the reception granted to *The Hatchet Man* would encourage Balchin to write more for television, initially for the BBC and later for the commercial channel, as the decade progressed.

*

Within a year of moving to Tufton Place the Balchins experienced two domestic setbacks of differing magnitude, both of which made headlines in the national newspapers.

In the first week of January 1963—the coldest month ever recorded in England, as the stunningly cold winter of 1962–1963 approached its icy midpoint—a water pipe in the roof space of the venerable dwelling had frozen. The Balchins sent for a plumber to thaw it out, but what they received instead, in Yovanka's evocative phrase, was 'the village idiot with the blowtorch'.[28] This gentleman defrosted the frozen pipe successfully but, unbeknown to anyone at the time, set fire to the rafters whilst doing so. The interior structure of the house therefore smouldered for many hours, but while they lay in their beds that night the Balchin family were blissfully unaware that their house was steadily combusting.

Early the next morning, Yovanka was outside tending to her livestock when she spotted that the roof of one wing of Tufton Place was ablaze, the fire having burnt its way through to the outside of the house in the vicinity of Cassandra's nursery. She yelled to warn Balchin but he had already been alerted to the danger by the sight of smoke drifting past the window of his study, where he was engaged on the task of 'trying to get a new novel started'.[29,30] He raced to the nursery to save the infant who, in contrast to her panic-stricken parents, gave the impression that she had been thoroughly enjoying herself, as Balchin told the *Sunday Express*:

"The fire seemed to be coming from beneath Cassandra's cot and shooting up towards the roof," he said.

"I was terrified," said Mr. Balchin. "But not my baby. She looked at me and laughed like a drain."[31]

Like her father before her, who had survived the experience of tipping a kettle of boiling water over himself when about eighteen months old, Cassandra had cheated death at a very tender age.[32] Balchin later played down his bravery when he recounted the story of the dramatic rescue to the national press: 'don't get the idea that it was heroic. I've been in much hotter and smokier rooms... at cocktail parties.'[33]

When Balchin was not making light of his courage he did admit that the conflagration could have had grave consequences: 'It might so nearly have been a dreadful tragedy [...] But as it is we have just had part of the house ruined.' Fortunately for its residents, the firefighters confined the blaze to the twentieth century section of the house, but the nursery wing and kitchens were destroyed and the water used to extinguish the fire damaged Balchin's collection of sixteenth century oil paintings. It was many weeks before the family were able to move back into their house, just in time to be burgled. An opportunistic thief climbed a tree to gain access to the upper floor, broke into Yovanka's bedroom while she and Balchin were downstairs and made off with a considerable quantity of valuable jewellery. For the Balchins, Tufton Place was fast turning out not to be the dream house they had taken it for when it had become available for them to purchase.

22

Return Journeys

In November 1962, nearly six months after he and his family had moved into Tufton Place, Balchin's love affair with his magnificent house in the Sussex countryside was showing no signs of waning when he invited a reporter from the *Daily Sketch* to take a look round the new estate and hinted to the journalist that he intended to go on living there for some time to come:

> "Life is fairly short. After rushing round the world in a frenzy never having time to enjoy the operation I began to wonder just what it is worth."
>
> "Now all I want to do is stay in one place."[1]

This proved to be a forlorn hope. Less than two years after the Balchins had bought it, Tufton Place was being advertised in the property pages of *The Times* and 'The world wanderer', as the *Daily Sketch* had dubbed him, was preparing to up sticks again.

The sheer scale of Tufton Place, combined with a rapid turnover of unreliable staff sourced from the locality, meant that the house was impossible to manage and too expensive to maintain, even for a man who had accrued a small fortune by working in the film industry. Balchin wanted to be closer to London. Yovanka, as she had been in Italy, was 'bored stiff'[2] and thus, in her words, 'The inevitable move followed'.

Enviably located on the edge of two attractive green spaces, Regent's Park and Primrose Hill, 48 Regent's Park Road is an imposing Georgian townhouse in north-west London and it was here that Balchin brought his family in May 1964. The four-storey building was enormous, and although it could not compete with the forty-eight rooms that Tufton Place and its outbuildings had run to, there was still more than enough square footage to accommodate four people. The senior Balchins commandeered the lower two floors as their territory, the top floor was rented out and the children and their nanny were installed on the intermediate floor, which led, as Balchin's youngest daughter Cassandra remembered, to a physical barrier being erected between the older and younger generations of the family:

> There were huge stairs between the floors and there were even lockable doors so it really was very self-contained. The unit where my brother and I and the nanny lived and the unit downstairs were separate worlds completely.[3]

Yovanka admits with hindsight that this policy of segregation, which had also been employed in Florence and at Tufton Place, was '[not] all that clever (history repeating itself)'.[4]

With his own dedicated study in the basement and the assistance of 'a sweet girl as his secretary', as Yovanka described her, Balchin established a working environment that allowed his writing to prosper and during the five years or so that he spent at Regent's Park Road he duly produced his final two novels. But aware perhaps that his powers as a novelist were dwindling, and in the face of the continued requirement to maximize his earnings so as to finance the upper-class form of living that he and Yovanka were still determined to pursue, Balchin sought fresh outlets for his writing, whilst concomitantly widening its scope. Three contrasting pieces released to the world during 1964 were characteristic of this new trend, but in one way or another they were all backward-looking and a sizeable proportion of Balchin's writing for the remainder of the decade would see him either reworking old material or else revisiting ground that had been thoroughly trampled before. But then at this point in his life perhaps Balchin's past held greater appeal for him than his future…

The first of Balchin's 1964 commissions would have enchanted readers of the *Sunday Times* with a penchant for his prose when they opened their newspaper's colour supplement over the breakfast table on a summer's morning in August. 'Rim of the Plain'[5] was part of a series entitled 'Return Journey' in which prominent people were taken back to a place they had known well in their younger days and asked to compare its present-day appearance with their earlier memories of it. Balchin chose to write about 'the rural Wiltshire where he spent his childhood' and visited not just Potterne, his birthplace, but also nearby Devizes, where he was photographed outside St John's Church, a building inside which he had 'once played the cello in the Brahms Requiem'. In Potterne, Balchin searched for the house he had been born in but discovered that it had been razed to the ground at some point during the intervening fifty-six years ('All that I could see of the place on a recent visit was what used to be the wall of the garden'). The writer's tour of central Wiltshire also took in West Lavington, where he would appear to have had better luck tracking down the house he had lived in as a Dauntsey's schoolboy:

One of the pubs in Lavington has been rebuilt, and is now a place with a smart snack bar and dining room. But the cottages[6] opposite it are still as they always were, their thatched roofs bright green with moss.

Balchin's article for the *Sunday Times* is the first recorded example of him writing an extensive non-fictional account of his childhood, but within about six weeks of 'Rim of the Plain' appearing in print he was once more in nostalgic mood. 'The Knowledge Explosion' was a *Horizon* documentary transmitted by the BBC on 21 September, and it contained a segment in which Balchin gave his personal view, in his capacity as a trained scientist, of 'The explosion of scientific knowledge in the 20th century',[7] this being the only time that television, unlike radio, made use of Balchin's professional expertise. In the programme, he discussed scientific progress since his birth in 1908, but added a personal touch by linking inventions and technical breakthroughs with contemporaneous occurrences in his own life.

The last of Balchin's new pieces for 1964 was his contribution to a book called *Fatal Fascination*.[8] Published in the autumn, and subtitled *A Choice of Crime*, the volume comprised four long essays, each on the subject of a particular crime or criminal that had seized the imagination of a celebrated writer, the other three being C. S. Forester, Eric Linklater and Christopher Sykes.[9]

Balchin's essay ('Burnt Njal—The Irredeemable Crime') evolved from the love of the Norse sagas that had exerted such a profound influence on his fiction. The Saga of Burnt Njal is 'an account of a blood feud and the crimes which sprang from it' and represents, in Balchin's opinion, 'the greatest and most perfect of all the Sagas'. In its original Norse form the saga had occupied some 350 pages and so it is a tribute to Balchin's ability to précis that he succeeded in boiling it down to just under fifty.

'Burnt Njal' is Balchin's longest and most accomplished essay and a very rare example of a piece of his longer non-fiction that can tolerate comparison with one of his better novels, the essay format providing a setting in which Balchin's storytelling gifts were showcased to their best advantage. 'Burnt Njal' is a light and inviting ingress to the Norse sagas, with Balchin's playful tone, satirical sideswipes and mordant pen portraits of some of the characters who become embroiled in the feud helping a bloodthirsty tale come to life in an entertaining (and even charming) fashion, so much so that he almost succeeded in making the ancient tale read as if it was his own work. The essay is a brightly polished miniature that rivals any of the author's other writing from the 1960s.

Balchin had also spoken about the Norse sagas—and 'Burnt Njal' in particular—on the BBC's *Bookstand* programme in November 1961, and an approximate transcript found its way into the *Listener* the following month.[10] For Balchin, three standout features of the Icelandic sagas that he admired (and tried to reflect in his own writing) were their pacy delivery ('the story [...] is always moving forward'), their objectivity ('One is never told what people thought or felt: one is told only what they were seen to do and heard to say') and their quality of emotional restraint ('The Norsemen never tear a passion to tatters').

As virtually no moving pictures of Balchin have survived

into the twenty-first century in publicly accessible sources, it is worth dwelling for a moment on his physical appearance as revealed in the two television programmes he contributed to in the opening half of the 1960s. On both *Bookstand* and *Horizon*, Balchin bore a marked resemblance to the photographs—and especially a frequently reproduced image from the early 1950s in which he was pictured holding a cigarette, every bit the successful author—that had adorned his book jackets at the height of his post-war fame. Facially, Balchin had altered little in the ten years or so since those photographs had been taken: the large oval-shaped head topped by a dome-like forehead; the thick black slicked-back hair, worn slightly longer than was normal for men of his generation; the prominent aquiline nose; and the alert, piercing eyes all remained largely unchanged. His mouth was by far the most expressive feature of his face, but here time had evidently taken its toll as it now provided a home for a calamitous set of 'tombstone' teeth, stained and irregular, that were reminiscent of the haphazard arrangement of gravestones, canted over at gravity-defying angles, that inhabit shady corners of English country churchyards. *Guardian* journalist John Rosselli is another who paid attention to Balchin's memorable physiognomy when he interviewed him just a few weeks before *Bookstand* was transmitted, although he was transfixed more by Balchin's eyes than by his lamentable dentition:

> Reading Nigel Balchin you expect him to have one of those faces that look as though they had been cut and polished out of some tough material. [...] Meeting him you find that on the contrary he has an affable long face, extraordinarily mobile and given, as he thinks out an answer, to screwing itself up and then opening out in a smile and an efflorescence of blue eyes.[11]

But it was Balchin's voice that made the greatest impression on me when I watched his two 1960s television performances. As no audio records now exist of Balchin's many radio broadcasts, the television appearances remain the only occasions on which I have ever heard him speak. I was aware that the Wiltshire twang of his childhood had been supplanted whilst he was at school by a 'niminy-piminy, plum-in-the-mouth accent'[12] that the BBC had complained about in 1938 because they felt it was 'affected and somewhat condescending',[13] but I wasn't expecting the tones that reached my ears to be quite as deep, rich and plummy as they were. Balchin's slow, measured intonation (he weighed every word with great care) seemed more appropriate to an aristocrat than a grocer's son from a humble background. Like his predilection for presenting himself as a man of means, this is, I think, an example of Balchin pretending to be someone he wasn't; on television in the 1960s he was impersonating a 'literary gent', whether knowingly or not, and despite his oft-professed loathing for that species.

In addition to simply appearing on television as a 'talking head', Balchin was still striving to write fiction for the medium. In the autumn of 1963, he reactivated an old project for the BBC to consider. A novel with the title *Mind of Nicholas Hurst* had been mentioned to Blanche Knopf when Balchin took sherry with the American publisher in September 1949, and this had probably developed from an earlier play entitled *The Fool of Time* that had also featured a character called Nicholas Hurst.[14] Balchin told Knopf that he was anticipating finishing his novel during the following year, but other projects intervened and *Mind of Nicholas Hurst* was put on indefinite hold. Fourteen years on, the flexible Balchin realized that his novelistic conception was in fact ideally suited to television serialization.

Balchin envisaged an eight-part serial with the title *The Nine Lives of Nicholas Hurst*. The idea underpinning it was that 'Hurst is a sort of Everyman, seen consecutively against a series of different environments and backgrounds'.[15] In other words, the central character would have been witnessed each week living a new life, i.e. inhabiting a different persona and pursuing a different profession. Balchin had written four episodes when the project was terminated (with regret) by the BBC. The mandarin who turned it down was very keen on many facets of Balchin's serial, but one of the major stumbling blocks was the necessity for some sort of 'time travel' mechanism to be incorporated within its structure in order to make it work.[16] After the BBC declined to develop the series, the author tried to reformat it as a novel, but although he wrote a full-length manuscript the book remained unpublished when Balchin died, joining a select group of such works (see Appendix).

Balchin's 'Nicholas Hurst' project has a dark edge to it—its themes include marital unfaithfulness and borderline criminal activity and an air of slightly seedy unhappiness permeates its manuscript pages—but the next project that he pitched to the BBC was jet black all the way through. Written originally for the stage (it would not appear ever to have been performed), *Lennie's Point of View* was examined for both radio and television presentation—but was rejected by both media—during the summer of 1965.

Lennie is a salesman whose wife wants a fur coat. He says no and so she retaliates by refusing to have sex with him until she gets her way. Lennie picks up a prostitute who takes him back to her place and disports herself in a fur coat for his amusement. While her back is turned he steals the coat and takes it home for his wife. When this peace offering provokes no reaction, Lennie phones the police to report a murder: the salesman had inadvertently and unknowingly killed his wife earlier in the evening when he had attacked her in a violent rage after they had argued about the fur.

The BBC were not at all enamoured with *Lennie's Point of View*. The reader who examined the play for radio production described it as a 'macabre piece'[17] and a colleague working for television complained that it was 'unfashionable'. It is easy to see why the flimsy unreality of *Lennie's Point of View* failed to impress the Corporation. Misanthropic and resolutely gloomy (when he assessed the play as a possible for the 'Theatre 625' slot on the new BBC2 channel, the reader commented that 'the persistent misery of Lennie's condition is hard to take'), the work was riveted together from indelicate component parts and peppered with salty language that would have made it decidedly out of place on the BBC in 1965.

'A certain dislike of women' was another detrimental feature of *Lennie's Point of View* that was mentioned inside Broadcasting House. This criticism was thoroughly justified: the women in the play exist only to be abused, either verbally or physically, or used for the purpose of sexual gratification. In turn, they exhibit few, if any, redeeming qualities and none of the kindness or generosity of spirit commonly associated with their gender. Balchin had displayed a rather condescending attitude towards women in some of his earlier fiction, but at the same time he had given the impression that, deep down, he loved them. In works such as *Lennie's Point of View* it appears as if he hates them. The misogynistic streak that crept into Balchin's writing during the 1960s would get him into hot water before too much longer. One can only assume that the ongoing unhappiness of his second marriage—and a steady accumulation of romantic troubles since the late 1940s—had by now coloured Balchin's opinion of women and that his discontentment with them occasionally expressed itself unwisely in the production of unwholesome revenge fantasies such as *Lennie's Point of View*.

There was little appetite at the BBC for adapting any more of Balchin's novels in the mid-1960s but there was of course now another potential televisual outlet for his work. Shortly before Independent Television (ITV) had begun broadcasting in the autumn of 1955, Balchin had moved abroad to work as a film scriptwriter and so had missed the opportunity to have his work transmitted on the new channel. This omission was rectified ten years later when Rediffusion, London, the ITV franchise serving the capital and surrounding areas, broadcast an eighty-minute-long version of *The Fall of the Sparrow* on 1 March 1965.

Reviewing this 'Rediffusion Play of the Week' in the *Guardian*, Mary Crozier[18] characterized it as 'very dated' and said that it had been 'skating on very thin ice at times', although she did concede that *The Fall of the Sparrow* represented 'an interesting curiosity' and that it was 'the sort of play you can't stop watching'. In the *Daily Telegraph*, Lyn Lockwood[19] was more generous with her praise, describing *The Fall of the Sparrow* as 'a very effective piece of work' that had succeeded in 'capturing the authentic Balchin flavour in a number of scenes'.

In the early months of 1967, six stories extracted from *Last Recollections of My Uncle Charles* were also broadcast by Rediffusion, with Raymond Huntley (who had played the Cabinet Minister Gatling in *Suspect*) starring as the incorrigible 'smoking-room wizard' who recites the tales in a series called simply *Uncle Charles*. A repeat run was brought to a premature end in the summer of 1968 when Rediffusion lost its franchise and Balchin's chance of building up a profitable long-term working relationship with the channel had gone, which was a pity for him because he could undoubtedly have used the money that such an arrangement would have brought in.

*

The linked subjects of children, the growing-up process and inter-generational friction engaged Balchin's mind during 1965, not unreasonably considering that he was the middle-aged father of a nine-year-old boy and a three-year-old girl. The cogitation he undertook culminated in the publication of one of his most important non-fiction articles. On 9 October the American magazine the *Saturday Evening Post*, which had carried Balchin's short story 'Now We Are Broke My Dear' in 1950, published a rather more controversial offering from the British author. The new piece was called 'Children are a Waste of Time',[20] and if the title alone didn't raise eyebrows among the *Post*'s readership then the inclusion within the main body of the article of inflammatory statements such as 'every child in its early years is a potential Hitler', '[children] are destructive of the emotional life of the average man' and 'children are fundamentally antisocial. They are cruel, ruthless, cunning, and almost incredibly self-centered' would certainly have done so. When a shortened version of Balchin's essay was published in Britain a month later, the editorial team in Fleet Street took care to distance themselves from some of his more toxic statements:

> The Sunday Express too disagrees with Mr. Balchin's conclusions. But it publishes his article as a challenging viewpoint at a time when ideas about the place of children in the modern world are in ferment.[21]

The novelist's primary contention in 'Children are a Waste of Time'[22] was that parents dissipated their time, money and energy in bringing up their offspring, in the hope that they would 'produce somebody really exceptional', but often emerged from the process unrewarded. Balchin hinted that the personal resources he had devoted to child-rearing could have been redirected in the service of a more creative purpose, namely the composition of literature:

> More talent and creative ability have been lost to the world through the necessity to provide for children than from any other single cause.

This is in effect a restatement of Cyril Connolly's famous warning that the arrival of children in the home of a writer can sabotage a promising artistic career:

> There is no more sombre enemy of good art than the pram in the hall.[23]

In 'Children are a Waste of Time',[24] Balchin criticized the automatic deferment of parents to their children ('I oppose the idea that every child by the mere virtue of being a child is a *superior* citizen, to whose wisdom and development all must be sacrificed') before the final paragraph of his article took him into intriguing and more speculative territory. Thinking perhaps of the vast gulf in age between himself and his two young children, which had led them to regard their father as a benevolent but somewhat distant figure, a state of affairs not helped by the parent–child segregation practised first in Italy and then continued at Tufton Place and 48 Regent's Park Road, Balchin suggested that scientific expertise should be harnessed in an attempt to bridge this age gap:

> The world would be revolutionized if some means could be found by which the human child became fully grown and physically mature very young, as are the offspring of most other animals.

Ironically, in view of the fact that, within a year of his article appearing in America, Balchin would return to that country to begin researching a novel about the space programme, he concluded his diatribe by predicting that the acceleration of childhood development he desired would inevitably be pushed down the scientists' agenda in preference to concentration on the race to the stars:

> There are so many other more important things on which to spend our time, our genius and our money, such as going to the moon.

*

Published in June 1966, *In the Absence of Mrs Petersen*, the penultimate novel that Balchin wrote, is also one of his most autobiographical, as he confessed to the *Daily Express* in a promotional interview conducted to coincide with the book's appearance:

> "It must always be so. In the last decade of my life I've spent most of the time abroad, script-writing in Hollywood and so on.
>
> That's why the hero of my book is a script-writer and why the action swings from America to Yugoslavia."[25]

Balchin said that the idea for *In the Absence of Mrs Petersen* had come to him in the mid-1950s, during a holiday with Yovanka in Yugoslavia, but he didn't specify a particular incident that had sparked his imagination.[26] Yovanka suggests that the impetus to write the novel had been provided by her transatlantic flight landing badly in Los Angeles on one occasion when she had been on her way to visit Balchin in Hollywood. In the early chapters of *In the Absence of Mrs Petersen* her husband therefore imagined what might have happened had the jet caught fire instead of coming to a safe standstill alongside the terminal building.

The novel is set in Beverly Hills, Paris, Venice and in and around Belgrade, all locations that were fairly well known to

In the Absence of Mrs Petersen (1966)

Jim Petersen, an English scriptwriter working in Los Angeles, sends his wife Sarah to New York for a holiday because she is bored with the Hollywood life. He arrives at the airport hoping to wish her bon voyage but is only in time to watch her plane accelerate down the runway and then burst into flames. Sarah is killed in the resulting fireball.

Dazed after the tragedy, Jim flies to Paris where he meets a young woman who is almost an exact replica of his recently deceased spouse. The girl, a Yugoslav called Katherina Feldic, puts a proposition to Jim. She tells him that she is planning to go to Yugoslavia, where her grandparents are hoarding a sizeable quantity of valuables for her. In return for the use of Sarah's passport and his assistance in smuggling the gold and jewellery out of the country, Jim is offered the chance of a well-paid holiday in Yugoslavia with his beautiful new companion. He accepts.

The couple travel to Belgrade via Venice. Whilst in the Yugoslav capital, Jim discovers that Katherina is in love with a dissident called Pelic who has been causing embarrassment for the Communist government. But as the authorities will never allow Pelic to leave the country or Katherina to marry the man and then live in Yugoslavia with him, Katherina implores Jim to get her back to Paris as quickly as possible.

Jim therefore drives Katherina to a village outside Belgrade to collect the valuables, noticing as he does so that they are being tailed by the police. When they arrive at their destination they find that Pelic is lying in wait for them, armed with a Luger...

Balchin. But in order to obtain some up-to-date local colour he sensibly used his family's 1965 summer holiday on the Adriatic as something of a research trip. In a dry run for Petersen's journey to Yugoslavia with his new 'wife', Balchin and Yovanka travelled from London to Venice by train, stayed there for some days and then proceeded by boat to Rijeka. Balchin also met several of his elderly Yugoslav relatives during his holiday, useful background perhaps for the portraits of Katherina's grandparents that later found their way into the book.

Petersen, the extravagantly remunerated Hollywood scriptwriter (he earns even more than Balchin had a few years before) who narrates *In the Absence of Mrs Petersen*, is another in the author's expanding gallery of staid, urbane, domineering protagonists and thus has some character traits in common with his creator. To give an insight into Petersen's character, his attitude towards women is exquisitely distilled by a thought that occurs to him in a Parisian restaurant:

> I remembered that in our last few years together I had been in the habit of making Sarah choose the wine, because it was good practice for her in knowing what the whole wine affair is about.

The apparent self-confidence of Yugoslavian émigré Katherina masks insecurities that often flare up in outbursts of sulkiness or truculence. Many decades after the book was written, Balchin's widow realized that some of her less endearing personal qualities had been abstracted by her husband and assigned to both Katherina and Petersen's dead wife Sarah (who shares a birthday with Yovanka):

> ...I wouldn't have recognized it at the time but I do now with hindsight. [...] I used to do that or I used to be childish and react in this or that way.[27]

The combustible relationship between Petersen and Katherina (the pair spend much of their time together quarrelling and sniping at each other) probably shares some similarities with that between Balchin and Yovanka.

Balchin told the *Daily Express* that *In the Absence of Mrs Petersen* contained 'some of my deepest thoughts about women and what makes a marriage tick'.[28] However, the most memorable of those thoughts seem to have found their way into the newspaper profile, not the novel, in the columns of which Balchin confided that 'Women are not so much a different sex as a different species' and 'Women live on emotional peaks, they see things in black and white. They either like a person or they hate him—often for no good reason.' Prefiguring a complaint about him that would be made by the BBC three years later, Balchin told the newspaper that his views on women 'will probably get me assassinated one day'.

The novel's thriller-style ending (and the Yugoslavian portion in general) evoked comparisons in the review columns with the works of Eric Ambler. The poet and novelist Roy Fuller,[29] writing in *The Times Literary Supplement*, felt that Balchin had come off second best having chosen to invade the other writer's territory: 'Mr. Ambler himself has come in his post-war novels to do such a *tour de force* with far greater subtlety and power.' It is not known whether Balchin had read Ambler, but *In the Absence of Mrs Petersen* does bear some resemblance to post-war novels—especially *The Schirmer Inheritance*—by the writer with whom Balchin had clashed so memorably after a V2 rocket launch in 1945.

Evidence of some slackening in Balchin's ability as a novelist during the 1960s can be divined from reading *In the Absence of Mrs Petersen* and as a consequence the book generated a very mixed bag of newspaper clippings. The implausibility of the plot—considerable quantities of disbelief have to be suspended before the doppelgänger conceit can be swallowed whole—caused much consternation among the reviewers, a typical comment being that voiced by Frederic Raphael[30] in the *Sunday Times*: 'In The Absence Of Mrs Petersen is a story shamelessly unlikely to the point of fantasy.' In *The Times*, an anonymous reviewer[31] made the valid observation that 'Mr. Balchin's skill is for most of the time enough to conceal the improbability of the whole thing, and the book is consistently readable' but did add pointedly that 'The main disappointment is that we know that the author of *The Small Back Room* is capable of much more'. And Irving Wardle[32] in the *Observer*, despite grouching about the novel's 'B-picture plot', lauded it memorably as 'another expert tale of the middle-aged man on the flying trapeze'.

Anthony Burgess[33] penned a typically thoughtful review of *In the Absence of Mrs Petersen* for the *Listener*. Although he could not resist joining in with the general mood of incredulity regarding the book's narrative arc ('The plot seems preposterous'), the author of *A Clockwork Orange* did at least give the impression that he had enjoyed reading it:

> …the skills of the author who aims primarily for readability
> are deployed, as they always were, quite ravishingly.

Prudently, Balchin was working in America when *In the Absence of Mrs Petersen* was published, and had thus put several thousand miles of ocean between himself and the gun sights of any enraged British feminists who might have been offended by the views on women that he had allowed to infiltrate the pages of *In the Absence of Mrs Petersen* and expostulated in the accompanying *Daily Express* profile. He had also cunningly adopted a disguise to fool any would-be assassins, the *Express* reporter informing his readers that Balchin was 'lean with a craggy, bronzed face to which he has lately added a beard'.[34] Balchin may have joked about this piece of facial decoration ('with a face like mine almost any change is an improvement') but he liked it well enough to retain it for most of the rest of his life.

23

Failing to Achieve Lift-Off

> Oh God! I could be bounded in a nutshell, and count myself
> a king of infinite space, were it not that I have bad dreams.
>   – William Shakespeare, *Hamlet*

Before Collins had even begun dispatching copies of *In the Absence of Mrs Petersen* to bookshops, Balchin had already started work on the follow-up. On 3 June 1966 he left England, in company with Yovanka, and sailed to New York at the start of a six-week fact-finding mission, as reported on by the *Daily Express*:

> ...with the full co-operation of the authorities, he will tour space stations in Florida, Texas, and California, and meet astronauts.[1]

After the 'shamelessly unlikely'[2] jewel-smuggling escapades detailed within the pages of *In the Absence of Mrs Petersen*, Balchin's next book promised to be 'something totally different—a novel about space'.[3] The written product of Balchin's research trip was a realistic account of the American space programme disguised as a piece of science fiction and entitled *Kings of Infinite Space*. It was the first Balchin novel to have been fitted with a scientific spine since 1949's *A Sort of Traitors* and would also turn out to be his final novel.

Balchin had readily admitted that much of the content of *In the Absence of Mrs Petersen* had been autobiographical and several real events that he experienced in America during the summer of 1966 also appeared in his new book in lightly fictionalized forms. The most striking of these was a Titan-IIIC rocket launch that took place in Florida on the morning of 17 June. Balchin and Yovanka were among the spectators at Cape Kennedy during the first stage of NASA's deployment of a series of communications satellites. This launch, which Yovanka later described in her scrapbook as 'The most stimulating experience of my life', is almost exactly paralleled by a Titan-propelled mission with the same purpose ('placing each satellite in orbit at planned distances around the earth, like a milkman delivering milk to the right addresses') which is observed by the narrator of *Kings of Infinite Space*, Frank Lewis:

> The big puff of white vapour and yellow-orange flame burst out precisely at their [sic] appointed time. The white rocket slowly rose on its flaming tail, as though courteously waiting for the photographers, and then shot away [...] But nothing had prepared me for that colossal pulsating sound that literally filled the air, so that it seemed to come from all directions at once and to press on me with almost tangible weight...

Balchin also visited the NASA Manned Spacecraft Center at Clear Lake near Houston (which features prominently in *Kings of Infinite Space*), walked on a simulation of the moon's surface and attended a press briefing prior to the launch of the Gemini X manned space flight.[4] Lewis is present at a comparable press briefing and when he discovers why one of the astronauts is unpopular with the media—'Bill's a great guy, but he doesn't come across well to the press, or give them anything very interesting to write about, so they don't want any part of him.'—one cannot help but be reminded of the fact that, despite the author's routine insistence that his novel 'contains no reference to any living person', Neil Armstrong also gave the impression of being decidedly uncomfortable when positioned behind a bank of microphones:

> His diffident nature made him appear ill at ease at news conferences, and the brevity and occasional evasiveness of his answers led to some unfavourable comment...[5]

It is not known which astronauts Balchin met in 1966, but Armstrong had already returned from his first space flight—Gemini VIII—a few months before Balchin arrived in America, and would have been preparing for the crucial part he later played in the Apollo programme while the novelist was assiduously gathering colour for his book.

An absorbing documentary about the US space programme was released into cinemas in 2007. *In the Shadow of the Moon* featured interviews with most of the surviving moonwalkers, interspersed with archive footage of the Apollo missions. Watching the film, one is made aware that Balchin's novel, despite its many narrative deficiencies, does at least perform a useful function by presenting a faithful representation of actual NASA procedures circa 1966. This is reflected by details such as Balchin's astronauts in training, like their factual counterparts, being intimately involved in designing the spacecraft that they hope will enable them to break free of the Earth's gravitational field and the fact that each crew member in the book is required to become an expert on a specific technical aspect of the astronautical business. The team of aspiring astronauts that Lewis joins in *Kings of Infinite Space* seems to have been inspired by a real grouping referred to by NASA as 'Astronaut Group Four (The Scientists)'. This intake began their duties in June 1965 and consisted of three physicists, two physicians and a geologist. This was a marked contrast from prevailing NASA practice: up until this time, all astronauts had either been test pilots or at least had experience of flying jet aircraft.

Disappointingly, the scientific details of the astronauts' preparations for space flight contained in *Kings of Infinite Space* make little positive impression on the reader, which is odd given that Balchin had repeatedly proven himself to be greatly skilled at integrating relatively abstruse technical matter within a fictional framework. In earlier novels such as *The Small Back Room*, *Mine Own Executioner* and *A Sort of Traitors* the factual material that gives those books substance had been meshed far more harmoniously with the story elements. Two theories can be advanced to explain why the technical background of *Kings of Infinite Space* is rendered less compellingly than in some of Balchin's other novels. Either his writing ability had by now been seriously degraded by his reliance on alcohol or else his interest and imagination had never been fully engaged by the project in the first place because, as Yovanka suggests, her husband's decision to write about the space race had been dictated more by financial than creative considerations:

> He didn't particularly enjoy writing the book [...] It wasn't something that he really wanted to do, it was just a question of the money.[6]

'My general reaction was to find myself with my mouth open with astonishment all the time',[7] Balchin said of the weeks he spent shadowing NASA operations, and he added that 'The technical skill involved in the space programme really is amazing.' But the sense of wonderment that the novelist experienced in Florida and Texas was largely absent from the piece of fiction he completed on his return to England.

At the beginning of *Kings of Infinite Space*, the Harvard professor who arranges for Lewis to work for NASA asks the Cambridge physiologist to endeavour to find out 'what's happening to the human *mind* in all this [astronautical] work'. As the novel also makes mention of 'the human factor in space flight' it is apparent that *Kings of Infinite Space* was not after all 'something totally different' for Balchin and that, with regard to at least one of its themes, he had been transported right back to where he had begun as a novelist in 1934. *No Sky*, his debut, described the application of industrial psychology in the engineering industry. Thirty-three years later, the setting for Balchin's fiction may have been relocated from grimy northern England in the 1930s to the shiny neon-and-chrome space-age world of late-1960s America, but some of the author's preoccupations remained the same. Condensed to the sort of snappy one-line note that Balchin was accustomed to writing as an aide-memoire when beginning work on a new novel, the content of *Kings of Infinite Space* can be summarized

Kings of Infinite Space (1967)

The story begins in autumn 1969. Cambridge physiologist Frank Lewis accepts an opportunity to work for NASA to investigate the decline in the performance of astronauts caused by fatigue, and possibly also to become an astronaut himself.

When Lewis flies to Houston to join NASA the Russians have already accomplished a manned lunar landing but suffered a fatality in the process. The Americans ran them a close second, and having now successfully landed a man on the moon themselves are pressing ahead with ambitious plans to return there and also to explore deep space.

Lewis is assigned to an international team of prospective space pilots and scientific observers, and following a round of interviews, medicals and psychiatric tests is accepted for the programme. As his training schedule proceeds, he watches a rocket launch and is permitted to sit in at the flight surgeon's console during a lunar landing in order to monitor the astronauts' fatigue levels. In parallel with his training, he also begins to design and construct a 'fatigue accumulation detector'.

After a great deal of soul-searching, Lewis decides that he would like to go into space. He is therefore earmarked to be a scientific observer on a deep space mission so that he can test the performance of his fatigue machine. The aim of Project Ulysses is to fly two and a half million miles in the general direction of Mars (further than man has ever gone before), turn around and return to Earth. But shortly before Lewis is due to blast off he is involved in a car crash and taken to hospital, jeopardizing his chances of becoming an astronaut.

as 'industrial psychology in outer space'.

After *Kings of Infinite Space* was published in Britain in October 1967, Balchin came under attack from some reviewers because his statement that 'the engineering aspects of the space effort have developed more rapidly than its philosophy or its art', which he included as part of his prefatory Author's Note, was treated as something of an old saw that did not require restating. So when he quoted Lewis's synonymous observation in the fictional text that 'Our technical skill has outrun our imagination', Martin Levin[8] in the *New York Times* felt obliged to append the sarcastic rejoinder 'Excellent deduction, Lewis'. However, it is worth noting that a number of the astronauts themselves, including two members of the three-man crew of Apollo 11, have expressed the opinion in recent years that a significant failing of the US space programme was its inability to explain what going into space or landing on the moon was really *like*. The many millions across the globe who watched the Apollo missions on television were kept thoroughly informed about the technical details of space travel but were left in the dark regarding the emotions being experienced by the men in the rockets. Buzz Aldrin lamented that, of those who went to the stars, NASA 'never sent anyone who could really communicate what was happening'.[9]

Michael Collins, the member of the Apollo 11 crew who remained in orbit around the moon while his two colleagues walked on its surface, concurred with Aldrin. He admitted that 'Being a military test pilot was the best background from a technical point of view but was probably, I would add, the worst background from a public relations or public understanding or emotional point of view'.[10] Balchin (an artist himself of course, albeit one masquerading as a scientist on this occasion) was perceptive to have drawn attention to this emotional illiteracy among NASA's courageous, experienced and supremely technically qualified personnel and to have suggested at the end of the novel, via the mouthpiece of Lewis, that 'You can't 'think' about space, but by God you can feel it, and write a poem about it, or symphony, or paint it'.

It was not just the science versus art theme of *Kings of*

Infinite Space that evoked criticism. Robin Cook[11] in the *Sunday Telegraph* suggested that Balchin had been forced to administer 'injections of sex' to prevent his story from suffering a premature death. Balchin had wielded a hypodermic in much the same way in his two previous novels and, considered in tandem with some of the suggestive material to be found in his late television scripts, the belated importation of sexual matter into his fiction perhaps represented an ill-advised attempt by the author to adapt and modernize his work in order to fit in with the zeitgeist of the 1960s. The titillating content of *Kings of Infinite Space* includes Lewis's girlfriend Julian disporting herself in skin-tight clothing to excite her lover, the physiologist going to bed with women on both sides of the Atlantic, Lewis and a fellow astronaut-in-training visiting a strip club in New Orleans and the latter petting a colleague's wife whilst simultaneously driving Lewis's Aston Martin at top speed. Almost all of the women in *Kings of Infinite Space* function primarily as sex objects, and not as interesting three-dimensional characters in their own right, another example of the misogynism that steadily infiltrated Balchin's work as the 1960s unfolded.

In addition to the lack of impact made by the technical matter, Balchin's final book is also badly hobbled by its less than stellar plot. One possible reason for what Maurice Richardson[12] in the *Observer* referred to as 'some narrative weakness' in *Kings of Infinite Space* is that the novel had not undergone the requisite gestation period. Balchin generally allowed something in the region of ten years to elapse between conceiving the concept for a new novel and starting to write it (and the idea for *In the Absence of Mrs Petersen* had brewed in his mind for well over a decade). *Kings of Infinite Space*, written partly on the hoof in the American summer of 1966 and completed during the English winter that followed, underwent a drastically truncated pregnancy by comparison. Balchin once likened his novel-writing process to that used by cooks when making a stew:

> "The basic ingredients of the story are shoved in a mental oven. I take the lid off now and then till I find it's cooked."[13]

For a Balchin dish, *Kings of Infinite Space* tasted underdone, contained some gristly, indigestible lumps and had been inadequately seasoned.

Balchin's space novel is arguably the worst of his many works of fiction, and the majority of the reviews reflected this fact, albeit in a variety of tones ranging from the respectful to the downright offensive. Richardson,[14] who had been very kind about Balchin's output in the recent past, described *Kings of Infinite Space* as 'a fascinating book, one of the most interesting he has written, but I doubt if it is his best novel' and was generally equivocal about the merits of the work.

Somewhat surprisingly, given its history of scepticism regarding the worth of Balchin's fiction, the *Times Literary Supplement* printed one of the most complimentary reviews of the novel to be found just about anywhere in the British press. In its pages, David Williams[15] drew attention to 'the deftness and sparkling narrative skill' displayed in *Kings of Infinite Space*.

It was left to Cook[16] to administer the critical thrashing that the other reviewers had shied away from, almost as if they had sportingly resisted the temptation to kick a man when he was down. Nancy Spain aside, Cook's review is the worst that Balchin received during his long career as a novelist. It was a cruel and prolonged sarcasm-tipped assault, but it is difficult to deny the validity of many of the points he made, the first of which was one of the kindest:

> Nigel Balchin's new novel, Kings of Infinite Space, slowly deals with what the averagely well-informed already know about the ordeal of manned space flights.

The quality of Balchin's prose in *Kings of Infinite Space* does not remotely approach that of his more celebrated novels and Cook ruthlessly exposed its overdependence on cliché:

> Every familiar narrative device ("...Things were moving very fast now..." "...Then a number of things began to happen very quickly indeed..." "...As soon as she started to say it

I realised what she was getting at and how almost perfectly apt it was…") is there to haunt us, and no stylised agréments in the bedroom will exorcise the ghost.

The *Sunday Telegraph* reviewer also declared that *Kings of Infinite Space* evidenced a failure on the part of Balchin 'to create interest in his work' and that structural deficiencies in the novel's construction seemed to be 'a matter of indifference to the author'. Cook's final trenchant observation, despite being an obvious one to make, was indisputably true: 'Unlike those rockets, Mr. Balchin's text just will not blast off.'

After Balchin's death in May 1970, an unnamed leader writer in the *Guardian* condemned *Kings of Infinite Space* as 'almost totally unreadable'.[17] This was wholly inaccurate, as the book is as readable as virtually any of Balchin's post-war novels, but the salient question that begs to be asked is this: why should anyone want to read it *today*, more than forty years after the last of the moon landings took place? Now that the general public's earlier interest in spacefaring has declined to a level of almost complete apathy, it is tough to construct a persuasive argument in favour of *Kings of Infinite Space*, which lacks the energy of Balchin's finest work and is likely to appeal only to readers with a keen interest in the history of the US space programme. Balchin's final novel put a lacklustre full stop to his fiction-writing career, one that spanned thirty-three years and fifteen books, began inauspiciously with *No Sky* and then flowered magnificently in the 1940s and 1950s before tailing off in the last few years of his life.

*

The Greyhound in Glemsford is a fifteenth century thatched cottage set back a little way from the main road passing through the heart of this attractive Suffolk village. The building functioned as a public house for many years, before losing its licence in 1907. On the night on which it closed its doors for the final time, the villagers, after gargantuan consumption of free beer, processed to the churchyard carrying a coffin they had specially procured for the purpose. Either this coffin or a mock-up was later sent to the brewery in protest at the loss of a popular watering hole and The Greyhound was converted from a public to a private house.[18]

Sixty years after the last pint was pulled in The Greyhound, Nigel Balchin relocated his family there. Yovanka was delighted by her husband's purchase, which for her comprised a cornucopia of diverse attractions:

> A cottage which had been a pub, a barn, a bakery, lots of outhouses, a separate garage with a room above, charming gardens, in a village.[19]

It may have offered him ample room in which to practise his favourite hobby of woodcarving but Balchin was less enchanted than his wife by the attributes of the house. Charles recalls how his father had duplicated the mistake made by C. P. Snow at Oast Cottage by 'banging his head on those bloody low ceilings'.[20] As a natural teller of tales, Balchin did revel though in his new property's connection with an extra-corporeal presence, taking delight in reciting a condensed ghost story to a representative of the local press:

> "I've never seen it [the ghost] but the story goes that one of the people who lived here a long time ago got into financial difficulties and hanged himself.
>
> He owned a white horse that now and then comes looking for him. It goes into what used to be a loose box and then when it's had enough it just goes away."[21]

Balchin commissioned a local artist to paint 'the principal ornament' that adorned the front elevation of the former pub, namely a 'swinging inn sign of a greyhound put there by Mr. Balchin to guide visitors so they might not be delayed when on their first journey to Glemsford'. This small piece of thoughtfulness later backfired on the Balchins. Yovanka remembers a number of occasions on which unwelcome visitors arrived outside their house very late in the evening and proceeded to rap loudly on the front door, anxious to gain admittance and wary of the imminent approach of 'closing time'. They would reluctantly depart, in a foul temper, once they had been informed that The Greyhound was no longer licensed premises and that there was thus no prospect of slaking their thirst beneath its ancient roof.

The proximity of Glemsford to Toppesfield, not much more than ten miles across the border in neighbouring Essex, allowed Balchin to maintain contact with his first wife Elisabeth and her second husband Michael Ayrton. There are also reports of cultural gatherings in Pentlow, a village very close to Glemsford, in which both Ayrton and Balchin participated. The psychological battle enacted between the two men to secure Elisabeth's affections in the late 1940s had not been allowed to destroy their close friendship, which remained intact twenty years later. After his divorce, Balchin also supported Ayrton financially by purchasing artworks from him, particularly during the 1950s.

Yovanka 'adored'[22] her country cottage, but rural life held much less appeal for Balchin simply because, as an individual described by his second wife as 'very sedentary',[23] he found nothing much to do in Glemsford. (This after all is the man who, when living in Sussex in the 1950s, had said that the advantage of the countryside was that it did *not* contain 'a lot of charming people with whom to waste one's time talking'.[24]) By contrast, London offered the attractions of the Savile Club, the presence of friends and acquaintances and the prospect of sexual encounters that could be conducted at a considerable remove from the prying eyes and wagging tongues of a small rural community.

Reflecting on the time she had spent at The Greyhound, Yovanka remarked that 'Sadly, although it was my favourite house, it was also where I was the unhappiest'.[25] This was partly because her husband was continuing to drink copiously when in residence, but also because he was away from her for long periods and thus open to temptation where other women were concerned. As Balchin remained the owner of the vast

48 Regent's Park Road, he chose to write there in preference to The Greyhound, using one floor of the house as his working quarters and installing a live-in secretary, a single mother from Clacton, on the floor above. Balchin's relations with his employee soon developed beyond the purely professional, as Yovanka remembers:

> She became Nigel's mistress and I was told after his death by the Americans [who lived on the ground floor] that they used to hear frightful screaming matches above in the flat.

For a while, it looked as if Balchin might actually leave Yovanka in order to live with his secretary. But, as had already happened several times before, the Balchins decided that they would be better off together than apart and so agreed to prolong their turbulent marriage. For Yovanka, her husband's fling had not seemed real anyway:

> I never took the relationship seriously because by then he was an alcoholic so there wasn't anybody who would really want to take him on.[26]

Beset by problems in his private life, Balchin derived scant succour from his writing. With good ideas for novels continuing to elude him, he turned once more to the BBC as a possible source of employment. In April 1968, he was invited to adapt William Makepeace Thackeray's novel *Henry Esmond* for television. The work that Balchin produced in response to this commission proved to be unusable, the BBC's Production Department commenting in September that his were 'the worst scripts they had seen in four years'.[27]

Undaunted, Balchin tried his luck again the following year. A new project occupied him during the early months of 1969, its progress being reported on by the *East Anglian Daily Times* at the start of February:

> He is now engaged on, and about three-quarters of the way towards completing, a series of open letters with the title "To

all you ladies" an attempt to explain characteristic male and female misunderstandings.[28]

On 12 March, Balchin was interviewed about this work and his thoughts were broadcast in the form of a six-minute segment of the family magazine programme *Home This Afternoon* on Radio 4 at the end of the month.

The day after he had recorded the interview, 'To All You Ladies' was sent to the BBC for possible inclusion, logically enough, in *Woman's Hour*, a staple of Radio 4's daytime output aimed principally at its female listenership. The young writer Virginia Browne-Wilkinson had befriended Leonard Woolf, widower of Virginia Woolf, in the autumn years of his life. In the words of Leonard Woolf's biographer, Victoria Glendinning, Browne-Wilkinson was 'in charge of books for the BBC's 'Woman's Hour' '.[29] In this capacity, she examined Balchin's potential contribution to the programme but was scathing about the chauvinistic attitude that pervaded it:

> I started reading these very hopefully because I liked the idea & thought they might be used in place of short stories on W.E.W.H.[30] But they are *horrid*. They are superficially good humoured, but just under the skin he really dislikes women very much (evidently) & wants to say humiliating & physically offensive things with a would-be urbane smile.[31]

'To All You Ladies' was forcefully rejected by *Woman's Hour*; like *Lennie's Point of View* a few years before, it seems to have been turned down by the BBC primarily as a result of the misogynistic sentiments contained within its pages.

To the catalogue of woes that afflicted Balchin while he was the owner of The Greyhound—alcoholism, continued indifferent health, difficulty placing his writing, an uncertain future with Yovanka—one must also add worries over money. Several years after the completion of *Kings of Infinite Space*, the income that Balchin was receiving from his writing had now shrivelled to almost nothing, but he was still required to make mortgage payments on sizeable properties in both town and country as well as providing for his wife and children. The novelist's financial situation when he was living in East Anglia became so parlous that Yovanka was obliged to sell some of her finest pieces of jewellery in order to keep her husband afloat:

> ...he realized that he was going to be made bankrupt by Lloyds for the princely sum of £75 [just over £1,000 today] that he owed the wine merchant in Bury St Edmunds. But then he had a lot of debts as well. So I got together whatever jewellery I had and went to London. I had a beautiful diamond ring which my grandparents had given me (it was a four and a half carat diamond) which today would be worth about £40,000 and I sold it. I went to Bond Street and sold it and [...] paid off the debts and stopped him from being publicly humiliated.[32]

Faced with an obvious need to downsize, Balchin and Yovanka chose to return to London. The writer's wife told the *Daily Mail* in October 1968 that they had decided to put their Suffolk house up for sale. The reason for press interest in the Balchins' movements is that the couple were trying to send Cassandra to school in Yugoslavia, Yovanka explaining their reasoning to the reporter:

> 'My husband hasn't been very well,'[33] she says, 'and we have had schooling difficulties with our daughter, so we have decided to go abroad for about six months.
> We once lived in Italy, but we don't want to go anywhere so obvious this time. We want to do something mildly silly.'[34]

Appropriately, given this sombre period in Balchin's life, not even mild silliness resulted, the Balchins wintering in England instead of pursuing frivolity overseas. Cassandra spent a year and a half at the American School in Belgrade, residing with her maternal grandmother, and when she returned to England in the first few months of 1970 she found that, in her absence, the family home had been relocated fifty miles or so southwards.

Marlborough Mansions is a large red-brick block of flats in Cannon Hill, West Hampstead situated about a mile to the south-west of Hampstead Heath. The Balchins had the conductor Adrian Boult for a neighbour while they inhabited Number 89 but, after occupying a succession of expansive properties since 1962, they had slid quite a long way down the housing ladder (and the social scale) having gone from being the owners of an enormous country house in Sussex (Tufton Place) to the owners of a mere flat in north-west London in the space of not much more than five years.

Balchin's career was now in free fall: he had burnt his boats with the film world, was out of favour with the BBC and, with his sixtieth birthday already well behind him, was too old to resume his original occupation of industrial psychologist but too young and too short of money to ease gently into retirement. All he could do was write, but about what? It was Elizabeth Jane Howard's belief that 'like so many writers he ran out of material. You're only likely to continue to have material if you continue to move on in your life: mature, expand, develop. And I think he got stuck.'[35] Balchin had become stuck because, having distanced himself from the world of work that had helped to kick-start his career as a writer, there was now insufficient material at his disposal to spark his imagination. When he tried to write fiction that concerned events outside of his own experience it lacked conviction, was often tarnished by unwholesome preoccupations and/or tainted by misogynism and therefore found its way inexorably into the wastepaper baskets of his intended clients. Remarkably, a near-perfect solution to Balchin's writing dilemma did present itself within months of leaving The Greyhound. But unfortunately for him, it would have tragic consequences.

24

Balchin and Drink

> ...I think he was far more of a serious alcoholic than you
> have perhaps realized. He was basically an alcoholic...
> — Yovanka Balchin[1]

Outside of my own work, I have only ever encountered one
published mention of Nigel Balchin's relationship with alcoholic
drink. In the *Oxford Dictionary of National Biography*, Peter
Rowland stated that, for Balchin, the appeal of working in
Hollywood in the late 1950s had 'soon palled owing to his growing
reliance on alcohol'.[2] Mentions of Balchin's drinking habits are
completely absent from all of the many obituaries for him that
I have read; it is uncertain whether this taciturnity sprang from
press reluctance, in 1970, to speak ill of the dead or whether it
can be attributed instead to simple ignorance of an unpalatable
fact that was known to those closest to Balchin for many years
before his untimely death. For it has to be stated here and now
that Balchin was, emphatically and indisputably, an alcoholic.

Drink had not exercised such a powerful hold on Balchin
in his early years as a writer. It is Yovanka's belief that her
husband 'didn't drink until he was about thirty-six'.[3] Although
it is unclear what prompted him to begin experimenting with
alcohol, he had turned thirty-six just before the end of 1944, and
as he told Yovanka that he had suffered a breakdown during the
final year of the Second World War then it is permissible I think
to conjecture that those two occurrences may have been linked.

Balchin's friend and fellow novelist Elizabeth Jane Howard
met him for the first time at the beginning of the 1950s. While
getting to know each other they would often dine together in

London, sometimes at Boulestin in Covent Garden. Howard confirmed that Balchin was an established social drinker at this point in his life, but certainly not a drunk:

> ...if he took me out for dinner we had Martinis or cocktails of some kind. And then we'd have a bottle of wine and then we might have some brandy. And I didn't think anything of that because that's what people did, it was very usual. I don't remember seeing him drunk.[4]

The collapse of Balchin's first marriage is one traumatic episode in his personal life that may have transformed his relationship with alcohol from a relatively benign one into something more malignant. When they were courting in the early 1950s, shortly before Balchin obtained his divorce, Yovanka noted that her future husband's consumption of alcohol was copious enough to suggest to her that he had a problem: 'he had been drinking a lot throughout these years, although I would not say he was a drunk. [...] He was a very damaged person already but certainly not a confirmed alcoholic.'[5] If a breakdown of relations with Elisabeth was the trigger for Balchin to increase his alcohol intake to damaging levels then marrying again in 1953 did nothing to resolve the problem. The novelist continued to drink to excess on occasions throughout the course of his second marriage and Yovanka admits that her youth and headstrong nature were destined not to moderate the amount he imbibed:

> Can you imagine how he must have felt married to someone 20 years younger who thought she knew better! No wonder he continued drinking.[6]

So if Balchin was not a confirmed alcoholic by the early 1950s, when did he become one? The transition would definitely appear to have been completed by 1964 because Yovanka recalls that, when her family left Tufton Place in Sussex in May of that year to return to London, her husband 'was I would say an alcoholic'.[7]

It was while Balchin was living at The Greyhound in

Suffolk between 1967 and 1969 that he seems to have plumbed rock bottom as far as his drinking was concerned. If there had previously been any doubt regarding whether he was an alcoholic then it had all been erased by the late 1960s. Balchin's addiction was now an open secret, being apparent to both family members and strangers alike, and it was not a pretty sight. Aged about five at the time, Cassandra remembered her father falling down the stairs at The Greyhound:

> I found it very frightening; he'd sort of bashed himself. Now with adult hindsight I presume it was from drinking, because he was in a pretty bad state by then.[8]

On another occasion, a visitor to the house unexpectedly encountered Balchin in a pitiful condition, Yovanka recalling that 'the vicar's wife, who had called to ask me to open the church fete, came to walk round the orchard with me and we found Nigel dead drunk in the grass'.[9]

There are many reasons why Balchin continued to drink to the point of stupefaction right up until his death. Among the most pertinent that can be put forward are being married to a wilful, occasionally infuriating woman who was many years his junior, the fact that he was under constant pressure to maximize his earnings in order to finance the extravagant lifestyle that he and Yovanka chose to adopt from the mid-1950s onwards and having the responsibility for bringing up two small children thrust upon him when he was already well into middle age. Two of Balchin's immediate family also point a finger at the American film industry as a pertinent factor that may have contributed to his alcoholism. 'I think he was [an alcoholic] in Hollywood'[10] remarks his daughter Freja, and Yovanka considers that it was when Balchin was separated from her and their young son and living the lonely, unrewarding existence of the Hollywood scriptwriter in the late 1950s that 'the foundation was laid for his unavoidable alcoholism'.[11] Theatre critic Blanche Marvin, the writer's former literary executor, has an alternative take on why Balchin was driven to drink. She believes that he sought solace in alcohol because he felt his work had not been accorded the respect that it had rightfully deserved and that, as a result, 'he was a broken man at the end'.[12]

The last photograph of Balchin that I have seen was taken to accompany a local newspaper interview that he gave in February 1969, not long before he made the permanent move from Suffolk back to London and only fifteen months before he died. With his sad, rheumy eyes, careworn expression and straggling salt-and-pepper beard, Balchin looks much older than he had done in photographs taken only about five years earlier and more like an octogenarian than the sexagenarian he had recently become. As the image is in black-and-white it is not possible to detect the florid complexion that is often a telltale sign of long-term alcohol abuse, but it would probably have been apparent to the photographer and had certainly been observed by Howard some years before:

> I didn't realize he was an alcoholic. I should have, from his face really. He had [...] grog-blossom...[13,14]

Yovanka remembers that her husband was once described by his doctor as being 'a circumstantial alcoholic'.[15] Not an expression that would appear to be in mainstream circulation as an accepted piece of medical terminology, its meaning is nevertheless fairly clear. Balchin drank to excess whenever he was confronted by difficult or unhappy circumstances, alcohol having become his chosen palliative to take the edge off the pain inflicted by any sort of reverse, be it the frustration of having his work interfered with in Hollywood, harsh criticism of his writing or a difference of opinion with Yovanka, who states that 'you only had to say one thing [...] and he was off'. As an example of what could transpire when Balchin's work was criticized or rejected, Yovanka recalls an occasion, after the publication in 1967 of *Kings of Infinite Space*, when a piece of his writing was turned down by A. D. Peters:

> ...one of the people at the agency sent the article back and more or less saying [sic] that it was dreadful, that we can't

offer this to any publisher. That's when he got blindingly drunk: that really upset him terribly.

As the end of his writing career approached, Balchin had trapped himself inside a vicious alcohol-driven circle: every time his work was rejected he drank heavily, the after-effects of his drinking bouts caused him to produce further inferior work and that work was then more likely to be rejected.

Balchin's deployment of alcohol as a crutch when his ego had taken a battering is reflected in his fiction. Bill Sarratt drinks in *Darkness Falls from the Air* when his superiors meddle with his work; both Sammy Rice in *The Small Back Room* and Jim Manning in *A Way Through the Wood* reach for the bottle when their partners abandon them; Felix Milne in *Mine Own Executioner* gets drunk after arguing with the principal of the psychiatric clinic where he works and then resigning his position there; and almost the first reaction of Lawrence Spellman in *Sundry Creditors* when he is accused of making improper advances towards a young female worker in his factory is to steady his nerves with a slug of alcohol: "What I need at the moment is a drink." Balchin's GP would undoubtedly have diagnosed circumstantial alcoholism in many of his patient's characters…

Living in London, not rural Suffolk, during the final months of his life did nothing to alleviate Balchin's alcoholism. In Yovanka's opinion, her husband was now 'beyond cure'[16] and she recalls several occasions on which he injured himself on returning home the worse for wear after a night out:

I would hear him come through the front door in Marlborough Mansions and there'd be a cut on his forehead and he'd be bleeding because he'd fallen on the stone stairs going up.

In fact a cure was attempted at around this time. Yovanka drove Balchin from London to Nottingham very late one night to admit him to an alcohol addiction clinic but he only lasted two days before discharging himself. In her opinion, modern-day therapeutic concepts may have been more successful in her husband's case: 'if only The Priory had existed,[17] he might have stood a chance, so many birds of a feather would have been easier to take'.[18]

*

> I had a drink while I waited for Ted and it went down very well and I had another, and that went down very well too. I told myself that I was beginning to drink too much and ordered another and shut my eyes.
>   – Nigel Balchin, *Darkness Falls from the Air*

Balchin's alcoholism exacerbated his other health problems, hurt those closest to him, almost certainly shortened his life and, I believe, negatively impacted his written work for the majority of the decade preceding his death: as his alcohol consumption increased the quality of his writing deteriorated and it seems scarcely believable that the two events were unconnected. It is of course no consolation at all for those that Balchin left behind but the one positive corollary of his addiction to alcohol is that his fiction is enriched by scenes in which drinking is at the heart of the action. Balchin's legacy of fine novels would be impoverished if some of their characters were not in the habit of drinking far more than is good for anyone and if so many memorable, vibrantly written set pieces located in pubs, bars, night clubs and restaurants, at dances or parties were not swimming in alcohol. Had Balchin, after the age of thirty-six, never allowed anything stronger than lemonade to pass his lips then he would not have succeeded in getting so convincingly inside the heads of some of his most notable fictional creations. Balchin wrote so well about damaged people because, as Yovanka has said, he was 'a very damaged person'[19] himself. That damage had been inflicted initially by Elisabeth's decision to leave him so that she could live with Michael Ayrton and was later compounded by ill health and a stormy relationship with Yovanka. Balchin drank to try to ameliorate difficult situations but, like so many other creative artists before and since, found that the answer to his problems did not lie halfway down a bottle.

25

Death of a Famous Writer

"There are two things about being a writer," says Nigel Balchin. "One is that you can never stop working. The other is that whatever happens to you can be turned to advantage."[1]

Nigel Balchin never stopped writing. Some of the material he wrote in the final years of his life remains elusive but Yovanka is adamant that he was still producing it right up until his death:

No way had he retired. [...] He was in his study every day writing.[2]

Although Balchin never retired as a writer, by the end of the 1960s he had been marginalized by those creative industries that had previously regarded his work with such respect and admiration. His writing was now being rejected more often than it was being accepted, a situation that evoked the period in the lead-up to the Second World War during which he had struggled to achieve recognition. The BBC had turned down *The Nine Lives of Nicholas Hurst* in 1964, as well as Balchin's adaptation of Thackeray's *Henry Esmond* four years later, and they had lost considerable sums of money on both projects. When his series of 'open letters' to women was rejected by *Woman's Hour* in 1969, a policy of 'three strikes and you're out' seems to have been triggered because Balchin never received another cheque from the Corporation, bringing to an end an association that had lasted for very nearly thirty-five years. Two of his other stalwart supporters during his better days had now also decisively altered their opinion of him, as Yovanka explains:

...he had had one or two rebuffs from Collins and unpleasant criticism from his editor there, and also what he felt as neglect from his agent, A. D. Peters, who had told him something he had written was rubbish.[3]

Balchin's work was being returned to him because it had dipped well beneath his usual standard and two reasons can be put forward to account for this deterioration in quality. The first—and most obvious—is that the work was emanating from the study of an alcoholic. The second reason is that nothing was happening to Balchin in his day-to-day life that could be turned to advantage when he sat down at his desk, lit a cigarette, paused for thought, stubbed out the cigarette and then picked up his pencil to begin writing. With all his links to industry and business now broken, he had to rely on the products of his own imagination to stimulate a flow of words and, as Yovanka elucidates, this was not one of her husband's strengths: 'invention was not his thing. He had to embellish things that he had experienced'.[4] In 1961, when Balchin was planning his return to England from Italy, he had spoken about the possibility of finding another job, more than a quarter of a century on from his last, as an industrial psychologist. This aspiration came to nothing, but had he succeeded in securing such employment then it might just have revitalized his fiction. A position in a 1960s industrial environment would have been new and strange to Balchin and had he obtained one then he would have succeeded in reconnecting himself to the supply of material he required in order to both initiate and invigorate his writing.

Balchin may have become persona non grata at the BBC but the commercial channel was still willing to entertain him as a creator of drama. On 12 July 1969, four days before Apollo 11 set its course for the moon, *Better Dead* was aired by Anglia Television as part of their 'Saturday Night Theatre' strand. But the final Balchin-authored piece broadcast on either television or radio before his death was a strictly earthbound entertainment and when the credits rolled one reviewer was surprised to learn that the Wiltshireman's name was attached to it.

In common with his two previous original television

screenplays (*The Leader of the House*, which had been about politics, and *The Hatchet Man*, set in Hollywood), *Better Dead* took Balchin outside his familiar 'man at work' milieu and into another new realm, this time that of the murder mystery. When a solicitor is found dead in his house it looks at first sight as if the man has taken his own life. While the dead man's wife is being consoled by her friend the family doctor, a police inspector begins investigating the death and is unconvinced by the suicide hypothesis. Sylvia Clayton[5] in the *Daily Telegraph* explained why the investigation was more complex than it had initially appeared:

> The police bewilderment in the case on view was understandable. After all, who would suspect a respectable family doctor of not only having an affair with a solicitor's wife, helping to murder her husband and blacken his name, but also of living a secret life as a transvestite?

The policeman therefore seeks advice from his friend Colonel James James, an amateur sleuth who is consulted by Scotland Yard whenever they are baffled by a case. Clayton compared James with both Sherlock Holmes, a crime-solver whom Balchin was very well acquainted with (in 1962 he had revealed that 'I don't read detective stories [...] except Sherlock Holmes'[6]), and Miss Marple.

Ron Moody's performance as Colonel James was an evident highlight of the play, the star of Lionel Bart's *Oliver* being referred to as 'so good' by Stanley Reynolds[7] in the *Guardian*, although the reviewer found little else to admire in *Better Dead*, which for him constituted 'an old-fashioned thriller with a cumbersome plot which, coming from a man with Nigel Balchin's reputation, was surprising'. Clayton[8] was more complimentary about Balchin's screenplay, commending it as 'a neatly-slotted old-fashioned piece of crossword puzzle fiction, with Ron Moody enjoying his chance to display the colonel's superior intelligence', but she did complain that this latest addition to the panoply of fictional detectives appeared 'to have been assembled by Nigel Balchin on Identikit principles'.

Like the two Balchin television dramas that were turned down

by the BBC in the mid-1960s—*The Nine Lives of Nicholas Hurst*
and *Lennie's Point of View*—*Better Dead* displays a fascination with
the darker, more unsavoury aspects of the human condition. All
three pieces featured a prostitute in their cast lists and took their
writer into more risqué territory than ever before The type of
material he had marshalled in order to create *Better Dead* was totally
alien to Balchin, and the end result was a predictably shaky slice
of television. Clayton concluded her review by suggesting that the
combination of murder and transvestism that Balchin had essayed
had not been a winning one by any stretch of the imagination:

> The disappointment was that this artificial situation
> had been created by Nigel Balchin, a novelist capable of
> producing genuine excitement.

*

As the 1970s began, Balchin's fortunes showed some signs of
revival. Although he remained an alcoholic right up until the end
of his life, his drinking was no longer quite such an agonizing
problem for him and his wife to deal with—partly because they
had become accustomed to it—and his marriage, which hitherto
had been characterized by almost perpetual turbulence, at last
entered a more tranquil phase. Yovanka recollects that, during
their last few years together, 'we were finding a sort of modus
vivendi'[9] and she offers a poignant illustration of the strength of
her partner's feelings for her:

> …I had just brought him a cup of tea in bed—and this was
> in Marlborough Mansions—and he told me that I was the
> only person he'd ever really loved.

Despite the many difficulties that the pair had endured during
their seventeen years of matrimony, Yovanka confirms that
their union had been constructed on the bedrock of a very deep
mutual affection:

> …however much our relationship was stormy (which of course
> it was, it had to be) I also really, really loved him very much.

With his personal life therefore on a more even keel than it had been for some while, Balchin prepared to take on another major writing project. Although he no longer had fresh first-hand experience of factories or offices to draw upon as a source of inspiration there was still one form of labour that he could write about authoritatively purely from recent memory: writing. The mechanics of authorship had supplied the backbone for a couple of appearances he had made on radio and television in the 1950s, as well as providing material for miscellaneous pieces of journalism, and so penning articles about the writing process itself should have been something that he could have handled with aplomb. The famous writer of the 1940s and 1950s was about to become a Famous Writer of the 1970s.

The Famous Writers School (FWS), headquartered in Westport, Connecticut, was a purveyor of correspondence courses in creative writing designed to teach its 65,000 American customers how to write best-selling novels.[10] Already established as an American institution, with an annual turnover of $48 million (about £190 million today), the FWS was looking to spread its wings and open an outpost in the UK. In the early months of 1970, Balchin was approached and asked if he would like to assist in this endeavour. As Yovanka remembers, 'His first reaction was negative'.[11]

In 1936, in a chapter of his book on personal budgeting, *Income and Outcome. A Study of Personal Finance*, devoted to the topic of Insurance, Balchin had declared that 'I have rather less than no use for any married man without capital who does not insure his life'. Almost literally taking a leaf out of one of his own books, Balchin therefore decided to accept the lucrative proposal he had received from the FWS but also to insure his life at the same time. Yovanka outlined the principal benefit of the insurance policy that her husband took out:

> …he decided to do a financial deal involving a life insurance of £30,000 [just under £400,000 today] […] To that effect, he was asked to go to a medical of their choice and much to our joint surprise passed with flying colours.[12]

Other well-known British writers were also signed up by the FWS. These included Elizabeth Taylor (author of many finely turned novels, including the Booker Prize-shortlisted *Mrs Palfrey at the Claremont*), Richard Gordon of *Doctor in the House* fame, Christianna Brand (author of thrillers such as *Green for Danger*, which was brilliantly filmed by Launder and Gilliat in 1946 with Alistair Sim in the starring role) and the comedy writer, television personality and noted bowtie-wearer Frank Muir. The financial carrots being dangled in front of these famous writers were undeniably alluring: as recompense for agreeing to have their names linked with the FWS, prospective employees were tempted with a retainer that, in Gordon's words, equated to 'the price of 100 TV sets a year'[13] or, as Taylor's biographer Nicola Beauman put it, with greater precision, 'an enormous fee, (allegedly £4,000 a year, £45,000 nowadays)'. The demands placed on the writers in return for these astronomical sums were hardly onerous. Members of the Guiding Council of the International Writers School, as the English version of the FWS became known, were asked to do no more than write a few pieces for the instruction manuals, spend one afternoon a month discussing the project with their fellow scribes at a swanky London hotel (on which occasions they were invited to take advantage of a prodigiously stocked drinks trolley) and promise to make at least one trip to Westport during their association with the FWS.

Balchin attended several meetings of the Guiding Council in London, in the course of which the curriculum for the writing course began to take shape. Gordon reported that 'The teachers of the Famous Writers School got along famously'[14] and he personally enjoyed the time he had spent in the company of 'the excellently entertaining Nigel Balchin'.

In May, Balchin flew to New York and then travelled on to Westport, some fifty miles distant, for his mandatory visit to FWS headquarters. As recounted by Yovanka it was a whistle-stop trip—'that awful thing where you arrive and you go straight to meetings and back to the hotel'[15]—and, despite having only recently passed his insurance company's medical, an alcoholic sexagenarian with many years of indifferent health behind him was perhaps insufficiently robust to withstand the rigours of crossing the Atlantic twice at high altitude (and inside a pressurized cabin) in quick succession. Balchin returned from Westport with bronchitis and immediately entered a nursing home not far from Marlborough Mansions (the Greenaway in Fellows Road, NW3) for a spell of recuperation. Three days after being admitted he was dead.

Balchin died in the early hours of the morning of 17 May, aged sixty-one. His death sent a huge shockwave through his family because it was so completely unexpected. Perhaps the writer himself had been aware of the sands of time running out when he had drawn up a new will less than three months before departing England for Westport, but his demise had not been foreseen by those closest to him and the rapidity of her husband's deterioration after entering the nursing home took Yovanka completely by surprise. On the evening of the day on which Balchin died, she informed readers of the *Daily Mail* of the sequence of events during the previous twenty-four hours:

'I saw him yesterday and he seemed to be getting along well. Today he had a sudden heart attack.'[16]

His death certificate records that Balchin died from a combination of coronary thrombosis—the precursor to a heart attack—and pneumonia.

Balchin's flirtation with the FWS ended tragically for him and had no positive financial repercussions for Yovanka because her husband had not survived long enough to enable the life insurance policy to be triggered:

If he'd lived another three weeks the thing would have been through and I would have been very, very, very, well-off...[17]

With the exception of a handful of large cheques, working for the FWS also produced few obvious benefits for the likes of

Gordon and Taylor. Two months after Balchin's death, the American literary magazine *The Atlantic Monthly* published an article by Jessica Mitford[18] that was deeply critical of both the teaching methods of the FWS and the organization in general. In the wake of a rash of letters from irate Americans complaining that they had been duped, the FWS filed for bankruptcy in 1972. The first volume of the teaching manual that Balchin had contributed to, *The International Writers Course—Principles of Good Writing*, was typeset but never published, leaving Gordon to record wistfully that 'I prize my set of our oatmeal volumes, now among the world's rare books'.[19]

Like Balchin, Taylor had signed up with the FWS almost solely for monetary reasons, in her case as a way of compensating for the significant dip in her earnings that had resulted when a long-established and very profitable association with the *New Yorker*—they published dozens of her short stories from 1949 onwards—came to an abrupt end in 1969. The gifted author of *Palladian* and *Angel* was bashful about having agreed to work for the FWS, refusing to tell her editor at the *New Yorker* on what pretext she was coming to America when she travelled there in spring 1970 to attend a meeting at Westport and, in Beauman's opinion, was naive to have had 'anything to do with an organisation notorious in American literary circles for peddling wares not much better than those sold by vacuum-cleaner or encyclopedia salesmen'. Gordon confessed that 'We were a teeny bit ashamed of ourselves'[20] but added that 'we honestly hoped we might instil a little of the literacy it was becoming unfashionable to teach in schools'.

As far as Balchin was concerned, Yovanka considers that once he had overcome his initial distaste at being involved with the FWS ('he was, in fact, ashamed of doing the job, but was doing it for us [i.e. her and their two children]'[21]), her husband had absorbed himself in the task of writing pieces for the instruction manual and that his labours had undoubtedly been productive: 'he was working very well on it: it was a very good period.'[22]

He was the love of my life and when he died my life died too.
— Yovanka Balchin[23]

Nigel Balchin's funeral was held on 20 May at Hampstead Cemetery. The surviving members of his family can now recall only the sketchiest details of his internment, attesting perhaps to the numbing sense of shock they had all experienced when he died. Penelope Leach is not even entirely sure that she attended the service, but feels on balance that she must have done. Yovanka remembers little of the three-day period between her husband's death and the funeral, with the exception of trying to find a black hat to wear and telephoning her father in Paris to inform him that his son-in-law was dead and receiving in reply a cryptic message perhaps intended to function, when translated, as a rough Yugoslavian equivalent of the English proverb 'You reap what you sow':

If you go out into the rain without an umbrella you get wet.[24]

A large crowd of mourners gathered in Hampstead to pay their last respects to one of Britain's pre-eminent popular novelists, cramming inside what his son Charles describes as a 'Pretty full church'.[25] Despite his father's strong connections with the worlds of books and film he recalls that 'There certainly weren't a lot of 'stars' on show but many of the people who had played a part in his life were there'. In keeping with her husband's near-subterranean public profile in the last few years before he died, Yovanka considers that it was 'a low-key funeral'.[26] The newsreader and broadcaster Richard Baker, like Balchin a Petrean (albeit one of a later vintage), gave the eulogy, and A. D. Peters and William Collins were among the congregation, as was the head of the FWS, who in Yovanka's opinion seemed 'decidedly miffed at the let-down!'.[27]

Balchin's gravestone is to be found adjacent to one of the paths that snake through the vast Hampstead Cemetery, final resting place for the likes of antiseptic pioneer Joseph Lister and music-hall star Marie Lloyd. It is situated very close to the main entrance on Fortune Green Road and only a few metres away from the grave of the writer's long-time literary agent David Higham. The headstone is carved in the form of two facing pages of an open book, the verso[28] bearing the simple inscription 'NIGEL MARLIN BALCHIN 1908–1970' and, underneath, the words 'LORD, I WAS AFRAID', chosen by Yovanka in recognition of the fact that this experimental work of fiction was the book he was most proud of having written. The stone has weathered now, and the metallic lettering is partly dilapidated, but the simplicity and unobtrusiveness of the memorial would perhaps have appealed to Balchin, who found himself thrust into the limelight on occasions but never felt truly at ease in its unforgiving glare.

In October 1970, Balchin's wealth at the time of his death was revealed by probate to have been £41,891 gross (about £500,000 today). In the same month, Yovanka informed the *Evening Standard* that she had not been left 'on the bread line'[29] but her husband had hardly bequeathed her a fortune, and an anonymous diarist in the newspaper pondered why this should have been so:

> The size of Nigel Balchin's estate—only £10,949 net—may have puzzled some people…

At the end of this head-scratching exercise, several factors had occurred to the journalist to explain the modest extent of the novelist's wealth ('Balchin had not written a book for three years before his death and he was also ill'), although the excessive profligacy of the final dozen or so years of Balchin's life, launched on the back of his screenwriter's income, would have provided a more salient explanation had it been more widely known at the time. As Elizabeth Jane Howard remarked, during their time together, Balchin and Yovanka 'spent money like water'.[30]

The gross value of Balchin's estate was overshadowed by those of two other famous British novelists revealed in the same year that Balchin died: John Wyndham left £70,799 and

E. M. Forster bequeathed £68,298. And when Michael Ayrton died in 1975, five years after Balchin, the money he left to Balchin's first family (£93,672) was more than double that which Balchin had passed on to his second.[31]

*

Balchin's passing attracted considerable attention, with obituaries appearing in most of the British national newspapers and also in the *New York Times*. The unattributed obituary that appeared in the *Guardian*[32] on the day after Balchin's death was the most considered (and illuminating) of those published in the British broadsheets. Here, Balchin was described as 'greatly gifted' and the writer declared that 'To some good judges, Balchin, rather than C. P. Snow, was the novelist of men at work'. In the *Guardian*'s opinion, Balchin had 'a narrative power and a breadth of worldly knowledge that would have suited a Victorian novelist', he could 'render with exactitude and wry wit' the speech of the professional classes within whose world he had set his most successful works of fiction and he had been underrated for much of his career as a consequence of his 'no-nonsense, unliterary pose'.

Some of Balchin's fiction, including the likes of *A Sort of Traitors* and *Lord, I Was Afraid*, came in for criticism, but *The Small Back Room* ('his best book') was exalted by the writer, who declared that Balchin's most famous novel 'may well endure as one of the sharpest pictures of how people lived and felt in Britain in the Second World War'. In the *Guardian*'s view, Balchin had sometimes been 'obsessed to the point of self-parody' by his insistence on writing about characters with physical and emotional handicaps in the middle years of his career and, in a justified attack on some of the novelist's weaker material, the obituarist opined that 'now and again both psychology and style came too pat'. But the most penetrating piece of analysis was left to last, and can usefully serve as an apt and poignant epitaph for an author whose work, as Roy Fuller observed in 1966, 'never competed in the senior league of contemporary fiction',[33] despite Balchin's creation of at least half a dozen captivating and memorable novels:

Balchin had everything of a first-rate novelist except the
ultimate fusing, transmuting power of the imagination.
At any time this would be a big exception; Balchin was,
however, unlucky in living at a time when this, of all gifts,
was prized most and all the other gifts he could offer were
prized least.[34]

So what exactly is Balchin's legacy? As a young man he was
a skilled and thoughtful industrial psychologist who transformed
the fortunes of some of the companies, such as Rowntree's,
that he worked for in the 1930s and was instrumental in the
introduction of a box of chocolates, Black Magic, that we can
still enjoy today. During World War Two, Balchin was given
the opportunity to demonstrate his ability as 'a gifted logistical
thinker—a natural critical path analyst with a remarkable
capacity for absorbing the detail of new fields'[35] and his
extraordinary gifts in this arena helped to rejuvenate the British
Army at one of the most critical junctures in its history. After
the war, he proved himself to be a successful business executive,
a supple and profound thinker on the subject of incentives and a
talented screenwriter, responsible for scripting serious films such
as *Mandy* and *The Man Who Never Was* that remain moving
and extremely watchable more than half a century after they
were originally released into cinemas.

Balchin was 'perhaps the most successful British author to
emerge during the war'[36] and undoubtedly one of the best. He
wrote about 'timeless things, the places in the heart'[37] and his
body of work was consistently stimulating, with novels such as
*The Small Back Room, Mine Own Executioner, Darkness Falls from
the Air* and *The Fall of the Sparrow* standing out as some of the
most absorbing and mesmerically readable books ever written.

*

The Balchin industry has been largely dormant since his death.
The centenary of Balchin's birth in 2008 was marked by a BBC
radio documentary,[38] but the most important piece of Balchin-
related activity during the last decade has been the making of
a new film based on one of his novels. The movie in question

was entitled *Separate Lies* and represented the directorial debut of Julian Fellowes, Oscar-winning scriptwriter of the superb country house murder mystery *Gosford Park*. Fellowes's loose adaptation of *A Way Through the Wood*—only one or two scenes were retained from the book and the characters and situations were transported from their original 1950s setting to the present day—premiered in London in October 2005.

The standout feature of *Separate Lies* is the acting: Fellowes was extravagantly well served by his cast, especially the two principals. As James Manning, Tom Wilkinson is exceptional, and if the picture can be said to be a success then much of the credit must be given to him. His use of gesture and body language is supreme and every little twitch of his conscience as he tiptoes agonizingly through the moral minefield he is obliged to negotiate is beautifully conveyed. Emily Watson is almost as good as his wife (here renamed Anne) and if she just fails to convince us that her somewhat vapid character could be a real person then the blame should surely be attributed more to Balchin—for devising such an unreal figure in the first place—than to a fine actress doing the best she can with a tricky assignment. Rupert Everett is entertainingly louche and acid-tongued as Bill Bule but his eye-catching performance cannot disguise the fact that he was badly miscast in the role.

Despite its clever use of locations (particularly the idyllic village of Turville, near Henley-on-Thames), sumptuous set designs, exquisite photography and one or two memorable scenes, such as the poignant reconciliation between James and Anne shot at night in pouring rain outside Bule's London flat, *Separate Lies* fails to exceed the sum of its parts and makes for a very watchable but frustrating and ultimately unsatisfying viewing experience.

Why should this be so? The main reason is that the film loses momentum as it approaches its conclusion; the high point occurs roughly halfway through, when Anne discharges her twin revelations that she has been having an affair with Bule ("I do fuck Bill. Or rather, he fucks me.") and that she was driving the car that hit Joe Pearce, and there is too much talking and hand-wringing—and far too little action—in the second half of the picture. Also, in common with other cinematic interpreters of Balchin's work, notably Michael Powell, Fellowes could not resist the temptation to tinker with the text on which his film was based, substituting a somewhat artificial happy ending for the much bleaker and more realistic unresolved ending that Balchin had written for *A Way Through the Wood*.

Several film critics pointed out that *Separate Lies* is insufficiently cinematic, and that it would perhaps have fared better had it been made for a different medium. Thus Peter Bradshaw[39] in the *Guardian* said that the film 'looks like the most addictive sort of Sunday-night telly' and Nicholas Barber[40] in the *Independent on Sunday* was in agreement with him: '*Separate Lies* seems more suited to television than to the cinema. But if it were a TV drama, it would get rave reviews.' There was also consensus among the reviewers that *Separate Lies* suffered from being too quiet, too reserved, too English. The most damning such brickbat was lobbed by Tim Robey[41] in the *Daily Telegraph*, who observed that the film 'doesn't so much weave a tangled web of deceptions as draw a polite diagram of one'.

At odds with almost everybody else who reviewed the movie was Christopher Tookey[42] in the *Daily Mail*, who awarded *Separate Lies* a five-star rating and characterized it as a 'Brilliant, heart-breaking dissection of a marriage'. And, in an online update to his 1970s article on Balchin, Clive James[43] considered that Fellowes had made 'a stunning directorial debut'. Yet the reception given to *Separate Lies* was generally much more muted, with two- and three-star reviews being the order of the day across the newspapers and film magazines. I half-remember Mark Kermode on BBC Radio Five Live describing *Separate Lies* as 'A hmm movie' and that remains a fair summary of the most recent attempt to bring Balchin's world to the big screen.

Afterword

- In later life, **Elisabeth Balchin** continued (under the name Elisabeth Ayrton) to write a mixture of novels and cookery books. She died in 1991.
- After the death of her husband Nigel, **Yovanka Balchin** (b. 1930) worked for many years as an antiques dealer before retiring to Suffolk, where she still lives today.
- Following his dalliance with Elisabeth Balchin in the early months of World War Two, **Christian Darnton** continued to plough an eclectic furrow as a classical composer and latterly as a poet and essayist. He died in 1981.
- At the time of his death in 1975, **Michael Ayrton** had established himself as one of Britain's foremost painters and sculptors.
- The author of fifteen novels, **Elizabeth Jane Howard** died at her home in Suffolk in January 2014; she was ninety.
- **Prudence Balchin** married the screenwriter John Hopkins in 1954. After he divorced her in order to marry actress Shirley Knight, she ran a zoo in company with her second husband. She died in 2004.
- Since the 1960s, **Penelope Balchin** (b. 1937) has pursued a highly successful career as a writer and academic and, as Penelope Leach, is now renowned as one of the world's leading child psychologists. Her most recent book is *Family Breakdown* (2014).
- **Freja Balchin** (b. 1944) worked for her husband, psychologist Richard Gregory, upon graduating from Cambridge University. After separating from him, she then ran an antiques shop with her mother and sister Prudence before

becoming a teacher. She now lives in Bristol.

- **Charles Balchin** (b. 1955) has spent the bulk of his career working in television, including stints at the BBC and Sky Sports. He is currently Head of Programmes at IMG Productions, lives on the outskirts of London and also looks after the Nigel Balchin estate.
- **Cassandra Balchin** worked for many years as a journalist in Pakistan. On returning to the UK in 2000, she became a freelance development consultant, specializing in the rights of women in Muslim countries. She died in 2012.

*

In 2015, Nigel Balchin's reputation remains mummified within the same sarcophagus of 'unfocussed semi-respectability'[1] in which Clive James found it when he analysed Balchin's work in 1974. There are numerous reasons why Balchin's reputation evanesced so rapidly after his death, a few of the more pertinent explanations being outlined below.

The seven-year hiatus in Balchin's fiction chronology between 1955 and 1962, during which time he concentrated solely on writing film scripts, badly damaged his critical standing as a novelist. Balchin also made the mistake in the mid-1950s of cutting himself off from the rich seams of real-life experience that had helped to make his earlier novels so fresh, interesting and unusual; his later books tended to be weaker in the absence of an absorbing work background.

When Balchin did resume writing novels after his Hollywood interlude, the sense that he was a man whose time had been and gone permeated the reviews. Already considered an unfashionable writer by the mid-1960s, the decline of Balchin's reputation accelerated after his death, when more experimental and elliptical modes of writing began to hold sway and his expertly constructed linear narratives—the novelist Philippa Gregory has commented that the average Balchin novel 'has a splendid shape […] it goes from A through to Z in a very logical sequence'[2]—began to resemble museum pieces. If only Balchin's alcoholism had not prevented him from writing a late work of fiction that rivalled his great wartime trilogy then his reputation would have been buttressed before his death and he would probably be better thought of today than he actually is.

Balchin was never associated with any literary movements suitable for a twenty-first century critical re-examination that might enable his work to be rediscovered at the same time. Had he remained in Britain instead of relocating to Hollywood in 1955 then he could have become profitably embroiled in the Angry Young Men movement, as 1953's *Sundry Creditors* can in some senses be seen as a progenitor of that genre, but here Balchin's timing was badly awry and by plumping for film over literature he was unable to achieve the same level of recognition in the late 1950s as the likes of Kingsley Amis, John Braine and Alan Sillitoe.

Although Balchin received a British Film Academy award for his script for *The Man Who Never Was*, it did not confer the same worldwide kudos as winning an Oscar. His other screenplays have been accorded much less attention, and unfortunately for him the only really well-known film he was involved with was the monumental cinematic farce that constituted *Cleopatra* and it was not his intelligent and lucid script—'the first folio edition'[3]—that won the approval of the front office at Twentieth Century Fox. Association with a hugely popular film can of course significantly burnish a novelist's reputation: the name Nevil Shute remains known to the British public today probably as much for the successfully filmed *A Town Like Alice* as for his other twenty novels put together.

Finally, as a result of the three excellent novels that he wrote between 1942 and 1945, Balchin has been unfairly pigeonholed as a writer whose career was neatly and decisively terminated as soon as Germany surrendered to the Allies and his reputation consequently abandoned amongst the air-raid sirens and bombed-out buildings of that era. (Writer and critic Andrew Sinclair's comment that Balchin's pen had 'stuck in dried blood'[4] after 1945 is representative of this school of thought.) Balchin's subsequent work has therefore tended to be either completely disregarded or, at best, badly undervalued.

James considers Balchin to be 'the missing writer of the

Forties'[5] but it is high time that he was seen instead as one of the most important missing writers of the entire twentieth century, for Balchin to be celebrated as being among the finest popular novelists that Britain has ever produced and for his work to be widely known and enjoyed again, as it was seventy years ago.

Acknowledgements

This book could not have been written without the very considerable input of Yovanka Balchin. During the course of my first meeting with Yovanka in 2006 my tentative plan to write a biography of her late husband was transformed in the space of a few hours from a nice idea on paper into a viable proposition, and over the many years that followed Yovanka continued to respond to my frequent questions with great forbearance and thoroughness and provided me with much useful material, including a highly informative memoir of her life with Nigel and an extract from his personal notebook. If I have succeeded in any way in bringing the Nigel Balchin story to life then it is to Yovanka that I owe the greatest debt of gratitude.

All of the other Balchin family members that I spoke to willingly agreed to relate their memories of Nigel and patiently submitted to my faltering and inexpert attempts to interview them. I am indebted therefore to the following: Penelope Leach, Freja Gregory, Charles Balchin, the late Cassandra Balchin, Justine Hopkins and Milena Vasich.

I am especially grateful to Julie Kaveney, who showed me around Dauntsey's School and introduced me to that establishment's archival holdings; Philip Pattenden, who performed a similar function at Peterhouse, Cambridge and has subsequently been both outstandingly helpful and tireless in his quest to unearth new information concerning Balchin's time at the College; David McDine, who took me on a very informative tour of Stelling Minnis and the surrounding locale; and the late David Duncan, who spoke to me at length and with infectious enthusiasm about Balchin's connections with industrial psychology. Andrew Plant graciously sent me a copy of his PhD thesis on Christian Darnton and then read (and helpfully commented on) Chapter 7 of this book, which was significantly influenced by my study of Dr Plant's work. And the late Elizabeth Jane Howard, despite being in the throes of writing a new novel at the time, kindly gave up an afternoon to relate her memories of Balchin to me.

I am grateful to all the librarians and archivists that I approached during my research for responding to my enquiries with courtesy and diligence. I am particularly indebted to Monica Thapar at the BBC Written Archives Centre in Caversham and to Felicity Windmill and Dawn Sinclair at HarperCollins, all of whom went well beyond the call of duty to try to furnish me with the information I was seeking. Others who provided notable help include Colin Merton and Patrizia Cox at the Savile Club, Michael Meredith at Eton College, Jacqueline Cox at Cambridge University, Hannah Lowery at the University of Bristol Special Collections, Janet Moat at the British Film Institute, Alex Wicks at JWT London, Alex Hutchinson at Nestlé and Jessica Bueno De Mesquita at the Royal Automobile Club.

Numerous other people provided me with useful information about Balchin or some of the activities he was involved in during his lifetime. Not all of that information subsequently found its way into this book but it was gratefully received nonetheless. I would therefore like to thank the following for their contributions: Jim Hodges, Eddie Look, John Cox, Pat Grassick, Blanche Marvin, Geoff Bunn, Andrew Biswell, John Stein, Rick Stein, Rob Stammers, Jeremy Stewart, Andrew Putnam, Rupert Mallin, Pat Brabon, Richard Kwiatkowski, Frederic Stansfield, Janet Few, Pat Critchlow, Mark Curthoys, Michael Weatherburn, Alex Jasinski and Nicola Beauman.

Nigel C. Balchin of the Balchin Family Society (www. balchin-family.org.uk) was a valuable contact during the earliest days of my research into his namesake. I am also grateful to the Balchin Family Society in general, and especially to its Chairman Sir Robert Balchin, for their support of my work.

Phillip Thwaites took me on a fact-finding motor tour of Wiltshire and was accosted by an irate local for his trouble. This did not however dissuade him from subsequently designing and implementing the first version of my Nigel Balchin Website in 2010 (www.nigelmarlinbalchin.com). Andrew Chapman assumed the mantle of webmaster in 2012 and I am indebted to him not just for having smoothly and expertly elevated the site to another level but also for his friendship, sage advice and keen interest in all aspects of my Nigel Balchin project. I am also grateful to all the subscribers to my Nigel Balchin Newsletter for their advice, stimulating suggestions and encouragement.

Within my family, my mother Jennifer was extremely supportive when I first embarked on this project but tragically did not live long enough to see it brought to fruition—this book is therefore dedicated to her memory. The financial support provided by my father Barry since 2008 made it possible for me to finish this biography without being declared bankrupt in the process. My brother Philip took me on an earlier (unaccosted) motor tour of Wiltshire and my cousins Natasha Bowers (and her husband David) and Jacqueline Edgecumbe (and her husband Andy) provided assistance in an assortment of practical ways.

Pauline Kiernan gave many useful suggestions on an early draft of the opening chapters and helped to put me on the right path towards writing the version of the book that you now hold in your hands. I am grateful to the former Publishing Director of Duckworth Publishers, Andrew Lockett, for first spotting the potential of my work and to an anonymous reviewer at Duckworths who made many intelligent suggestions for revisions to the manuscript, most of which I acted upon. Peter Hughes kindly and repeatedly permitted me to print out large chunks of the manuscript in return for only the occasional bowl of Singapore noodles, commented intelligently on various portions of the text and has been perpetually supportive ever since I first began researching Balchin. I also gratefully acknowledge the help and support that have been forthcoming from, among others, Yvonne James, Lesley Brewer, Ivan Fisher, Masumi Murase, Jonathan Moseley, Laura Elliott and Alan and

Anna Colgan. Especial thanks to Anna for bravely reading the entire manuscript in 2013 and astutely identifying how it could be strengthened and also for printing out the entire manuscript for me on one occasion at her (then) employer's expense! Many thanks also to Helen Hart, Bronwen Wotton and all the staff at SilverWood Books for steering this project smoothly and competently towards completion.

Finally, a big thank you to anyone else I may inadvertently have omitted to mention and to all those people who took the time and trouble to get in touch with me via my website, either to provide information or to offer their appreciation of my ongoing efforts to keep Nigel Balchin's name alive and help make him better known.

Photo Credits

Appendix: Selected Works of Nigel Balchin

Unless stated otherwise, all of these items were published or made in the UK.

When this book went to press all of Balchin's books were out of print but Orion Books were planning to reissue *Darkness Falls from the Air* and *The Small Back Room* in September 2015, with *A Way Through the Wood* scheduled to follow in March 2016.

Novels

No Sky (Hamish Hamilton, 1934)
Simple Life (Hamish Hamilton, 1935)
Lightbody on Liberty (Collins, 1936)
Darkness Falls from the Air (Collins, 1942)
The Small Back Room (Collins, 1943)
Mine Own Executioner (Collins, 1945)
The Borgia Testament (Collins, 1948)
A Sort of Traitors (Collins, 1949)
Mind of Nicholas Hurst (unfinished, 1949)
A Way Through the Wood (Collins, 1951)
Sundry Creditors (Collins, 1953)
The Fall of the Sparrow (Collins, 1955)
Seen Dimly Before Dawn (Collins, 1962)
In the Absence of Mrs Petersen (Collins, 1966)
Kings of Infinite Space (Collins, 1967)
King Beer (or *Rich Man* or *The Last Indecency*, unpublished, 1950s?)
Nine Lives of Nicholas Hurst (unpublished, 1960s?)

Non-fiction books

How to Run a Bassoon Factory; or Business Explained (as Mark Spade; Hamish Hamilton, 1934)
Business for Pleasure (as Mark Spade; Hamish Hamilton, 1935)
Fun and Games: How to Win at Almost Anything (as Mark Spade; Hamish Hamilton, 1936)

Income and Outcome. A Study of Personal Finance (Hamish Hamilton, 1936)
The Anatomy of Villainy (Collins, 1950)
How to Run a Bassoon Factory; or Business Explained and *Business for Pleasure* (as Mark Spade, with an Introduction by Balchin; Hamish Hamilton, 1950)
The Language of Sex (unfinished, 1960s?)

Other books

Lord, I Was Afraid (play; Collins, 1947)
Last Recollections of My Uncle Charles (short stories; Collins, 1954)

Selected short stories not included in *Last Recollections of My Uncle Charles*

'Publicity Pays' (*The Passing Show*, 16 September 1933)
'That Feller Oates' (*20 Story Magazine*, November 1933)
'The Heriot' (*Evening News*, 2 July 1934)
'The Service of Miss Eyles' (Regional Programme, BBC radio, 25 August 1935)
'The Salamander' (*Illustrated London News*, Christmas Number 1945)
'Major Cole's Third Shot' (BBC TV, 26 July 1952)
'Dover Incident' (In: *Did It Happen?*, Oldbourne Press, London, 1956)
'The Phantom Gardener' (*The Saint Mystery Magazine*, December 1964)

Selected other works

The Aircraft Builders. An Account of British Aircraft Production 1935–1945 (monograph; HMSO, London, 1947)
'Writing in Pictures' (essay; In: J. Sutro (Ed.), *Diversion*, Max Parrish & Co. Ltd., London, 1950)
'The Private Gentleman' (essay; In: N. Branch (Ed.), *This Britain: Tradition and Achievement*, Macdonald, London, 1951)
The Worker in Modern Industry (pamphlet; Institute of Personnel Management, London, 1954)
'Burnt Njal—The Irredeemable Crime' (essay; In: N. Balchin, C. S. Forester, E. Linklater & C. Sykes, *Fatal Fascination. A Choice of Crime*, Hutchinson, London, 1964)
Foreword to *Pig and Pepper: A Comedy of Youth* by David Footman (Derek Verschoyle, London, 1954)
Preface to *Lucrezia Borgia. A Study* by Joan Haslip (Heron Books, London, 1968)

Scientific and technical articles

'Movement Study in Packing' (*Journal of the National Institute of Industrial Psychology*, 1931;V:274–5)
'Time Experiments on Hoeing' (*The Human Factor*, 1932;VI:12–25)
'The Psychological Difficulties of the Institute's Work' (*The Human Factor*, 1933;VII:257–65)
'A Psychological Approach to Market Research' (*The Human Factor*, 1933;VII:375–85)
'On Wasting Time' (*The Human Factor*, 1934;VIII:1–15)

'Package Appeal' (*The Human Factor,* 1934;VIII:229–35)
'First Impressions' (*The Human Factor,* 1934;VIII:303–8)
'Sales versus Production' (*The Human Factor,* 1935;IX:8–12)
'Satisfactions in Work' (*Occupational Psychology,* 1947;21:125–34; later reprinted in *The Free Mind,* Part I: Winter 1947/8, Part II: Spring 1948)
'The Nature of Incentives' (*The Nineteenth Century and After,* 1948;CXLIV:247–54)
'The Development of Industry. Its Impact on the Worker' (*Personnel Management— The Journal of the Institute of Personnel Management,* 1953;XXXV(324):66–77)

Articles published in *Punch*

Ninety articles beginning with the first part of the ten-part series 'The Compleat Modern' in issue dated 4 October 1933 and ending with 'Chateau d'Espagne' in issue dated 16 March 1938

Articles published in *The Aeroplane*

Seventy-one Pobottle articles beginning with 'Pobottle on Publicity' in issue dated 19 August 1936 and ending with 'Vital Secrets and All That' in issue dated 24 May 1940

Other articles

'Keeping the Peace' (*Time and Tide,* 10 October 1936)
'The Next Song Will be a Dance' (*Night and Day,* 15 July 1937)
'Trotsky or Notsky' (*Night and Day,* 19 August 1937)
'An Inventory of Inventors' (*Lilliput,* April 1944)
'Notes on the Way' (*Time and Tide,* 18 and 25 October 1947)
'An Alphabet of Literary Prejudice' (*The Windmill,* 1947;2(8):1–8)
'Scientists in a Hurry' (*Lilliput,* December 1947)
'Notes on the Way' (*Time and Tide,* 2 and 9 July 1949)
'The Uses of Criticism' (*Listener,* 6 October 1949)
'Nigel Balchin' (pen portrait; *New York Herald Tribune Book Review* (US), 8 October 1950)
'Creative Talent in Harness' (*The Times,* 18 October 1962)
'Return Journey III: Rim of the Plain' (*Sunday Times,* 9 August 1964)
'Children are a Waste of Time' (*Saturday Evening Post* (US), 9 October 1965)
'Must we sacrifice our lives for our children?' (*Sunday Express,* 28 November 1965; slightly amended UK version of 'Children are a Waste of Time')

Film screenplays (years shown refer to original cinema release dates)

Fame is the Spur (GFD/Two Cities/Charter, UK, 1947)
Mine Own Executioner (London Films, UK, 1947)
Mandy (Ealing Films, UK, 1952)
Malta Story (GFD/British Film Makers, UK, 1953)
Josephine and Men (Charter, UK, 1955)
Twenty-Three Paces to Baker Street (Twentieth Century Fox, US, 1956)
The Man Who Never Was (Sumar Films, UK, 1956)

Sea Wife (uncredited; Sumar Films, UK, 1957)
The Barbarian and the Geisha (uncredited; Twentieth Century Fox, US, 1958)
The Blue Angel (Twentieth Century Fox, US, 1959)
Suspect (British Lion, UK, 1960)
Circle of Deception (Twentieth Century Fox, US, 1961)
The Singer Not the Song (Rank, UK, 1961)
Barabbas (Columbia, Italy/US, 1962)
Cleopatra (uncredited; Twentieth Century Fox, US, 1963)

Screenplays for films not made (years shown are approximations only)

A Sort of Traitors (1949)
The Bandits (1951)
Ingram's Peace (1953)
Black Wings (1956)
Hassan (1957)
Lucy Crown (1957)
March the Ninth (1958)
Dragon Tree (1959)
The Two Enemies (1960)
Seen Dimly Before Dawn (1963)

Stage plays

Power (1935)
Peace in Our Time (1936)
Miserable Sinners (1937)
Profit and Loss (1938)
The Leader of the House (1960)

Unperformed stage plays (dates unknown)

Carted Stag
Bored Residents
Square Deal
Modern Harmony
The Highway Code
Active Service
Lord, I Was Afraid (revue)
Lennie's Point of View

Television screenplays

The Leader of the House (BBC, 1955)
The Hatchet Man (BBC, 1962)
Better Dead (Anglia TV, 1969)

Unrealized television screenplays

The Nine Lives of Nicholas Hurst (BBC TV series; 1964)

Lennie's Point of View (BBC, 1965)

Radio productions

'The Master' (short story later included in *Last Recollections of My Uncle Charles*; BBC, 1951)
The Leader of the House (Home Service, BBC, 1955)

Unrealized radio productions

Lennie's Point of View (BBC, 1965)

Notes

Foreword

1. W. Hooper (Ed.), *Selected Literary Essays by C. S. Lewis*, Cambridge University Press, Cambridge, UK, 1969.
2. N. Shrapnel, 'Balchin's burden', *Guardian*, 19 January 1962.
3. R. Winnington, 'Korda Produces a Good Film', *News Chronicle*, 22 November 1947.
4. B. Macintyre, *Operation Mincemeat. The True Spy Story that Changed the Course of World War II*, Bloomsbury, London, 2010.
5. 'What They Did to Me in Hollywood', *Daily Mail*, 18 January 1962.
6. C. James, 'Prisoners of clarity—1. Nigel Balchin', *The New Review*, 1974;1(1):64–72. Available at www.clivejames.com/pieces/hercules/Balchin
7. Letter from Yovanka Balchin to author, 15 August 2007.
8. N. Balchin, Pen portrait published in the *New York Herald Tribune Book Review*, 8 October 1950.
9. C. James, 'Prisoners of clarity—1. Nigel Balchin', *The New Review*, 1974;1(1):64–72. Available at www.clivejames.com/pieces/hercules/Balchin
10. J. Fellowes, Foreword to *Separate Lies*, Phoenix Paperbacks, London, 2005.

Chapter 1

1. In order of their occurrence, these phrases are taken from the following reviews: *Daily Herald*, 26 September 1945; *Daily Telegraph*, 21 September 1945; *Sketch*, 31 October 1945; *Observer*, 21 October 1945; *Time and Tide*, 27 October 1945.
2. *New Statesman and Nation*, 13 October 1945.
3. *John o'London's Weekly*, 5 October 1945.
4. N. Balchin, 'Rim of the Plain', *Sunday Times*, 9 August 1964.
5. According to Balchin's second wife Yovanka, the sliver of family history related in this Author's Note is broadly true. Some details, such as the year in which his grandfather died, were changed by Balchin, but the way in which his family's fortune was lost would appear to have been accurately presented.
6. The name 'Marlin' or 'Marlen', which is believed to be a corruption of George's middle name, was handed down to successive generations of Balchins, including Nigel, and is still in use in the family today.
7. N. Balchin, 'Children are a Waste of Time', *Saturday Evening Post*, 9 October 1965.

8. From the script of 'The Knowledge Explosion' (*Horizon*, BBC Television, 21 September 1964) held by the BBC Written Archives Centre, Caversham, UK.

9. *Parishes: Potterne, A History of the County of Wiltshire*, 1953;7:207–17. Available at www.british-history.ac.uk/report.aspx?compid=115473

10. T. Smith, *In a Wiltshire Village*, Wiltshire Family History Society, Devizes, UK, 1993.

11. N. Balchin, 'Rim of the Plain', *Sunday Times*, 9 August 1964.

12. From the script of 'The Knowledge Explosion' (*Horizon*, BBC Television, 21 September 1964) held by the BBC Written Archives Centre, Caversham, UK.

13. N. Balchin, 'Rim of the Plain', *Sunday Times*, 9 August 1964.

14. Extract from Balchin's notebook dated 13 June 1952.

15. N. Balchin, 'Rim of the Plain', *Sunday Times*, 9 August 1964.

16. From the script of 'The Knowledge Explosion' (*Horizon*, BBC Television, 21 September 1964) held by the BBC Written Archives Centre, Caversham, UK.

17. Some of the information in this paragraph and the following one is derived from my previously published article 'Potterne to Hollywood: Balchin's Rise to Fame', *Wiltshire Life*, September 2010.

18. School records of the period do not establish definitively when Balchin started at Dauntsey's. A plaque erected on the front of his childhood home in West Lavington High Street by the Old Dauntseians Association suggests that it would have been in 1919; on Balchin's application form for admission to Peterhouse, perhaps a more reliable guide, he claims that he first attended the school in 1918 and so this is the year I have used henceforth.

19. *Dauntsey's School Millennium CD-ROM*, Dauntsey's School, 2000.

20. According to Awdry, Balchin invigilated the examination in his role as head of school. Awdry would seem to have been mistaken in that assertion because Balchin was not made captain of school (the Dauntsey's synonym for head boy or head of school) until 1927 and Awdry's examination took place before the end of 1924. Balchin had though been a prefect since 1923, and so it would probably have been in that position of authority that he had served as an invigilator.

21. *Dauntsey's School Millennium CD-ROM*, Dauntsey's School, 2000.

22. N. Balchin, 'Rim of the Plain', *Sunday Times*, 9 August 1964.

23. This account is taken from the edition of the *Wiltshire Gazette* dated 2 July 1925.

24. Letter to the author from John Cox (undated but received in 2005).

25. Letter to the author from Eddie Look (undated but received in 2005).

26. Balchin's application form for admission to Peterhouse. Nigel Balchin's personal file, Peterhouse, Cambridge, UK. Quoted with permission from the Master and Fellows of Peterhouse.

27. Yovanka Balchin, Interview with author, 24 April 2007.

28. The programme was broadcast on the BBC Home Service on 29 October 1954.

29. *Music and People*, London Calling Asia, BBC Radio, 25 November 1954.

30. N. Balchin, 'Rim of the Plain', *Sunday Times*, 9 August 1964.

31. Letter from R. H. Adie (School of Agriculture, Cambridge) to P. C. Vellacott, 20 August 1926. Nigel Balchin's personal file, Peterhouse, Cambridge, UK. Quoted with permission from the Master and Fellows of Peterhouse.

32. *Dauntsey's School Millennium CD-ROM*, Dauntsey's School, 2000.

Chapter 2

1. D. E. Broadbent, 'Bartlett, Sir Frederic Charles (1886–1969)', rev. H. Series, *Oxford Dictionary of National Biography*, Oxford University Press, Oxford, UK, 2004.

2. D. E. Broadbent, 'Frederic Charles Bartlett', *Biographical Memoirs of Fellows of the Royal Society*, 1970;16:1–13.

3. From the script of 'The Knowledge Explosion' (*Horizon*, BBC Television, 21 September 1964) held by the BBC Written Archives Centre, Caversham, UK.

4. E. St Johnston, *One Policeman's Story*, B. Rose, London, 1978.

5. Yovanka Balchin, Interview with author, 24 April 2007.

6. Penelope Leach, Interview with author, 14 November 2006.

7. J. Trevelyan, *Indigo Days. The Art and Memoirs of Julian Trevelyan*, MacGibbon & Kee, London, 1957.

8. The student reminiscences of Frank Walbank and James Gerstley are taken from a feature entitled 'Memories of Peterhouse' which appeared in the 2001/2002 edition of the *Peterhouse Annual Record*.

9. A number of different methods can be used to convert monetary values from the past into modern-day equivalents. Throughout this book, unless stated otherwise, I have used the increase in the retail price index over the intervening period as the basis for my conversions. See www.measuringworth.com for the rationale behind this procedure.

10. The information in this paragraph about Peterhouse is largely derived from the College's website: www.pet.cam.ac.uk

11. R&Co 93/IX/20. Rowntree Archive, held at the Borthwick Institute for Archives, University of York, York, UK.

12. Sir Frederick Gowland Hopkins, Professor of Biochemistry in Balchin's time at Cambridge, was the first person to isolate the amino acid tryptophan and he won the 1929 Nobel Prize for Physiology or Medicine for his discovery of vitamins. John Burdon Sanderson (J.B.S.) Haldane was appointed Reader in Biochemistry at Cambridge under Hopkins in the early 1920s. He subsequently forged a reputation for himself as both an eminent geneticist—his quantitative theory of evolution reinforced Darwin's view of natural selection—and as a popularizer of science with a gift for lucid communication of his ideas. Haldane's use of himself as a guinea pig when researching physiology at Oxford just after World War One, together with the bravery he showed during World War Two when he performed experiments on deep-sea submersion for the Admiralty, suggests that he may have been the inspiration for the recklessly gallant self-experimenter Professor Gates in Balchin's 1945 short story 'The Salamander' (see Chapter 18).

13. N. Balchin, 'Talking Without the Book', *Punch*, 17 November 1937.

14. The student reminiscences of Frank Walbank and James Gerstley are taken from a feature entitled 'Memories of Peterhouse' which appeared in the 2001/2002 edition of the *Peterhouse Annual Record*.

15. Letter from P. C. Vellacott to H. A. Roberts (Secretary, University of Cambridge Appointments Board), 26 October 1929. Nigel Balchin's personal file, Peterhouse, Cambridge, UK. Quoted with permission from the Master and Fellows of Peterhouse.

16. N. Balchin, ''Little Fleas Have Lesser Fleas'', *Punch*, 14 October 1936. The quotation refers to 'John', who is in fact Mason. See Chapter 5 for a more detailed explanation of this name confusion.

17. N. Balchin, Pen portrait published in the *New York Herald Tribune Book Review*, 8 October 1950.

18. M. Powell, *A Life in Movies. An Autobiography*, Mandarin, London, 1986.

19. 'Famous Writer at the Sign of the Greyhound', *East Anglian Daily Times*, 4 February 1969.

20. The Sexcentenary Club was the undergraduate common room of the College and was so named because it had been established to celebrate the 600th anniversary of the founding of Peterhouse in 1884.

21. No. 92, Lent term, 1929.

22. No. 93, May term, 1929.

23. Letter from P. C. Vellacott to H. A. Roberts (Secretary, University of Cambridge Appointments Board), 26 October 1929. Nigel Balchin's personal file, Peterhouse, Cambridge, UK. Quoted with permission from the Master and Fellows of Peterhouse.

24. Yovanka Balchin, Interview with author, 24 April 2007.

25. The student reminiscences of Frank Walbank and James Gerstley are taken from a feature entitled 'Memories of Peterhouse' which appeared in the 2001/2002 edition of the *Peterhouse Annual Record*.

26. N. Balchin, 'Time Experiments on Hoeing', *The Human Factor*, 1932;VI:12–25.

27. Letter from P. C. Vellacott to F. C. Bartlett, 21 May 1930. Nigel Balchin's personal file, Peterhouse, Cambridge, UK. Quoted with permission from the Master and Fellows of Peterhouse.

28. Letter from Balchin to the Ministry of Agriculture, 13 February 1930. Nigel Balchin's personal file, Peterhouse, Cambridge, UK. Quoted with permission from the Master and Fellows of Peterhouse.

29. The Wiltshire Club and Ground squad would probably have consisted primarily of young players on the verge of selection for the full county team.

30. Beckett, the only first-class cricketer to have won a Nobel Prize (that for Literature in 1969), played twice for Dublin University against Northamptonshire in 1925 and 1926. Conan Doyle participated in ten first-class games for the MCC in the very early years of the twentieth century and once dismissed W. G. Grace.

31. 'The Author of the May Book', *World Books Broadsheet*, World Books, London, May 1947.

Chapter 3

1. N. Balchin, 'The Psychological Difficulties of the Institute's Work', *The Human Factor*, 1933;VII:257–65.

2. Unless stated otherwise, the information presented in this chapter about Balchin's tenure at the NIIP is derived from the NIIP Archive held at the London School of Economics (LSE) Library. Specific items from this archive are referenced where appropriate.

3. D. C. Doyle, 'Aspects of the Institutionalisation of British Psychology: The National Institute of Industrial Psychology 1921-1939', Unpublished PhD thesis, University of Manchester, Manchester, UK, 1979.

4. This information is derived from the following article: 'Annual report for the year 1933–4', *The Human Factor*, 1934;VIII:448.

5. C. B. Frisby, 'The development of industrial psychology at the NIIP', *Occupational Psychology*, 1970;44:35–50.

6. Presumably this was Leonard Hunt.

7. Letter from Balchin to P. C. Vellacott, 16 November 1930. Nigel Balchin's personal file, Peterhouse, Cambridge, UK. Quoted with permission from the Master and Fellows of Peterhouse.

8. This information is derived from the NIIP's annual report for the year 1930 (*Journal of the National Institute of Industrial Psychology*, 1931;V:304).

9. N. Balchin, 'Movement study in packing', *Journal of the National Institute of Industrial Psychology*, 1931;V:274–5.

10. 'Staff Social', *Cocoa Works Magazine*, Easter 1931, Rowntree Archive, held at the Borthwick Institute for Archives, University of York, York, UK.

11. Balchin gently satirizes assorted representatives of the Rowntree family in *Sundry Creditors*. Here, the target for his mockery is Oscar Rowntree, Seebohm's brother, a one-time member of the Rowntree's Board. Oscar was first and foremost a pig farmer: he resigned as a Board member after less than a year in order to return to his livestock.

12. £396 is equivalent to a present-day value of just over £22,000 according to the increase in the retail price index over the intervening period; however, if one considers Balchin's 1931 salary as a proportion of Gross Domestic Product then he would have enjoyed the same economic status as someone earning about £100,000 a year today.

13. The information contained in this sentence is taken from the following book: P. Clarke, *Hope and Glory: Britain 1900–1990*, Penguin, London, 1990.

14. H. J. Welch & C. S. Myers, *Ten Years of Industrial Psychology*, Pitman, London, 1932.

15. R/B3/BSR/2. Rowntree Archive, held at the Borthwick Institute for Archives, University of York, York, UK.

16. C. B. Frisby, 'The development of industrial psychology at the NIIP', *Occupational Psychology*, 1970;44:35–50.

17. G. Bunn, '"A flair for organization": Charles Myers and the establishment of psychology in Britain', *History & Philosophy of Psychology*, 2001;3:1–13.

18. D. C. Duncan, quoted in S. Shimmin & D. Wallis, *Fifty Years of Occupational*

Psychology in Britain, British Psychological Society, Leicester, UK, 1994.

19. G. H. Miles, 'An autobiography (conclusion)', *Occupational Psychology*, 1950;24:31–9.

20. The information in this paragraph describing the background to the creation of Black Magic is derived from the following book: R. Fitzgerald, *Rowntree and the Marketing Revolution, 1862-1969*, Cambridge University Press, Cambridge, UK, 1995.

21. G. H. Miles, 'An autobiography (conclusion)', *Occupational Psychology*, 1950;24:31–9.

22. T. Rayfield, *Fifty in 40: The Unofficial History of JWT London 1945-1995*, Rayfield Writers, Radnage Common, UK, 1996.

23. The information in this paragraph and subsequent paragraphs regarding the market research conducted prior to the launch of Black Magic is derived from the following article: 'Black Magic', *Cocoa Works Magazine*, Easter 1933, Rowntree Archive, held at the Borthwick Institute for Archives, University of York, York, UK.

24. Herman Hollerith (1860–1929) was an American statistician and engineer who, during the 1880s, devised the first punched-card system to help with the processing of the colossal volume of data anticipated to be generated by the 1890 US census. Holes were punched on cards to represent various pieces of personal information. By the time that Balchin chose to use punched-card technology to analyse the findings of the Black Magic market research project, it was possible to sort the punched cards automatically and the data held on them could be processed using a 'Hollerith machine'. The company that Hollerith founded in 1896 to sell his new technology later evolved into the modern-day information giant IBM.

25. T. Rayfield, *Fifty in 40: The Unofficial History of JWT London 1945-1995*, Rayfield Writers, Radnage Common, UK, 1996.

26. R/B2/2. Rowntree Archive, held at the Borthwick Institute for Archives, University of York, York, UK.

27. 'The Compleat Modern' was serialized in *Punch* in ten weekly instalments between 4 October and 6 December 1933.

28. 'The Author of the May Book', *World Books Broadsheet*, World Books, London, May 1947.

29. Letter from P. C. Vellacott to the Ministry of Agriculture, 22 February 1930. Nigel Balchin's personal file, Peterhouse, Cambridge, UK. Quoted with permission from the Master and Fellows of Peterhouse.

30. Minutes of the Investigations Subcommittee of the NIIP, 1 December 1932. From LSE Library's collections, NIIP/7/5.

31. W. Raphael, 'NIIP and its staff 1921 to 1961', *Occupational Psychology*, 1970;44:63–70.

32. N. Balchin, 'The Psychological Difficulties of the Institute's Work', *The Human Factor*, 1933;VII:257–65.

33. Letter from Leonard Moore to Charles Siepmann, 11 May 1934. BBC Written Archives Centre, Caversham, UK. Reproduced by permission of Sheil Land Associates Ltd.

Chapter 4

1. *Sunday Times*, 14 October 1934.
2. The factual information presented in this chapter about Balchin's books and working life is derived from two principal sources: (i) the Hamish Hamilton Collection at the University of Bristol Library Special Collections, University of Bristol, Bristol, UK; and (ii) the NIIP Archive held at the LSE Library. Specific items from these two archives are referenced where appropriate.
3. £30 in 1934 is roughly equivalent to £1,750 today. As comparators, George Orwell received £40 from Gollancz in 1932 for his first book *Down and Out in Paris and London* and Eric Ambler was advanced £30 in 1936 by Hodder & Stoughton for *The Dark Frontier*, his debut novel.
4. *We Write Novels*, BBC General Overseas Service, 7 April 1955.
5. *Daily Telegraph*, 28 September 1934.
6. 'I Don't Want To Be A Literary Gent says Nigel Balchin', *Books and Bookmen*, 1962;7(4):9–11.
7. *Sunday Times*, 14 October 1934.
8. *Daily Telegraph*, 28 September 1934.
9. This quotation is taken from the book jacket of Balchin's 1936 novel *Lightbody on Liberty*.
10. 'I Don't Want To Be A Literary Gent says Nigel Balchin', *Books and Bookmen*, 1962;7(4):9–11.
11. 'Famous writer at the sign of the Greyhound', *East Anglian Daily Times*, 4 February 1969.
12. The articles were serialized in weekly instalments between 7 March and 9 May 1934.
13. E. St Johnston, *One Policeman's Story*, B. Rose, London, 1978.
14. 'Famous writer at the sign of the Greyhound', *East Anglian Daily Times*, 4 February 1969.
15. *Financial Times*, 1 January 1951.
16. *The Times Literary Supplement*, 19 January 1951.
17. *Economist*, 16 December 1950.
18. Letter from Jamie Hamilton to Balchin, 5 February 1935. Hamish Hamilton Collection, University of Bristol Library Special Collections, University of Bristol, Bristol, UK.
19. John Hilton was Professor of Industrial Relations at Cambridge University and broadcast frequently on the radio in the 1930s.
20. Letter from Balchin to Jamie Hamilton, 29 January 1935. Hamish Hamilton Collection, University of Bristol Library Special Collections, University of Bristol, Bristol, UK.
21. 'I Don't Want To Be A Literary Gent says Nigel Balchin', *Books and Bookmen*, 1962;7(4):9–11.
22. G. H. Miles, 'An autobiography (conclusion)', *Occupational Psychology*, 1950;24:31–9.
23. G. Bunn, '"A flair for organization": Charles Myers and the establishment of psychology in Britain', *History & Philosophy of Psychology*, 2001;3:1–13.
24. W. Raphael, 'NIIP and its staff 1921 to 1961', *Occupational Psychology*,

1970;44:63–70.

25. Minutes of the Executive Committee of the NIIP, 7 February 1935. From LSE Library's collections, NIIP/2/4.

26. David Duncan, Personal communication to author (2008).

27. C. James, 'Prisoners of clarity—1. Nigel Balchin', *The New Review*, 1974;1(1):64–72. Available at www.clivejames.com/pieces/hercules/Balchin

28. Letter from Balchin to Jamie Hamilton, undated but probably written early in 1935. Hamish Hamilton Collection, University of Bristol Library Special Collections, University of Bristol, Bristol, UK.

29. *New Statesman and Nation*, 11 May 1935.

30. *Sunday Times*, 5 May 1935.

31. *John o'London's Weekly*, 11 May 1935.

32. *Observer*, 12 May 1935.

33. *Daily Telegraph*, 3 May 1935.

34. *Time and Tide*, 18 May 1935.

35. C. James, 'Prisoners of clarity—1. Nigel Balchin', *The New Review*, 1974;1(1):64–72. Available at www.clivejames.com/pieces/hercules/Balchin

36. The bulk of *Business for Pleasure* had been serialized in weekly instalments between 14 August and 16 October 1935.

37. *The Times Literary Supplement*, 30 November 1935.

38. Balchin made this claim on a form he completed upon joining the army in 1941. This form was among the documents relating to his wartime military service obtained by the author from the Army Personnel Centre.

39. T. Rayfield, *Fifty in 40: The Unofficial History of JWT London 1945-1995*, Rayfield Writers, Radnage Common, UK, 1996.

40. R/DH/CS/2/10–13. Rowntree Archive, held at the Borthwick Institute for Archives, University of York, York, UK.

41. *The Times Literary Supplement*, 28 March 1936.

42. Letter from Jamie Hamilton to Balchin, 10 July 1936. Hamish Hamilton Collection, University of Bristol Library Special Collections, University of Bristol, Bristol, UK.

43. Letter from Balchin to Jamie Hamilton, 5 April 1936. Hamish Hamilton Collection, University of Bristol Library Special Collections, University of Bristol, Bristol, UK.

44. Letter from Balchin to Jamie Hamilton, 9 August 1936. Hamish Hamilton Collection, University of Bristol Library Special Collections University of Bristol, Bristol, UK.

45. *New Statesman and Nation*, 14 November 1936.

46. I have been unable to trace this review but it was evidently a complimentary one.

47. Letter from Jamie Hamilton to Balchin, 22 November 1937. Hamish Hamilton Collection, University of Bristol Library Special Collections, University of Bristol, Bristol, UK.

Chapter 5

1. *We Write Novels*, BBC General Overseas Service, 7 April 1955.

2. 'The Theatre Spotlight on Nigel Balchin', Article printed in the programme

for *Power*, Croydon Repertory Theatre, Croydon, UK, April 1935.

3. *Croydon Times and Surrey County Mail*, 13 April 1935.
4. *Croydon Advertiser and Surrey County Reporter*, 13 April 1935.
5. 'The Theatre Spotlight on Nigel Balchin', Article printed in the programme for *Power*, Croydon Repertory Theatre, Croydon, UK, April 1935.
6. Elisabeth dealt with some of her husband's routine correspondence, typed his manuscripts and, as mentioned in Chapter 4, helped to prepare his 1936 book *Income and Outcome: A Study of Personal Finance* for publication.
7. *Croydon Advertiser and Surrey County Reporter*, 12 September 1936.
8. *The Times*, 14 September 1936.
9. Agatha Christie's *The Mousetrap* began its record-breaking run here in 1952.
10. J. Mason, *Before I Forget: An Autobiography*, Hamish Hamilton, London, 1981.
11. *The Times*, 26 April 1937.
12. *Era*, 29 April 1937.
13. *Stage*, 29 April 1937.
14. *Daily Telegraph*, 4 May 1938.
15. *The Times*, 4 May 1938.
16. C. James, 'Prisoners of clarity—1. Nigel Balchin', *The New Review*, 1974;1(1):64–72. Available at www.clivejames.com/pieces/hercules/Balchin
17. *Observer*, 27 September 1936.
18. *Sunday Times*, 11 October 1936.
19. 'Dora' is more commonly known nowadays as the Defence of the Realm Act 1916.
20. *The Times Literary Supplement*, 26 September 1936.
21. As 'Bunny' Barnes, Mason escaped from jail in the 1936 British film *Prison Breaker*.
22. *The Aeroplane*, 19 August 1936.
23. 'Coefficient of Expansion', *The Aeroplane*, 16 September 1936.
24. 'Pobottle on Publicity', *The Aeroplane*, 19 August 1936.
25. *The Aeroplane*, 13 October 1937.
26. *The Aeroplane*, 29 December 1937.
27. 'The Next Song Will be a Dance' was published in the edition dated 15 July 1937 and 'Trotsky or Notsky' appeared in that dated 19 August 1937.
28. Luker went up to Cambridge a year after Balchin but it is not known whether the two men had first encountered each other as undergraduates.
29. Most of the information contained in this chapter concerning Balchin's work for the BBC is derived from files on Balchin held by the BBC Written Archives Centre, Caversham, UK.
30. Issue dated 22 March 1938.
31. Issue dated 3 October 1938.
32. Issue dated 16 February 1939.
33. R&Co 93/IX/20. Rowntree Archive, held at the Borthwick Institute for Archives, University of York, York, UK.

Chapter 6

1. The information in this chapter is derived from two principal sources:

(i) files in the Rowntree Archive, held at the Borthwick Institute for Archives, University of York, York, UK; and (ii) R. Fitzgerald, *Rowntree and the Marketing Revolution, 1862-1969*, Cambridge University Press, Cambridge, UK, 1995. Specific files from the Rowntree Archive are referenced where appropriate.

2. The form Balchin completed upon joining the army was among the documents relating to his wartime military service obtained by the author from the Army Personnel Centre.

3. R/B4/WW/4. Rowntree Archive, held at the Borthwick Institute for Archives, University of York, York, UK.

4. R/B4/GJH/1. Rowntree Archive, held at the Borthwick Institute for Archives, University of York, York, UK.

5. R/B4/WW/7. Rowntree Archive, held at the Borthwick Institute for Archives, University of York, York, UK.

6. When Wallace joined Rowntree's in 1929, he worked initially as Seebohm Rowntree's private secretary. He had risen to become a director of the company and, like Balchin, was attending meetings of the MCA's Defence Committee when he was sent to work at the Ministry of Food in 1940. He later became Vice-Chairman of Rowntree's, before succeeding Harris as Chairman in 1952.

7. R/B4/GJH/2. Rowntree Archive, held at the Borthwick Institute for Archives, University of York, York, UK.

8. R/B4/WW/7. Rowntree Archive, held at the Borthwick Institute for Archives, University of York, York, UK.

9. R. Fitzgerald, *Rowntree and the Marketing Revolution, 1862-1969*, Cambridge University Press, Cambridge, UK, 1995.

10. As Wallace was eighteen years older than Balchin, apparently 'went native' whilst at the Ministry of Food and found his work there incredibly tiring, I believe that the clashes in *Darkness Falls from the Air* between Sarratt and his boss, Lennox, may have been influenced to some extent by the frustration that Balchin suffered having been forced to work alongside Wallace.

11. N. Balchin, 'Notes on the Way', *Time and Tide*, 9 July 1949.

12. Two Wartime Trades Associations (one for cocoa and chocolate, the other for sugar confectionery) were set up by Wallace and the MCA during 1941. These were industry-funded bodies under the (nominal) control of the Ministry of Food that were responsible for handling problems relating to the supply, production, distribution and costing of confectionery items. As Harris himself was Chairman of the Cocoa and Chocolate Wartime Trades Association, I think it is virtually certain that it is that body he is referring to here.

13. R&Co 93/IX/20. Rowntree Archive, held at the Borthwick Institute for Archives, University of York, York, UK.

14. This quotation appears on the back cover of the 2002 Cassell Military Paperbacks edition of *Darkness Falls from the Air*.

15. 'I Don't Want To Be A Literary Gent says Nigel Balchin', *Books and Bookmen*, 1962;7(4):9–11.

16. C. James, 'Prisoners of clarity—1. Nigel Balchin', *The New Review*,

1974;1(1):64–72. Available at www.clivejames.com/pieces/hercules/Balchin

17. The information in this paragraph about wartime paper rationing is taken from the following book: V. Holman, *Print for Victory: Book Publishing in England 1939–1945*, British Library, London, 2008.

18. 'I Don't Want To Be A Literary Gent says Nigel Balchin', *Books and Bookmen*, 1962;7(4):9–11.

19. *New Statesman and Nation*, 6 February 1943.

20. C. James, 'Prisoners of clarity—1. Nigel Balchin', *The New Review*, 1974;1(1):64–72. Available at www.clivejames.com/pieces/hercules/Balchin

21. 'I Don't Want To Be A Literary Gent says Nigel Balchin', *Books and Bookmen*, 1962;7(4):9–11.

22. *Tatler and Bystander*, 13 January 1943.

23. *New Statesman and Nation*, 6 February 1943.

24. *Sketch*, 18 November 1942.

25. *Time and Tide*, 21 November 1942.

26. According to sales figures unearthed by James (C. James, 'Prisoners of clarity—1. Nigel Balchin', *The New Review*, 1974;1(1):64–72. Available at www.clivejames.com/pieces/hercules/Balchin), the novel would go on to sell 14,000 copies in hardback and more than 99,000 in paperback in Collins imprints alone, i.e. not including much later reissues in other series, such as Abacus and Cassell Military Paperbacks.

27. *Daily Telegraph*, 24 June 1949.

Chapter 7

1. A. Plant, 'Darnton, (Philip) Christian (1905–1981)', *Oxford Dictionary of National Biography*, Oxford University Press, Oxford, UK, 2004.

2. Extract from Balchin's notebook dated 13 June 1952.

3. J. Hopkins, *Michael Ayrton: A Biography*, Andre Deutsch, London, 1994.

4. Yovanka Balchin, Interview with author, 24 April 2007.

5. 'Mummy was the light of my life', *Guardian*, 26 February 2003.

6. J. Hopkins, *Michael Ayrton: A Biography*, Andre Deutsch, London, 1994.

7. In *Darkness Falls from the Air*, Stephen has a cottage in the Buckinghamshire village of Penn, less than five miles away from the Darnton residence, to which he takes Marcia for a long weekend.

8. A. Plant, 'Darnton, (Philip) Christian (1905–1981)', *Oxford Dictionary of National Biography*, Oxford University Press, Oxford, UK, 2004.

9. A. Hallis, Letter to Christian Darnton, 1 March 1940, British Library, London, Add. MSS 62763.

10. I gratefully acknowledge the significant help that Dr Plant gave me with the writing of this chapter, parts of which are substantially based on his PhD dissertation.

11. A. Plant, 'The life and music of Christian Darnton', Unpublished PhD dissertation, University of Birmingham, Birmingham, UK, 2002.

12. J. Hopkins, *Michael Ayrton: A Biography*, Andre Deutsch, London, 1994.

13. Justine Hopkins, Personal communication to author (2012).

14. *We Write Novels*, BBC General Overseas Service, 7 April 1955.

15. *Sketch*, 18 November 1942.

16. *New Statesman and Nation*, 6 February 1943.
17. C. Darnton, Letter to Denis ApIvor, 19 August 1970, McMaster University, Hamilton, Ontario, Canada.
18. The Concise Oxford English Dictionary offers two definitions of the word 'fugue': '1 *Music* a contrapuntal composition in which a short melody or phrase (the subject) is introduced by one part and successively taken up by others. 2 *Psychiatry* a state or period of loss of awareness of one's identity, often coupled with flight from one's usual environment, associated with certain forms of hysteria and epilepsy.'
19. C. James, 'Prisoners of clarity—1. Nigel Balchin', *The New Review*, 1974;1(1):64–72. Available at www.clivejames.com/pieces/hercules/Balchin
20. Extract from Balchin's notebook dated 13 June 1952.

Chapter 8

1. 'No More Army Misfits', *Daily Telegraph*, 29 May 1942.
2. WO 165/101. The National Archives, London.
3. Balchin did not possess any formal psychological qualifications but had of course been trained as an industrial psychologist before the war.
4. E. Anstey, 'Reminiscences of a Wartime Army Psychologist', *The Psychologist*, 1989;2:475–8.
5. Anon., 'The Adjutant-General's Department in War', *Army Quarterly*, 1943;XLVI(2):217–24.
6. Officers on the General List were not assigned to a particular regiment or corps, except during their initial training period.
7. D. McMahon, '"Mr Nigel Balchin: Army years"', *The Times*, 26 May 1970.
8. E. Anstey, 'Reminiscences of a Wartime Army Psychologist', *The Psychologist*, 1989;2:475–8.
9. G. N. Tuck, 'The Army's use of psychology during the war', *Occupational Psychology*, 1946;20:113–8.
10. In the time that had elapsed since Balchin had performed the data analysis for the Black Magic market research project using a Hollerith machine, punched-card technology had evolved from being merely a data-processing tool to become a storage medium as well.
11. D. McMahon, '"Mr Nigel Balchin: Army years"', *The Times* 26 May 1970.
12. C. James, 'Prisoners of clarity—1. Nigel Balchin', *The New Review*, 1974;1(1):64–72. Available at www.clivejames.com/pieces/hercules/Balchin
13. D. McMahon, '"Mr Nigel Balchin: Army years"', *The Times*, 26 May 1970.
14. C. James, 'Prisoners of clarity—1. Nigel Balchin', *The New Review*, 1974;1(1):64–72. Available at www.clivejames.com/pieces/hercules/Balchin
15. E. Anstey, 'Reminiscences of a Wartime Army Psychologist', *The Psychologist*, 1989;2:475–8.
16. Ibid.
17. D. McMahon, '"Mr Nigel Balchin: Army years"', *The Times*, 26 May 1970.
18. HS 9/79/4. The National Archives, London.
19. Penelope Leach, Interview with author, 13 June 2008.
20. Note that Elisabeth Balchin's S.O.E. file at the National Archives contains only copies of the application forms she filled in when she attempted to join

the organization, together with related memoranda. There is nothing in the file about what she actually *did* as a member of S.O.E. Both Elisabeth's daughter Penelope Leach and her granddaughter Justine Hopkins believe that she vetted potential agents for the French Section headed by Maurice Buckmaster and I have therefore taken this information on trust in the absence of any supporting documentation.

Chapter 9

1. WO 222/130. The National Archives, London.
2. FD 1/6387. The National Archives, London.
3. The Directorate of Army Psychiatry.
4. WO 222/130. The National Archives, London.
5. This quotation is taken from documents relating to Balchin's wartime military service obtained by the author from the Army Personnel Centre.
6. CAB 98/28. The National Archives, London.
7. K. F. H. Murrell, 'Fitting the job to the sailor', *Occupational Psychology*, 1953;27:30–7.
8. WO 222/130. The National Archives, London.
9. WO 222/148. The National Archives, London.
10. 'The Authors and Their Books', Introduction to the Reader's Digest Condensed Books edition of *In the Absence of Mrs Petersen*, Reader's Digest Association, London, Sydney and Cape Town, 1967.
11. C. James, 'Prisoners of clarity—1. Nigel Balchin', *The New Review*, 1974;1(1):64–72. Available at www.clivejames.com/pieces/hercules/Balchin
12. 'I Don't Want To Be A Literary Gent says Nigel Balchin', *Books and Bookmen*, 1962;7(4):9–11.
13. C. James, 'Prisoners of clarity—1. Nigel Balchin', *The New Review*, 1974;1(1):64–72. Available at www.clivejames.com/pieces/hercules/Balchin
14. *New Statesman and Nation*, 23 July 1949.
15. 'I Don't Want To Be A Literary Gent says Nigel Balchin', *Books and Bookmen*, 1962;7(4):9–11.
16. C. James, 'Prisoners of clarity—1. Nigel Balchin', *The New Review*, 1974;1(1):64–72. Available at www.clivejames.com/pieces/hercules/Balchin
17. *Sphere*, 11 December 1943.
18. *Sunday Times*, 5 December 1943.
19. *Sketch*, 12 January 1944.
20. *New York Times*, 13 March 1945.
21. *New Statesman and Nation*, 8 January 1944.
22. C. James, 'Prisoners of clarity—1. Nigel Balchin', *The New Review*, 1974;1(1):64–72. Available at www.clivejames.com/pieces/hercules/Balchin
23. I am grateful to the late Elizabeth Jane Howard for informing me that, when writing about Sammy Rice's bomb disposal work, Balchin may have been inspired by the wartime exploits of Baron Victor Rothschild, who defused explosive devices in his capacity as head of the counter-sabotage section of MI5 during World War Two. In 1944, on the personal recommendation of Winston Churchill, Rothschild was awarded the George Medal after he dismantled a new type of Nazi bomb that had been secreted amongst a cargo

of Spanish onions sent to Britain.

24. 'The Authors and Their Books', Introduction to the Reader's Digest Condensed Books edition of *In the Absence of Mrs Petersen*, Reader's Digest Association, London, Sydney and Cape Town, 1967.

Chapter 10

1. 'The Author of the May Book', *World Books Broadsheet*, World Books, London, May 1947.
2. Unpublished memoir by Yovanka Balchin (undated but written in 2008).
3. Yovanka Balchin, Interview with author, 24 April 2007.
4. BSR 93/VIII/3. Rowntree Archive, held at the Borthwick Institute for Archives, University of York, York, UK.
5. 'The Author of the May Book', *World Books Broadsheet*, World Books, London, May 1947.
6. For the information in this chapter relating to the late Joe and Alice McDine and their connection with the Balchin family I am indebted to their son David, whom I spoke to at length in 2008 and who kindly gave me a copy of an undated interview with Alice he had conducted in 2003, and from which her quotations are taken.
7. HS 9/79/4. The National Archives, London.
8. J. Hopkins, *Michael Ayrton: A Biography*, Andre Deutsch, London, 1994.
9. 'Mummy was the light of my life', *Guardian*, 26 February 2003.
10. J. Hopkins, *Michael Ayrton: A Biography*, Andre Deutsch, London, 1994.
11. For the information in this chapter relating to the late Joe and Alice McDine and their connection with the Balchin family I am indebted to their son David, whom I spoke to at length in 2008 and who kindly gave me a copy of an undated interview with Alice he had conducted in 2003, and from which her quotations are taken.
12. 'Nigel Balchin's scalpel on love and marriage', *Daily Express*, 2 June 1966.
13. 'The Author of the May Book', *World Books Broadsheet*, World Books, London, May 1947.
14. C. James, 'Prisoners of clarity—1. Nigel Balchin', *The New Review*, 1974;1(1):64–72. Available at www.clivejames.com/pieces/hercules/Balchin
15. *The Times Literary Supplement*, 29 September 1945.
16. *Sketch*, 31 October 1945.
17. *Daily Herald*, 26 September 1945.
18. *New Statesman and Nation*, 13 October 1945.
19. N. Balchin, 'Writing in Pictures', In: J. Sutro (Ed.), *Diversion*, Max Parrish & Co. Ltd., London, 1950.
20. *Observer*, 21 October 1945.
21. C. James, 'Prisoners of clarity—1. Nigel Balchin', *The New Review*, 1974;1(1):64–72. Available at www.clivejames.com/pieces/hercules/Balchin
22. *Speaking Personally*, BBC Television, 11 August 1951.
23. Note that, although Balchin's claim may have been correct in 1951, if the sales figures located by James (C. James, 'Prisoners of clarity—1. Nigel Balchin', *The New Review*, 1974;1(1):64–72. Available at www.clivejames. com/pieces/hercules/Balchin) are correct then *The Small Back Room* proved

to have greater staying power, having emphatically overtaken *Mine Own Executioner* in terms of copies shifted by the time that James wrote his article on Balchin for *The New Review* in 1974.

24. T. H. Pear, 'Psychologists' and novelists' approaches to personal relations', *Bulletin of the British Psychological Society*, 1967;20:3–17.

25. *We Write Novels*, BBC General Overseas Service, 7 April 1955.

26. 'Famous writer at the sign of the Greyhound', *East Anglian Daily Times*, 4 February 1969.

27. Letter from Balchin to Val Gielgud, 30 July 1946. BBC Written Archives Centre, Caversham, UK.

28. T. H. Pear, 'Psychologists' and novelists' approaches to personal relations', *Bulletin of the British Psychological Society*, 1967;20:3–17.

29. *New Statesman and Nation*, 13 October 1945.

30. L. S. Hearnshaw, *A Short History of British Psychology 1840-1940*, Methuen, London, 1964.

31. E. Trist & H. Murray (Eds), *The Social Engagement of Social Science. Volume 1: The Socio-psychological Perspective*, Free Association Books, London, 1990.

32. *New Statesman and Nation*, 27 September 1947.

Chapter 11

1. C. James, 'Prisoners of clarity—1. Nigel Balchin', *The New Review*, 1974;1(1):64–72. Available at www.clivejames.com/pieces/hercules/Balchin

2. The information in this chapter about Operation Backfire comes from a file at the National Archives in London (WO 33/2554) and the biographical information about Eric Ambler is partly derived from his entry in the *Oxford Dictionary of National Biography*: M. Barber, 'Ambler, Eric Clifford (1909–1998)', *Oxford Dictionary of National Biography*, Oxford University Press, Oxford, UK, 2004.

3. C. James, 'Prisoners of clarity—2. Eric Ambler', *The New Review*, 1974;1(6):63–9.

4. In 1943, Korda had become the head of a new company formed following a merger between MGM's British arm and London Films. Balchin signed a contract to write scripts for the new company, MGM British Studios, in June 1944, as detailed in Chapter 13.

5. WO 291/2316. The National Archives, London.

6. None of the others would appear to have survived.

7. WO 291/2316. The National Archives, London.

8. This quotation is taken from Jeremy Stewart's appearance on the television programme *Who Do You Think You Are?*, the subject of which was Rick Stein, first broadcast on BBC Television on 16 February 2009.

9. Email from Stewart to author, 17 December 2008.

10. Email from Stein to author, 28 October 2008.

11. N. Balchin, C. S. Forester, E. Linklater & C. Sykes, *Fatal Fascination. A Choice of Crime*, Hutchinson, London, 1964.

12. Letter from Balchin to Val Gielgud, 30 July 1946. BBC Written Archives Centre, Caversham, UK.

13. A radio version of *Mine Own Executioner* was broadcast on the Light

Programme on 11 April 1951.

14. Romary was a factory in Tunbridge Wells in Kent that made wafer biscuits for Rowntree's.

15. T. Rayfield, *Fifty in 40: The Unofficial History of JWT London 1945-1995*, Rayfield Writers, Radnage Common, UK, 1996.

16. 'The Author of the May Book', *World Books Broadsheet*, World Books, London, May 1947.

17. The Sandpit is a lounge at the Savile Club.

18. G. Anderson, *Hang Your Halo in the Hall*, Savile Club, London, 1968. The information in this chapter about A. D. Peters is derived from this published history of the Savile Club.

Chapter 12

1. N. Balchin, 'Satisfactions in Work', *Occupational Psychology*, 1947;21:125–34.

2. This information is derived from the following book: D. Kynaston, *A World to Build. Austerity Britain 1945–48*, Bloomsbury, London, 2007.

3. Here, Rowntree is wondering what Balchin had done with himself after leaving Rowntree's when war broke out in 1939. When he refers to 'the Works' he means the Rowntree's Cocoa Works in York.

4. Letter from B. S. Rowntree to Lord Piercy, 10 October 1946. BSR 93/VIII/NIIP. Rowntree Archive, held at the Borthwick Institute for Archives, University of York, York, UK.

5. £2,000–3,000 in 1946 is worth about £65,000–100,000 today.

6. R&Co 93/IX/20. Rowntree Archive, held at the Borthwick Institute for Archives, University of York, York, UK.

7. Letter from Balchin to B. S. Rowntree, 15 November 1946. BSR 93/VIII/3. Rowntree Archive, held at the Borthwick Institute for Archives, University of York, York, UK.

8. N. Balchin, 'Satisfactions in Work', *Occupational Psychology*, 1947;21:125–34.

9. In 1947, Herbert Morrison was Lord President of the Council and Deputy Prime Minister in Clement Attlee's Labour administration.

10. N. Balchin, 'Satisfactions in Work', *Occupational Psychology*, 1947;21:125–34.

11. R. G. Ford, 'Paper of my lifetime: Balchin, N. (1947) "Satisfaction [sic] in Work"', *The Occupational Psychologist*, 1993;20:11–12.

12. N. Balchin, 'The Nature of Incentives', *The Nineteenth Century and After*, 1948;CXLIV:247–54.

13. Balchin wrote quite a lot about the aircraft industry in the 1930s and 1940s, despite the fact that he never had any direct involvement with it. In addition to *The Aircraft Builders*, he also wrote a play (1938's *Profit and Loss*) set in the world of aircraft manufacture as well as his Pobottle advertisements for High Duty Alloys. Balchin's sister Monica married Stuart Braund in 1936. Braund was an aeronautical engineer who worked for Rolls Royce in Bristol. Balchin's brother Bill also worked at various times for the Bristol Aeroplane Company and for the Air Ministry. Presumably these two gentlemen would

have been able to furnish Balchin with technical information whenever he was required to write about the aircraft industry. But as Balchin was greatly skilled at quickly absorbing the complexities of a new subject it is quite probable that he was able to manage perfectly well without any external assistance from members of his family.

14. C. James, 'Prisoners of clarity—1. Nigel Balchin', *The New Review*, 1974;1(1):64–72. Available at www.clivejames.com/pieces/hercules/Balchin

15. *News Chronicle*, 28 August 1947.

16. *Daily Mail*, 23 August 1947.

17. *Daily Telegraph*, 29 August 1947.

18. *New Statesman and Nation*, 27 September 1947.

19. The principal characters of *Lord, I Was Afraid* in fact comprise four men and three women.

20. N. Balchin, 'Children are a Waste of Time', *Saturday Evening Post*, 9 October 1965.

21. Extract from Balchin's notebook dated 13 June 1952.

22. *Observer*, 24 August 1947.

23. *John o'London's Weekly*, 5 September 1947.

24. *Manchester Evening News*, 28 August 1947.

25. *Daily Telegraph*, 29 August 1947.

26. *Daily Mail*, 23 August 1947.

27. *New Statesman and Nation*, 27 September 1947.

28. 'Taxes hold up new writing', *News Chronicle*, 24 July 1952.

29. *New Statesman and Nation*, 27 September 1947.

30. 'Coming Home', *Guardian*, 23 October 1961.

31. Yovanka Balchin, Interview with author, 24 April 2007.

32. R. Francis, *Francis Bacon*, Tate Gallery, London, 1985.

33. C. James, 'Prisoners of clarity—1. Nigel Balchin', *The New Review*, 1974;1(1):64–72. Available at www.clivejames.com/pieces/hercules/Balchin

34. The information in this chapter about the stage adaptation of *Lord, I Was Afraid* is partly derived from the following book: A. Biswell, *The Real Life of Anthony Burgess*, Picador, London, 2005.

35. *Nigel Balchin: The Small Back-Room Boy*, BBC Radio 4, 24 April 2008.

36. *The Times Literary Supplement*, 26 January 1962.

37. *JGB News*, Number 22, February 1994. Available at http://www.jgballard.ca/pringle_news_from_the_sun/news_from_sun22.html

38. N. Balchin, 'Notes on the Way', *Time and Tide*, 18 October 1947.

Chapter 13

1. N. Balchin, 'Writing in Pictures', In: J. Sutro (Ed.), *Diversion*, Max Parrish & Co. Ltd., London, 1950.

2. L. Halliwell, *Halliwell's Filmgoer's and Video Viewer's Companion*, 9th edition, Paladin, London, 1989.

3. B. MacFarlane, *An Autobiography of British Cinema*, Methuen, London, 1997.

4. *Observer*, 12 October 1947.

5. B. MacFarlane, 'Fame is the Spur: an honourable failure', In: A. Burton, T.

O'Sullivan & P. Wells (Eds), *The Family Way. The Boulting Brothers and Postwar British Film Culture*, Flicks Books, Trowbridge, UK, 2000.

6. B. MacFarlane, *An Autobiography of British Cinema*, Methuen, London, 1997.
7. *Time and Tide*, 6 December 1947.
8. *Monthly Film Bulletin*, 31 December 1947.
9. M. Powell, *A Life in Movies. An Autobiography*, Mandarin, London, 1986.
10. B. MacFarlane, *An Autobiography of British Cinema*, Methuen, London, 1997.
11. M. Powell, *A Life in Movies. An Autobiography*, Mandarin, London, 1986.
12. B. MacFarlane, *An Autobiography of British Cinema*, Methuen, London, 1997.
13. The name of this gentleman remains a mystery.
14. B. Meredith, *So Far, So Good. A Memoir*, Little, Brown and Company, Boston, MA, 1994.
15. Unfortunately, she did not explain what that background consisted of.
16. B. MacFarlane, *An Autobiography of British Cinema*, Methuen, London, 1997.
17. *New Statesman and Nation*, 29 November 1947.
18. *News Chronicle*, 22 November 1947.
19. *New Statesman and Nation*, 29 November 1947.
20. *News Chronicle*, 22 November 1947.
21. *Daily Telegraph*, 24 November 1947.
22. *Sight and Sound*, Winter 1947/8.
23. The figures in this paragraph are taken from the following article: V. Porter, 'The Robert Clark Account: films released in Britain by Associated British Pictures, British Lion, MGM, and Warner Bros., 1946-1957', *Historical Journal of Film, Radio and Television*, 2000;20(4):469–511.
24. *We Write Novels*, BBC General Overseas Service, 7 April 1955.
25. *Time and Tide*, 6 December 1947.
26. *New Statesman and Nation*, 29 November 1947.
27. A. Ross, *The Forties. A Period Piece*, Weidenfeld & Nicolson, London, 1950.
28. *Sweet and Low* opened at the Ambassadors Theatre in London's Covent Garden (the scene of Balchin's own greatest theatrical triumph, the one-night run of his James Mason vehicle *Miserable Sinners* in 1937) on 10 June 1943 and ran for 264 performances. It starred Hermione Gingold and did indeed feature a song entitled *The Borgias are Having an Orgy*. This information is derived from the following book: S. Green, *Encyclopedia of the Musical Theatre*, Dodd, Mead & Company, New York, 1976.
29. In his preface to Joan Haslip's book about Lucrezia Borgia (J. Haslip, *Lucrezia Borgia. A Study*, Heron Books, London, 1968) Balchin supplied the additional information that the actors representing Rodrigo, Cesare and Lucrezia Borgia had 'explained to the audience, with ghastly glee, that all the food was poisoned'.
30. 'I Don't Want To Be A Literary Gent says Nigel Balchin', *Books and Bookmen*, 1962;7(4):9–11.
31. *New Statesman and Nation*, 18 September 1948.

32. *Evening Standard*, 27 July 1948.
33. *Manchester Evening News*, 21 July 1948.
34. *Daily Mail*, 17 July 1948.
35. *Time and Tide*, 11 September 1948.
36. *The Times Literary Supplement*, 24 July 1948.
37. *Time and Tide*, 11 September 1948.
38. *Tatler and Bystander*, 18 August 1948.
39. C. James, 'Prisoners of clarity—1. Nigel Balchin', *The New Review*, 1974;1(1):64–72. Available at www.clivejames.com/pieces/hercules/Balchin
40. *Sunday Times*, 31 December 1950.
41. 'I Don't Want To Be A Literary Gent says Nigel Balchin', *Books and Bookmen*, 1962;7(4):9–11.
42. Extract from Balchin's notebook dated 13 June 1952.
43. *John o'London's Weekly*, 23 July 1948.
44. N. Balchin, C. S. Forester, E. Linklater & C. Sykes, *Fatal Fascination. A Choice of Crime*, Hutchinson, London, 1964.
45. J. Haslip, *Lucrezia Borgia. A Study*, Heron Books, London, 1968.
46. *We Write Novels*, BBC General Overseas Service, 7 April 1955.
47. C. James, 'Prisoners of clarity—1. Nigel Balchin', *The New Review*, 1974;1(1):64–72. Available at www.clivejames.com/pieces/hercules/Balchin

Chapter 14

1. *Daily Telegraph*, 24 June 1949.
2. C. James, 'Prisoners of clarity—1. Nigel Balchin', *The New Review*, 1974;1(1):64–72. Available at www.clivejames.com/pieces/hercules/Balchin
3. *New Statesman and Nation*, 23 July 1949.
4. *Daily Telegraph*, 24 June 1949.
5. *Listener*, 7 July 1949.
6. *Sunday Chronicle*, 19 June 1949.
7. *The Times Literary Supplement*, 24 June 1949.
8. *Sketch*, 20 July 1949.
9. *Sunday Times*, 19 June 1949.
10. *Daily Telegraph*, 24 June 1949.
11. *Illustrated London News*, 9 July 1949.
12. This fact was reported in the magazine *John Bull*, 9 July 1949.
13. M. Powell, *A Life in Movies. An Autobiography*, Mandarin, London, 1986.
14. According to a biography of Pressburger (K. Macdonald, *Emeric Pressburger: The Life and Death of a Screenwriter*, Faber and Faber, London, 1994), *The Small Back Room* was the first film that he and Powell made for Korda having re-entered his employ after a period working for the Rank Organisation. Originally intended to be filmed in 1946 for Rank by Powell alone, the movie was delayed by squabbles between Powell and Pressburger and the eventual transfer of the duo to Korda's London Films stable.
15. M. Powell, *A Life in Movies. An Autobiography*, Mandarin, London, 1986.
16. B. MacFarlane, *An Autobiography of British Cinema*, Methuen, London, 1997.
17. M. Powell, *Million-Dollar Movie: The Second Volume of his Life in Movies*,

Mandarin, London, 1993.

18. *Sunday Chronicle*, 23 January 1949.
19. M. Powell, *Million-Dollar Movie: The Second Volume of his Life in Movies*, Mandarin, London, 1993.
20. B. Forbes, *Notes for a Life*, Everest Books, London, 1977.
21. *Time and Tide*, 29 January 1949.
22. B. MacFarlane, *An Autobiography of British Cinema*, Methuen, London, 1997.
23. *Spectator*, 28 January 1949.
24. *New Statesman and Nation*, 29 January 1949.
25. *Tatler and Bystander*, 2 February 1949.
26. *Star*, 21 January 1949.
27. In order of their occurrence, these comments are taken from the following reviews: *Sunday Chronicle*, 23 January 1949; *Sunday Graphic*, 23 January 1949; *Spectator*, 28 January 1949; *Sunday Chronicle*, 23 January 1949; *Illustrated London News*, 5 February 1949.
28. M. Powell, *Million-Dollar Movie: The Second Volume of his Life in Movies*, Mandarin, London, 1993.
29. V. Porter, 'The Robert Clark Account: films released in Britain by Associated British Pictures, British Lion, MGM, and Warner Bros., 1946-1957', *Historical Journal of Film, Radio and Television*, 2000;20(4):469–511.
30. M. Powell, *Million-Dollar Movie: The Second Volume of his Life in Movies*, Mandarin, London, 1993.
31. The most recent of these adaptations, a new version of *The Small Back Room*, was made by BBC Radio 4 in 2008 to commemorate the centenary of Balchin's birth and starred Damian Lewis in a pre-*Homeland* role as Sammy Rice.
32. *Daily Telegraph*, 6 April 1959.
33. *The Times*, 6 April 1959.
34. *Observer*, 12 April 1959.
35. *Daily Telegraph*, 5 August 1959.
36. *The Times*, 5 August 1959.
37. S. Zuckerman, *From Apes to Warlords. The Autobiography (1904–1946) of Solly Zuckerman*, Collins, London, 1988.
38. Letter from P. C. Vellacott to H. A. Roberts (Secretary, University of Cambridge Appointments Board), 26 October 1929. Nigel Balchin's personal file, Peterhouse, Cambridge, UK. Quoted with permission from the Master and Fellows of Peterhouse.
39. The information in this chapter concerning Balchin's negotiations with Blanche Knopf is derived from the Alfred A. Knopf correspondence held by the Harry Ransom Center, The University of Texas at Austin, Austin, TX and reproduced by permission of the Harry Ransom Center and Alice L. Knopf.

Chapter 15

1. Extract from Balchin's notebook dated 13 June 1952.
2. In order to write this chapter I have leant heavily on information gleaned

from the following book: J. Hopkins, *Michael Ayrton: A Biography*, Andre Deutsch, London, 1994.

3. *John o'London's Weekly*, 4 December 1942.
4. In later paperback editions the epigraph was amended so that the first word read 'Brightness', thus agreeing with Nashe's text.
5. T. G. Rosenthal, 'Ayrton, Michael (1921–1975)', *Oxford Dictionary of National Biography*, Oxford University Press, Oxford, UK, 2004.
6. J. Hopkins, *Michael Ayrton: A Biography*, Andre Deutsch, London, 1994.
7. Penelope Leach, Interview with author, 13 June 2008.
8. J. Hopkins, *Michael Ayrton: A Biography*, Andre Deutsch, London, 1994.
9. Yovanka Balchin, Interview with author, 24 April 2007.
10. Unpublished memoir by Yovanka Balchin (undated but written in 2008).
11. Although she has never officially changed her name, Yovanka Balchin is known today amongst her friends and family as Jane, an anglicized version of her forename.
12. Penelope Leach, Interview with author, 13 June 2008.
13. Unpublished memoir by Yovanka Balchin (undated but written in 2008).
14. Yovanka Balchin, Interview with author, 24 April 2007.
15. D. Souhami, *The Trials of Radclyffe Hall*, Weidenfeld & Nicolson, London, 1998.
16. Unpublished memoir by Yovanka Balchin (undated but written in 2008).
17. Penelope Leach, Interview with author, 14 November 2006.
18. J. Hopkins, *Michael Ayrton: A Biography*, Andre Deutsch, London, 1994.
19. *Desert Island Discs*, BBC Radio 4, 13 September 1992.
20. Extract from Balchin's notebook dated 13 June 1952.
21. J. Hopkins, *Michael Ayrton: A Biography*, Andre Deutsch, London, 1994.
22. Letter from David Higham to Mike Watkins, 1 February 1950. David Higham Associates correspondence, Harry Ransom Center, The University of Texas at Austin, Austin, TX. Reproduced by permission of the Harry Ransom Center and David Higham Associates.
23. N. Balchin, Pen portrait published in the *New York Herald Tribune Book Review*, 8 October 1950.
24. Extract from Balchin's notebook dated 13 June 1952.
25. 'Keeping up with Balchin', *Saturday Evening Post*, 8 July 1950.
26. Penelope Leach, Interview with author, 13 June 2008.
27. Extract from Balchin's notebook dated 13 June 1952.
28. J. Hopkins, *Michael Ayrton: A Biography*, Andre Deutsch, London, 1994.
29. Yovanka Balchin, Interview with author, 24 April 2007.
30. Extract from Balchin's notebook dated 13 June 1952.
31. J. Hopkins, *Michael Ayrton: A Biography*, Andre Deutsch, London, 1994.
32. N. Balchin, Undated fragment, Nigel Balchin Collection, British Film Institute, London.
33. Penelope Leach, Interview with author, 13 June 2008.
34. *Desert Island Discs*, BBC Radio 4, 13 September 1992.
35. *Front Row*, BBC Radio 4, 15 November 2005.
36. Extract from Balchin's notebook dated 13 June 1952.

Chapter 16

1. Penelope Leach, Interview with author, 14 November 2006.
2. This title derived from the epigraph that Balchin chose for the novel, which in turn came from Montaigne's essay 'Of Solitariness': 'Oh Lord deliver me from feeling of this losse; for Thou knowest as yet they have touched nothing that is mine.'
3. *Daily Telegraph*, 8 June 1951.
4. C. James, 'Prisoners of clarity—1. Nigel Balchin', *The New Review*, 1974;1(1):64–72. Available at www.clivejames.com/pieces/hercules/Balchin
5. Penelope Leach, Interview with author, 14 November 2006.
6. 'The Authors and Their Books', Introduction to the Reader's Digest Condensed Books edition of *In the Absence of Mrs Petersen*, Reader's Digest Association, London, Sydney and Cape Town, 1967.
7. C. James, 'Prisoners of clarity—1. Nigel Balchin', *The New Review*, 1974;1(1):64–72. Available at www.clivejames.com/pieces/hercules/Balchin
8. Extract from Balchin's notebook dated 13 June 1952.
9. Penelope Leach, Interview with author, 14 November 2006.
10. *Speaking Personally*, BBC Television, 11 August 1951.
11. Extract from Balchin's notebook dated 13 June 1952.
12. *Evening Standard*, 5 June 1951.
13. *Daily Mail*, 9 June 1951.
14. *Manchester Guardian*, 8 June 1951.
15. *Sunday Times*, 3 June 1951.
16. *New Statesman and Nation*, 30 June 1951.
17. Extract from Balchin's notebook dated 13 June 1952.

Chapter 17

1. *Speaking Personally*, BBC Television, 11 August 1951.
2. These statistics are derived from the following article: H. Mount, 'The King is dead – long live the Queen', *Daily Telegraph*, 6 February 2012.
3. *Radio Times*, 9 October 1953.
4. *Radio Times*, 5 March 1954.
5. *New Statesman and Nation*, 16 May 1953.
6. This information is derived from the jacket of the World Books edition of *Sundry Creditors* published by the Reprint Society, London, 1954.
7. C. James, 'Prisoners of clarity—1. Nigel Balchin', *The New Review*, 1974;1(1):64–72. Available at www.clivejames.com/pieces/hercules/Balchin
8. *The Times Literary Supplement*, 8 May 1953.
9. N. Balchin, 'The Development of Industry. Its Impact on the Worker', *Personnel Management – The Journal of the Institute of Personnel Management*, 1953;XXXV(324):66–77.
10. R. Fitzgerald, *Rowntree and the Marketing Revolution, 1862-1969*, Cambridge University Press, Cambridge, UK, 1995.
11. John Quail, Personal communication to author (2014). I am indebted to Dr Quail for confirming my suspicion that *Sundry Creditors* is to some extent a roman-à-clef, informing me of George Harris's treatment of Peter Rowntree

and pointing out the existence of information about Balchin in the Rowntree Archive at the Borthwick Institute in York that had previously eluded me.

12. R. Fitzgerald, *Rowntree and the Marketing Revolution, 1862-1969*, Cambridge University Press, Cambridge, UK, 1995.

13. *Evening Standard*, 4 May 1953.

14. *Talking of Books*, BBC Home Service, 24 May 1953.

15. *Daily Telegraph*, 8 May 1953.

16. *Observer*, 3 May 1953.

17. *Daily Express*, 7 May 1953.

18. C. Sykes, *Evelyn Waugh. A Biography*, Collins, London, 1975.

19. *Daily Express*, 7 May 1953.

20. H. Puffmore, 'Under Review', *Bookseller*, 16 May 1953.

21. 'Collins v. their authors', *Bookseller*, 24 July 1948.

22. P. Snow, *Stranger and Brother, A Portrait of C. P. Snow by Philip Snow*, Macmillan, London, 1982.

23. Extract from Balchin's notebook dated 13 June 1952.

24. Elizabeth Jane Howard, Interview with author, 26 September 2007.

25. Yovanka Balchin, Interview with author, 24 April 2007.

26. Elizabeth Jane Howard, Interview with author, 26 September 2007.

27. Letter from P. C. Vellacott to H. A. Roberts (Secretary, University of Cambridge Appointments Board), 26 October 1929. Nigel Balchin's personal file, Peterhouse, Cambridge, UK. Quoted with permission from the Master and Fellows of Peterhouse.

28. Yovanka Balchin, Interview with author, 24 April 2007.

29. The information on the links between Balchin, MacKendrick and JWT is contained in the following book: T. Rayfield, *Fifty in 40: The Unofficial History of JWT London 1945-1995*, Rayfield Writers, Radnage Common, UK, 1996.

30. C. Barr, *Ealing Studios*, Studio Vista, London, 1993.

31. P. Kemp, *Lethal Innocence. The Cinema of Alexander MacKendrick*, Methuen, London, 1991.

32. J. Hawkins, *Anything for a Quiet Life*, Elm Tree Books, London, 1973.

33. *Sunday Times*, 3 August 1952.

34. P. Kemp, *Lethal Innocence. The Cinema of Alexander MacKendrick*, Methuen, London, 1991.

35. *The Times*, 4 August 1952.

36. *Sunday Times*, 3 August 1952.

37. *The Times*, 4 August 1952.

38. L. Halliwell, *Halliwell's Film Guide* (edited by J. Walker), 8th edition, HarperCollins*Publishers*, London, 1991.

39. Extract from Balchin's notebook dated 13 June 1952.

40. Unpublished memoir by Yovanka Balchin (undated but written in 2008).

41. Extract from Balchin's notebook dated 13 June 1952.

42. Unpublished memoir by Yovanka Balchin (undated but written in 2008).

43. Yovanka Balchin, Interview with author, 24 April 2007.

44. Yovanka Balchin, Interview with author, 25 April 2007.

Chapter 18

1. Letter from Yovanka Balchin to author, 15 August 2007.
2. Unpublished memoir by Yovanka Balchin (undated but written in 2008).
3. Yovanka Balchin, Interview with author, 9 December 2009.
4. Unpublished memoir by Yovanka Balchin (undated but written in 2008).
5. Obituary for Angharad Rees published in the *Daily Telegraph*, 23 July 2012.
6. BBC Home Service, 29 October 1954.
7. *Any Questions?*, BBC Light Programme, 10 December 1954.
8. BBC General Overseas Service, 7 April 1955.
9. Yovanka Balchin, Interview with author, 24 April 2007.
10. BBC General Overseas Service, 7 April 1955.
11. Unpublished memoir by Yovanka Balchin (undated but written in 2008).
12. The information in this chapter about Ronald Millar and the genesis of *Waiting for Gillian* is derived from Millar's autobiography: R. Millar, *A View from the Wings. West End, West Coast, Westminster*, Weidenfeld & Nicolson, London, 1993.
13. The role of Gillian had been written by Millar specifically with Glynis Johns in mind, but the Welsh actress pulled out when negotiations were at an advanced stage because she had already committed herself to other acting projects. Johns would get her opportunity to appear in a Balchin-authored work the following year when she took the title role in the film *Josephine and Men*, the script of which was developed by Balchin from his short story 'Among Friends', as detailed later on in this chapter.
14. *Observer*, 25 April 1954.
15. *New Statesman and Nation*, 1 May 1954.
16. *Plays and Players*, June 1954.
17. *Spectator*, 30 April 1954.
18. *Observer*, 20 November 1955.
19. Originally published in the *Evening Standard* under the title 'Custom House Incident', Balchin's tale was later included in the multi-author story compendium *Did it Happen?* (Oldbourne Press, London, 1956). 'Dover Incident' is a true story about a journey that Balchin had taken from Florence to London by train and boat. On the train between Florence and Calais he had taken pity on a gauche and physically repellent woman who had gratefully latched onto him in the hope that he would pilot the two of them through customs without her luggage being subjected to anything more than a cursory inspection. But instead she was stopped and searched at Dover and revealed to be an unlikely-looking smuggler ("they'd found forty watches when I came away, and that was only the start").
20. 'The Salamander' (*Illustrated London News*, 'Christmas Number', 8 November 1945) probably arose from Balchin's wartime work for the army although, as mentioned in one of the Notes to Chapter 2, the central character may perhaps have been partly inspired by one of Balchin's university lecturers, J.B.S. Haldane. The story describes the bravery of Professor Gates, who is made a Companion of the Bath during World War Two after using himself as a human guinea pig to test

the weapons potentiality of flame-throwers. He also earns himself the nickname The Salamander, after the mythical lizard-like creature that is unafraid of fire. The irony is that, in peacetime, Gates is employed in academia, one of his duties being to give lectures on organic chemistry. But he is scared stiff of his students, who mercilessly rag him whilst he attempts to lecture them.

21. *The Times*, 14 November 1955.

22. Letter from William Collins to Balchin, 30 November 1954. University of Glasgow Archive Services, Glasgow, UK, William Collins, Sons & Co Ltd collection, GB0248 UGD243/1/11/9.

23. Letter from William Collins to A. D. Peters, 13 December 1954. University of Glasgow Archive Services, Glasgow, UK, William Collins, Sons & Co Ltd collection, GB0248 UGD243/1/11/9.

24. C. James, 'Prisoners of clarity—1. Nigel Balchin', *The New Review*, 1974;1(1):64–72. Available at www.clivejames.com/pieces/hercules/Balchin

25. Jeremy Stewart.

26. *Any Questions?*, BBC Light Programme, 10 December 1954.

27. Email from Stein to author, 5 February 2009.

28. *Daily Dispatch*, 26 November 1954.

29. *The Times*, 10 November 1954.

30. *Tatler and Bystander*, 22 December 1954.

31. Harvey was a British playwright and scriptwriter who worked on several memorable Boulting brothers' productions, including *Seven Days to Noon*, *Private's Progress* and *I'm All Right Jack*.

32. *The Times*, 14 November 1955.

33. *Tatler and Bystander*, 23 November 1955.

34. *Time and Tide*, 19 November 1955.

35. BBC General Overseas Service, 7 April 1955.

36. *Illustrated London News*, 17 September 1955.

37. *The Times Literary Supplement*, 16 September 1955.

38. Anon., 'Mr Nigel Balchin', *Guardian*, 18 May 1970.

39. C. James, 'Prisoners of clarity—1. Nigel Balchin', *The New Review*, 1974;1(1):64–72. Available at www.clivejames.com/pieces/hercules/Balchin

40. *Daily Mail*, 2 September 1955.

41. *Tatler and Bystander*, 21 September 1955.

42. *Evening News*, 3 September 1955.

43. *Observer*, 4 September 1955.

44. *Daily Express*, 7 May 1953.

45. The information concerning Waugh's spat with Spain is derived from the following two books: (i) C. Sykes, *Evelyn Waugh. A Biography*, Collins, London, 1975; and (ii) R. Collis, *A Trouser-wearing Character. The Life and Times of Nancy Spain*, Cassell, London, 1997.

46. *Daily Express*, 7 May 1953.

47. *Daily Express*, 3 September 1955.

48. Elizabeth Jane Howard, Interview with author, 26 September 2007.

49. Yovanka Balchin, Interview with author, 24 April 2007.

Chapter 19

1. Yovanka Balchin, Interview with author, 24 April 2007.
2. Elizabeth Jane Howard, Interview with author, 26 September 2007.
3. *The Times*, 12 March 1956.
4. According to Ben Macintyre's recent book (*Operation Mincemeat. The True Spy Story that Changed the Course of World War II*, Bloomsbury, London, 2010), although the cadaver was carrying letters signed by Mountbatten, the one suggesting that the Allies would invade Greece and Sardinia instead of Sicily was in fact signed by General Sir Archibald Nye, Vice Chief of the Imperial General Staff.
5. *Sunday Telegraph*, 10 March 1956.
6. L. Halliwell, *Halliwell's Film Guide* (edited by J. Walker), 8th edition, HarperCollins*Publishers*, London, 1991.
7. *Sunday Telegraph*, 10 March 1956.
8. L. Halliwell, *Halliwell's Film Guide* (edited by J. Walker), 8th edition, HarperCollins*Publishers*, London, 1991.
9. D. Kynaston, *Modernity Britain. Opening the Box, 1957–59*, Bloomsbury, London, 2013.
10. ''Identity card' for film', *The Times*, 13 March 1956.
11. In its issue dated 13 December 1956, the trade paper *Kinematograph Weekly* described the film as having 'scored fluently' at the box office, and they bracketed it with *The Ladykillers* and *Cockleshell Heroes* as being among the 'Other Money-makers of the Year', i.e. it occupied a position just behind the three most lucrative British films of 1956, namely *Reach for the Sky*, *Trapeze* and *Private's Progress*.
12. *The Times*, 20 August 1956.
13. L. Halliwell, *Halliwell's Film Guide* (edited by J. Walker), 8th edition, HarperCollins*Publishers*, London, 1991.
14. *The Times*, 20 August 1956.
15. Letter from Balchin to Yovanka dated 8 May 1956 and in the possession of Yovanka Balchin.
16. 'Six thousand miles to be born in England', *Evening News*, 8 September 1955.
17. Yovanka Balchin, Interview with author, 24 April 2007.
18. 'Between Friends', *Woman's Own*, 8 March 1956.
19. *Radio Times*, 23 December 1955.
20. 'Between Friends', *Woman's Own*, 8 March 1956.
21. D. Spoto, *Grace Kelly and Hollywood*, Hutchinson, London, 2009.
22. 'Balchin's return', *Evening Standard*, 29 September 1961.
23. Yovanka Balchin, Interview with author, 9 December 2009.
24. Yovanka Balchin, Interview with author, 24 April 2007.
25. 'What they did to me in Hollywood', *Daily Mail*, 18 January 1962.
26. In order of their occurrence, these values are taken from the following newspaper articles: 'What they did to me in Hollywood', *Daily Mail*, 18 January 1962; 'The world wanderer settles for a farm', *Daily Sketch*, 21 November 1962; 'Balchin's return', *Evening Standard*, 29 September 1961. If

one conflates fact and fiction, then perhaps the figure of 'about one hundred and fifty thousand miles' that Jim Petersen had flown 'in the last ten years' in the course of his duties as a film scriptwriter, as detailed in Balchin's penultimate novel, *In the Absence of Mrs Petersen*, is nearest to the mark.

27. Letter from Yovanka to Balchin dated 27 November 1957 and in the possession of Yovanka Balchin.
28. Unpublished memoir by Yovanka Balchin (undated but written in 2008).
29. 'Exploding with sexual chemistry', *Daily Telegraph*, 1 October 2012.
30. Unpublished memoir by Yovanka Balchin (undated but written in 2008).
31. This figure is derived from the following book: P. Clarke, *Hope and Glory: Britain 1900–1990*, Penguin, London, 1996.
32. 'Taxes hold up new writing', *News Chronicle*, 24 July 1952.
33. 'Notes for meeting of the Brains Trust', Personal document written by Balchin on 2 May 1959 and in the possession of Yovanka Balchin.
34. These notes were written at a time when Balchin thought he was on the brink of losing Yovanka to Steven Dedijer, a Yugoslav academic (see Chapter 20 for details).
35. L. Halliwell, *Halliwell's Film Guide* (edited by J. Walker), 8th edition, HarperCollins*Publishers*, London, 1991.
36. *Monthly Film Bulletin*, January 1961.
37. Balchin was unable to collect the award in person as he was working in Hollywood when the presentations were made in London on 11 July 1957. The film's producer, André Hakim, therefore picked up the award on Balchin's behalf.

Chapter 20

1. Unpublished memoir by Yovanka Balchin (undated but written in 2008).
2. J. Huston, *An Open Book*, Virgin Books, London, 1994.
3. Unpublished memoir by Yovanka Balchin (undated but written in 2008).
4. 'Notes for meeting of the Brains Trust', Personal document written by Balchin on 2 May 1959 and in the possession of Yovanka Balchin.
5. Unpublished memoir by Yovanka Balchin (undated but written in 2008).
6. 'Balchin's return', *Evening Standard*, 29 September 1961.
7. Unpublished memoir by Yovanka Balchin (undated but written in 2008).
8. Yovanka Balchin, Interview with author, 24 April 2007.
9. Unpublished memoir by Yovanka Balchin (undated but written in 2008).
10. Yovanka Balchin, Interview with author, 24 April 2007.
11. L. Halliwell, *Halliwell's Film Guide* (edited by J. Walker), 8th edition, HarperCollins*Publishers*, London, 1991.
12. 'What they did to me in Hollywood', *Daily Mail*, 18 January 1962.
13. 'Balchin's return', *Evening Standard*, 29 September 1961.
14. Yovanka Balchin, Interview with author, 24 April 2007.
15. This quotation is taken from the following book: L. Mosley, *Zanuck. The Rise and Fall of Hollywood's Last Tycoon*, Granada, London, 1984. Other information in this chapter about the genesis of *Cleopatra* is derived from this book as well as from the television documentary *Cleopatra: The Film that Changed Hollywood* (Prometheus Entertainment, Los Angeles, CA, 2001).

16. Unpublished memoir by Yovanka Balchin (undated but written in 2008).
17. *Daily Cinema*, 14 November 1960.
18. *Daily Telegraph*, 12 November 1960.
19. *Tatler and Bystander*, 23 November 1960.
20. *New Statesman and Nation*, 19 November 1960.
21. *Daily Herald*, 11 November 1960.
22. *Illustrated London News*, 26 November 1960.
23. *New Statesman and Nation*, 19 November 1960.
24. *Time and Tide*, 19 November 1960.
25. *Monthly Film Bulletin*, December 1960.
26. *Sunday Times*, 13 November 1960.
27. Letter from William Collins to Balchin, 27 November 1959. University of Glasgow Archive Services, Glasgow, UK, William Collins, Sons & Co Ltd collection, GB0248 UGD243/1/11/12.
28. Letter from Balchin to William Collins, 9 December 1959. University of Glasgow Archive Services, Glasgow, UK, William Collins, Sons & Co Ltd collection, GB0248 UGD243/1/11/9.
29. R. Ward Baker, *The Director's Cut*, Reynolds & Hearn, London, 2000.
30. *Monthly Film Bulletin*, February 1961.
31. R. Ward Baker, *The Director's Cut*, Reynolds & Hearn, London, 2000.
32. B. MacFarlane, *An Autobiography of British Cinema*, Methuen, London, 1997.
33. Interview with Roy Ward Baker on the 2006 DD Home Entertainment DVD release of *The Singer Not the Song*.
34. R. Ward Baker, *The Director's Cut*, Reynolds & Hearn, London, 2000.
35. Interview with Roy Ward Baker on the 2006 DD Home Entertainment DVD release of *The Singer Not the Song*.
36. Although unable to identify the cause of the 'extraordinary enmity' between the two actors, who he said had worked together only once before, on 1952's *The Gentle Gunman*, John Coldstream, in his book *Dirk Bogarde. The Authorised Biography* (Weidenfeld & Nicolson, London, 2004), did offer two examples of how the feud was perpetuated during filming of *The Singer Not the Song*, with unhappy repercussions for Roy Ward Baker and the rest of the crew. The first concerned a remark uttered on set by one of the film's carpenters ('Of course it's Johnnie Mills who's going to walk off with this picture') that was overheard by Bogarde and incensed him. The other involved the fourteen-year-old son of Bogarde's male partner, who had been hanging out on location, drinking brandy and smoking. Mills was asked about this by the boy's mother and reassured her that it was just a case of 'boys being boys'. The woman then reported to Bogarde what Mills had told her. In Bogarde's opinion, Mills had 'sneaked' on him and he never forgave him for this piece of perceived treachery.
37. B. MacFarlane, *An Autobiography of British Cinema*, Methuen, London, 1997.
38. R. Ward Baker, *The Director's Cut*, Reynolds & Hearn, London, 2000.
39. *Daily Telegraph*, 7 January 1961.
40. *The Singer Not the Song* was in fact filmed in southern Spain.

41. *Monthly Film Bulletin*, February 1961.
42. *Evening Standard*, 5 January 1961.
43. *The Times*, 6 January 1961.
44. R. Ward Baker, *The Director's Cut*, Reynolds & Hearn, London, 2000.
45. Unpublished memoir by Yovanka Balchin (undated but written in 2008).
46. The three other writers who received a screenwriting credit were Christopher Fry, Ivo Perilli and Diego Fabbri.
47. *Monthly Film Bulletin*, June 1962.
48. L. Halliwell, *Halliwell's Film Guide* (edited by J. Walker), 8th edition, HarperCollins*Publishers*, London, 1991.
49. *Monthly Film Bulletin*, June 1962.
50. 'I Don't Want To Be A Literary Gent says Nigel Balchin', *Books and Bookmen*, 1962;7(4):9–11.
51. Elizabeth Jane Howard, Interview with author, 26 September 2007.

Chapter 21

1. 'What They Did to Me in Hollywood', *Daily Mail*, 18 January 1962.
2. Yovanka Balchin, Interview with author, 24 April 2007.
3. 'I Don't Want To Be A Literary Gent says Nigel Balchin', *Books and Bookmen*, 1962;7(4):9–11.
4. Yovanka Balchin, Interview with author, 24 April 2007.
5. Unpublished memoir by Yovanka Balchin (undated but written in 2008).
6. 'The Return of Nigel Balchin', *Sunday Times*, 1 October 1961.
7. 'What They Did to Me in Hollywood', *Daily Mail*, 18 January 1962.
8. Letter from Balchin to Yovanka dated 1 December 1961 and in the possession of Yovanka Balchin.
9. Yovanka Balchin, Interview with author, 24 April 2007.
10. Letter from Balchin to Yovanka dated 1 December 1961 and in the possession of Yovanka Balchin.
11. Yovanka Balchin, Interview with author, 24 April 2007.
12. 'Coming Home', *Guardian*, 23 October 1961.
13. J. Hopkins, *Michael Ayrton: A Biography*, Andre Deutsch, London, 1994.
14. *Sunday Telegraph*, 21 January 1962.
15. Yovanka Balchin, Interview with author, 24 April 2007.
16. *Sunday Telegraph*, 21 January 1962.
17. 'I Don't Want To Be A Literary Gent says Nigel Balchin', *Books and Bookmen*, 1962;7(4):9–11.
18. *Sunday Telegraph*, 21 January 1962.
19. *Guardian*, 19 January 1962.
20. *Sunday Times*, 21 January 1962.
21. *The Times Literary Supplement*, 26 January 1962.
22. 'I Don't Want To Be A Literary Gent says Nigel Balchin', *Books and Bookmen*, 1962;7(4):9–11.
23. *Radio Times*, 7 June 1962.
24. *Observer*, 17 June 1962.
25. *Sunday Telegraph*, 17 June 1962.
26. *Observer*, 17 June 1962.

27.   *Daily Telegraph*, 15 June 1962.
28.   Yovanka Balchin, Interview with author, 24 April 2007.
29.   'The happy ending to Nigel Balchin's drama', *Daily Express*, 7 January 1963.
30.   It is not known whether Balchin was working on 1966's *In the Absence of Mrs Petersen*, the next novel of his to be published, or something entirely different.
31.   'Nigel Balchin Saves Daughter', *Sunday Express*, 6 January 1963.
32.   Tragically, Cassandra died of cancer in 2012 having only just turned fifty.
33.   'The happy ending to Nigel Balchin's drama', *Daily Express*, 7 January 1963.

Chapter 22

1.   'The world wanderer settles for a farm', *Daily Sketch*, 21 November 1962.
2.   Unpublished memoir by Yovanka Balchin (undated but written in 2008).
3.   Cassandra Balchin, Interview with author, 30 December 2006.
4.   Unpublished memoir by Yovanka Balchin (undated but written in 2008).
5.   N. Balchin, 'Rim of the Plain', *Sunday Times*, 9 August 1964.
6.   Balchin's childhood home, Holly Cottage in West Lavington High Street, was a thatched cottage situated across the road from a pub.
7.   This quotation is taken from the entry for 'The Knowledge Explosion' (*Horizon*, BBC Television, 21 September 1964) in the television programmes catalogue held at the BBC Written Archives Centre, Caversham, UK.
8.   N. Balchin, C. S. Forester, E. Linklater & C. Sykes, *Fatal Fascination. A Choice of Crime*, Hutchinson, London, 1964.
9.   All four contributors were clients of A. D. Peters.
10.   'Did You Hear That?', *Listener*, 14 December 1961.
11.   'Coming Home', *Guardian*, 23 October 1961.
12.   N. Balchin, 'Rim of the Plain', *Sunday Times*, 9 August 1964.
13.   Letter from N. G. Luker to C. A. Siepmann, 16 December 1938. BBC Written Archives Centre, Caversham, UK.
14.   As many of the items in the British Film Institute's Nigel Balchin Collection are undated, it is not possible to establish for certain when they were written. However, those that have Balchin's address on them can usually be tentatively dated to within a couple of years.
15.   N. Balchin, 'Notes for "Nicholas Hurst"', Nigel Balchin Collection, British Film Institute, London.
16.   In televisual terms, Balchin was perhaps just a few years ahead of his time. His idea can in some ways be seen as simply a less surreal variant of the influential late-1960s Independent Television show *The Prisoner*, in which Patrick McGoohan as renegade British secret service agent 'Number Six' was placed in an array of different settings from week to week, with little explanation as to why.
17.   The quotations in this paragraph and the following one are taken from files on Balchin held by the BBC Written Archives Centre, Caversham, UK.
18.   *Guardian*, 2 March 1965.
19.   *Daily Telegraph*, 2 March 1965.
20.   N. Balchin, 'Children are a Waste of Time', *Saturday Evening Post*, 9 October 1965.

21. N. Balchin, 'Must we sacrifice our lives for our children?', *Sunday Express*, 28 November 1965.
22. N. Balchin, 'Children are a Waste of Time', *Saturday Evening Post*, 9 October 1965.
23. C. Connolly, *Enemies of Promise*, Routledge, London, 1938.
24. N. Balchin, 'Children are a Waste of Time', *Saturday Evening Post*, 9 October 1965.
25. 'Nigel Balchin's scalpel on love and marriage', *Daily Express*, 2 June 1966.
26. This information is derived from the following source: 'The Authors and Their Books', Introduction to the Reader's Digest Condensed Books edition of *In the Absence of Mrs Petersen*, Reader's Digest Association, London, Sydney and Cape Town, 1967.
27. Yovanka Balchin, Interview with author, 24 April 2007.
28. 'Nigel Balchin's scalpel on love and marriage', *Daily Express*, 2 June 1966.
29. *The Times Literary Supplement*, 30 June 1966.
30. *Sunday Times*, 26 June 1966.
31. *The Times*, 7 July 1966.
32. *Observer*, 26 June 1966.
33. *Listener*, 30 June 1966.
34. 'Nigel Balchin's scalpel on love and marriage', *Daily Express*, 2 June 1966.

Chapter 23

1. 'Nigel Balchin's scalpel on love and marriage', *Daily Express*, 2 June 1966.
2. F. Raphael, *Sunday Times*, 26 June 1966.
3. 'Nigel Balchin's scalpel on love and marriage', *Daily Express*, 2 June 1966.
4. Gemini was an equipment-testing precursor of the Apollo programme. Gemini X was crewed by John Young (later the ninth man to land on the moon as a member of the Apollo 16 mission) and Michael Collins (the astronaut who orbited the moon during the first moon-landing Apollo mission, Apollo 11).
5. Obituary for Armstrong published in the *Daily Telegraph*, 27 August 2012.
6. Yovanka Balchin, Interview with author, 24 April 2007.
7. 'Dull on the Moon', *Evening Standard*, 12 October 1967.
8. *New York Times*, 14 July 1968.
9. M. Hanlon, 'One Giant Leap Into the Dark', *Daily Telegraph*, 27 August 2012.
10. *In the Shadow of the Moon*, Channel 4 DVD, 2008.
11. *Sunday Telegraph*, 1 October 1967.
12. *Observer*, 1 October 1967.
13. 'I Don't Want To Be A Literary Gent says Nigel Balchin', *Books and Bookmen*, 1962;7(4):9–11.
14. *Observer*, 1 October 1967.
15. *The Times Literary Supplement*, 2 November 1967.
16. *Sunday Telegraph*, 1 October 1967.
17. Anon., 'Writers Who Mean to be Read', *Guardian*, 18 May 1970.
18. The information in this paragraph is derived from the following booklet: K. W. Glass, *A Short History of Glemsford*, 1962. Available at www.foxearth.org.

uk/GlemsfordGlass.html

19. Unpublished memoir by Yovanka Balchin (undated but written in 2008).
20. Charles Balchin, Personal communication to author (2008).
21. 'Famous writer at the sign of the Greyhound', *East Anglian Daily Times*, 4 February 1969.
22. Unpublished memoir by Yovanka Balchin (undated but written in 2008).
23. Yovanka Balchin, Interview with author, 24 April 2007.
24. This information is derived from the jacket of the World Books edition of *Sundry Creditors* published by the Reprint Society, London, 1954.
25. Unpublished memoir by Yovanka Balchin (undated but written in 2008).
26. Yovanka Balchin, Interview with author, 9 December 2009.
27. Files on Balchin held by the BBC Written Archives Centre, Caversham, UK.
28. 'Famous writer at the sign of the Greyhound', *East Anglian Daily Times*, 4 February 1969.
29. V. Glendinning, *Leonard Woolf*, Simon & Schuster, London, 2006.
30. *Weekend Woman's Hour*.
31. Files on Balchin held by the BBC Written Archives Centre, Caversham, UK.
32. Yovanka Balchin, Interview with author, 24 April 2007.
33. It is not known what form of ill health Balchin had been suffering from.
34. 'Faraway school for Miss Balchin (aged six)', *Daily Mail*, 25 October 1968.
35. Elizabeth Jane Howard, Interview with author, 26 September 2007.

Chapter 24

1. Yovanka Balchin, Interview with author, 24 April 2007.
2. P. Rowland, 'Balchin, Nigel Marlin (1908–1970)', *Oxford Dictionary of National Biography*, Oxford University Press, Oxford, UK, 2004.
3. Yovanka Balchin, Interview with author, 24 April 2007.
4. Elizabeth Jane Howard, Interview with author, 26 September 2007.
5. Unpublished memoir by Yovanka Balchin (undated but written in 2008).
6. Letter from Yovanka Balchin to author, 15 August 2007.
7. Unpublished memoir by Yovanka Balchin (undated but written in 2008).
8. Cassandra Balchin, Interview with author, 30 December 2006.
9. Unpublished memoir by Yovanka Balchin (undated but written in 2008).
10. Freja Gregory, Interview with author, 14 January 2007.
11. Unpublished memoir by Yovanka Balchin (undated but written in 2008).
12. Blanche Marvin, Interview with author, 22 September 2006.
13. Elizabeth Jane Howard, Interview with author, 26 September 2007.
14. The Oxford English Dictionary offers the following definition of the word grog-blossom: 'a redness or pimple on the nose caused by excessive drinking'.
15. Yovanka Balchin, Interview with author, 24 April 2007.
16. Ibid.
17. The Priory (a mental health hospital in south-west London) had in fact opened its doors as far back as 1872 but did not become established as a leading centre for the treatment of celebrities with drink problems until the 1980s. According to Penelope Leach, her father was a patient there for a brief period.
18. Unpublished memoir by Yovanka Balchin (undated but written in 2008).
19. Ibid.

Chapter 25

1. 'The Authors and Their Books', Introduction to the Reader's Digest Condensed Books edition of *In the Absence of Mrs Petersen*, Reader's Digest Association, London, Sydney and Cape Town, 1967.
2. Yovanka Balchin, Interview with author, 9 December 2009.
3. Unpublished memoir by Yovanka Balchin (undated but written in 2008).
4. Yovanka Balchin, Interview with author, 9 December 2009.
5. *Daily Telegraph*, 14 July 1969.
6. 'I Don't Want To Be A Literary Gent says Nigel Balchin', *Books and Bookmen*, 1962;7(4):9–11.
7. *Guardian*, 14 July 1969.
8. *Daily Telegraph*, 14 July 1969.
9. Yovanka Balchin, Interview with author, 24 April 2007.
10. Unless stated otherwise, the information in this chapter about the Famous Writers School and its English offshoot is derived from the following book: N. Beauman, *The Other Elizabeth Taylor*, Persephone Books, London, 2009.
11. Email from Yovanka Balchin to author, 19 June 2009.
12. Ibid.
13. R. Gordon, *Fifty Years a Fisherman. Memoirs of an Angling Man*, Harrap, London, 1985.
14. Ibid.
15. Yovanka Balchin, Interview with author, 24 April 2007.
16. 'Heart attack kills Nigel Balchin', *Daily Mail*, 18 May 1970.
17. Yovanka Balchin, Interview with author, 24 April 2007.
18. J. Mitford, 'Let Us Now Appraise Famous Writers', *Atlantic Monthly*, July 1970.
19. R. Gordon, *Fifty Years a Fisherman. Memoirs of an Angling Man*, Harrap, London, 1985.
20. Ibid.
21. Email from Yovanka Balchin to author, 19 June 2009.
22. Yovanka Balchin, Interview with author, 24 April 2007.
23. Yovanka Balchin, Personal communication to author (2006).
24. Yovanka Balchin, Interview with author, 24 April 2007.
25. Charles Balchin, Personal communication to author (2008).
26. Yovanka Balchin, Interview with author, 24 April 2007.
27. Email from Yovanka Balchin to author, 19 June 2009.
28. The recto of Balchin's memorial was purposely left blank by Yovanka. Although she purchased a double plot in the cemetery so that she could be buried alongside her husband she has since had second thoughts, and now intends that her ashes should be scattered from the Rialto Bridge, reflecting the fact that she and Balchin had spent some of their happiest times together in Venice.
29. 'Balchin's money', *Evening Standard*, 22 October 1970.
30. Elizabeth Jane Howard, Interview with author, 26 September 2007.
31. The values of these three estates are taken from the three men's entries in the *Oxford Dictionary of National Biography*, Oxford University Press, Oxford,

UK, 2004.

32. Anon., 'Mr Nigel Balchin', *Guardian*, 18 May 1970.
33. *The Times Literary Supplement*, 30 June 1966.
34. Anon., 'Mr Nigel Balchin', *Guardian*, 18 May 1970.
35. C. James, 'Prisoners of clarity—1. Nigel Balchin', *The New Review*, 1974;1(1):64–72. Available at www.clivejames.com/pieces/hercules/Balchin
36. 'Keeping up with Balchin', *Saturday Evening Post*, 8 July 1950.
37. R. Rendell, 'In the Second-hand Bookshops', *Sunday Telegraph*, 21 January 1990.
38. *Nigel Balchin: The Small Back-Room Boy*, BBC Radio 4, 24 April 2008.
39. *Guardian*, 18 November 2005.
40. *Independent on Sunday*, 20 November 2005.
41. *Daily Telegraph*, 18 November 2005.
42. *Daily Mail*, 18 November 2005.
43. C. James, 'Prisoners of clarity—1. Nigel Balchin', *The New Review*, 1974;1(1):64–72. Available at www.clivejames.com/pieces/hercules/Balchin

Afterword

1. C. James, 'Prisoners of clarity—1. Nigel Balchin', *The New Review*, 1974;1(1):64–72. Available at www.clivejames.com/pieces/hercules/Balchin
2. *Front Row*, BBC Radio 4, 15 November 2005.
3. 'What they did to me in Hollywood', *Daily Mail*, 18 January 1962.
4. A. Sinclair, *War Like a Wasp. The Lost Decade of the 'Forties*, Hamish Hamilton, London, 1989.
5. C. James, 'Prisoners of clarity—1. Nigel Balchin', *The New Review*, 1974;1(1):64–72. Available at www.clivejames.com/pieces/hercules/Balchin

Index

Balchin's works can be found in the index both as individual entries and listed at the end of the entry for Balchin, Nigel Marlin. Page numbers in bold indicate plot summaries of the novels. The letters n and pl. indicate notes and photographic plates, respectively. The abbreviation NMB is used in places to refer to Nigel Balchin.

Active Service (revue, date unknown) 189

Adam, Lieutenant-General Sir Ronald 133

Aero chocolate 85–86

The Aeroplane magazine 102–4

agents *see* Higham, David; Moore, Leonard; Peters, A. D.; Watkins, Mike

Agriculture, Ministry of 31, 35, 47, 50–51

The Aircraft Builders. An Account of British Aircraft Production 1935–1945 (1947) 187–89

aircraft industry 187–89, 415–16n13

alcohol, in NMB's fiction 123, 370, 371

alcoholism, NMB's 14, 272, 298, 308–9, 324, 354, 361, 366–71, 387–88, 431n17

Aldrin, Buzz 356

Alfred A. Knopf, Inc., publisher 223–24

Alison, Dorothy 265

Allen, Walter
    interview with 69–70, 167, 274–76, 283

    reviews by 204, 249

Allingham, Margery 123

Ambler, Eric 172–74, 349

America *see* American space programme; Famous Writers School (FWS); Hollywood

American space programme 351–53

'Among Friends' (short story) 91, 279, 281–83

The Anatomy of Villainy (1950) 208–10

Anglia Television 373–75

Angry Young Men movement 252, 388

Anstey, Edgar 135, 136, 138, 139, 140

Any Questions? (radio programme) 274, 280

Apollo space missions 356

Armstrong, Neil 352–53

army
    Directorate of Army Psychiatry 169–70
    Directorate of Biological Research (D.B.R.) 144–50
    Directorate of Selection of Personnel (D.S.P.) 133–41, 170
    NMB's enrolment 110–11, 118, pl.6, pl.8

Operation Backfire (V2 rocket testing) 172–74
Scientific Adviser to the Army Council (S.A.A.C.) 144, 147–50, 172–74
astronauts 351–53, 356
Atholl, Katharine Stewart-Murray, Duchess of 27–28
The Atlantic Monthly (American magazine) 379
Attenborough, Richard 216, 313
Awdry, Rev. W. 25–26, 31–32
Ayrton Gould, Barbara 227
Ayrton, Joan 227–28, 229
Ayrton, Michael pl.10
  and break up of NMB's marriage 13, 209, 225–29, 232–33, 236–37, 238, 239
  death 382, 386
  NMB's generosity of spirit towards 14
  influence on NMB's fiction 244–45
  later friendship with NMB 271, 361

Bacon, Francis 193
Baker, Richard 380
Baker, Roy Ward 315–17, 318
Balchin, Ada Elizabeth (née Curtis) (mother) 19, 29, 107
Balchin, Cassandra Marlin (daughter) 325, 334–35, 337, 364–65, 368, 387, 429n32
Balchin, Charles Zoran Marlin (son)
  birth 296–97
  early life 300, 304, 305, 307, 308, 310, 325, 337, pl.17
  later life and career 387
  recollections of NMB 360
  recollections of NMB's funeral 380
Balchin, Elisabeth Evelyn (née Walshe) (first wife)
  appearance 47, pl.7
  birth of first child, Prudence 67–68
  death 386
  employment: early career after Cambridge 93; wartime 111–12, 114, 141–43, 159, 411n20
  graduation 60
  marriage with NMB: meets NMB at Cambridge 47–50; courtship and marriage 56, 63–64; helps with NMB's work 88–89, 93, 408n6; affair with Darnton 125–28, 129–31, 132, pl.9; resentment builds at Leigh Barton 157–61; accompanies NMB to Venice 203; affair with Ayrton: marriage disintegrates 225–39; divorce 236, 367; maintains contact with NMB after divorce 270–71, 361
  and NMB's work: helps with *Income and Outcome* 88–89; works as NMB's secretary 93, 408n6; influence on NMB's female characters 164; advises not to throw novel away 167
  writing 160, 237, 386
Balchin, Freja Mary (daughter) 157, 233, 368, 386–87
Balchin, George Martin (grandfather) 18–19
Balchin, Monica Coralie (sister) 19, 29, 30, 107, 415n13
Balchin, Nigel Marlin 11–15, 387–89, pl.1, pl.18
  alcoholism 14, 272, 298, 308–9, 324, 354, 361, 366–71, 387–88, 431n17

appearance 19–20, 28–29, 36, 138, 179, 323–24, 339–40, 350, 369, pl.1, pl.18

army service: enrolment 110–11, 118, pl.6, pl.8; Directorate of Selection of Personnel (D.S.P.) 133–41, 170; Directorate of Biological Research (D.B.R.) 144–50; Scientific Adviser to the Army Council (S.A.A.C.) 144, 147–50, 172–74; promotion to brigadier 149–50, 166, 175; Operation Backfire (V2 rocket testing) 172–74; demobilization 172, 174–75

awards and nominations 221, 265, 277, 303, 426n37

birth and childhood 18, 19–25, 29–31, 429n6, pl.2

characteristics: anti-child sentiment 191, 238, 344–46; biblical knowledge 29; extravagance 296, 312, 326, 381; generosity of spirit 13–14; an individualist 109; insecurity after divorce 261–62, 269, 270, 326; intellectual abilities 138, 150; loneliness 70–73; love of the outdoors 22–24; loyalty and disloyalty 267–68, 270–71, 305; misogynistic streak 342–43, 349, 357, 363; pride and boastfulness 262–63; pride in own competence 243–44; quiet, studious, modest 28; a quitter of employment 109, 183; rationality 132, 207–8; reaction to criticism and rejection 369–70; reproduced in his novels 243–44, 348; self-confidence 138; self-righteousness 243–44; sense

of humour 45–46, 74–75, 84, 87–88; serious, rational, 'a bore to women' 132; shyness 262; speaking voice 27, 105, 107, 340–41; wit 141

death and burial 378, 380–81, 432n28

education at Dauntsey's School 25–29, 31–32, 41

education at Peterhouse, Cambridge 33–50, pl.3; academic studies 33–37, 41–42, 46–47, 50; admission process 29, 31; extra-curricular activities 40–41, 43–44, 45–46; friends and contemporaries 37–39, 43–45, 47–50; rooms and lodgings 39–40, 42–43; writing for, and editing, *The Sex* 45–46

employment as scientist: career summary 383; National Institute of Industrial Psychology (NIIP) 51, 53–63, 64, 66–67, 181–87; Rowntree's 55–59, 60–63, 76–80, 85–86, 108–9, 117–18, pl.5; creates Black Magic 60–63, pl.5; wartime 108–9, 110–11, 112–17; Ministry of Food 110–11, 113–17; Manufacturing Confectioners Alliance (MCA) 111, 112–13; post-war consultancy work for Rowntree's and JWT 177–78, 255; incentives to work and 'London Lecture' 180–87; considers returning to industrial psychology 323; *Horizon* documentary 338

family: background 18–19, 24–25, 29, 107–8; births of children

67–68, 105, 157, 296–97, 325; mother's funeral and subsequent distancing from family 107–8; relationship with his children 232–33, 235–36, 310, 337, 345, pl.17

friends: Michael Ayrton (*see* Ayrton, Michael); John and Roy Boulting 139–40, 159, 196–203, 282, 312, 314; cricket: 'Mr. Nigel Balchin's XI' 259; entertains Elizabeth Taylor at Villa di Tizzano 312; entertains Noël Coward at Leigh Barton 265; Elizabeth Jane Howard (*see* Howard, Elizabeth Jane); John Huston 304; Dorrie Jackson (later Stewart, then Stein) 48–50, 60, 72, 175, 280; Maurice Kendall 38; lack of 262–63; Major and Beryl Lester 272; Alexander MacKendrick 263–64, 265; James Mason 43–45, 94–95, 102, pl.4; on not putting them in novels 244; A. D. Peters 178, 234, 323, 369–70, 373, 380; socializing technique 179; Eric St Johnston 36, 74, 164; Eric Stein 72, 175, 280, 295; Alan Stewart 48–49, 53, 55, 60, 175; Eric Trist 170

health and illness: alcoholism 14, 272, 298, 308–9, 324, 354, 361, 366–71, 387–88, 431n17; final illness 378; ulcerated stomach 307, 321–22, 323–25; wartime breakdown 366

hobbies 14, 258–59; cine camera 309–10; music 29–30, 43–44, 158, 273; sport 26–27, 28, 40–41, 46, 51–52, 93, 158, 258–59 (see also *Fun and Games*); woodcarving 158, 309

homes: childhood 20–21, 429n6; Cambridge, student rooms and lodgings 39–40, 42–43; London lodgings with Winifred Raphael 59–60; Portsdown Road, Maida Vale, London 63–64, 67–68; Highpoint, Highgate, London 86; Robbery Bottom, Welwyn, Hertfordshire 105; wartime: London 108, 118, 142; wartime: North Wales 114; Leigh Barton, Kent 157–61, 228–29, 237, 243; Hamilton Terrace, St John's Wood, London 229; Oast Cottage, Sussex 234–36, 246–47, 259; Connaught Place, London 295–96; Florence 304, 305–6, 307–9; Tufton Place, Sussex 325–26, 334–35, 336; Regent's Park Road, London 336–37, 362; The Greyhound, Suffolk 359–61, 367–68; Marlborough Mansions, London 364–65, 375

interviews (*see* press interviews; radio: interview with Walter Allen)

legacy and reputation 387–89

marriage with Elisabeth Walshe: meets E. at Cambridge 47–50; courtship and marriage 56, 63–64; E. helps with NMB's work 88–89, 93, 408n6; E.'s affair with Darnton 125–28, 129–31, 132, pl.9; E.'s resentment builds at Leigh Barton 157–61; takes E. to Venice 203; E.'s affair with

Ayrton: marriage disintegrates
225–39; divorce 236, 367;
maintains contact with E. after
divorce 270–71, 361
marriage with Yovanka Tomich:
meets Y. and starts relationship
229–32, 261; marries Y.
246–47, 266–68; they soon
separate 269–73; Y.'s affair with
Milicevic 276; back together
and birth of Charles 276,
295–97; rift with Y. widens
299–301; moves with Y. to
Florence 28, 304–12, 318;
Y.'s affair with Dedijer 305–7;
NMB's health deteriorates
321–24; problems with the
marriage 324–25; return
to England: Tufton Place
325–26, 334–35, 336; birth
of Cassandra 336; back
in London: Regent's Park
Road 336–37, 361–62; life
in Suffolk: The Greyhound
359–61, 367–68; affair with
his secretary 362; return
to London: Marlborough
Mansions 364–65, 370–71; a
tranquil phase 375; final illness,
death and burial 378, 380–81
money: extravagance 296, 312,
326, 337, 381; financial legacy
381–82; insures his life 376,
378; problems 363–64, 368;
remuneration as a scientist
58, 63, 78, 86, 118, 177;
remuneration as a writer 69, 80,
83, 106, 181–82, 363–64; tax
301–2, 306
obituaries 285, 382–83
on himself: character sketch in
theatre programme 93; his

abilities as an employee 108;
his failure as a person 225;
his marriage breakdown 236,
237, 238, 239, 243–44; his
relationship with Yovanka 247,
266; his wartime work 116–17,
150; illness and dying 321, 323;
needing opportunity to think
273; the post-war period 329;
reading detective stories 374;
tax and financial responsibilities
301–2, 306; wanting to stay in
one place 336
on his writing: 'book-making'
208–9; combining work with
authorship 161, 178, 276,
332; his working routine 157,
248–49; his writing technique
72, 357; impact of war on
his novels 121–22; novelists'
knowledge of industry 250; the
pressure to produce more books
of the same type 192; reasons
for novel-writing 69–70, 152;
source of characters 244,
346; writer's creed 243, 372;
writing novels 69–70, 152,
154, 274–75, 283, 357; writing
screenplays 196
on other matters: children 191,
238, 344–46; grounds for
divorce 274; incentives to work
180, 184, 185, 187; marriage
and jealousy 161; psychological
warfare 174; rural life 361; the
war 109, 121–22, 152; women
132, 260, 261, 349
pseudonym 73, 88 (see also
*Business for Pleasure; Fun and
Games; How to Run a Bassoon
Factory*)
radio: adaptations 176–77, 221,

222, 419n31; appearances
29–30, 105–7, 176, 273–76,
280, 363; documentary on
NMB 383; interview with
Walter Allen 69–70, 167,
274–76, 283; unrealized
projects 68

relationships with women:
chauvinism 159–60; 'girl
hunting' as teenager 30;
misogyny in his writing
342–43, 349, 357, 363;
predilection for partner-
swapping 227, 272; sense of
inadequacy 132, 260–62

Savile Club membership 14,
178–79, 196–97, 225–26, 234,
263, 309

sex and sexuality: with Elisabeth
126, 237–38; in his novels 330,
357; interest in psychology of
36–37, 186, 296; unsure of
himself 261–62; with Yovanka
301

speaking engagements 183–87,
222–23

speaking voice 27, 105, 107,
340–41

television: adaptations
221–22, 277, 343–44, 419n31;
appearances 248–49, 338,
339–41; screenplays 278,
332–34, 373–75; unrealized
projects 341–43, 362, 372

travel pl.16; Famous Writers School
meetings 377–78; 'Hollywood
years' globetrotting 299–300,
302, 304–5, 308; Italy with
Elisabeth 203; Italy with
Elisabeth and Ayrton 228,
241; Italy with Yovanka 28,
231, 304–6, 307–12, 321–22,

432n28; researching US space
programme 351–53

writing (see also works below):
autobiographical aspects
191, 241–44, 346–49,
351–53, 371; deathbed scenes
65–66; disabled characters 152,
264–65, 294–95, 382; Famous
Writers School 376–78, 379;
female characters: improvement
at depicting 251, 286, 328–29;
female characters: weakness
at depicting 81, 94 200,
261, 283, 288, 293, 357;
historical writing 203–10;
humorous writing 45–46,
74–75, 83–84, 87–88, 98–104,
213; journalism 42, 64, 67,
101–5, 147–48, 149, 194–95;
love triangle plots 65–66,
81, 131–32, 163–64, 279,
317, 327; runs out of ideas
for writing 365; sources for
characters 127–31, 164, 244,
285–86, 328, 346, 348–49;
stage plays 91–98, 194; style
67, 72, 120–21, 153–54, 155,
213, 250–51; themes in novels
11–12, 70, 121, 153; treatment
of minor characters 164–65,
213; work as material for
writing 70, 73–74, 332–33;
writing career summary 11–13

works (listed alphabetically; for listing by
genre and date, see pages 395–399)
Active Service (revue, date
unknown) 189
The Aircraft Builders. An Account
of British Aircraft Production
1935–1945 (1947) 187–89
'Among Friends' (short story) 91,
279, 281–83

The Anatomy of Villainy (1950)
208–10

Barabbas (screenplay, 1962) 318–19

'Battle Study. Some Aspects of
Psychological Warfare' (report)
174

Better Dead (television screenplay,
1969) 373–75

The Blue Angel (screenplay, 1959) 310

The Borgia Testament (1948)
203–8, **205,** 210

'Burnt Njal' (see *Fatal Fascination*)

Business for Pleasure (1935) 75, 76,
83–84

Carnival in Venice (screenplay,
unrealized, 1948) 203

Carted Stag (stage play,
unperformed, date unknown)
91, 282

'Children are a Waste of Time'
(essay, 1965) 344–46

Circle of Deception (screenplay,
1961) 302–3

'The Compleat Modern' (*Punch,*
1933) 64

Darkness Falls from the Air (1942)
110, 118–24, **119,** 125, 127–29,
131–32, 153, 222, 226, 370,
371, 409n10, 410n7, 410n26

'Dover Incident' (short story, 1956)
278, 423n19

The Fall of the Sparrow (1955) 39,
147, 165, 283–90, **289,** 329

The Fall of the Sparrow (television
adaptation, 1965) 343

Fame is the Spur (screenplay, 1947)
197–98

Fatal Fascination: A Choice of Crime
(1964; with Forester, Linklater
and Sykes) 176, 210, 339

*Fun and Games. How to Win at
Almost Anything* (1936) 87–88

The Hatchet Man (television
screenplay, 1962) 333–34

Heir and Heiress (see *Sundry
Creditors*)

The Highway Code (stage play,
unperformed, date unknown)
91, 98

*How to Run a Bassoon Factory; or
Business Explained* (1934) 32,
60, 61, 73–76

In the Absence of Mrs Petersen
(1966) 165, 270, 320, 346–50,
347

*Income and Outcome. A Study of
Personal Finance* (1936) 72,
88–90, 103, 105–6, 376

'An Inventory of Inventors'
(*Lilliput,* 1944) 148

Kings of Infinite Space (1967)
351–59, **355**

The Language of Sex (unfinished)
37

*Last Recollections of My Uncle
Charles* (short stories, 1954) 18,
91, 209, 278–81, 344

The Leader of the House (television
screenplay, 1955) 278

Lennie's Point of View (stage play,
unperformed, date unknown)
342–43

Lightbody on Liberty (1936)
98–101, **99,** 120

"Little Fleas Have Lesser Fleas…"
(*Punch,* 1936) 102

Lord, I Was Afraid (1947) 29,
130–31, 189–94, 210, 381

Malta Story (screenplay, 1952) 265

The Man Who Never Was
(screenplay, 1956) 66, 291–94,
303, 425n11, pl.14

Mandy (screenplay, 1952) 263–65

Mind of Nicholas Hurst

(unfinished, 1949) 224,
341–42

Mine Own Executioner (1945)
17–18, 33–34, 35, 129–30,
161–70, **162,** 176–77, 228, 370

Mine Own Executioner (screenplay,
1947) 198–203, pl.12

Mine Own Executioner (television
adaptation, 1959) 221–22

Miserable Sinners (stage play, 1937)
94–96

'Mrs Sludge' (short story) 209

'Nicholas Hurst project' 224,
341–42

No Sky (1934) 65, 69–73, **71,** 121

'Patience' (short story) 91

Peace in Our Time (stage play,
1936) 93–94

Pobottle articles (*The Aeroplane,*
1936–40) 102–4

Power (stage play, 1935) 91–93

Profit and Loss (stage play, 1938) 96

'The Psychological Difficulties of
the Institute's Work' (journal
article, 1933) 67

'Publicity Pays' (short story, 1933) 65

Punch magazine articles 42, 64, 73,
84, 101–2

The Risk (see *Suspect*)

'The Salamander' (short story,
1945) 278, 423n20

'Satisfactions in Work' (lecture
for NIIP, 'London Lecture')
183–87

'Scientists in a Hurry' (*Lilliput,*
1947) 149

Seen Dimly Before Dawn (1962)
194, 321–22, 323, 326–32, **331**

'The Service of Miss Eyles' (short
story, 1935) 83

Simple Life (1935) 22–23, **79,**
80–83, 121, 327

The Singer Not the Song (screenplay,
1961) 315–18, 427n36, 427n40

The Small Back Room (1943)
23–24, 144, 145, 148–49,
150–56, **151,** 164, 370, 382,
413n23; radio and television
adaptations 221–22, 419n31

The Small Back Room (Powell
and Pressburger film, 1949)
216–21, pl.13

A Sort of Traitors (1949) 153,
211–16, **212,** 222 (see also
Suspect)

Square Deal (stage play,
unperformed, date unknown)
91

Sundry Creditors (1953) 57–58,
185–86, 211–13, 249–58,
253, 370

Suspect (screenplay, 1960) 216,
312–14

'That Feller Oates' (short story,
1933) 65–66

Twenty-Three Paces to Baker Street
(screenplay, 1956) 294–95

A Way Through the Wood (1951)
21, 29, 37, 91, 131, 160, 202,
222, 240–46, **242,** 370 (see
also *Separate Lies* (Fellowes);
Waiting for Gillian (Millar))

Balchin, Prudence Ann (daughter)
67–68, 86, 111, 114, 232–33, 386

Balchin, William Edwin (father) 19,
23, 24–25, 29, 107, 160

Balchin, William Edwin ('Bill')
(brother) 19, 24–25, 29, 30, 107,
415–16n13

Balchin, Yovanka Zorana (née
Tomich) (second wife)
background, family and early life
27, 229–30, 270, pl.11
marriage with NMB: meets NMB

and starts relationship 229–32, 261; marries NMB 246–47, 266–68; they soon separate 269–73; affair with Milicevic 276; back together and birth of Charles 276, 295–97; rift with NMB widens 299–301; with NMB in Florence 28, 304–12, 318; affair with Dedijer 305–7; NMB's health deteriorates 321–24; problems with the marriage 324–25; return to England: Tufton Place 325–26, 334–35, 336; birth of Cassandra 336; back in London: Regent's Park Road 336–37, 361–62; life in Suffolk: The Greyhound 359–61, 367–68; NMB's affair with his secretary 362; return to London: Marlborough Mansions 364–65, 370–71; a tranquil phase 375; NMB's final illness, death and burial 378, 380–81, 432n28
and NMB's work: influence on characters 285–86, 328, 348–49; influence on plots 346; interprets for NMB and de Laurentiis 318
recollections of NMB: alcoholism 366, 367, 368, 369–71; boastfulness 263; his script for *Cleopatra* 311; did not enjoy writing *Kings of Infinite Space* 354; did not retire 372; dislike of Hollywood 298; should have been a don 275; Dorrie Jackson in love with him 48; expense of bathroom for Elizabeth Taylor 312; financial problems 364; and the Famous Writers School 376, 379; great picker-upper of people 126; illness 321, 324; lack of confidence 326; lack of friends 262; his love for her 375; love of fruit trees 158; making wrong choice of her 269; proud of *Lord, I Was Afraid* 193, 381; reaction to criticism and rejection 290, 369–70; religion 29; Savile Club 179; sex with him 301; sexual interest 37, 296; writing: invention not his thing 373
sells jewellery to pay NMB's debts 364
widowhood and retirement 386
witnesses eclipse of the sun 321
Ballard, J. G. 194
Banks, Leslie 218
Bannen, Ian 313
Barabbas (screenplay, 1962) 318–19
The Barbarian and the Geisha (film, John Huston) 304–5
Barber, Nicholas 385
Barker, Ronald 277
Bartlett, F. C. (Frederic) 34–35, 51, 134, 170, 182–83
'Battle Study. Some Aspects of Psychological Warfare' (report) 174
BBC 68, 83, 105–7, 176–77, 221–22, 341–43, 362–63, 372, 383
Beauman, Nicola 377, 379
Bechhofer Roberts, C. E. 82–83
Beckett, Samuel 52
Bell, Joan 126
Betjeman, John 165, 240, 257
Better Dead (television screenplay, 1969) 373–75
Biswell, Andrew 194
Black Magic chocolates 60–63, 112, pl.5
The Blue Angel (screenplay, 1959) 310

Bogarde, Dirk 315, 316–17, 427n36
Books and Bookmen magazine,
    interview with NMB 322, 332–33
Bookseller magazine 258
Bookstand (television programme) 339
Boots Booklovers Library 81–82
The Borgia Testament (1948) 203–8,
    205, 210
Boulting brothers (John and Roy)
    139–40, 159, 196–203, 282, 312,
    314
Bowen, Elizabeth 123, 207, 281, 286
Boyd, Stephen 292
Bradfields, Toppesfield, Essex 233,
    271, 361
Bradshaw, Peter 385
Brandt, Carol 223
Braund, Stuart (brother-in-law)
    415–16n13
British Association for the
    Advancement of Science 187
British Film Academy awards 221,
    265, 303, 426n37
Britton, Tony 313
Brooks, Jeremy 330
Brophy, John 82
Brown & Polson Ltd. 53
Brown, Ivor 277
Browne-Wilkinson, Virginia 363
Bruce Lockhart, Freda 198, 202, 219,
    220
Buchanan, Jack 283
Buckinghamshire 126, 410n7
Burgess, Anthony 194, 330–32, 350
'Burnt Njal' see *Fatal Fascination*
Burton, Richard 316
Bushell, Anthony 218
Business for Pleasure (1935) 75, 76,
    83–84
Butler, George 61
Byron, Kathleen 219–20

Cadbury, John 112–13
Cadbury's 60–61, 77, 112–14
Calvert, Phyllis 265
Cambridge 29, 31, 33–50, 56, 223
Cambridge University Farm 50
Cannon, Esma 96
Carnival in Venice (screenplay,
    unrealized, 1948) 203
Carted Stag (stage play, unperformed,
    date unknown) 91, 282
characters in NMB's fiction
    disabled 152, 264–65, 294–95,
        382
    female, improvement at depicting
        251, 286, 328–29
    female, weakness at depicting 81,
        94, 200, 261, 283, 288, 293,
        357
    minor, treatment of 164–65, 213
    sources 127–31, 164, 244, 285–86,
        328, 346, 348–49
Charques, Richard 164
'Children are a Waste of Time' (essay,
    1965) 344–46
chocolate packaging 62–63
chocolate packing 56–57
Christy & Moore, literary agency
    68, 98
church 29
Circle of Deception (screenplay, 1961)
    302–3
Clayton, Sylvia 374, 375
Cleopatra (film) 310–12, 316
Collins, Michael 356, 430n4
Collins, publisher *see* William Collins,
    publisher
Colwyn Bay, North Wales 114
'The Compleat Modern' (*Punch,*
    1933) 64
confectionery industry rationalization
    112–17
Connell, John 286

Connolly, Cyril 82, 345
Cook, Robin 357, 358–59
Coward, Noël
    guest at Leigh Barton 159
    Private Lives 300
Cox, Anthony Berkeley ('Francis Iles')
    70, 73, 82
Cox, John, contemporary at
    Dauntsey's 28
Crew, Brigadier F. A. E. 145
cricket 26–27, 41, 51–52, 258–59
Croft-Cooke, Rupert 215
Croydon Advertiser and Surrey County
    Reporter reviews 92, 94
Croydon Times and Surrey County Mail
    reviews 92
Crozier, Mary 343
Curtis, Anthony 328, 329, 330
Cusack, Cyril 218–19
Cushing, Peter 313

Daily Dispatch reviews 280–81
Daily Express
    interview with NMB 346, 349,
        350, 351
    reviews 257, 287–90
Daily Herald reviews 165, 313
Daily Mail
    award for best drama 277
    interview with NMB 298–99,
        310–11, 322, 323
    item on Cassandra's schooling 364
    item on NMB's death 378
    reviews: Peter Quennell 189,
        191–92, 206, 245, 286;
        Christopher Tookey 385
Daily Sketch 336
Daily Telegraph
    report of 'No More Army Misfits'
        133
    reviews: John Betjeman 240, 257;
        Sylvia Clayton 374, 375;

W. A. Darlington 96;
    Campbell Dixon 201–2;
    Patrick Gibbs 312; Francis Iles
    70, 73, 82; Pamela Hansford
    Johnson 211, 214, 215; Lyn
    Lockwood 334, 343; Harold
    Nicolson 189–90, 191; Tim
    Robey 385; Eric Shorter
    317–18; Charles Spencer 300;
    'K. Y.' 221
A Dance to the Music of Time (Anthony
    Powell) 284
Dark, Noah, lamp-lighter in Potterne 21
Darkness Falls from the Air (1942)
    110, 118–24, **119**, 125, 127–29,
    131–32, 153, 222, 226, 370, 371,
    409n10, 410n7, 410n26
Darlington, W. A. 96
Darnton, Christian 125–28, 129–31,
    386, pl.9
Dauntsey Agricultural School 25–29,
    31–32, 41
Davenport, John 38, 286–87
D.B.R. (Directorate of Biological
    Research) 144–50
de Laurentiis, Dino 318
deathbed scenes 65–66
Dedijer, Steven 305–7
Dehn, Paul 218
Denham, Maurice 96
Dent, Alan 313
Dent, John Yerbury 130
Desert Island Discs (radio programme)
    29–30, 233, 273
detective fiction 373–75
Directorate of Army Psychiatry
    169–70
Directorate of Biological Research
    (D.B.R.) 144–50
Directorate of Selection of Personnel
    (D.S.P.) 133–41, 170
disabled characters in novels and films

152, 264–65, 294–95, 382
Dixon, Campbell 201–2, 292, 293
Donne, John 161
'Dover Incident' (short story, 1956)
    278, 423n19
Doyle, Arthur Conan 52
D.S.P. (Directorate of Selection of
    Personnel) 133–41, 170
Dyer, Peter John 315, 318–19

Ealing Studios 220, 263–64
East Anglian Daily Times 362–63
eclipse of the sun 321
Economist reviews 75
Egan, Beresford 102–3
employment and psychology *see*
    National Institute of Industrial
    Psychology (NIIP); psychology
Empson, William 38
Era reviews 95
Erskine Lindop, Audrey: *The Singer
    Not the Song* 315, 316
eternal triangle *see* love triangle plots
Evening News
    news item 295
    reviews 286
Evening Standard
    'Balchin's money' article 381
    'Balchin's return' article 311, 322
    reviews 206, 245, 256, 318
Everett, Rupert 384

Fairchild, William 266
The Fall of the Sparrow (1955) 39, 147,
    165, 283–90, **289**, 329
The Fall of the Sparrow (television
    adaptation, 1965) 343
Fame is the Spur (screenplay, 1947)
    197–98
Famous Writers School (FWS)
    376–79
Fane, Vernon 154

Farrar, David 217, 219, 220, pl.13
Fatal Fascination: A Choice of Crime
    (1964; with Forester, Linklater and
    Sykes) 176, 210, 339
Fellowes, Julian: *Separate Lies* 15,
    383–85, pl.15
female characters
    NMB's improvement at depicting
        251, 286, 328–29
    NMB's weakness at depicting 81,
        94, 200, 261, 283, 288, 293,
        357
filming of gun drills 146
filming of V2 rocket tests 172–74
films
    adaptations of NMB's work
        165–66, 216–21, 312–14,
        383–85, pl.12, pl.13, pl.15
    screenwriting 196–203, 263–66,
        282, 298–99, 302–3, 304–5,
        310–14, 315–20
Financial Times reviews 75
Fitzgerald, Walter 201
Florence, Italy 28, 231, 304, 307–12,
    321–22
Food Manufacturers' Federation 112
Food, Ministry of 110–11, 112–17,
    409n12
Forbes, Bryan 219
Fox *see* Twentieth Century Fox
Frisby, Clifford 55
Fryer, Frederick 108–9
fugue, NMB's use of term 130, 411n18
Fuller, Roy 349, 382
*Fun and Games. How to Win at Almost
    Anything* (1936) 87–88

George, Daniel 166
Gerstley, James, contemporary at
    Peterhouse 42–43
Gestetner, Sigmund 86
Gibbs, Patrick 312

Gielgud, Val, NMB writing to 177
golf 46, 158
Gordon, Richard 377, 379
Gough, Michael 218
Gould, Gerald 100–101, 227
Graham, Virginia 219
Grahame, Gloria 292, 293
Grant, Elspeth 283, 313
Gray, Dulcie 199, 200
Green, Charles Reginald 84
Gregory, Philippa 387
Gregson, John 221
The Greyhound, Glemsford, Suffolk
    359–61, 367–68
Griffin, Josephine 293
Guardian (formerly *Manchester
    Guardian*)
    John Rosselli interview with NMB
        192–93, 322, 326–27, 340
    obituary 285, 366, 382–83
    reviews: anon 359; Peter Bradshaw
        385; Mary Crozier 343;
        Stanley Reynolds 374; Norman
        Shrapnel 245, 330
gun drills, time-and-motion studies
    146
Gwynn, Michael 222

Haldane, J. B. S. 42, 402n12, 423n20
Hale, Lionel 259
Halliwell, Leslie 196, 266, 292, 293,
    295, 303, 319
Hamilton, Jamie 69, 73, 76, 80, 88,
    89, 90, 98
Hamish Hamilton, publisher 69, 73,
    75, 87, 88, 90, 98
Hanray, Lawrence 201
Harris, George 109, 112–13, 115,
    117–18, 181–82, 254–56, 409n12
Hartley, Anthony 277
Hartley, L. P. 82, 123, 128, 155, 165,
    206, 207

Harvey, Frank 282
Haslip, Joan 210
The Hatchet Man (television
    screenplay, 1962) 333–34
Hathaway, Henry 295
Hawkins, Jack 218, 265
Heir and Heiress see *Sundry Creditors*
Hertfordshire 105
High Duty Alloys (HDA) 102–4
Higham, David 98, 224, 234, 381
Highpoint apartments, Highgate
    86
The Highway Code (stage play,
    unperformed, date unknown)
    91, 98
historical writing 203–10
hockey 26, 27, 28, 41
Hollerith cards 61, 137–38, 405n24
Hollywood 166, 203, 291, 294–95,
    297–99, 320, 332–34, 368
Hopkins, John (son-in-law) 221–22,
    386
Hopkins, Justine (granddaughter)
    126, 160, 237, 327
Hopkins, Sir Frederick Gowland 42,
    402n12
Horizon (television programme) 338
Houghton Mifflin, publishers 223,
    224
Hour of Glory (American title of *The
    Small Back Room* film) 216–21,
    pl.13
Houston, Penelope 208, 303, 314
*How to Run a Bassoon Factory; or
    Business Explained* (1934) 32, 60,
    61, 73–76
Howard, Elizabeth Jane 234, 386
    recollections of NMB:
        extravagance 381; first
        impressions 261–63, 326; his
        drinking 366–67, 369; his
        writing 319, 365, 412n23; and

Nancy Spain 288; retainer
from Fox 291
humorous writing 45–46, 74–75,
83–84, 87–88, 98–104, 213
Hunt, Leonard 55–56, 404n6
Huntley, Raymond 313, 344
Huston, John 304

Iceland, Norse sagas 176, 339
identity cards, publicity stunt with
fake 293–94
Iles, Francis (pseudonym of Anthony
Berkeley Cox) 70, 73, 82
Illustrated London News reviews
215–16, 284, 313
In the Absence of Mrs Petersen (1966)
165, 270, 320, 346–50, **347**
incentives to work 180–88
*Income and Outcome. A Study of
Personal Finance* (1936) 72, 88–90,
103, 105–6, 376
Independent on Sunday reviews 385
industrial psychology
at Cambridge University Farm 50
consumer psychology 60–63,
76–80
and *How to Run a Bassoon Factory*
73–75
incentives to work 180–87
NMB joins NIIP 51
NMB writes for NIIP journal 64,
66–67
and NMB's novels 354–56
at Rowntree's 53–63
International Writers School (Famous
Writers School) 376–79
inventors and their inventions
148–49
'An Inventory of Inventors' (*Lilliput,
1944*) 148
Italy
with Elisabeth 203

with Elisabeth and Ayrton 228, 241
with Yovanka 28, 231, 304–6,
307–12, 321–22, 432n28
ITV (Independent Television)
343–44

J. Walter Thompson (JWT) 61, 63,
86, 177–78, 263–64
Jackson, Dorothy ('Dorrie') (later
Stewart, then Stein) 48–50, 60, 72,
175, 280
James, Clive, on NMB ('Prisoners
of clarity' (*The New Review*)) 15,
388–89
The Aircraft Builders 188–89
book sales 120, 167, 280
The Borgia Testament 207–8
Jason Pellew in *The Fall of the
Sparrow* 285
Julian Fellowes's *Separate Lies*
385
Lightbody on Liberty 100, 120
love triangles 81, 131, 163
Mine Own Executioner 163, 167
NMB's character and gifts 138,
150, 207–8, 243
NMB's demobilization 172
NMB's life and his fiction 137,
207–8, 241, 243
NMB's writing style 100, 121,
154
Simple Life 80, 81, 83
The Small Back Room 153
A Sort of Traitors 213
Sundry Creditors 250
A Way Through the Wood 241,
243
John, K. 215–16, 284
John o'London's Weekly reviews 17, 82,
191, 210, 226
John, Rosamund 197
Johns, Glynis 283, 423n13

Johnson, Pamela Hansford 17, 123, 154, 191, 210, 211, 214, 215, 226
Johnson, Van 294
journalism 42, 64, 67, 101–5, 147–48, 149, 194–95

Kellino, Pamela 94, 95
Kelly, Grace 297
Kemp, Philip 264
Kendall, Maurice 38
Kent *see* Leigh Barton
Kermode, Mark 385
Kimmins, Anthony 199, 201, 216
Kings of Infinite Space (1967) 351–59, **355**
Kit Kat chocolate bars 85–86
Knopf, Alfred 223–24
Knopf, Blanche 223–24
Korda, Alexander 216–17, 418n14

The Language of Sex (unfinished) 37
Laski, Marghanita 257
Last Recollections of My Uncle Charles (short stories, 1954) 18, 91, 209, 278–81, 344
Laurie, John 201
Leach, Penelope (daughter) 105, 111, 114, 232–33, 235–36, 386, pl.7
    on her father: characters in *A Way Through the Wood* 244; chauvinism 159; collapse of marriage 227, 238, 241; desire to be psychoanalyst 37; his deception and her resentment 232; his funeral 380; horrible second half of life 240; patient at The Priory 431n17
    on her mother 126, 142, 238
    on Yovanka (Jane) 230
The Leader of the House (television screenplay, 1955) 278
Leigh Barton, Stelling Minnis, Kent

157–61, 228–29, 237, 243
Lennie's Point of View (stage play, unperformed, date unknown) 342–43
Lester, Beryl 272
Lester, Major 272
Levin, Martin 356
libraries 81–82
Lightbody on Liberty (1936) 98–101, **99**, 120
Lilliput magazine, NMB writing for 147–48, 149
Listener magazine
    reviews 214, 350
    transcript of NMB on 'Burnt Njal' 339
"Little Fleas Have Lesser Fleas…" (*Punch,* 1936) 102
Liverpool Post reviews 73
Llandudno, North Wales 114
Lockwood, Lyn 334, 343
London
    lecture on satisfactions in work 183–87
    NMB's homes (*see* Balchin, Nigel Marlin: homes)
    wartime, described in novels 12, 122
Look, Eddie, contemporary at Dauntsey's 28
Lord, I Was Afraid (1947) 29, 130–31, 189–94, 210, 381
love triangle plots 65–66, 81, 131–32, 163–64, 279, 317, 327
Lubetkin, Berthold 86
Luker, Norman 105, 106–7, 408n28
Lynd, Robert 191

MacDonald, Philip: *The Nursemaid Who Disappeared* 294–95
MacKendrick, Alexander 263–64, 265
Maclaren-Ross, Julian 251

Macnee, Patrick 219

Majdalany, Fred 283

Malta Story (screenplay, 1952) 265

The Man Who Never Was (screenplay, 1956) 66, 291–94, 303, 425n11, pl.14

Manchester Evening News reviews 191, 206

Manchester Guardian see *Guardian*

Mandy (screenplay, 1952) 263–65

Manufacturing Confectioners Alliance (MCA) 111, 112–15, 409n12

Marlborough Mansions, West Hampstead 365, 375

Marvin, Blanche 368–69

Maskell, Virginia 313

Mason, James 43–45, 94–95, 102, pl.4

Maugham, Somerset, comparison with 281

Mavrogordato, Eustratius Emmanuel 101

McDine, Alice 159, 160, 413n6

McGregor, M. T. 219

McMahon, Denis 135, 137–38, 140–41

Men Talking (radio programme) 105–7

Meredith, Burgess 199–200, pl.12

MGM (Metro-Goldwyn-Mayer) 196, 203

Miles, George 60, 61, 76–77

Milicevic, Jovan 276

Millar, Ronald: *Waiting for Gillian* 97–98, 222, 277–78, 423n13

Miller, Mandy 265

Milligan, Spike 313

Mills, John 316–17, 427n36

Mind of Nicholas Hurst (unfinished, 1949) 224, 341–42

Mine Own Executioner (1945) 17–18, 33–34, 35, 129–30, 161–70, **162**, 176–77, 228, 370

Mine Own Executioner (screenplay, 1947) 198–203, pl.12

Mine Own Executioner (television adaptation, 1959) 221–22

miner, the absentee 185

Ministry of Agriculture 31, 35, 47, 50–51

Ministry of Food 110–11, 112–17, 409n12

Ministry of Supply 141–42

Miserable Sinners (stage play, 1937) 94–96

Mitford, Jessica 379

Montgomery, General Bernard L. 155

Monthly Film Bulletin reviews
    anon 198–99
    Peter John Dyer 315, 318–19
    Penelope Houston 303, 314

Moody, Ron 374

Moore, Kieron 200–201, pl.12

Moore, Leonard 68, 69, 98

Morell, André 97

Morgan, W. John 313

Morrison, Herbert 184

'Mrs Sludge' (short story) 209

Murrell, Hywel 146

music 29–30, 43–44, 158, 273

NASA 352–53, 356

Nashe, Thomas 225–26

National Institute of Industrial Psychology (NIIP) 51, 53–63, 64, 66–67, 73, 74–75, 76–80, 134, 181–87

Neame, Ronald 293

New Statesman and Nation reviews
    Walter Allen 204, 249
    anon 89–90
    Cyril Connolly 82
    W. John Morgan 313
    John Raymond 245–46, 256
    Henry Reed 17, 165, 168
    J. D. Scott 153, 214

Philip Toynbee 121, 123, 129, 155–56
William Whitebait 200, 201, 203, 219
T. C. Worsley 170–71, 190, 192, 277
New York Times reviews 155, 356
Newby, P. H. 214
News Chronicle
  NMB quoted in 192
  reviews 189, 200, 201
'Nicholas Hurst project' 224, 341–42
Nicolson, Harold 189–90, 191
Nicolson, Nigel 280–81
Night and Day magazine 105
NIIP *see* National Institute of Industrial Psychology
The Nine Lives of Nicholas Hurst (television screenplay; novel) 341–42
No Sky (1934) 65, 69–73, **71**, 121
Norden, Christine 200
Norman, Leslie 265
Norse sagas 176, 339

Observer reviews
  anon 198
  Ivor Brown 277
  John Davenport 286–87
  Daniel George 166
  Gerald Gould 100–101
  L. P. Hartley 82
  Marghanita Laski 257
  Robert Lynd 191
  Maurice Richardson 221, 278, 333–34, 357, 358
  Irving Wardle 350
Olive, George, headmaster at Dauntsey's 26
Operation Backfire 172–74
Operation Mincemeat 291–92, 425n4
Orwell, George 83

paper, wartime shortages 120
Parachute Training School, human 'wastage' at 146–47
Paris 147, 228, 241, 302
Parker, Cecil 295
The Passing Show magazine 65
'Patience' (short story) 91
Peace in Our Time (stage play, 1936) 93–94
Pearn, Pollinger & Higham, literary agency 98, 234
Peterhouse, Cambridge *see* Balchin, Nigel Marlin: education at Peterhouse, Cambridge
Peters, A. D. 178, 234, 323, 369–70, 373, 380
Plant, Andrew 127, 129, 130
Plays and Players reviews 277
plays for stage 91–98, 194
Pleasence, Donald 313, 333
Pobottle articles (*The Aeroplane*, 1936–40) 102–4
Portsmouth, fake identity card stunt 293–94
post-war Britain 180–81
Potter, Stephen 189
Potterne, Wiltshire 19–21, 338
Powell, Anthony 206–7, 215, 284
Powell, Dilys 265, 314
Powell, Michael 24, 44, 199, 216–21
Power (stage play, 1935) 91–93
Prescott, Orville 155
press interviews 322–23
  Books and Bookmen magazine 322, 332–33
  Daily Express 346, 349, 350, 351
  Daily Mail 298–99, 310–11, 322, 323
  Guardian (John Rosselli) 192–93, 322, 326–27, 340
Pressburger, Emeric 216, 218, 418n14

The Priory (mental health hospital)
431n17
Private's Progress (film, Boulting
brothers) 139–40
Profit and Loss (stage play, 1938) 96
psychiatry
in *Josephine and Men* 282
in *Mandy* 264–65
in *Mine Own Executioner*
129–30, 166–67, 168–70, 177,
199–200, 221
Yovanka seeks advice 272–73
'The Psychological Difficulties of the
Institute's Work' (journal article,
1933) 67
psychological warfare 174
psychology *see also* National Institute of
Industrial Psychology (NIIP)
army personnel selection 134–41
consumer psychology 60–63, 76–80
gun drills, time-and-motion
studies 146
incentives to work 180–87
NMB studies at Cambridge
33–37, 50
in NMB's novels 317
in NMB's writing 73–75, 207–8,
302–3, 354–56
taxi anecdote 195
'Publicity Pays' (short story, 1933) 65
Punch magazine, NMB writing in 42,
64, 73, 84, 101–2
punched cards 61, 137–38, 405n24
Purser, Philip 333

Quail, John 421–22n11
Quennell, Peter 189, 191–92, 206,
245, 286

radio
adaptations of NMB's work
176–77, 221, 222, 419n31
appearances by NMB 29–30,
105–7, 176, 273–76, 280,
363
documentary on NMB 383
interview with Walter Allen 69–70,
167, 274–76, 283
unrealized projects 68
Radio Times magazine 83, 106
Raphael, Frederic 349
Raphael, Winifred 59–60, 66, 77,
78
Ray, Cyril 214–15
Raymond, John 245–46, 256
Redgrave, Michael 38, 197, 198
Rediffusion London 343–44
Reed, Henry 17, 165, 168
Rees, John Rawlings 169–70
religion 29
remuneration
as a scientist 58, 63, 78, 86, 118,
177
as a writer 69, 80, 83, 106, 181–82,
363–64
Reynolds, Stanley 374
Richardson, Maurice 221, 278,
333–34, 357, 358
The Risk see *Suspect*
Robey, Tim 385
Rogerson, Sidney 259
Rosenthal, Tom 226
Rosmer, Milton 218
Ross, Alan 203
Rosselli, John, interview with NMB
192–93, 322, 326–27, 340
Rothschild, Baron Victor 412n23
rowing (sport) 87
Rowland, Peter 366
Rowntree & Co. Ltd. 55–59, 60–63,
77, 78, 85–86, 108–9, 112–14,
115, 117–18, 177, 254–56
Rowntree, Oscar 254, 404n11
Rowntree, Peter 255

Rowntree, Seebohm 57, 59, 63, 77, 78, 108, 111, 158, 181–83, 254

rugby 26, 28, 41

S.A.A.C. *see* Scientific Adviser to the Army Council

Sachs, Leonard 97

'The Salamander' (short story, 1945) 278, 423n20

Salisbury Plain, Wiltshire 22–24

'Satisfactions in Work' (lecture for NIIP, 'London Lecture') 183–87

Saturday Evening Post (American magazine) 235, 243, 344

Savile Club 14, 178–79, 196–97, 225–26, 234, 263, 309

Scientific Adviser to the Army Council (S.A.A.C.) 144, 147–50, 172–74

'Scientists in a Hurry' (*Lilliput,* 1947) 149

Scott, J. D. 153, 214

screenwriting 196–203, 263–66, 282, 298–99, 302–3, 304–5, 310–14, 315–20

Second World War 108–9, 110–24, 133–43, 144–56 *see also* Balchin, Nigel: army service; *Darkness Falls From the Air; The Small Back Room*
army personnel selection 133–41
Darnton injured 130
and Elisabeth's affair with Darnton 125–26
Elisabeth's war work 111–12, 114, 141–43, 159, 411n20
NMB has breakdown 366
and NMB's novels 12, 121–24, 153, 163
NMB's war work 108–9, 110–11, 112–17

Seen Dimly Before Dawn (1962) 194, 321–22, 323, 326–32, **331**

Sempstead *see* Oast Cottage, Sussex

Separate Lies (film, Julian Fellowes) 15, 383–85, pl.15

'The Service of Miss Eyles' (short story, 1935) 83

sewage workers 187

The Sex (The Magazine of the Peterhouse Sexcentenary Club) 45–46

sex and sexuality
NMB's interest in 36–37, 186, 296
in NMB's novels 330, 357
in NMB's relationships 126, 227–28, 237–38, 261–62, 272, 301

Shakespeare, William 351

Shepley, Michael 201

shooting accident 27–28, 307

short stories 64–66, 83, 91, 209, 278–81, 423n19, 423n20

Shorter, Eric 317–18

Shrapnel, Norman 245, 330

Siepmann, Charles 68

Sigal, Clancy 314

Sight and Sound reviews 202

Simple Life (1935) 22–23, **79**, 80–83, 121, 327

Simpson, Ronald 259

Sinclair, Andrew 388

The Singer Not the Song (screenplay, 1961) 315–18, 427n36, 427n40

Sketch reviews
Rupert Croft-Cooke 215
L. P. Hartley 123, 128, 155, 165

The Small Back Room (1943) 23–24, 144, 145, 148–49, 150–56, **151**, 164, 370, 382, 413n23
radio and television adaptations 221–22, 419n31

The Small Back Room (Powell and Pressburger film, 1949) 216–21, pl.13

Snow, C. P. (Charles) 215, 245, 259

Snow, Philip 259
S.O.E. (Special Operations Executive) 142–43, 411–12n20
A Sort of Traitors (1949) 153, 211–16, **212**, 222 see also *Suspect*
space programme, American 351–53
Spade, Mark (pseudonym of NMB) 73, 88 see also *Business for Pleasure; Fun and Games; How to Run a Bassoon Factory*
Spain, Nancy 257, 287–90
Speaking Personally (television programme) 248–49
Special Operations Executive (S.O.E.) 142–43, 411–12n20
Spectator reviews 219, 277
Spencer, Charles 300
Sphere reviews 154
sport 26–27, 28, 40–41, 46, 51–52, 87–88, 93, 158, 258–59
Spring, Howard: *Fame is the Spur* 197–98
Square Deal (stage play, unperformed, date unknown) 91
St Johnston, Eric 36, 74, 164
stage plays 91–98, 194
Stage reviews 95
Star reviews 219–20
Stein, Dorrie (formerly Stewart, née Jackson) 48–50, 60, 72, 175, 280
Stein, Eric 72, 175, 280, 295
Stein, John 48
Stein, Rick 280
Stelling Minnis, Kent *see* Leigh Barton
Stewart, Alan 48–49, 53, 55, 60, 175
Stewart, Dorrie (later Stein, née Jackson) 48–50, 60, 72, 175, 280
Stewart, Jeremy 48–49, 175
Stonier, George ('William Whitebait') 200, 201, 203, 219
Straus, Ralph 69, 73, 101, 154

Street, A. G. 25
Suffolk (The Greyhound) 359–61, 367–68
Sumar Films 291
Sunday Chronicle reviews 214–15, 218
Sunday Express 334–35, 344
Sunday Telegraph reviews
    Robin Cook 357, 358–59
    Anthony Curtis 328, 329, 330
    Campbell Dixon 292, 293
    Philip Purser 333
Sunday Times
    reviews: Jeremy Brooks 330; Penelope Houston 208; Dilys Powell 265, 314; Frederic Raphael 349; C. P. Snow 215, 245; Ralph Straus 69, 73, 101, 154; Doreen Wallace 82
    'Rim of the Plain' article by NMB 337–38
Sundry Creditors (1953) 57–58, 185–86, 211–13, 249–58, **253**, 370
Suspect (screenplay, 1960) 216, 312–14
Sussex *see* Oast Cottage; Tufton Place
Sykes, Christopher 257
Symons, Julian 191, 206, 285

Tatler and Bystander reviews
    Elizabeth Bowen 123, 207, 281, 286
    Freda Bruce Lockhart 219, 220
    Elspeth Grant 283, 313
Tavistock Clinic, London 169–70
taxation 301–2, 306
taxis at Charing Cross Station 195
Taylor, Elizabeth (actor) 311, 312
Taylor, Elizabeth (novelist) 377, 379
television
    adaptations of NMB's work 221–22, 277, 343–44, 419n31
    appearances by NMB 248–49, 338, 339–41

screenplays 278, 332–34, 373–75
unrealized projects 341–43, 362, 372
Thackeray, William Makepeace: *Henry Esmond* 362
'That Feller Oates' (short story, 1933) 65–66
Thomas, Gilbert 176–77
Thomas, Mary, NMB's first crush 30
Thomson, George Malcolm 206, 245, 256
Time and Tide magazine
    NMB writes for 104–5, 194–95
    reviews: Margery Allingham 123; C. E. Bechhofer Roberts 82–83; Freda Bruce Lockhart 198, 202; L. P. Hartley 206, 207; Fred Majdalany 283; M. T. McGregor 219; Clancy Sigal 314
The Times
    NMB letter on incentives 184
    reviews 94, 95, 96, 221, 222, 265, 279, 281, 282, 291–92, 294–95, 318, 349–50
The Times Literary Supplement reviews
    anon 75, 88
    Anthony Burgess 194, 330–32
    Richard Charques 164
    Roy Fuller 349
    Charles Reginald Green 84
    Julian Maclaren-Ross 251
    Eustratius Emmanuel Mavrogordato 101
    Anthony Powell 206–7, 215
    Julian Symons 285
    David Williams 358
Tizzano, Villa di, Florence 28, 307–12, 316, 318, 321
Tomich, Vera (Yovanka's mother) 229–30, 268, 270, 305
Tomich, Yovanka Zorana *see* Balchin, Yovanka Zorana

Tomich, Zoran (Yovanka's father) 229–30, 268, 380
Tookey, Christopher 385
total eclipse of the sun 321
Toynbee, Philip 121, 123, 129, 155–56
travel pl.16
    Famous Writers School meetings 377–78
    'Hollywood years' globetrotting 299–300, 302, 304–5, 308
    Italy with Elisabeth 203
    Italy with Elisabeth and Ayrton 228, 241
    Italy with Yovanka 28, 231, 304–6, 307–12, 321–22, 432n28
    researching US space programme 351–53
Trevelyan, Julian 38
triangle *see* love triangle plots
Trist, Eric 170
Troubridge, Una 231
Tufton Place, Sussex 325–26, 334–35, 336
Twentieth Century Fox 291, 293, 294–95, 302–3, 310, 312, 320
Twenty-Three Paces to Baker Street (screenplay, 1956) 294–95
20 Story Magazine 65

Ungerson, Bernard 135, 136, 259

V2 rockets 172–74
Vellacott, Paul 29, 31, 43, 47, 50, 55–56, 66, 223, 263
Venice 203, 432n28
Vesselo, Arthur 202

Waiting for Gillian (Ronald Millar) 97–98, 222, 277–78, 423n13
Walbank, Frank, contemporary at Peterhouse 39, 40, 49

Walker, Alexander 318
Wallace, Doreen 82
Wallace, William 115, 116, 409n6, 409n10, 409n12
Walshe, Douglas (father-in-law) 48, 93–94
Wanger, Walter 311
war *see* Second World War
War Office Selection Boards (WOSBs) 139–40, 141, 170
Wardle, Irving 350
Watkins, Mike 224, 234
Watson, Emily 384, pl.15
Waugh, Evelyn 287
A Way Through the Wood (1951) 21, 29, 37, 91, 131, 160, 202, 222, 240–46, **242**, 370 see also *Separate Lies* (Fellowes); *Waiting for Gillian* (Millar)
Wayne, John 304–5
We Write Novels (radio programme) 274–76
Webb, Clifton 292, pl.14
Welwyn, Hertfordshire 105
West Lavington, Wiltshire 24–25, 29–30, 51, 107, 338, 429n6 *see also* Dauntsey Agricultural School
What's My Line? (television programme) 249, 296
Wheatley, Alan 96–97
White, Barbara 200
Whitebait, William (pseudonym of George Stonier) 200, 201, 203, 219
Whittingham, Jack 264
Wilkinson, Tom 384, pl.15
William (family dog) 307
William Collins, publisher 98, 118, 120, 170, 190, 209, 258–59, 279–80, 314–15, 323, 373, 380
Williams, David 358
Wilson, A. E. 219–20
Wiltshire 51–52, 338
Wiltshire Gazette 24, 29, 30, 107
Winnington, Richard 200, 201
Woman's Hour (radio programme) 363
Woman's Own magazine 296–97
women
    at Cambridge 49–50
    NMB and (*see* Balchin, Nigel Marlin: relationships with women)
Woolton, Lord (Frederick Marquis, 1st Earl of Woolton) 114–16
work and psychology *see* National Institute of Industrial Psychology (NIIP); psychology
work incentives 180–88
work, NMB as the novelist of 11
World War Two *see* Second World War
Worsley, T. C. 170–71, 190, 192, 277

Yugoslavia 229, 230, 276, 346–48, 364